Adirondacks

Adirondacks

A Great Destination

Annie Stoltie

The Countryman Press * Woodstock, Vermont

SEVENTH EDITION

Maps by Erin Greb Cartography, © The Countryman Presss
Book design by Bodenweber Design
Composition by Eugenie S. Delaney
Previous spread: St. Regis Canoe Area photograph courtesy of Mark Bowie, www.markbowie.com.

Explorer's Guide Adirondacks, 7th edition
ISBN: 978-0-88150-973-1

Published by The Countryman Press, P.O. Box 748, Woodstock, VT 05091
Distributed by W. W. Norton & Company, Inc., 500 Fifth Avenue, New York, NY 10110
Printed in the United States of America

10 9 8 7 6 5 4 3

For Drew, Asa, and Orra.

Acknowledgments

IT'S BECAUSE OF ELIZABETH "BETSY" FOLWELL that this guidebook exists. In 1992, Betsy wrote the first edition of what was called *The Adirondack Book*, a clearinghouse for all things Adirondack, in meticulous, exhaustive detail, with the usual dining and lodging material but also folksy stuff, like firehouse suppers and where to score Stoddard stereoviews. She invited me to join her, as coauthor, for the book's sixth edition, and then handed over the whole thing for this, the seventh. Although I've updated and added and changed and reorganized, this book's foundation is all Betsy—I've even double-checked much of what you'll read in these chapters with her, my Adirondack guru.

In fact, I wouldn't have come to the Adirondack Park—wouldn't have lived and worked here for more than a decade now—if it hadn't been for Betsy's giving me a chance at *Adirondack Life* magazine, a publication I had admired from afar. Betsy introduced me to this wild place, with its characters and culture and beauty that, honestly, still takes my breath away. I'm grateful for the opportunities she's given me and for all she's taught me, but most of all I'm grateful for her friendship.

I'm also thankful for help from my Adirondack friends, all intrepid reporters who shared their thoughts and meals and experiences with me as I compiled this book. They include Galen Crane, of Lake Placid; Tom Henry, of Charlotte, Vermont; Mary Thill, of Saranac Lake; and my *Adirondack Life* colleagues Lisa Bramen, Niki Kourofsky, and Kelly Hofschneider. A special thank you goes to Saratogian Amy Godine, too, whose knowledge of Adirondack history and Spa City happenings—tossed with super, snappy writing—make the Adirondack history section and the Gateway Cities chapter so much fun.

Ted Comstock, of Saranac Lake, deserves thanks: we spent a chunk of time together sorting through his extensive collection of Adirondackana to find just the right historical postcards for this book.

This, the first color edition of the book, shares the best of the Adirondacks through the talents of some of the finest photographers in the Northeast. I am indebted to Adirondack photographers Nancie Battaglia, Mark Bowie, John DiGiacomo, Eric Dresser, Johnathan Esper, Drew Haas, Carl Heilman II, Mark Kurtz, Kevin and Deb MacKenzie, Jeff Nadler, Shaun Ondak, Ben Stechschulte, and Melody Thomas. If you like what you see in these pages, check out these photographers' websites.

My husband, Drew Sprague, is also all over this book. Not in text or imagery, but in spirit. We have two little kids and we both work demanding, full-time jobs. A proj-

In August 2011 Tropical Storm Irene devastated parts of the Adirondacks, including roads, homes, and businesses in Upper Jay. Courtesy of Deb MacKenzie, www.mackenziefamily.com

ect like this guide meant Drew's constant help and support. In him I have everything and then some. I know how lucky I am.

And as an Adirondacker, I'm compelled to mention all that our communities have endured this past year. In summer 2011, Tropical Storm Irene pushed our rivers, such as the Ausable and Boquet and their tributaries, to record levels, flooding much of the northern and eastern Adirondacks: water surged through living rooms, ripped apart businesses, disintegrated roads, devastated farms, killed livestock, carried away part of a fire station. After the flood, hamlets Au Sable Forks, Jay, Upper Jay, Keene, Keene Valley, and Elizabethtown, among others, looked as though they'd been bombed by an unrelenting army. As I write, some families and businesses still await flood relief, but many have mopped up the mess, rebuilt, and reopened. In Upper Jay, Paul Johnson's Bakery, underwater during the deluge, is ready for customers. Elizabethtown's Woodruff House B & B was sopping wet, but now it's better than ever. In no time the silt in Keene's Cedar Run Bakery was shoveled out and its coolers were stocked and its coffee ready. All of this is a testament to Adirondack will, to what makes our mountain towns so great, and to why I love this place.

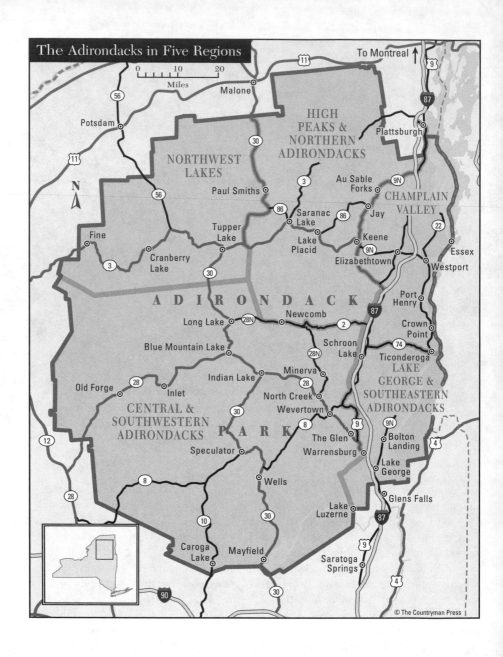

The Adirondacks in Five Regions

Miles
0   10   20

To Montreal ↑

HIGH
PEAKS &
NORTHERN
ADIRONDACKS

NORTHWEST
LAKES

CHAMPLAIN
VALLEY

A D I R O N D A C K

CENTRAL &
SOUTHWESTERN
ADIRONDACKS

P A R K

LAKE
GEORGE &
SOUTHEASTERN
ADIRONDACKS

Malone
Potsdam
Paul Smiths
Au Sable Forks
Plattsburgh
Fine
Saranac Lake
Jay
Tupper Lake
Keene
Lake Placid
Essex
Cranberry Lake
Elizabethtown
Westport
Newcomb
Port Henry
Long Lake
Schroon Lake
Crown Point
Blue Mountain Lake
Ticonderoga
Indian Lake
Minerva
Old Forge
Inlet
North Creek
Wevertown
The Glen
Bolton Landing
Speculator
Warrensburg
Lake George
Wells
Glens Falls
Lake Luzerne
Caroga Lake
Mayfield
Saratoga Springs

8

Contents

Courtesy of ORDA/Dave Schmidt

Introduction

NEW YORK'S ADIRONDACK PARK is a big park: bigger than Yellowstone and Yosemite put together and larger than any of the national parks in the lower 48. This park is better than national parks in many ways, too. You don't pay an entry fee when you cross the so-called Blue Line, the park's boundary; you don't need a permit to hike, climb a mountain, canoe, or explore the backcountry. People make this park their home and have lived here for many generations, giving this region a distinctive culture and offering an array of services to visitors.

The park has a year-round population of about 130,000 residents, and covers 6 million acres, about the size of the state of Vermont. Land owned by New York State—the Adirondack Forest Preserve—is about 2.5 million acres, and large landowners own another million acres and contribute significantly to the forested landscape and the local economy.

Through the years I've enjoyed visiting many different communities, exploring wild places, and learning about the region. Although the territory appears timeless, human endeavors change frequently. That's the impetus behind the seventh edition of this book—to supply information about new places and updates on classic spots. I hope that these pages encourage you to explore this great place.

Cascade Falls, in the Pigeon Lake Wilderness Area. Courtesy of Shaun Ondak, www.shaunondak.com

The Way This Book Works

TO COVER THE ADIRONDACK REGION, there are 10 chapters in this book—
"History," "Transportation," "Gateway Cities," "Central and Southwestern Adirondacks," "Northwest Lakes," "High Peaks and Northern Adirondacks," "Champlain
Valley," "Lake George and Southeastern Adirondacks," "If Time Is Short," and
"Information"—and many maps and indexes. Each geographic section of the park—
and the towns, listed alphabetically within those sections—have been broken down
to better serve those who are planning a trip to, say, Old Forge. However, in the
Adirondack Park it's not unusual to spend a day in multiple regions: Perhaps you'll
pass a morning at the Wild Center, in Tupper Lake, grab lunch in Lake Placid, spend
the evening at the theater in Westport, then stay the night in Keene Valley.

Although the first chapter, "Gateway Cities," includes travel information on two
places that are outside the Blue Line, Saratoga Springs and Glens Falls are fascinating destinations in themselves. Because these cities have long been the civilized
gateways to the great woods to the north, they deserve a place in this book. In this
chapter you'll find descriptions of lodgings, restaurants, museums, and recreational
opportunities available in both towns.

Throughout the book, many of the entries have phone numbers, websites,
addresses (although many Adirondack hamlets are so rural, all that's available is the
name of a street or route), and so forth. These facts have been checked as close to
the book's publication date as possible, but businesses do change hands and change
policies. It's always a good idea to call ahead—a long-distance call is a whole lot
cheaper than a tank of gas.

For the same reason, you won't find specific prices listed for, say, restaurants,
lodging, and greens fees; descriptions for these should explain whether they're high-
end or middle-of-the-road, which is typical of most places in the Adirondacks.

Early Warrensburg homestead. Courtesy of Ted Comstock, Saranac Lake

History

THE PEOPLE'S PARK

PLANNING A TRIP TO THE ADIRONDACKS in northern New York? Bring a road map, bring your bug spray, and by all means bring this book. But above all, bring your love of mystery and your capacity for wonder, for nothing is exactly as it seems here, and a taste for contradiction can only sweeten your encounter with a park bigger than the state of Vermont.

How did it come to pass that a vast swath of forest so relatively close to so many eastern cities was among the last in the lower 48 to gain the eye and expertise of the surveyor, cartographer, and lawmaker? Such marvelous proximity, and yet, for so long, so lightly valued and little known! So proudly venerable—yet so recent an addition to our pantheon of great parks! Like the proverbial girl next door who turns out to be a heart-stopping knockout, the Adirondack region has been, in terms of our appreciation of it, a very late bloomer. It took time for us to get wise to its rare beauty, time to learn to see and cherish the quiet treasure in our own backyard.

And maybe that's just as well, because the same forces that delayed a loving valuation of the region also stalled our rolling in and making an unholy hash of it (though the combined assault of such extractive industries as mining, logging, and tanning took a hard toll). Start with the Native Americans, for whom the Champlain Valley corridor was long a borderland between hereditary enemies, the Iroquois and the Algonquin, or more particularly, the easternmost Iroquois tribe, the Mohawks, and from the other side of the lake, the Abenaki, westernmost of the wide-ranging Algonquin. Borderlands that double as sporadic war zones are no place to settle down, and permanent Native encampments were accordingly unknown. (Migratory visitations, on the other hand, have been going on for some 8,000 years, the summer-to-fall residency that accounts for those relics you'll keep seeing in the local village museum display case.)

The Adirondack region was not a draw for European settlers in the 17th and 18th centuries, when a distant, long-lived imperial conflict pitted the British Crown against the soldiers of New France in one bloody raid and skirmish after another, culminating, of course, in the French and Indian War. In the Champlain Valley, in

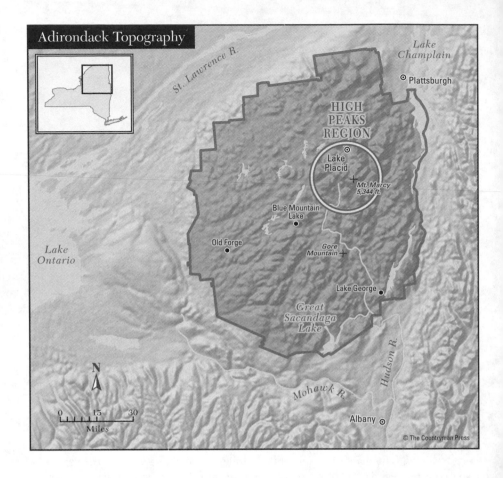

Adirondack Topography

Lake Champlain

Plattsburgh

St. Lawrence R.

HIGH PEAKS REGION

Lake Placid

Mt. Marcy 5,344 ft.

Blue Mountain Lake

Lake Ontario

Old Forge

Gore Mountain

Lake George

Great Sacandaga Lake

Hudson R.

N

0   15   30
Miles

Mohawk R.

Albany

© The Countryman Press

particular, much more was at stake than a show of military muscle. Each nation was as hot to lay claim to this commercially strategic thoroughfare as it was keen to edge the other out. This key waterway (Lake Champlain and Lake George) was the conduit for the kind of abundant timber (including arrow-straight white pines that could mast a royal navy) that a wood-starved Europe hadn't seen for a century. It provided habitat and transport for enough furs to cloak all of gay Paris. Indeed, whosoever ruled these waters owned the markets that lined the royal purse. The upshot of this imperial conflict for the Adirondacks was inevitable. The eastern region on the west flank of Lake Champlain gained a reputation of, if not a full-blown war zone, at least a pretty darned dicey place to settle. And so, for the first two thirds or so of the 18th century, settlers stayed away.

Or mostly. In 1730, soldier-farmers from New France colonized a settlement on the west side of Lake Champlain where the banks are close as pincers. Fort Saint Frederic, at present-day Crown Point, thrived for another 30 years, time enough for the French pioneers to raise families; build a trading post, mill, and chapel; and befriend the traveling bands of Native Americans. But in 1758, hearing of the imminent approach of British troops under the tireless Lord Jeffrey Amherst, the French homemakers of the region's first European enclave destroyed their Adirondack Roanoke and fled to Canada, leaving the charred remains to be rebuilt and reinvented as His Majesty's massive fort, Crown Point.

The French and Indian War also gave American and British soldiers their first glimpse of this virgin wilderness, and some of them liked what they saw well enough to come back at the conflict's end. Bands of Quakers found the region, too, and gave Quaker names to several early settlements in the southern and eastern Adirondacks, among them Wing's Falls, later called Glens Falls, the bustling mill town at the Adirondack's southeastern edge. Laboring under the delusion that the underpopulated Adirondack region might somehow escape the ever-growing tension between native-born Americans grown restive under British rule and those loyal to the Crown, the peaceable Quakers were in for a rude surprise. Once again, during the American Revolution and for some years after, the eastern Adirondack corridor between Montreal and Saratoga emerged as a bloody frontier warpath, and settlers hunkered down at their peril.

Among the ranks of the veterans who were nonetheless attracted to this dangerous frontier were many Scots, survivors of the Highlander regiments that fought with fabled valor at Lake George and Fort Ticonderoga. In the southern Adirondacks, Sir William Johnson, the high-living Irish-born veteran and brilliant liaison between the Iroquois and the British Crown, bought himself a sweet chunk of real estate from the British-allied Mohawk and set about parlaying his riverside homestead into a wilderness fiefdom. (Proud local legends insist that the tireless Johnson sired 700 progeny, donned a kilt with his Scottish Highlander immigrant tenants, and reveled with the Mohawk braves who routinely camped and feasted on his baronial front lawns.) But the Johnson family was pro-British, and when William Johnson died and the patriotic fever of the Revolution took the Mohawk Valley by storm, his sons exiled themselves to Canada, their faithful Scottish tenants with them, and the old man's upstate kingdom was seized and broken up, never to be restored.

The Scotsman Sir Philip Skene sowed his fertile corner of the Adirondacks near today's Whitehall (formerly Skenesborough) with sawmills, iron forges, settlers, and his own small crew of African American slaves. Sir William Gilliland, a Scots-Irish immigrant, and like Skene and Johnson, a veteran of His Majesty's Forces, set his dogged sights on the "howling wilderness" (his words) at the mouth of the Boquet River, near Willsboro (which he named for himself). Come the Revolution, the exiled Skene saw his shipyard seized, his slaves dispersed, and his pioneering iron forges used to fashion the cannonballs that stalled the British navy at the Battle of Valcour. Gilliland should have had better luck: He, at least, backed the winning party, even feeding 3,000 shell-shocked American soldiers in weary retreat from a disastrous foray into Canada. But patriot or not, Gilliland's grand feudal ambitions were ill suited to the democratic temper of his times. Benedict Arnold (of all people!) charged Gilliland with treason: Gilliland went to jail, lost his holdings and his farms to marauding Loyalists, landed in debtor's prison, and wound up freezing to death in the Adirondack woods, leaving a handful of Adirondack villages to honor his good work with Gilliland family names.

To the names of Johnson, Gilliland, and Skene, add Alexander Macomb,

Seventeenth- and 18th-century imperial conflicts shaped the region—and the country.

Surrender of Burgoyne. Postcard courtesy of Ted Comstock, Saranac Lake.

brief owner in 1791 of almost four million Adirondack acres; add the Rhode Island merchant John Brown, whose "tract" would encompass much of today's park before it reverted to New York State for taxes; add John Thurman, the New York City businessman who recruited Scottish pioneers to the region near the village that bears his name today. Their stories make such satisfying copy. The energetic Thurman: gored to death in his prime by a bull! The ever-hopeful Brown (who gave his ghostly, never-settled townships such names as Frugality, Sobriety, and Perseverance) lost his land agent, a son-in-law, to suicide, and his holdings to the state! The impecunious Macomb, who wound up in debtors' prison, half mad!

More enduring, if less flamboyantly dramatic, was the experience of the nameless pioneers who discovered the region in the half century or so after the Revolution when a close-to-bankrupt New York State took over the crown lands of the northern wilderness and sold upstate parcels by the thousands. Only then did the region see anything like a real influx of settlers, many of them veterans of the Continental Army. In they poured from the worked-over, exhausted hill farms of New England, and it wasn't long—maybe a decade, maybe two—before sod huts and log shanties donned neat suits of locally milled clapboard, and every crossroads settlement could boast an inn, tavern, and makeshift church. Historians call it the Yankee Migration, and Puritan-descended Yankees these land-starved settlers mostly were. But there were Hessians, too, and bands of Scots-Irish from northern Ireland, and once again Quakers trickling northward from the Hudson Valley, and coming south after 1816, both French and Anglo-Canadian homesteaders looking to make a fresh start after the quashing of the failed Canadian Rebellion.

Some came of their own accord, others in response to the propagandistic broadsides and handbills of land agents working for downstate speculators—speculators who had every reason to assume their settler-tenants would improve the value of their investment with each swing of the ax, even when they failed to pay rent or give over a portion of their crops. This time-honored colonial strategy had worked well enough elsewhere along the Eastern Seaboard. What went wrong up here? Why did one Adirondack empire after another fail to prosper?

It is true that many of these so-called harpy land barons would not live on or anywhere near their tracts, and not a few tenant farmers chafed under the high-handed, semifeudal expectations of their absentee landlords. But far more demoralizing than a long-distance landlord was the daily, blunt, implacable resistance of the terrain. If it wasn't the bitter thinness of the Adirondack soil (a few lush river valleys aside), it was the length and harshness of the winters, the stinginess of the growing season, the roughness of the topography, or the dread ferocity of predators—wolves and panthers, bugs and bears. Nor was the situation eased by the absence of transportation routes that might have eased the settlers' transition from subsistence to a market economy. What did it profit them to grow the sweetest hops, the fattest turnips, the reddest apples in their township, if they lacked wagon route or railhead or boat landing to get their crops to market? To be sure, there were snug farming settlements in places as far-flung as Lake Placid and Lake Luzerne, but once other options were open (tourism, especially), agriculture as the prime force of the local economy quickly took a backseat.

The fact that the 19-century Adirondack region was unvisited by marauding bands of horse-borne, painted Natives, or masked banditos, has made it hard for us to see it as a frontier territory every bit as dangerous and seemingly remote as the highlands of New Mexico or Arizona, but this is surely how it felt to the first lonely, forest-bound pioneers. As Adirondack cultural historian Philip Terrie has observed,

"The only thing that distinguished the Adirondacks from western frontier regions was that exploitation of local riches—real or imaginary—did not involve the removal or slaughter of indigenous peoples."

Everybody knew the Adirondacks was no place for a farmer with any kind of means. Settlers moved there mostly when they couldn't afford better pickings elsewhere. But how many of these hopeful pioneers could guess at a glance that such fair-seeming country could make a poor man poorer still? Little wonder that so many from this first generation of Adirondack pioneers pushed on to greener pastures farther west when the Erie Canal opened for business in 1825, or hastened home to long-settled New England. At the same time, as the rough reality of Adirondack climate and topography eroded the Jeffersonian dreamscape of a thousand well-tended, self-sufficient little farms, another kind of vision cast its own enduring spell—the view of the Adirondack woodlands not as a hindrance to a farmer's fortune but as a fortune in itself, rich as Croesus in the two crops that are the bane of any farmer's existence: tall trees and big rocks thickly seamed with iron ore.

It wasn't that these native crops weren't right there for the harvesting all along or that the colonists and the Native Americans before them were unmindful of them. But in 1700, what New Hampshire homesteader was thinking about the red spruce of the Adirondack interior? All the timber a colonist could hope for was right there in the back forty. It would take the depletion of the New England and southern New York forests to force a deeper move into northern New York, an advance that only quickened as innovations in the woods industries made it easier to get trees out. In the early 1800s, legislation that declared New York rivers public highways launched the great age of the Adirondack river drive. By midcentury, fast-running Adirondack rivers—the Saranac, the Grasse, the Schroon, the Hudson—were sometimes so densely shingled over with floating logs a skilled river driver could hop from log to log for half a mile with nary a glimpse of the water roiling beneath.

By 1850, New York State led the nation in timber production. Tiny sawmills that once catered to the basic needs of pioneers now shipped and sledded their product north to Canada or south to Albany. The feudal land baron was supplanted by the capitalist lumber baron, and the homesteader once as game to burn a tree as look at it now added skilled logger or river driver to his résumé. Every tree, it seemed, had its use: white pine and red spruce for ships' masts and house construction; hardwood for charcoal; hemlock for the bark whose tannin-rich liquor was essential in the curing of leather, a particularly vital Adirondack industry from 1860 to 1880. In the last two decades of the 19th century, the shift from rags to wood pulp in the paper-making industry brought a whole new world of trees into the loggers' line of fire. Pulp-grinding machinery didn't care how straight or true or old or

As industralization stepped up the demand for the extractive products of the wilderness, the logging meant work for hardscrabble farmers, immigrants, and migratory workers.

Moose River postcard courtesy of Ted Comstock, Saranac Lake

long the wood it used. Cellulose fiber did the trick, and trees as skinny as 3 inches round were fair game.

As for that other bumper Adirondack crop, iron ore, it, too, owned a hearty appetite for vast stands of wood. Ore was so abundant in the northeastern Adirondacks you could see it plainly in the outcrops along Lake Champlain, and so famously pure, some of it, you could work it fresh from the seam. Better than 200 forges operated in the 19th-century Adirondacks, almost half of them along the iron-russet banks of two Adirondack rivers, the Ausable and the Saranac. Of the scores of remote hamlets that owed their founding to these charcoal-hungry forges, many are now ghost towns or little more than a cluster of leafy sinkholes in the woods, but in 1850, New York State led the nation in iron ore production. The lumber barons who had overtaken the "harpy land barons" were now joined in their pursuit of wood by mining magnates, whose prolific crews of woodchoppers and colliers (charcoal makers) kept their forges bright with burning charcoal. Thanks to those mining magnates, the Adirondack forest suffered its first scarifying clear-cut. Indeed, it was the mining industry, much more than lumbering, that did so much to load the quills of illustrators whose before-and-after engravings of the Adirondacks (virgin, then denuded) in such magazines as *Harper's* and *Frank Leslie's Illustrated Weekly*, spurred an outraged readership to support the notion of an Adirondack forest preserve. Consider: It took two and a quarter cords of wood to make 100 bushels of charcoal, and up to 500 bushels of charcoal to generate a ton of Adirondack ore. The hills were alive with the sound of crashing hardwoods.

As industrialization stepped up the demand for the extractive products of the northern New York wilderness—tanbark, logs, pulpwood, ore—settlers found plenty of pickup work to buttress the meager output from their hardscrabble farms. And a good thing, too: The flexible, seasonally responsive diversification of the Adirondack home economy—a potato farm in the summer, a logging gig in the winter, a little

Courtesy of Ted Comstock, Saranac Lake

Old Rocks, New Mountains

The rocks beneath Adirondack peaks and valleys were formed from sediments laid down in shallow seas some 1.3 billion years ago. Although that sounds like a tranquil enough beginning, the intervening millennia between the Grenville period and modern times was a chaotic riot of rumpling, folding, shearing, compressing, cracking, and colliding. Himalaya-like peaks rose, then were beaten down by weather and wave; the land was then stretched and cloven as continents crashed into one another. The metamorphic rocks we walk on today, atop Mount Marcy or even along a southern Adirondack stream, were once buried 15 to 20 miles beneath the surface.

Today's mountain ranges, though, were ultimately shaped by the scraping action of a mile-thick glacier 10,000-plus years ago. This moving wall of ice took the jagged peaks down to their hardest bedrock, deposited sand as sinuous eskers, and left behind giant boulders—erratics—as calling cards. The Adirondack Mountains are rising still, reaching up at a rate of 2 to 3 millimeters a year, about the length of Lincoln's nose on a penny, thanks to a hot spot deep within the Earth.

From the high points of land, hundreds of rivers drain north into the Saint Lawrence River, east to Lake Champlain, and south to the Hudson and Mohawk Valleys. Lakes often fill the ancient fault valleys, in diagonal lines between the mountains.

The Adirondack Mountains are rising at a rate of 2 to 3 millimeters a year, about the length of Lincoln's nose on a penny.

High Peaks photograph courtesy of Johnathan Esper, www.wilder nessphotographs.com

hauling, a little millwork, a job guiding city fishermen to favorite streams—was the key to survival, and this tradition, long honored by migratory bands of Native Americans, defines the Adirondack lifestyle even now.

But when local hands proved too few to meet the labor needs of fast-growing mining towns, tannery hamlets, and logging camps, another source of labor was introduced: immigrants and migratory workers. To an extent, different industries generated different ethnic enclaves. Irish immigrants, for example, were often drawn to tannery towns. French Canadians worked in the woods, Italians on the railroad tracks, Poles and Lithuanians in the mines. But no single ethnic group monopolized any single industry to the exclusion of any other. Saint Regis Mohawk Indians worked on river drives and in Adirondack tanneries as well. In Lyon Mountain, Witherbee, or Mineville, eastern European miners worked cheek by jowl with Italians, Spaniards, Irish laborers, and African Americans; indeed, the first iron miners in the Adirondacks were the land baron Philip Skene's black slaves. The logging camp at Wanakena featured a Swedish sauna, and up near Chazy an encampment of Italian stonemasons built themselves a hive-shaped bread oven in the woods.

Because these rough-hewn, company-built settlements rose and dispersed with

Ads, Dacks, and Adirondacks

The word "Adirondack" reportedly comes from an Iroquois word that means "they eat bark," an insult referring to the Algonquin's allegedly lousy woodcraft skills. That can't be proven, though (neither their ineptitude nor the etymology); using romantic Native-sounding words has long been a favorite pastime of mapmakers, writers, and even politicians. What can be defined are some North Country specifics:

The Adirondack Park: Established in 1892, it covers 6.1 million acres of public and private land in a shield shape that includes much of the northern third of New York State. It's the largest state park in the nation. It's not all wilderness: Everything within, from the summits of the highest peaks to the most remote bog to Main Street in Lake Placid, is in the park.

The Adirondack Forest Preserve: Established in 1885, this is about 42 percent of the Adirondack Park that is public land, and preserved as wilderness, wild forest, or primitive areas. It comprises many scattered parcels, not one contiguous unit, although some wilderness areas are vast enough to take days to cross on foot. In a nutshell, if you're on Forest Preserve land you're free to hike, hunt, fish, canoe, and do almost whatever else you want, although wilderness areas are off-limits to motorized vehicles (e.g., snowmobiles, ATVs, and motorboats). If you're not on public land, you're trespassing on somebody's property, unless you have permission to be there. Odd as it may seem to come across private land inside a state park, please respect it. If you want to go for a walk in the woods, look for trailheads with state Department of Environmental Conservation signs; they are on public land.

The Adirondack Mountains: The tallest summits—the celebrated High Peaks—occupy the northeast quarter of the Adirondack Park, but there are chains of mountains and scattered monadnocks throughout the region. They generally lie in parallel fault valleys, making a southwest–northeast diagonal across the park.

the success and decline of the industries that founded them, their story has excited little notice among Adirondack historians. If anything, the Adirondacks has enjoyed a certain nativist reputation as a demographic land apart, free and clear of "outsiders," the monolithic stronghold of the Yankee pioneer. But northern New York was never exempt from the demographic trends that salted so much of rural America with ethnic enclaves during the great age of industrialization. If a migratory lifestyle deprived many of these immigrant communities of a place in the written historical record, you can still trace the evidence of an ethnic presence in the tongue-twisting nomenclature of early headstones, the sunken remains of one-time railroad tracks, the French or Irish street names in Adirondack towns.

Not every 19th-century Adirondack railroad spur bore carloads full of hemlock bark or iron ore, pulpwood, or massive logs. Some were built specially to ferry a special cargo *to* the woods: the sightseers and "city sports" for whom, from 1870 to 1910 or so, a visit to the distant Adirondacks held all the exotic cachet of an African safari. The burgeoning resort scene was an inevitable extension of the "Grand Tour" of the North Country that already encompassed tony Saratoga Springs and elegant Lake George. And where railroad sleepers left off, stagecoaches and steamboats picked up—another source of seasonal employment for enterprising locals, some who would parlay modest stagecoach routes into backwoods transportation empires.

This new, bourgeois resort clientele expected rather different lodgings than the circuit riders and traveling peddlers who preceded them, and Adirondack hostelries made haste to adjust. The proverbial backcountry tavern with its rough pallets in the attic begat the North Country inn, which in turn begat the double-balconied hotel, with uniformed black waiters, Irish cooks, and ready stable of picturesque, authentically gruff Adirondack guides. More socially positioned visitors were lucky enough to enjoy an invitation to one of the Adirondack Great Camps, private compounds sometimes as built up as small towns. Here, guests were plied with the bubbliest champagne, the mildest Cuban stogies, and the most delicious six-course feasts that the ruthlessly gotten gains of the Gilded Age could buy.

Wilderness no longer had to justify itself as a means to an agricultural or industrial end; it was increasingly an end in itself and it was held for spirit, soul, and body, especially those bodies in the early grip of tuberculosis. Lots of rest and good clean air—that pretty much summed up the homely prescription of Dr. Edward Livingston Trudeau, the great champion of the "Adirondack cure," and that's what a six-week stint in the screened-in porch of a Saranac Lake village cure cottage delivered. In this hill-bound hamlet, there were, in addition to Trudeau's well-known sanatorium, cure cottages for Lower East Side tenement girls, for Cuban aristocrats, for show business mavens, and for Hungarian aesthetes. Robert Louis Stevenson did a turn at Saranac Lake. So did baseball star Christy Mathewson and the gangster "Legs" Diamond. You sat, you ate, you rested, you got bored out of your mind. But as often as not, you did get better. And if you didn't, your problem was you found the Adirondacks just too late to do you good.

What happened when the tourists and the travelers collided with the worked-over, roughed-up landscape of the Adirondack industrialist and his heavy-booted teams of loggers, tanners, river drivers, and mill workers? No matter how pristine the eventual destination, the view from the stagecoach or sleeper window almost certainly exposed the Adirondack adventurer to the occasional glimpse of clear-cut hillsides and tangled slash. Sometimes it seemed the more prolific the newly converted admirers of the region, the faster it was changing—and not for the better. Was it an accident that in the same year (1864) an anonymous editorial in the *New York Times* suggested that the Adirondack region be preserved as a "Central Park for the world" and George Perkins Marsh published his seminal book, *Man and Nature*, on the delicate relationship between a healthy forest and a secure watershed?

Cut too much, Marsh argued, and you set the scene for a tidal wave of muddy runoff and unleash the threat of flood and drought. Too much cutting can even make the climate change and diminish rainfall, which in turn would damage agricultural production. No more rain: no more farms, no more food—worst-case scenario, no more people! In New York State specifically, as surveyor Verplanck Colvin pointed out, a ravaged watershed in the north could mean lower water levels for the Hudson River and the Erie Canal—a disaster for commercial and transportation interests and for downstate politicians. A healthy watershed was also a safeguard against waterborne disease, a concern of no small moment to the epidemic-leery voters of metropolitan New York.

Although it would take a few more decades to gather steam enough to win the necessary political support, here was a perfectly utilitarian rationale for the founding of a preserve. No early advocate ever argued for the Adirondack Park in aesthetic terms alone. It helped that the region was gorgeous, but it was health and public safety, not good looks and recreation, that won the day in 1885 with the creation of the Adirondack Forest Preserve, then comprising almost 700,000 acres scattered across 11 counties. Five years later, the state began to consolidate its holdings with additional purchases, and the expectation was expressed that someday all the land

Presidents in Residence

Although we can't claim that George Washington slept here, the father of our country was certainly aware of the vital importance of fortifications at Ticonderoga and Crown Point along Lake Champlain's western shore. **Thomas Jefferson** and **James Madison** visited Lake George in 1791, on a summer reconnoiter to Vermont that doubled as a vacation; Jefferson, a seasoned world traveler, described the lake as one of the most beautiful he'd ever seen.

In 1817, **James Monroe** skirted the wild edge of what would become the Adirondack Park during a trip from Champlain to Sackets Harbor, on the Saint Lawrence River.

Andrew Jackson, who served in Congress from 1827 to 1829, was a close friend of Richard Keese II, after whom the village of Keeseville is named. Jackson ("Old Hickory") went north to see Keese, and in honor of the occasion, a hickory sapling was sought to plant in the front yard of the homestead. But no hickories could be found for miles around, so a bitter walnut was substituted. It thrived.

Chester A. Arthur stayed at Mart Moody's Mount Morris House, near Tupper Lake, in 1869, and slept on the floor like everyone else. When he was president, in 1881, Arthur named the guide and innkeeper postmaster of a new settlement named—surprisingly enough—Moody.

Grover Cleveland also knew Moody as a guide. While hunting near Big Wolf Pond, Cleveland reportedly said to him, "There's no wolves, here, darn it! But—there ain't a hundred pencils here, either, goin' every minute to take down everything I say." The president returned to the Adirondacks for his honeymoon, and also stayed at posh places in and around Lake Placid.

President **Benjamin Harrison** visited his vice-presidential candidate Whitelaw Reid at Loon Lake during the 1892 campaign, and he whistle-stopped in Crown Point, Lyon Mountain, Bloomingdale, and Saranac Lake. Along the way, he was feted with band concerts and pageants and given gifts of iron ore and wildflower arrangements. In 1895, Harrison built a rustic log camp named Berkeley Lodge on Second Lake, near Old Forge.

William McKinley made a special trip here to John Brown's grave in 1897, but it was his assassination that led to one of the most exciting footnotes in Adirondack history.

within the penciled "Blue Line" that outlined the edges of this new park would comprise "One Grand, Unbroken Domain."

In 1892, the Adirondack Park was officially defined. Three years after that, a new state constitution declared these Forest Preserve lands should be "forever kept as wild forest lands." Private land could still be logged, but state land was off-limits, allowed to grow up and fall down without interference from humans. It was, notes historian Philip Terrie, a provision that made the Adirondack Forest Preserve "one of the best protected landscapes in the world." And enacted not a day too soon: Late-19th-century innovations in pulp making meant that virtually *all* the woods were fair game for the lumber magnates, and between 1890 and 1910, the very years the park was birthed, logging activity on privately held lands within the park actually peaked. Of course, the more frenetic the pace of logging, the faster the non-state-owned forest was depleted, and as shortages occurred, many lumber companies began to move their logging operations elsewhere, to tree-cloaked Quebec, for instance, or to the temperate South.

And what was moving in about this time, sputtering exhaust and spitting gravel and scaring horses half to death? Infernal combustion. Automobiles were rare enough in the Adirondack region in the early 1900s, but within a generation roads

Berkeley Lodge, on Second Lake, the summer cottage of former president Benjamin Harrison.

Courtesy of Ted Comstock, Saranac Lake

Theodore Roosevelt, who first came to the mountains as a teenager in 1871, was climbing Mount Marcy when news of McKinley's imminent demise was cabled north. A guide scrambled up the peak to tell TR, who made it down in record time. Three relays of teams and wagons whisked him in the murk of night from the Tahawus Club to North Creek, and Roosevelt learned in the North Creek railroad station that he had become the twenty-sixth president on September 14, 1901.

Calvin Coolidge established a summer White House at White Pine Camp, on Osgood Pond, in 1926. This was at the height of Prohibition; silent Cal's place was a mere stone's throw away from Gabriels, a hotbed of bootleg activity.

Franklin D. Roosevelt was no stranger to the North Country. He officiated at the opening of the 1932 Winter Olympics, dedicated the Whiteface Veterans Memorial Highway in 1935, and celebrated the fiftieth anniversary of the Forest Preserve in Lake Placid that same year.

Bill Clinton's August 2000 visit to Lake Placid included golf and plenty of fresh air, but what locals remember is how a young woman flashed the commander in chief as he waited for a cone at Ben & Jerry's ice-cream shop on Main Street.

George W. Bush came to Wilmington to promote his "Clear Skies" initiative in April 2002. Heavy snows, perhaps laden with noxious chemicals described in the initiative, forced the speeches from a beach on the Ausable River to the lodge at Whiteface Mountain.

were snaking between passes. In their dusty wake followed not only carloads of vacationers but trailheads that met the roads and led hikers to remote summits; roadside auto courts, housekeeping cabins, and filling stations; and roadside attractions with music, dancing, and even dancing bears.

Was it the end of the Adirondack Park or the beginning? Certainly the age of the automobile spelled the death of the Adirondacks' vaunted isolation and mystique. You didn't need to come for a season anymore. From the necklace of midsize cities that outline the Adirondack region (Glens Falls, Plattsburgh, Ogdensburg, Watertown, Amsterdam, Gloversville, Massena, Malone), you could do it in a day. Or chug up from Albany or even Brooklyn for a nice long weekend: Pack the trunk with tent and camping gear, throw the kids in back under a blanket, check the oil, kick the tires—you're off. No two-week stay at one hotel; you could play connect-the-dots between lakeside campgrounds under the towering white pines, cook your own chow over an open fire instead of dealing with a stuck-up waiter in a uniform at some swank hotel. You didn't need to hire a guide; a good map and one of those new wood-canvas canoes could do you just as well.

Roads democratized the Adirondack experience as no paper legislation ever could, and with the ease of access, the reputation of the region as a recreational

Virgin Trees and Charismatic Megafauna

The Adirondack forest primeval—which survives today in scattered tracts of old growth in remote wilderness areas such as the Five Ponds and West Canadas—varies according to elevation and soil. At the very tops of some mountains, only alpine shrubs and flowers grow, and below them are stunted trees known as **krummholz**, which can be hundreds of years old yet only a few feet high. Lower down, thick **spruce** and **fir** forests grow; on steep, inaccessible slopes some patches have remained undisturbed for centuries. **White pine** and spruce take over at an elevation of 2,500 feet or so, with mixed hardwood forests—**yellow birch**, **beech**, **sugar maple**, plus **eastern hemlock**—covering miles and miles of the central Adirondacks. The understory in this woodland is the classic Adirondack landscape, with beautiful ferns and wildflowers such as **trillium**, **lady's slipper**, and **jack-in-the-pulpit**.

White pine towering 150 feet tall and enormous spruce were the first to fall before the woodsman's ax. These logs were floated downstream to towns and sawmills as early as 1812, and following the Civil War, when paper-making technology made the great leap from rags to wood pulp, softwood forests were stripped bare. Hemlocks, too, had great commercial value; bark was a necessary ingredient in leather tanning, but the wood itself was left to rot where it fell. Many towns in the central and southern Adirondacks owe their existence to tanneries that processed South American hides into American shoe parts.

Early records show a wide variety of wildlife ranging through the different habitats of woods and waters. **Elk** lived in the Saint Lawrence and Mohawk River Valleys as late as the 1820s, and moose were common throughout the lake country until about 1870 (they've since made a comeback). **Mountain lions** and **wolves** posed a serious threat to settlement, but generous bounties paid out by counties (in the mid-1800s, some locales paid more for bounties in a year than they spent on schools) decreased the numbers of predators considerably. Mountain lions are occasionally spotted today, although conservation officials deny any breeding population; questions linger about wolves. Did gray wolves ever really live in upstate New York, or are the smaller, reddish canines we call **coyotes** the historic Adirondack wolf?

Black bears have adapted remarkably well to life with humans; their numbers have been stable over this century. Other carnivores such as **fishers**, **pine martens**, and **bobcats** are thriving in the forest. **Lynx** once were found in the High Peaks and other rugged countryside, preying on **snowshoe hares**, but disappeared due to hunting and habitat

nirvana grew by leaps and bounds. Small towns reeling under the recent loss or exodus of the extractive industries rebounded with a plethora of services aimed squarely at the car-borne tourist: diners, supper clubs (maybe, during Prohibition, with a speakeasy in back), motels, and souvenir shops. As the century wore on, those small town storefronts increasingly would include the recreational outfitter and the real estate office. Nothing like the completion of a superhighway, the "Northway," or Interstate 87, in 1967, to whet the appetite of city dwellers keen to build their Adirondack getaway.

Indeed, so rapid was the proliferation of Adirondack second homes in the 1960s, and so potentially damaging was their impact on the landscape, that Governor Nelson Rockefeller appointed a commission that recommended a new agency just to oversee land use and development. Thus was spawned the controversial Adirondack Park Agency (APA) in 1974. Many are the local objections to the APA's unwieldy bureaucratic mandate (to guide development on public and private lands), but on one thing its critics can almost all wholeheartedly agree: The establishment more

Lynx once were found in the High Peaks and other rugged countryside, preying on snowshoe hares, but disappeared due to hunting and habitat changes. Courtesy of Eric Dresser, www.ecdphoto.addr.com

changes. Efforts to reintroduce the species in the 1980s have proven fruitless.

The big reintroduction success story is the **beaver**. For three centuries, well before maps and military expeditions, there was lively trade in beaver pelts, with furs shipped to Fort Orange (now Albany) and Montreal. Beaver hair pressed into felt was used in fashionable hats, and demand soon exceeded the supply. By 1894 beavers were virtually extinct; in the early 1900s, they were reintroduced to the Old Forge area. By 1910 the animals had spread throughout the central Adirondacks, busily building dams and flooding woodlands. Today you can see evidence of their engineering on almost any Adirondack waterway.

These beavers' efforts create habitat for the Adirondack bird population. **Loons**, revered for their haunting songs, inhabit many larger Adirondack lakes and ponds. With luck you may see an **ospreys**, **peregrine falcons**, or **bald eagles** soaring on warm currents over a lakeshore or cliff. **Hawks** are fairly easy to spot; songbirds—especially **warblers**—are plentiful during warm weather; and at least 10 varieties of **ducks** nest near the waterways of the park.

Moose have also made a comeback. There are believed to be more than 800 of these creatures in the Adirondacks, with the largest population not in the Moose River Plains, as most would assume, but near Upper Chateaugay Lake, in the northern park.

than a hundred years ago of the Adirondack Park was a miracle of timing, foresight, and good luck. It could not have happened any sooner, and it certainly could not have happened since. Love the park for its variety and beauty, and you won't be disappointed, but love it for its hidden history as well—the lost loggers, the vanished tannery towns, the boarded-over mine shafts, the stagecoaches, the peddlers, and the wedding cake hotels—and your love and understanding of it can only be enhanced.

Transportation
OVER THE RIVER AND THROUGH THE WOODS

ON ANY ROAD MAP OF NEW YORK STATE, the Adirondack Park shows up as a green, shield-shaped polygon. Looking closer, you'll notice that the park boundary encloses much empty space, crossed by few highways and sparsely dotted with towns. This reflects the large portion of the park that's public land, and it doesn't mean that those spidery thin lines are bad roads. Major highways through the Adirondacks are well-maintained two-lane blacktop, the lifelines of the region. Come winter, platoons of snowplows and sand trucks keep the roads clear; 2 feet of snow causes far less trouble here than 2 inches, in say, Washington, D.C.

On that road map, you'll notice lots of blue rivers and lakes, the original travel corridors. By canoe or by snowshoe over the ice, Native Americans and the first Europeans followed these paths of least resistance. Although no single river provided passage through the entire rugged region, it was possible to travel from the southwest to northeast corners via the Moose, Raquette, and Saranac River systems with but a few short *carries*, the Adirondack word for "portages." The importance of the rivers is underscored by the fact that in the early 1800s, many streams were declared public highways for floating logs to downstream markets.

The first roads were hacked out of the forest to transport iron ore, charcoal, and other commodities between settlements. Later, some of these dirt tracks were paved with logs (known as corduroy roads), but they were not much more than wide, slightly less primitive trails. A stagecoach ride on one could be a bone-jarring, tooth-loosening experience, and a special passenger wagon, the "buckboard"—with a long springy board between the front and back wheels—evolved to make the best of terrible thoroughfares.

Even into the beginnings of the tourist era, waterways remained principal transportation routes, and most towns were built along a lake or river that allowed people to connect with the larger world. In response, specific vessels were developed: the guideboat—light, fast, and maneuverable, easy for one man to carry—with oars rather than paddles, marvelous for fishing and hunting on Adirondack ponds; and tiny steamboats, built to fit the small lakes of the interior.

The first widespread, modern, means of movement was the railroad. Originally built to haul out timber, the railroads quickly became a profitable, convenient way to haul in tourists. Beginning about 1900, a web of lines throughout the region offered several passenger trains a day speeding north from East Coast cities to destinations in the woods. One of the most popular targets, Blue Mountain Lake, could be reached by a remarkable trip that involved an overnight train ride from New York to Utica, transfer to a steamboat, change to the world's shortest standard-gauge railroad (less than a mile long), and a final leg on another steamboat for delivery to your hotel of choice.

Road to Eagle Bay postcard courtesy of Ted Comstock, Saranac Lake.

By the 1920s, with the growing popularity of the automobile, roads were gradually improved until they surpassed the railroads, although such special offerings as ski trains enabled passenger service to struggle along until well after World War II. The late 1960s were a watershed time; the last passenger train serving the interior, the Adirondack Division of the New York Central (the Utica–to–Lake Placid line), rolled to a stop in 1965, and the Adirondack Northway, the only interstate highway in northeastern New York, was completed along the eastern edge of the park in 1967. This event seemed at once to ensure that the family car would be the way the vast majority of people would travel to the Adirondacks for years to come and to discourage the development of a public transportation system.

So, if you want to get around in the 21st-century Adirondacks, you'll need your own wheels. If you don't own a car, rent one before you get to the North Country. Even if you come here by some other means, once you arrive it can be difficult to do much without one. Public transportation is scarce and not always convenient.

The following information gives you the best routes for access to the Adirondacks and for getting around once you're here. We start with the most practical means of transportation—your car—and also provide details on bus, train, and air service. Routes that incorporate a Lake Champlain ferry crossing are also described.

BY CAR

Highways to Get You Here

Major highways can get you to the perimeter of the Adirondack Park from all points:

- *From New York City:* Take I-87 north. This is the New York State (or Thomas E. Dewey) Thruway, a toll road, to Albany (Exit 24); then it becomes the toll-free Adirondack Northway (I-87). Principal exits off the Northway for the interior are: 14 and 15 for Saratoga Springs; 18 for Glens Falls; 21 for Lake George (roughly four hours from metro New York); 23 for Warrensburg and the central Adirondacks; 28 for Schroon Lake and Ticonderoga (about five hours from New York); and 30 for Lake Placid, Saranac Lake, and the High Peaks.

Winter Driving

The Adirondack climate that dumps 10 or more feet of snow in an average winter may be great news for skiers and snowmobilers, but what about the road conditions, you might wonder. Throughout the Adirondack Park, the state and county highway departments have plenty of snowplows that toil night and day to keep roads clear. For several years, a "bare roads" policy has been in effect, meaning that sand and salt are applied liberally when roads may be slippery. Another plus for winter driving these days is the prevalence of four-wheel- and front-wheel-drive cars, which handle better on slick roads than the traditional rear-wheel-drive vehicles. (If you're coming to the wintry Adirondacks in a pickup truck, van, or passenger car with rear-wheel drive, try putting at least 150 pounds of weight—concrete blocks, sandbags, whatever—over your rear axle to help traction.)

The worst driving scenarios often occur at the beginning or end of winter, when temperatures hovering at the freezing point can cause a mixture of snow, rain, and sleet, with fog near lakes and low cold spots. Then it's best to consider your options: Can you wait out the storm at your lodgings, or are you prepared to rest at a remote pullout if conditions deteriorate? Every winter traveler's car should carry a sleeping bag, a small shovel, a snow scraper, extra windshield-washing fluid, a powerful flashlight, and some candy or granola bars and bottled water, just in case you need to dig out of a snowbank or sit quietly beside the road for a few hours as the weather takes its course. Cell-phone owners beware: Coverage is spotty, so don't count on it.

- *From Philadelphia and South:* Take the Northeast Extension of the Pennsylvania Turnpike and then I-81 north to Syracuse. From Syracuse take I-90 east to entry points such as Utica and Amsterdam, or I-81 farther north and then east on NY 3 at Watertown to reach the northern areas. Either way, it's not as far as you might think—you can reach the southwest edge of the park in about six hours from Philadelphia. Or you can take I-88 from Binghamton to Schenectady, go east two exits on I-90 and head north on I-87 from Albany; see above, "From New York City." And there's always the Garden State Parkway to the New York Thruway, then proceed as above.
- *From Buffalo, Cleveland, and West:* Take I-90 east to Syracuse, then proceed as directed above ("From Philadelphia"). From Buffalo to the edge of the park north of Utica is a little more than four hours.
- *From Toronto and Detroit:* Take NY 401 toward Montreal. Three toll bridges cross the Saint Lawrence River. The one that provides the most direct access not only to the edge of the park but also to such interior locations as Lake Placid and Blue Mountain Lake leaps from Prescott (Highway 16 exit) to Ogdensburg; the toll in 2012 for a car is $2.75 U.S. one way. On the U.S. side, take NY 37 west a couple of miles to NY 68 south to Colton, and NY 56 into the park. From Toronto it's about five hours to the edge of the park and seven to the center. Travelers are required to present an enhanced driver's license, passport, or birth certificate at the border.
- *From Ottawa:* Take Highway 16 to the Prescott–Ogdensburg toll bridge and proceed as directed above ("From Toronto"). Allow two hours to the edge of the park, four to central points.
- *From Montreal:* Take Highway 15 south; this becomes I-87, the Adirondack Northway, at the border. Principal jumping-off exits for the interior are 38

(Plattsburgh), only an hour (plus customs wait, which can be lengthy) from the outskirts of Montreal; and 34 (Keeseville), twenty minutes south of Exit 38.

- *From Boston:* Take the Massachusetts Pike, I-90, to I-87, then head north and follow the directions given under "From New York," above, to get past Albany. Or, take I-93 north to I-89, to one of the Lake Champlain ferry crossings described below. Via Albany, the Adirondacks is about four hours from Boston; via the ferries it's closer to five, but the ferries are fun.

Highways to Get You Around Once You Get Here

North and South

Not surprisingly, four of the five north–south highways that traverse the Adirondacks do so in the narrow corridor between Lake Champlain and the mountains. This is where much of the region's population and many of its attractions are located, and it's also on a direct line between two concentrations of population: New York City and Montreal. These routes are:

Inlet postcard courtesy of Ted Comstock, Saranac Lake.

- *NY 9N,* which rambles through lovely rolling countryside from Saratoga Springs northwest to Corinth and Lake Luzerne, then east to Lake George village, then up to Hague, and to Lake Champlain at Ticonderoga, where it meets:
- *NY 22,* which hugs Lake Champlain all the way from Whitehall up to Ticonderoga, where it joins 9N. The combined routes have expansive views of the lake on the east and farmland in the valley beneath the High Peaks on the west, passing through Crown Point and Port Henry. At Westport, NY 22 follows the lake valley north to Willsboro, while 9N heads west to Elizabethtown, over Spruce Hill and on to Keene. This historic route passes through Upper Jay, Jay, and Au Sable Forks, paralleling the Ausable River, and connects again with NY 22 at Keeseville.
- *US 9* begins in the park just north of Glens Falls and skirts Schroon Lake and the Schroon and Boquet Rivers, but its route has been mostly supplanted by:
- *I-87,* the Adirondack Northway, an honest-to-goodness interstate highway named "America's Most Scenic Highway" in 1966–67.
- *NY 30,* the fifth north–south route, bisects the region from Gloversville via Speculator, Indian Lake, Blue Mountain Lake, Long Lake, Tupper Lake, and Paul Smiths to Malone. The remote and lightly populated western half of the region has no north–south highways.

East and West

Reflecting the reality that most travel in the Adirondacks always has been north–south, only three highways cross the entire region on the east–west axis, and two of them cover some of the same territory. These are:

- *NY 28,* which forms a semicircle from Warrensburg through North Creek, Indian Lake, Blue Mountain Lake, Inlet, Old Forge, and down to Utica.
- *NY 8,* which zigzags west from Hague, on Lake George, through Brant Lake,

Adirondack Access

Blue Mountain Lake is central—it's 1½ to 2 hours to the edge of the park in every direction—so this location will serve as a reference point in determining about how long a drive to the Adirondacks will take:

City	Miles to Blue Lake Mountain	Approximate Time to Blue Mountain Lake
Albany	105	2 hrs
Binghamton	220	4 hrs
Boston (via Albany)	270	5½ hrs
Buffalo	280	5½ hrs
Burlington, VT	100	3 hrs (involves ferry)
Montreal	165	3½ hrs*
New York	260	5½ hrs
Ottawa	150	3½ hrs*
Philadelphia	390	8 hrs
Rochester	210	4½ hrs
Syracuse	140	3 hrs
Toronto	320	7 hrs*
Utica	90	2 hrs

*plus possible delays crossing border

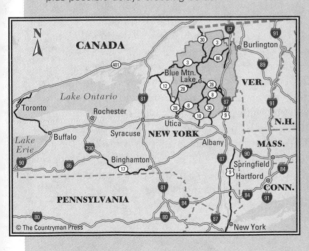

Chestertown, Johnsburg, Speculator, Lake Pleasant, Piseco, Hoffmeister, and southwest to Utica.
- *NY 3*, which crosses the northern part of the park from Plattsburgh, to Redford, Vermontville, Bloomingdale, Saranac Lake, Tupper Lake, Piercefield, Childwold, Cranberry Lake, Star Lake, and exits the Blue Line west to Watertown.

Additional Routes

Other shorter but scenic routes in the Adirondacks include:
- *Northeast on NY 73* from Underwood (Exit 30 of the Northway) to Lake Placid, which offers a 45-minute panorama of the High Peaks.

- *West on NY 86* from Jay, past the foot of Whiteface Mountain and through dramatic Wilmington Notch to Lake Placid, then on to Saranac Lake and Paul Smiths.
- *East on NY 374* from Chateaugay, past the Chateaugay Lakes and Lyon Mountain to Plattsburgh, which, in addition to views of the Adirondacks, provides a long-distance scan across Lake Champlain to the Green Mountains of Vermont as it drops down Dannemora Mountain.
- *Northwest on NY 28N* from North Creek on NY 28 to Long Lake. Be sure to stop at the roadside rest area at Newcomb, where a display identifies the High Peaks panorama to the north.
- *East on the "Number Four" Road* from Lowville, past Stillwater Reservoir and on to Big Moose and Eagle Bay, which is on NY 28. Rather than great views, this drive offers a sense of the forest depths. About half of the 45 miles is gravel or graded dirt, and there are no services over the full distance.

The Adirondack North Country Association has created driving tours in and around the Adirondacks. These are arranged to hit scenic vistas, historic markers, craft shops, sporting events and so on. You can check out these routes at www.adirondackscenicbyways.org.

By Bus

Considering the size of the Adirondack region—you could fit Connecticut inside it— it's astonishing how little bus service exists. There's only one round-trip a day that's of any use, and once you get off the bus you're dependent on traveling by foot or finding sparse taxi service and even sparser rental car possibilities. If you do plan to use bus service: Adirondack Trailways (1-800-776-7548; www.trailwaysny.com) makes stops in various locations in the park (stops at diners and shops remind you you're not in urban America anymore): Keene Valley (Noon Mark Diner), Lake George (Lake George Hardware), Lake Placid (Olympic Authority), Paul Smiths, Saranac Lake (Hotel Saranac), Schroon Lake (Mount Severance Country Store), and Warrensburg (Marco Polo Pasta). But these hubs come and go, and some are seasonal, so call ahead. Also, bus tickets can be purchased at these hubs. Call ahead or visit your local terminal for the latest bus schedule since it changes season to season. In 2012, a one-way bus ticket from Port Authority, in Manhattan, to Lake Placid, was $65.75.

By Train

Amtrak

Amtrak (1-800-872-7245; www.amtrak.com) operates one train a day each way between New York City and Montreal. The Adirondack leaves each city in the morning and reaches its destination the same evening (schedules are different on Saturdays and Sundays). The train closely follows the west shore of Lake Champlain for the better part of 90 scenic miles. The New York departure is from Penn Station. It makes stops in Saratoga Springs, Fort Edward, and the Adirondacks— Ticonderoga, Port Henry, Westport, and Port Kent—but how to get around once you are deposited at these places can be problematic. You may arrange, in advance, for shuttle service from the depot in Westport to Lake Placid (or Elizabethtown or Keene) by calling Ground Force One/Majestic Limousine (518-523-0294; www .groundforce1.net), Rick's Taxi (518-523-4741) or Polar Express (518-327-3331). Train travel may not be what it once was, but compared to buses and puddle-jumper airplanes, this remains the most relaxing, visually engaging way to get to the Adirondacks. The trip is spectacular, involving tunnels, high trestles, rocky ledges 150 feet above the waters of Lake Champlain, and vistas of farm and forest, river, lake, and mountain that simply cannot be had any other way. The least expensive Fort Edward–Plattsburgh one-way fare was $23 in 2012. One-way from Penn Station, in New York City, to Westport was $63.

Amtrak's Empire Service leaves New York's Penn Station several times a day and stops in Albany–Rensselaer, Schenectady, and Utica. One train a day from Boston hooks up with this route at Albany–Rensselaer. Coming from the west, Empire Service originates in Buffalo; Chicago–Boston/New York and Toronto–New York Amtrak trains also ply this route.

An Amtrak passenger train offers trips from Utica to Thendara/Old Forge, allowing at least semiregular train service to the southwestern Adirondacks. Trains run primarily Wednesday through Saturday, June through October. The ride takes approximately 2½ hours; an adult round-trip fare in 2012 was $37.50. Once you're in Old Forge, there's a shuttle bus to take you to McCauley Mountain and shops on Main Street. This route is not in Amtrak's database, so contact Adirondack Scenic Railroad's office (315-369-6290 or 1-800-819-2291; www.adirondackrr.com) for schedule and fare information.

North Creek–bound travelers can take Amtrak from Penn Station, in New York City, to Saratoga Springs, then transfer to the new Saratoga & North Creek Railway, a comfortable, elegant and postcard-view-packed ride to the Adirondack Park's interior (see below).

Tourist Trains

The Adirondack Scenic Railroad (ASR) operates a popular short line from its Thendara station (trains depart at 10 AM, 12:30 PM, and 2:45 PM) in spring through fall, with round-trip runs south along the Moose River to Otter Lake, and north to Carter Station. Look for special events (simulated train robberies, murder mysteries, the Polar Express) and unique travel opportunities (mountain bikers and canoeists—and their respective gear—may use the train as part of their explorations). Fares in 2012 were between $17 and $37.50 for adults, depending on the trip. For fare and schedule information, call 315-369-6290 or visit www.adirondackrr.com.

The Adirondack Railway Preservation Society, the nonprofit outfit that operates the Adirondack Scenic, runs an excursion line—though its future is currently unclear—on the 8 miles of track between Saranac Lake and Lake Placid. It's a loud but nostalgic ride. The round-trip fare in 2012 is $19.

The new Saratoga & North Creek Railway (1-877-726-7245; www.sncrr.com), which connects the Spa City to the central Adirondack ski town, revives a route—Saratoga, Corinth, Hadley/Luzerne, Stony Creek, Thurman, the Glen, Riparius, North Creek—that had been abandoned for half a century. North Creek's depot earned a place in history in September 1901 as the spot where Teddy Roosevelt, then vice president, learned that William McKinley had died in Buffalo, and that he was the next president of the United States (a museum in the station complex describes this event and showcases local history). Passengers are raving about the line's 1950s air-conditioned dome car that has upper and lower level seating and a fine menu, and its holiday Polar Express and ski-season snow trains. The S&NCR runs Thursday through Monday, July through October; in 2012, Saratoga to North Creek one-way fares were $13 for coach and $27 for dome. The snow train brings folks to the North Creek station Fridays, Saturdays, and Sundays, December through

Big-Game Crossing

Keep your eyes peeled for deer as you drive through the Adirondacks— not only to see them, which will be a pleasant memory of your trip, but also to avoid hitting them.

Deer are most active in the late afternoon and evening, and particularly just after sunset, when they're also hardest to see. They often travel in pairs or small groups; if one crosses the road ahead of you, others are likely to follow. They're especially mobile during fall, for several reasons: that's their breeding season; they have to travel more to find food at this time of year; and hunters disrupt their daily routines. In winter they seek out plowed roads since the going is easier. Around Old Forge, especially NY 28 and the South Shore Road, deer are as common as squirrels all year.

The moose population has grown steadily, and sadly, car-moose encounters are becoming more common. Courtesy of Eric Dresser, www.ecdphoto.addr.com

One more thing: The instinctive reaction of a deer caught by car headlights is to freeze, not to scramble out of the way. It's up to you to miss. Your best bet: Drive alertly, obey speed limits—and take those deer crossing signs seriously.

MOOSE CROSSING signs have been installed across the park; they're not just a tourist gimmick but a real warning of a potential hazard. The moose population has grown steadily, and sadly, car-moose encounters are becoming more common. Pay special attention in the fall, when thousand-pound bulls can come crashing out of the forest directly into your lane, and at night, when your headlights may shine under their bodies without reflecting in their eyes.

March, where a shuttle delivers them to Gore Mountain. One-way fares in 2012 were $18 for coach and $30 for dome.

By Ferry

The only way to get to the Adirondacks from the east is to cross Lake Champlain, the largest freshwater lake in America after the Great Lakes. You can do that via the brand new Lake Champlain Bridge, which connects Crown Point, New York, and Addison, Vermont, but has a nice view that lasts for just 30 seconds. Why not savor the journey and take one of the Lake Champlain ferries? The views last for up to an hour and you don't have to steer. Three of the four crossings are operated by Lake Champlain Transportation, the oldest continuously running inland navigation company in America (802-864-9804; www.ferries.com). Rates vary depending on type of vehicle, number and age of persons in it, and so forth; those shown were for car and one driver, one-way, in 2012. Credit cards are not accepted.

- *From Charlotte, Vermont, to Essex:* This may be the most scenic route, seeming to deliver you truly into the mountains. Crossing time is 20 minutes; trips run year-round, departing Charlotte starting at 6 or 7 AM, depending on the season. $9.80.

- *From Burlington, Vermont, to Port Kent:* This is almost as scenic, and delightful for its relaxing hour-long crossing of the widest part of the lake. Trips begin at 8 or 9 AM and run several times a day from mid-May through the beginning of October. $17.80.
- *From Grand Isle, Vermont, north of Burlington, to Plattsburgh:* A bit north of the Adirondacks, this route provides a decent if long-distance view of them. It operates 24 hours a day year-round, blasting through ice packs in even the coldest snaps, generally every twenty minutes (every 40 minutes in the dead of night). Crossing time is 12 minutes. $9.80.
- *From Shoreham, Vermont, to Ticonderoga:* This crossing is a living museum. Following a route that's been in use since the British army arrived in the 1700s, it brings you to the foot of the promontory on which the restored fort reposes. This is one of the few cable-guided ferries left in America: The cable is attached at each landing and a tugboat provides power. Crossing time is six minutes; the one-way fare is about $8 per car, and trips run from 8 AM to 5:45 PM, from mid-May through late October, and from 8 AM to 6:45 PM July 1 through Labor Day. There's no set schedule; "We just go back and forth," says the captain. For more information: 802-897-7999.

By Air

Commercial Airports

In all this vast territory there's only one commercial airport: Adirondack Regional Airport at Lake Clear (518-891-4600), about 15 minutes from Saranac Lake and 30 from Lake Placid. In 2012, it is served by the commuter line Cape Air (1-800-352-0714), which has daily service to and from Boston to connect travelers with national and international airline services, three times a week in winter and four times a week in summer. Fares depend on the time of year, how far ahead you purchase your ticket, and so forth. In a random sampling, the nonrefundable price in winter 2012 for a flight from Boston to Saranac Lake was about $120 round-trip or $58 one-way.

As these commuter airlines come and go, it's best to call first to make sure this one's still using Lake Clear. If you're calling another airport or a travel agent, ask about "Saranac Lake," not "Adirondack." Car rentals are available at the airport: Hertz (518-891-9044), Lavigne's Taxi (518-891-2444), Rick's Taxi (518-523-4741), Ground Force One/Majestic Limousine (1-800-397-2602) and Polar Express (518-327-3331) also provide transportation to nearby towns.

Cities just outside the Adirondacks that offer air service are Plattsburgh, Albany, Syracuse, and Burlington, Vermont (amenities such as jets and a variety of rental cars), and Watertown.

Private Airports

Private airports, ranging from a tarmac strip down to a patch of grass in the woods, can be found scattered about the Adirondacks, in such places as Schroon Lake, Ticonderoga, and Westport. Consult a good navigational map. The most significant is on the outskirts of Lake Placid, with a 4,200-foot runway, public lounge, and other facilities: 518-523-2473. Another is at Piseco (518-548-3415). Better be prepared to be met at most of the others; taxi service and cars to rent are nowhere to be found in most cases, and it can be a hike to get to town. For the truly adventuresome, you can charter a seaplane to pick you up on the East River, at 23rd Street and Waterside Plaza, New York City (see page 85 for seaplane services).

Glen Street, Glens Falls, N.Y.

Gateway Cities

SARATOGA SPRINGS AND GLENS FALLS

ALTHOUGH NEITHER SARATOGA SPRINGS NOR GLENS FALLS is in the Adirondack Park, that fact is merely technical for people from downstate heading north on I-87. After the three-hour push out of metropolitan New York and up the Hudson Valley, the exit signs for Saratoga and Glens Falls are the starting gates that signal the home stretch.

SARATOGA SPRINGS

Once in a blue moon the urge may overtake an Adirondacker to swap the warble of a loon for the strains of Yo-Yo Ma—and then it's off to Saratoga, which every summer serves up an arts and music calendar that leaves no day unfilled. This is the Adirondack region's favorite getaway, a retreat of high culture, fine dining, and matchless Victorian architecture. You can use Saratoga as a springboard to explore the North Country, or for its own hospitable, hedonistic self. Just peel off the Northway (I-87) at exits 13, 14, or 15, and as fast as you can say, "I got the horse right here," you're there.

From the beginning, Saratoga—Mohawk for "place of the rapid water"—has enjoyed a reputation as a bold exception to every imaginable rule. In the colonial era, when New York's wild country was a war zone for rival bands of Native Americans, Saratoga, home to scores of cherished therapeutic springs, was off-limits, an oasis of tranquility. Two centuries later, Prohibition-era gangsters honored a summer truce while ensconced in sumptuous Saratoga digs.

In the 19th century and through the next, dingy, river-driven mill towns all around the Spa City rose and fell, while Saratoga buffed its gleaming image as a world apart. Too self-impressed and naughty for the staid decorum of the Hudson Valley to the south, too frivolous for the rough-and-tumble Adirondacks to the north, the town played a vital role in both. Saratoga was the first stop on the Grand Tour of the Northern Wilderness, which introduced Gilded Age excursionists to the wonders of Ausable Chasm and Lake George. Halfway between Manhattan and Montreal,

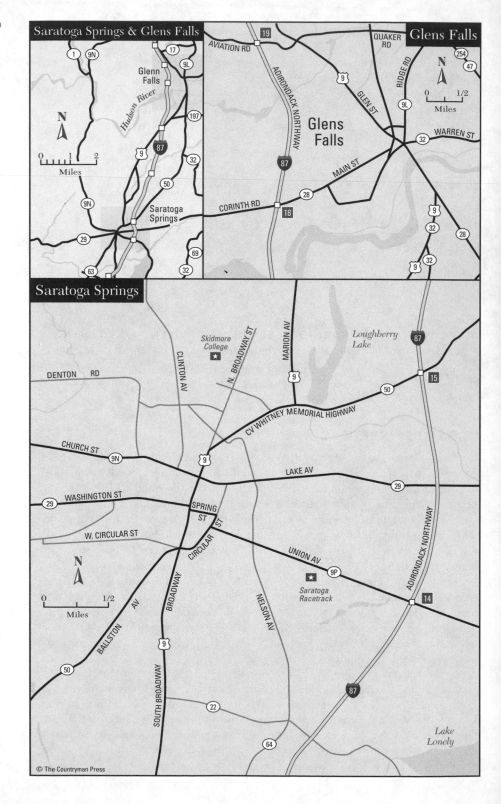

Saratoga Springs & Glens Falls

Glenn Falls

Hudson River

Glens Falls

Glens Falls

AVIATION RD

QUAKER RD

RIDGE RD

GLEN ST

ADIRONDACK NORTHWAY

WARREN ST

MAIN ST

CORINTH RD

Saratoga Springs

Saratoga Springs

Skidmore College

Loughberry Lake

DENTON RD

CLINTON AV

N. BROADWAY ST

MARION AV

CV WHITNEY MEMORIAL HIGHWAY

CHURCH ST

LAKE AV

WASHINGTON ST

SPRING ST

CIRCULAR ST

W. CIRCULAR ST

UNION AV

Saratoga Racetrack

BROADWAY

NELSON AV

ADIRONDACK NORTHWAY

BALLSTON AV

SOUTH BROADWAY

Lake Lonely

© The Countryman Press

here was founded the oldest running thoroughbred racetrack in the country; here constructed the nation's biggest hotel, the Grand Union (halls that went on for a mile and a half, carpets that stretched for 7 acres). And here was built a perfect stunner of a casino that the *New York Times* called "the finest hell on earth."

The grand piazzas have given way to street-side cafés, and Canfield Casino is now a respectable historical museum, but you can still play the odds at the world's prettiest racetrack—or skip the horseplay completely. In the six-week "season," Saratoga Springs is as good-times crazy as ever.

Nowadays, Saratoga's dozen-plus open-sided spring pavilions no longer draw dapper men and wide-hatted women waiting for a dipper boy to dole out a dram. Hydrotherapy fell from favor 50 years ago and with it the tradition of the two- or three-week "cure," a regimen of porch sitting, park promenading, mud soaking, and ritualized sipping of spring water reputed to be good for everything from eyestrain to arthritis. But Saratogians swear by the stuff; pick up a map at the Urban Cultural Park on Broadway and treat yourself to a walking tour of the downtown springs. Although the mud baths are gone, you can still savor the romance of an old-time spa in the porcelain tubs at the Roosevelt Baths and Spa (1-800-452-7275; www.gideon putnam.com) in Saratoga Spa State Park and other sip-and-soak options around town.

Broadway is a draw in its own right. Bracketed on the north by Victorian mansions and the woodsy campus of Skidmore College, on the south by the Spa State Park, this is the street that gives Saratoga Springs its architectural spine. The 1953 demolition of the landmark Grand Union Hotel was a wake-up call for preservation. Boarded-up Victorian storefronts and office buildings emerged from a deep sleep with smart new paint jobs and market-savvy agenda. Ethnic restaurants joined the steak-and-spuds stand-bys. An infusion of hip venues—a classy wine bar, an artisanal bakeshop, a gourmet food purveyor, brewpubs, and a city arts center—revived half dead façades. With the coming of many chain stores, the Parisian-profile Broadway is gone, but it is still hands-down the sprightliest downtown around.

The people-watching is fabulous, especially from the vantage of an espresso bar or outdoor bistro. On Broadway, you'll see high rollers in their summer whites, cigar-chomping gamblers straight out of *The Sopranos,* Hispanic horse walkers, and frock-coated Hasids from Brooklyn. Neon-headed skateboarders drift around in packs.

Then, when Broadway stales, stroll the side streets. Franklin Square, west of Broadway, is crammed with architectural gems, some fixed-up, some in seedy disrepair. To Broadway's east are Phila Street and Caroline Street, both chockablock with offbeat shops and restaurants. On Phila is the modest entrance to the legendary Caffè Lena, (518-583-0022; www.caffelena.org; 47 Phila Street), the longest-running coffeehouse in the country, a funky upstairs 1960s throwback serving up good folk music most every night. Bob Dylan, Dave Van Ronk, Arlo Guthrie, Greg Brown, Odetta, Rick Danko, and Emmylou Harris have played here. Keep walking and you come to Circular Street, the heart of Saratoga's venerable Victorian district. Follow Circular to Union Avenue, lined with graceful homes, one top-flight museum of horse racing, and the fabled Thoroughbred track itself.

Saratoga Springs is ideally positioned for day trips. The Adirondack Park is as handy as the top third of Saratoga County, as distant as a 2.5-hour drive if you're aiming for the drama of the High Peaks. Five miles southwest on NY 50 brings you to Saratoga's spinster aunt, Ballston Spa, once as chic as Saratoga was unknown, today a laid-back village with a main street favored by antique dealers and artists. West on NY 9N takes you through the Adirondacks' piney borderlands. You can also find the Adirondacks by way of Corinth, birthplace of International Paper, and the nearby village, Lake Luzerne, cherished for a summer music colony and some bite-size historical museums.

New England, or the feeling of it, finds you long before you reach Vermont in the spruced-up clapboard villages of Greenwich and Cambridge to Saratoga's east. This is farm country, rolling, open, early settled, a trove of early American architectural styles. Stop for the fresh-made cider doughnuts at Saratoga Apple, Inc. (518-695-3131; www.saratogaapple.com; 1174 NY 29), mosey through drowsy Schuylerville, make a stop at Old Saratoga Books (518-695-5607; www.oldsaratoga books.com; 94 Broad Street), and cross the Hudson River into Washington County. Hard by the county fairgrounds is the Hand Melon Market (518-692-7505; hand melonfarm.com; 533 Wilbur Avenue, Greenwich). Hand melon is a tasty cantaloupe, and if you like it, you might try the homemade melon ice cream down the street at the Ice Cream Man (518-692-8382; www.the-ice-cream-man.com; 417 NY 29, Greenwich); however long the line, it's worth the wait. Cafés, shops, and a popular bistro with a fine arts gallery, One One One (518-692-8016; www.111mainstreet.net; 111 Main Street), anchor the meandering main street of pretty Greenwich. High in the hills is a terrific used bookstore, the Owl Pen (518-692-7039; 166 Riddle Road— and don't try finding it yourself, ask for directions), or, if you press on, the scenic Batten Kill Railroad (518-692-2160; 1 Elbow Street). The next stop, Cambridge, is home to art galleries, and Hubbard Hall (518-677-2495; www.hubbardhall.org; 25 East Main Street), an old-time opera house where you can catch a fiddle contest or chamber music. The restored glorious old Cambridge Hotel (518-677-5626; www.cambridgehotel.com; 4 West Main Street) is the reputed birthplace of pie à la mode. And just north is Salem, home to Salem Artworks (www.salemartworks.com; 19 Cary Lane), a multitiered arts center and sculpture park that offers workshops, hosts gallery exhibitions, and nurtures established and emerging artists in the region.

Pick Your Spot
Lodging in Saratoga Springs

Accommodations in Saratoga Springs range from bare bones to celestial, in keeping with the wildly diverse ways and means of summer throngs. Modest but serviceable motels line US 9 along the north and south exurbs of Saratoga Springs. Chains, with restaurants, conference centers, indoor pools, and parking—the Saratoga Hilton (518-584-4000; www.thesaratogahotel.com; 534 Broadway), and Holiday Inn (518-584-4550; 232 Broadway)—anchor both ends of Broadway, with one plain-but-honest hometown standby, the Saratoga Downtowner Motel (518-584-6160; www.saratogadowntowner.com; 413 Broadway), pinning down the middle.

Whatever the class or quality of lodging, from a Depression-era housekeeping cottage to a palatial suite at the Batcheller Mansion Inn, one rule abides for all—when the track is open, rates go up. Waaaaayyyy up.

The Adelphi Hotel (518-587-4688; www.adelphihotel.com; 365 Broadway) was once the haunt of gangster types, but it's now a favorite of the New York City Ballet, and the undisputed jewel in the crown of Saratoga's elite hotels. Flanking Broadway at Caroline, it is the only surviving grand hotel from the Gilded Age, still boasting the original second-story piazza above the handsome entrance. Rooms are small but uniquely atmospheric; ask for one with a Broadway view. Late at night, the

Along Broadway, in Saratoga Springs   Courtesy of Kelly Kilgallon

lobby and moonlit patio are great places to order a drink and a dessert and lounge under hand-painted wallpaper on a Mae West fainting couch, ogling the celebrities. Open May through October.

Batcheller Mansion Inn (518-584-7012 or 1-800-616-7012; www.batcheller mansioninn.com; 20 Circular Street) is the ultimate for fans of Victorian Gothic design—your stay at this luxurious inn with its stunning mansard roof, clamshell arches, and dome-capped minaret will make you think you went to historic conservation heaven. This over-the-top B&B was the first residence in the United States to be patented (the minaret was inspired by the original owner's appointment as magistrate to Cairo under President Ulysses Grant). Rooms range from simply elegant to outright decadent, with canopy beds, double Jacuzzis, billiard tables, and, in the library, a large-screen TV, should Saratoga's nightlife fail to divert.

Saratoga Arms (518-584-1775; www.saratogaarms.com; 497 Broadway) is only a stone's throw from the heart of downtown. If the Adelphi is a giddy debutante, the 16-room Saratoga Arms is the oh-so-suave bachelor—quiet, eminently tasteful, scrupulously private,

and set up with every boutique treat (bathrobe, iron, WiFi, and hairdryer in each room, and, according to the *London Financial Times*, "the best coffee this side of the Hudson River"). Meticulously restored down to the antique wicker on the porch, this concierge hotel on the north end of Broadway is a getaway within a getaway.

Union Avenue, the elegant thoroughfare that runs from the artists' retreat Yaddo past the thoroughbred racetrack to Congress Park, is Saratoga's gold coast for upscale bed & breakfasts. Here are some of the better known, each commanding its own faithful clientele: Six Sisters Bed and Breakfast (518-583-1173; www.sixsistersbandb .com; 149 Union Avenue) offers a cheery vibe, designer coffee, hearty breakfasts, and expert insider advice that keep the patrons coming back. This Victorian favorite, with quirky gingerbread fretwork, is only a short stroll from the track. Particularly popular is a hotel-and-spa package deal with the Crystal Spa.

Union Gables (518-584-1558; www .uniongables.com; 55 Union Avenue) is a grand Queen Anne stalwart designed by R. Newton Brezee. In the early 1990s it underwent a massive restoration and emerged a sparkling kid-friendly B&B with all the trimmings: hot tub, exercise room, bikes for guests, and a refrigerator in every lavish room. While some are themed (the Adirondack-style room features branches for curtain rods), most hew faithfully to Saratoga's high Victorian style. There are 11 rooms, each with a distinctive "personality," and two guest rooms in an adjacent carriage house.

Westchester House (1-800-581-7613; www.westchesterhousebandb .com; 102 Lincoln Avenue), with its puckishly offbeat pastel paint job, seven rooms, lovely grounds, and the innkeepers' keen knowledge of the local scene, hosts regulars returning to this impeccably managed, longtime Victorian B&B. It's only blocks from Union Avenue in a city neighborhood called Five Points, centrally located between the track and the Saratoga Performing Arts Center.

Local Flavors
Where to Eat in Saratoga Springs

Saratoga Springs has always been a city with an outsized appetite. High-roller Diamond Jim Brady could pack away four dozen oysters, six lobsters, a whopping steak, and a dozen crabs at a sitting. You can still chow your way through a brace of country or Victorian-themed steak-and-salad joints, or find yourself an all-you-can-eat Chinese or Mexican buffet.

But you can also eat well. Very well. And spend a lot of money doing it—which Saratogians and a lot of other northern New Yorkers are evidently prepared to do. But humbler spots abound as well, down-home diners and night-owl getaways, ethnic take-out joints, and pizza parlors galore.

Beekman Street Bistro (518-581-

1816; www.thebeekmanstreetbistro .com; 62 Beekman Street) is a stylish hot spot in the Art District that takes advantage of Saratoga Springs's proximity to farm country. The freshest local products available, along with great wine and creative dishes that evolve with regional harvests, has turned Beekman Street Bistro into one of the most popular restaurants in the Spa City. Diners appreciate reading on the menu just where the ingredients for their meal come from, places like Flying Pigs and 3-Corners Field Farms. Dishes range from red wine marinated grilled hanger steak over mashed potatoes to grilled crème fraîche pizza with arugula, sundried tomatoes, caramelized onions and fontina cheese. Slow food never tasted so good.

Chianti Il Ristorante (518-580-0025; www.chiantiristorante.com; 18 Division Street) serves Roman cuisine that's as exuberant as the ochre-heavy, mural-rich décor. A nice range of pasta selections, rich risottos, and grilled meats fills the menu, with nightly specials. Good red wine, too, and lots of it. No pretense here, just lots of fun.

Hattie's (518-584-4790; www .hattiesrestaurant.com; 45 Phila Street) is probably the only spot in the North Country where you'll find soul food. The owners of this Depression-vintage downtown icon are determined to maintain Hattie Mosley's beloved legacy of solid Southern and New Orleans–style fare. On hot nights grab a table in the patio out back. You can't lose with the tried-and-true deep-fried chicken, pork chops, mac and cheese (with andouille sausage or chicken), or shrimp. If you're feeling like a break from convention, ever-changing specials such as Creole jambalaya and smothered pork chops are a welcome touch.

Karavalli (518-580-1144; www .karavallilatham.com; 47 Caroline Street) is a find. It has a superb Indian buffet, varied dinners, and a hopping take-out business. Karavalli's weekend brunch is popular with locals.

The Wine Bar 518-584-8777; www.thewinebarofsaratoga.com; 417 Broadway), featuring the cuisine of executive chef Dominic Colose, is an establishment with a full, creative menu—light plates, entrées, gourmet cheeses, and homemade desserts— served on two floors and, in summer, on the patio. The bar itself is still an elegant spot with live piano music and an endless wine list, but do venture to the dining room for vegetarian meat loaf with mushroom gravy, duck pro- sciutto with goat's milk Camembert and fig paste, or trout with fennel- citrus salad. And ask about the Wine Bar's overnight suite for a luxury get- away.

MORE MEALS IN THE SPA CITY

For a quick and easy morning fix, a poppy-seed bagel with a lox and cream cheese schmear at Uncommon Grounds Coffee & Tea (518-581-0656; www.uncommongrounds.com; 402 Broadway) is a winner every time. Many other spreads, toppings, and bagel flavors are available as well. Early-rising city workers pack no- nonsense Compton's (518-584-9632; 457 Broadway) for the swiftest and most reliable four-square breakfast on Broadway. Another town favorite, the cozy Country Corner Café (518-583- 7889; 25 Church Street) draws a Skid- more crowd with its Green Mountain coffee, berry pancakes, and orange juice in jelly jars. The menu at the Saratoga Family Restaurant (518-584- 4044; 153 South Broadway, in front of the Greyhound bus terminal) is enor- mous, and breakfasts are as filling as they are affordable. If you're visiting during the race season, breakfast at the track (518-584-6200) is a long- standing tradition. Get there early

because clubhouse tables fill up fast, starting at 7 AM. Or bring your own basket with juice and muffins and climb the bleachers to a long view. A free tram ride takes you to the barns.

Good, solid, fail-safe lunches are available at all of the above, but if you're after something more original, try Ravenous (518-581-0560; www .ravenouscrepes.com; 21 Phila Street) for spicy crepes and crisp *pommes frites;* or a local favorite, Sperry's (518-584- 9618; 30½ Caroline Street), for bistro fare—broiled cod, steak *au poivre*—is really tasty and as reliable as Big Ben. Scallions, too, has quality lunches of high-end California bistro fare with décor to match (518-584-0192; 44 Lake Avenue. Duo Modern Japanese Cuisine (518-580-8881; www.duo -japanese.com; 175 South Broadway) serves tasty lunches to stay or to go. The elegant Mouzon House (518-226- 0014; 1 York Street) makes mostly Creole-infused cuisine—never overdone Cajuny, just delicious. The wine list is nice, and High Rock Park is just a stroll away.

There's also Gotchya's Trattoria, which features homemade pasta and portraits of mobster thugs on its walls (518-584-5772; www.gotchyas.com; 68 Beekman Street); and Circus Café (518-583-1106; www.circuscafe.com; 392 Broadway) has the nicest staff in town and is a good place to take the kids. The Local Pub and Teahouse (518-587-7256; www.thelocalpubandtea house.com; 142 Grand Avenue) has sandwichy eats and beer and tea that people love. In summer head to PJ's for barbecue and shoofly pie (518-583-7427; www.pjsbarbq.com; South Broadway).

A wide range of delicious take-out fare may be found at neighborhood joints such as Spring Street Deli & Pizzeria (518-584-0994; 132 Spring Street). For a family-run Italian deli, go to Roma Foods (518-587-6004; 222 Washington Street).

FOOD PURVEYORS

So you've got a cooler, you've got a picnic blanket. Where's the view and what's for lunch? Well, there are long, wide vistas of the Hudson from the Saratoga National Historical Park (518-664-9821) off NY 32 and NY 4, the site of bloody American Revolution battles. In Schuylerville, the Fort Hardy Visitors Center (518-695-4159) on the Hudson offers tables, toilets, grills, and a beach to launch a canoe. A 1911 powerhouse flanks the picnic area at Lock 5 on the Champlain Canal, where boaters can put in (518-695-3919). Go north on I-87 to Exit 17, backtrack south to Moreau Lake State Park (518-793-0511), where great trails and a good small beach await you. Back in town, the public lawn and rose garden at Yaddo (518-584-0746; www.yaddo.org), a famous art colony, are lovely places to picnic—if you can manage to ignore I-87 roaring just behind the wall of white pines.

As for that picnic, Saratoga's food purveyors and take-out places will not disappoint. But let's start with coffee. This city even has an espresso bar in the library. You can't get more hard-core than that. Saratoga Coffee Traders (518-584-5600; www.saratogacoffee traders.com; 447 Broadway) is the perfect combination: aromatic all-organic Fair Trade coffee, retro candy, a light Mediterranean menu, and ice cream from the Ice Cream Man, of Greenwich. Uncommon Grounds Coffee and Tea (518-581-0656; 402 Broadway) keeps fresh flowers on the tables and has new art on the walls each month, giant burlap bags of beans, a rack of magazines and newspapers, a coffee roaster as big as a phone booth, and toothsome bagels. If there's a line, hang in there. It chugs along fast enough. Hard-hustling Skidmore students man the espresso bar. Featured soups change every day. Virgil's House (518-587-2949; www.virgilshouse.com; 86 Henry Street) has an old-school aura: lots of

Yaddo postcard courtesy of Ted Comstock, Saranac Lake.

board games, smushy chairs, chess, an old Victrola, and *Life* magazines from the 1960s.

NATURAL FOODS

Four Seasons Natural Foods Store and Café (518-584-4670; www.fourseasons naturalfoods.com; 33 Phila Street) has organic chips, exotic fruit pops, fruit leather, and kefir, plus a dining area bracketed on one side by an all-vegetarian, made-fresh-daily, surprisingly diverse buffet. The soups are hearty, the salads fresh, and the entrées are heavy on tofu, root vegetables, and grains. Also great: the baba ghanoush, focaccia, and rice pudding. Saratoga Farmers' Market (518-587-0766; www.saratogafarmers market.org; in summer: High Rock Park on High Rock Avenue, behind the City Center; in winter: Division Street Elementary) is always bursting with vendors peddling cut flowers, organic eggs, rare perennials, lamb sausage, free-range poultry, mesclun, fresh fava beans, beefalo soup bones, heirloom tomatoes, sweet corn, beeswax candles, raspberry jam, homemade soap, varietal melons, and apples for every palate, recipe, and plate.

SPECIALTY FOODS AND BAKE SHOPS

The Bread Basket Bakery (518-587-4233; www.saratogabreadbasket.com; 65 Spring Street) is where regulars line up for muffins, scones, bear claws, and a great array of sandwich breads. Mrs. London's Bakery and Café (518-581-1652; www.mrslondons.com; 464 Broadway) offers nothing but the real deal: Valrhona chocolate, Plugrá butter, and the purest of biodynamic grains. The prices are not for the fainthearted, but hard-core pastry lovers won't care. You won't find a better double-berry charlotte, cherry clafouti, or Ricard-flavored Gâteau Basque north of New York City, and the hot chocolate is divine. Putnam Market Place (518-587-3663; www .putnammarket.com; 435 Broadway), as close to Zabar's as Saratoga will ever get, is a zealously upmarket gourmet empo-

rium that provides smartly prepared food to go (great albacore tuna salad, thick rounds of pink beef tenderloin, cold poached salmon), ridiculously out-sized sandwiches, a terrific cheese board, and a bold miscellany of cold fruit drinks and teas. Come August, the place is mobbed. Cooking classes are given onsite. Roma Importing Company (518-587-6004; 222 Washington Street), a family institution, serves up hand-cut Italian subs (try the lean capicola), pillowy fresh mozzarella, and good olives. The breathless efficiency and wisecracking bonhomie of the staff make shopping fun and easy.

Nightlife
After-hours fun

Rumor has it that the dim-lit, moody, 40-seat jazz-scored 9 Maple Avenue (518-583-2582; www.9mapleavenue .com) has the largest selection of single-malt Scotch in New York State and a martini menu longer than your arm. The Wine Bar (518-584-8777; www.thewinebarofsaratoga.com; 417 Broadway) earns high marks for the courage and ambition of its list as well (for starters, 50 wines by the glass), and a waiter can help you match your tapas to your selection. The Parting Glass (518-583-1916; www.partingglasspub.com; 40–42 Lake Avenue) is for the Guinness-loving dart-and-penny-whistle crowd and acoustic music fans, and live jazz is the draw at the atmospheric One Caroline Street Bistro (518-587-2026; www.onecaroline.com). Here, the bar is always busy and the waiters bearing plates of hearty Italian food move with skill between the close-set tables. And don't miss a nightcap and a dessert on the patio of the Adelphi Hotel (518-587-4688; www .adelphihotel.com; 365 Broadway).

To Do
Attractions and activities in Saratoga

ARTS AND HISTORICAL CENTERS

If you like your history but museum captions make your eyes water, head to the Saratoga Springs Heritage Area Visitor Center (518-587-3241; www .saratogaspringsvisitorscenter.com; 297 Broadway) across from Congress Park. Built in the Beaux-Arts style in 1915 as a trolley station, the "VC" is the best place to load up on news of current events and walking tour brochures on Saratoga's historic districts, one of which includes a tour of its elegant old springs. Of the three Depression-era spa complexes developed by then governor Franklin D. Roosevelt, only the Lincoln Bath still brings the old-time fizz. The Spa Park itself is as serene and restorative as ever, even if day guests know it less for its constellation of mineral springs than for a lovely 18-hole championship golf course, a posh hotel (the Gideon

Putnam), and a great open-sided concert arena, the Saratoga Performing Arts Center, set like a moonstone in a grove of pines. The local volunteers are well informed and helpful; the location is as central as it gets.

Catercorner to the "VC" at the corner of Broadway and Spring is a building that resembles nothing more than the old city library, which it was. Today it houses the handsome Saratoga County Arts Council at the Arts Center (518-584-4132; www .saratoga-arts.org; 320 Broadway), home to a flourishing arts council; a theater space where the Saratoga Film Forum shows great indie flicks (518-584-FILM; www .saratogafilmforum.org for listings); and a roomy art gallery whose monthly exhibitions range from equine art to the hippest of video installations.

A mere two blocks away is the Saratoga Springs Public Library (518-584-7860; www.sspl.org; 49 Henry Street)—as big as a city hall with a nice restaurant and espresso bar, a superb little-used bookstore, a massive DVD collection, an always-booked community room—and books and books and books.

Exhibitions about social history in Saratoga County are featured at the Saratoga County Historical Society at Brookside (518-885-4000; www.brooksidemuseum.org; 6 Charlton Street, Ballston Spa). In a modest Georgian clapboard building thought to be the oldest hotel in the nation are a handful of galleries and exhibitions. Ballston Spa is also home to the National Bottle Museum (518-885-7589; www.nationalbottle museum.org; 76 Milton Avenue) in an old downtown commercial building. Arrayed here are thousands of hand-blown bottles, the tools that made them, and the stories of the 18th- and 19th-century settlements that manufactured New York's glassware for generations. The Bottle Museum also features a diorama of an 1880s glass furnace and hosts an annual antique bottle show in Saratoga Springs.

MUSEUMS

Children's Museum at Saratoga (518-584-5540; www.childrensmuseumatsaratoga .org; 69 Caroline Street) is a hands-on children's museum that will work your youngsters, ages seven and under, into a frenzy. A gaily colored mockup of a generalized downtown offers stations to play postal worker, storekeeper, short-order cook, and firefighter (slide down the pole, pull on the boots, climb on the fire truck, and you're off). Another floor features stations for making and hopping through giant bubbles, climbing into a tree house, suiting up in old-time clothes from "The Attic," and learning how to make music by breaking up electronic beams in a mini bandstand. Kids love serving up orders in the 1950s diner and practicing their hammering skills in the construction zone. Admission: $6; children under 1 free.

The Historical Society of Saratoga Springs (518-584-6920; www.saratogahistory .org; Canfield Casino, Congress Park) is a calm oasis in the middle of busy Congress Park. The city-managed Canfield Casino boasts a top-floor Victorian house museum, a permanent and in-depth exhibition on the history of Saratoga Springs, a revolving gallery (often focusing on some offbeat aspect of local history), and the architectural landmark, the casino itself. Although it was Richard Canfield who added the Beaux-Arts dining room, the gardens, and the Tiffany window when he bought the place in 1895, the real star of the Italianate structure is the scrappy spirit of prizefighter and Troy politico John Morrissey, who established it as a gaming club in 1870 and who, more than anyone, put Saratoga on the map. Gambling was outlawed when the casino fell into the hands of the city in 1911, and the building was overtaken by springs sippers and tea parties. But you can admire the old chips, roulette wheel, and cards in the "High Stakes Room," and even rent the glorious grand old place for a wedding party or a bash. Admission: $5 adults.

Saratoga's National Museum of Dance is the only museum in the country devoted to American professional dance.

Courtesy of the National Museum of Dance

See gorgeous jockey silks, gleaming trophies, and a first-rate equine art collection at the National Museum of Racing and Hall of Fame on Union Avenue.

Courtesy of the National Museum of Racing and Hall of Fame

National Museum of Dance (518-584-2225; www.dancemuseum.org; 99 South Broadway at the Saratoga Spa State Park) occupies the former Washington Bath House, an Arts and Crafts–style structure built in 1918. The museum—overseen by the Saratoga Performing Arts Center and located in the Saratoga Spa State Park—is the only one in the country devoted expressly to American professional dance. A recent exhibition celebrated the work of black dancers and choreographers, while a permanent Hall of Fame honors the abiding genius of Fred Astaire, Bill "Bojangles" Robinson, Ted Shawn, Martha Graham, Alvin Ailey, Jerome Robbins, and Trisha Brown, plus a hundred others. The interactive kids' Discovery Room allows future dancers to try on costumes and perform on a miniature stage. This is a lovely place for a break between your afternoon chamber music concert at the Little Theater and your next symphony at the Saratoga Performing Arts Center. Open late May through mid-October. Admission: $6.50 adults, $5 students and seniors, $3 children.

National Museum of Racing and Hall of Fame (518-584-0400; www.racingmuseum.org; 191 Union Avenue) is the place to go when your luck flags at the track and celebrity spotting loses its allure. You don't have to love or even like horse racing to be seduced by the interactive exhibits, the life-size starting gate with hidden soundtrack (hoofbeats drumming, the crowd roaring), the gorgeous jockeys' silks, gleaming trophies, first-rate equine art collection, and the Racing Hall of Fame. Admission is $7 adults, $5 seniors and students; members and children under 5 free.

New York State Military Museum (518-581-5100; 61 Lake Avenue) is located in a 19th-century armory and houses the records and stories of New York State's military forces and veterans. Some 10,000 artifacts from the Revolutionary War to World War II to contemporary conflicts have a permanent home here, everything from uniforms to weapons to flags (there are more than 1,000 state battle flags in this collection, more than half from the Civil War). Soldiers' experiences are captured in the Veterans Research Center, the museum's 2,000-volume library, which has endless photographs (more than 2,300 images from the Civil War), scrapbooks, maps, and letters. Appointments are recommended for the research center.

Saratoga Automobile Museum (518-587-1935; www.saratogaautomuseum.org; 110 Avenue of the Pines at Saratoga Spa State Park), in the handsome old bottling plant in the heart of the Spa Park, is a flashy place. Vintage car buffs and youthful gearheads alike are thronging to the colorful installations. The permanent exhibition "East of Detroit" features the automobile industry in New York State; another hall explores the world of racing; and a third, "Sprockets to Rockets," fires up the kids. The cars displayed at the museum change constantly. In summer, lawn shows bring hot rods, famous motorcycles (one ridden by Audrey Hepburn, another owned by Elvis), and all sorts of international models to the museum. Admission is $8 adults, $5 seniors, $3.50 ages 6–16 years old; children under 5 free.

The Frances Young Tang Teaching Museum and Art Gallery (518-580-8080; www.skidmore.edu/tang; 815 North Broadway) brings a touch of edginess in Saratoga. This Skidmore College museum can look like a giant foundering ship or a streamlined Incan monument. Exhibitions, which are always changing, are provocatively interdisciplinary and designed to make you think. The UpBeat on the Roof summer evening music series is very cool.

MUSIC AND PERFORMING ARTS

Saratoga Performing Arts Center (518-587-9330; www.spac.org; Saratoga Spa State Park, Hall of Springs 108 Avenue of the Pines) is the summer home of the New York City Ballet, the Philadelphia Orchestra, the Saratoga Chamber Music Festival, and Freihofer's Jazz Festival; the Homemade Theater (518-587-4427; www.homemade theater.org), and Opera Saratoga sojourn in Spa Little Theater, also in Spa Park. On the packed schedule, the opera and ballet go first (more or less through July). When Philly claims the stage you might expect to see the likes of Yo-Yo Ma, Sarah Chang, Lang Lang, and Joshua Bell. SPAC is touted for its outdoor sound, so if you'd sooner watch the stars than Maestro Charles Dutoit's back, buy a lawn ticket and bring a blanket to the big grassy slope in front of the amphitheater, along with binoculars and bug spray. In August, pop and rock events, such as performances by the Allman Brothers, Lucinda Williams, Bruce Springsteen, and Phish fill the place.

SPAC and other venues around town host dynamite annual events. Some of the best include the Saratoga Food & Wine Festival; the many free readings from the Writers Institute at Skidmore College (regular guests include novelist Russell Banks and Poet Laureate Robert Pinsky); the big-ticket Travers Stakes in late August (dress sharp, bet big, lose nice); the Saratoga Native American Festival; and the Nutcracker Tea Party.

The Saratoga Shakespeare Company (518-209-5514; www.saratogashakespeare .com), made up of professional directors, designers, and actors, puts on free productions in Congress Park in July.

FAMILY FUN

A few years back, die-hard historic preservationists protested the introduction of an Ilion carousel in Frederick Law Olmsted's historic Congress Park. Now that it's installed, complaints are few. The carousel runs weekend afternoons from late spring into fall—rides cost just $.50—and it's a stunner. So, for that matter, is Congress Park, famous with the stroller set for its ducks, ponds, and pretty fountains.

The Saratoga Spa State Park (518-584-2535; www.saratogaspastatepark.org; US 9) on the outskirts of town makes a big splash with its two vintage outdoor pools: The big shallow Peerless is pretty much for children only; the Victoria Pool is very nice for adults. A tree-shaded, somewhat unkempt but still hugely popular wading pool in the East Side Recreation Field on Lake Avenue (NY 29) keeps the toddlers cool in summer, and there are jungle gyms and sand boxes and swings for all (518-587-3550).

The Bog Meadow Brook Nature Trail, 3 miles from downtown, is a level, easy hike (518-587-5554). Another way to get some exercise: bring a bike and sample Saratoga's growing tangle of bike loops.

Family-friendly events include Sunday evening bandstand concerts in Congress Park and tailgate picnics at the Saratoga Polo Grounds (518-584-8108; www.saratoga polo.com; Bloomfield Road). Around the middle of July the Saratoga County Fair (518-885-9701; www.saratogacountyfair.org) comes to Ballston Spa. The fairgrounds in Greenwich, 15 miles to the east, host the more expressly agricultural and better-known Washington County Fair (518-692-2464; www.washingtoncountyfair.com) in late August—tractor pulls and pig races, a midway, and barns full of livestock.

A great family movie option is the old-time Malta Drive-In Theater (518-587-6077; www.maltadrivein.com) just south of town on US 9. And last but by no means least, in summer there is the horse track (518-584-6200; www.saratogaracetrack.com; 267 Union Avenue). As far as children go, forget the races—it's the paddock that brings the news. Small wiry men in giant polka dots, plus huge horses with swishy tails!

Shopping
Stores, boutiques, and antiques in Saratoga

Although some chain stores have moved into town, such stalwarts as Symmetry (518-584-5090; www.symmetrygallery .com; 348 Broadway), peddling art glass, and G. Willikers (518-587-2143; www .gwillikerstoys.com; 461 Broadway) upmarket toys hold firm, along with Gallery 100 (518-580-0818; www.gallery100.net; 462 Broadway), which exhibits a variety of fine art. Bibliophiles will lose themselves in the labyrinthine antiquarian bookshop, the Lyrical Ballad (518-584-8779; 7 Phila Street), and appreciate exotic pieces at deJonghe Jewelry (518-587-6422; www.dj originals.com; 470 Broadway). Also, on Saratoga's west side, check out the Candy Company (518-580-0499; www.saratogacandy.com; 5 Washington Street), all sorts of artistic endeavors at Beekman Street Artists Co-op (518-583-0086; Beekman Street Artists Studios; 79 Beekman Street), and paintings with horses and snazzy designer handbags at Mimosa Gallery (518-583-1163; www.mimosagallery.com; 70 Beekman Street).

Big-box retailers galore—Target, Lowes, Kohl's, and Home Depot—can be found just east of town on NY 50.

GLENS FALLS

If Saratoga Springs is the Emerald City, where many a cabin-fevered Adirondacker likes to steal away for a big night on the town, Glens Falls, the self-styled "Gateway to the Adirondacks" in southeastern Warren County, is Kansas. The Falls is as down to earth as Saratoga is razzle-dazzle.

Glens Falls was named "Hometown U.S.A." by the editors of *Look* magazine in 1944 and 19 years later voted America's "most typical town" by Swedish National Television. The little city is a true child of the Adirondacks, a hard-working, four-square mill town.

Economically, Glens Falls looks north; that's where many of its residents hail from, that's where many of them go to work. It even smells like the north, that sweet-and-sour whiff of wood pulp. In Glens Falls speech, the hard, evenly paced cadence may be a legacy of French Canada; Saratoga's accent blows north from New York City, with hints of Brooklyn and undertones of New Jersey.

Saratoga may own bragging rights to the "Turning Point of the American Revolution" (a distinction, it must be noted, claimed by several other towns with famous battlefields), but when it comes to really regional history, the story of the Adirondacks, surely Glens Falls commands center stage. Quakers founded the settlement in 1763, built a sawmill, ran a tavern, lost their shirts, and saw their homes go up in smoke during the Revolutionary War, their pacifism provoking the suspicion of Tory and patriot alike. After the Revolution, the settlement bounced back, buoyed by an influx of pioneers from New England and Warren County's emerging lumber industry and bolstered by the adoption of the fast-running Schroon and Hudson Rivers as highways for the log drives. Glens Falls earned a century of industrial fame and quiet fortune thanks to logging and papermaking. The Hudson, which winds through Glens Falls from west to east, gave rise as well to a smoky necklace of long-lived mills and factories—lime kilns, canal boat operators, foundries, cement mills, collar factories, railroad spurs, and, looming over all, the pulp and paper mills whose chimney-borne emissions give the city a fragrance all its own.

Finch, Pruyn & Company, for nearly 150 years the major employer in town as well as a major Adirondack landowner, drove the local economy, philanthropy, and even recreation, through its 160,000 acres of woodland. The Hudson River in Glens Falls remains the city's industrial heart. But it isn't really a company town—the city was also home to an impressive number of insurance companies, the largest of which, Glens Falls Insurance, built the blocky downtown edifice that is Glens Falls's skyscraper and has a helpful way of looming into view and getting you oriented when you're on the verge of getting lost. (The building is now office space—Glens Falls Insurance itself is gone.)

The city is far from all business. One of the finest little art museums in New York flourishes here on the high banks of the Hudson, and several other museums, too. The Hyde Collection Art Museum (see page 203) was the inspired notion of Charlotte Pruyn, daughter of lumber magnate Samuel Pruyn, and Charlotte's art-loving husband, Louis Fiske Hyde. Mentored by the savvy likes of Bernard Berenson, the world-traveling, fast-learning Hydes amassed an art collection that continues to delight visitors for its diversity and taste. Here, in the Hydes' former home (an Italian Renaissance–Revival mansion overlooking the mill that made the family fortune) are paintings by Rembrandt, Degas, Seurat, Rubens, El Greco, and Botticelli, as well as American masters Eakins, Hassam, Ryder, and Whistler. In 1952, 18 years after her husband's death, Charlotte Hyde bequeathed the art collection to Glens Falls. The museum opened in 1963, adding a stylish wing for temporary exhibitions in 1989 and undergoing a massive restoration and expansion project, completed almost a decade ago.

On the other side of town is another monument to the civic fealty of the local bourgeoisie: the former home of merchants, the DeLong family, now the Chapman Historical Museum (see page 54).

Today, in Glens Falls's center, old storefronts have been revitalized as toy stores, bookshops, a coffee roaster, gift galleries, and interesting restaurants. The former Woolworth's is now home to the Adirondack Theatre Festival as well as a huge, beautiful shop featuring New York wines.

Pick Your Spot

Lodging in and around
Glens Falls

Because it is not itself a tourist destination, Glens Falls doesn't have many cozy bed & breakfasts. Motels abound off Exit 19 on I-87 at Aviation Mall and along US 9 heading north and south out of Glens Falls, where such chains as Econo Lodge (518-793-3700; 543 Aviation Road) and Ramada Inn Glens Falls (518-793-7701; 1 Abby Lane, Queensbury) are available. Six Flags Great Escape Lodge & Indoor Waterpark (1-888-708-2684; 89 Six Flags Drive, Queensbury) means family fun year-round.

Inside the city proper, lodging choices winnow down to a fine few, each with comfortable rooms at sensible rates that—along with Saratoga room rates—shoot up in the "high season" of August.

Glens Falls Inn (646-824-8379; www.thegfinn.com; 25 Sherman Avenue) has brass beds and nice quilts among scrupulously period features that characterize this sunny bed & breakfast in a 100-plus-year-old Victorian home. The inn has five guest rooms with private bath, plus a roomy apartment suite.

The Manor Inn (518-793-2699; 514 Glen Street), a 1920s bed & breakfast in a leafy neighborhood full of historic homes, offers five guest bedrooms. As if the fireplace in the parlor and the period antiques weren't sufficiently enticing, the inn also serves a full breakfast by candlelight—surely an Adirondack first.

The Queensbury Hotel (518-792-1121; www.queensburyhotel.com; 88 Ridge Street) is the belle of the ball—if there were a ball, if the ballroom that once pulsed to the beat of Benny Goodman and Guy Lombardo hadn't changed to a reception room years ago. This historic 125-room full-service hotel in the heart of town is the darling of conventioneers and visiting politicos and stars. Ronald Reagan stayed at the Queensbury, as well as Bobby Kennedy, ZZ Top, Ozzy Osborne, Bob Dylan, and Phish. The Who also stayed here, in splendid anonymity, working out the kinks of a North American tour.

The Queensbury was built in 1924, when 100 local businessmen, bolstered by substantial start-up gifts from Finch, Pruyn and Glens Falls Insurance, joined forces to get a hotel built in the heart of their beloved boomtown. Today it remains a fine place to stay, handy to downtown with requisite shop and lounge, pool and Jacuzzi, restaurant, salon, and exercise room.

Local Flavors

Where to eat in Glens Falls

132 Glen Bistro (518-743-9138; www.132glenbistro.com; 132 Glen Street), a small, noisy, busy storefront—hip, colorful, and adorned with historic photographs—brings you into downtown and serves up wholesome fare. You'll find one of your favorite comfort foods on the limited menu. Chef-owner Kevin M. Bethel willingly creates lighter portions if that's your desire. Numerous entrées reflect his delight in seafood—the salmon and tuna dishes are terrific. Bethel's homemade salad dressings are inspired, and his Cuban sandwiches are really something special. You just can't go wrong here. Leave room for dessert. The Key lime pie is creamy and tangy. Carrot cake and ice creams appeal, also. In this beer-or-wine-only bistro, the lover of robust brews is in for a treat. Cooper's Cave beers, conceived and brewed locally (by a Bethel brother),

are served. If you'd like to eat this creative comfort food in the comfort of your own home, order a meal to go.

Bistro Tallulah (518-793-2004; adirondackminute.com/bistro-tallulah; 26 Ridge Street) is the chicest downtown offering in this mill city. Its superb New Orleans–style fare can be ordered as small or full portions. Some highlights are the Southern buttermilk fried quail, *cochon de lait,* and the chocolate bourbon pecan torte.

Siam Thai Sushi (518-792-6111; www.siamthaisushi.com; 200 Glen Street) serves delicious curry dishes, a pad thai house special, and the sushi a fine treat for a place so far from the Big Apple.

QUICK BITES AND SPECIALTY FOODS

Poopie's? Dirty John's? These beloved places reflect the owners' nicknames and not failed hygiene. The nickname thing is part and parcel of Glens Falls's mill town roots—where lunch counters are like Cheers, without beers.

Order ice cream or a frosty one at Cooper's Cave Ale Company (518-792-0007; www.cooperscaveale.com; 2 Sagamore Street)—the root beer is excellent. Find more suds at Davidson Brothers Restaurant & Brewery (518-743-9026; www.davidsonbrothers.com; 184 Glen Street) in a historic exposed-brick building with a courtyard for outdoor dining. Onion rings on a stick are the perfect accompaniment to a cold beer. Gourmet Café (518-761-0864;

www.downtowngourmet.com; 185 Glen Street) has soups, salads, sandwiches—served on Rock Hill bread—ample options for vegetarians, and an outdoor café. Check out New Way Lunch (518-792-9803; 21 South Street), famous for its Dirty John's hot dogs with meat sauce. Poopie DiManno's Lunch Inc. (518-792-6155; 54 Lawrence Street) has the best breakfasts. Since World War II, it's been run by the DiManno family, which serves huge portions, scrumptious slabs of ham, and attitude at no charge. Rock Hill Bakehouse (518-615-0777; www.rockhillbakehouse.com; 19 Exchange Street), near the hospital, serves lunch: smoked turkey and cranberry sandwiches with cheese, Black forest ham, roast beef, all on signature Rockhill breads. The chowders, minestrone, and beef barley soups are worth trying, too, plus good coffee and sweets.

In Queensbury, Silo Country Store (518-798-1900; 537 Aviation Road) is an atmospheric place—poke around the old barn for sandwiches, soups, and salads. And Sutton's Market Place (518-798-1188; www.suttonsmarketplace.com; US 9) has croissant sandwiches and excellent choices for ladies who lunch. In summer you just might run into Rachael Ray, who gushes about this hot spot.

And for nightlife in Glens Falls: get a dose of tunes with your martini or meal at Wallabee's Jazz Bar (518-792-8282; www.wallabeesjazzbar.com; 190 Glen Street).

To Do
Attractions and activities in Glens Falls

GALLERIES, LIBRARIES, AND MUSEUMS

Chapman Historical Museum (518-793-2826; www.chapmanmuseum.org; 348 Glen Street), part classic 19th-century house museum, it also offers a temporary exhibition gallery and space dedicated strictly to the work of the Adirondacks' best-known late-19th-century photographer, Seneca Ray Stoddard (1843–1917). In the mid- and late 19th century, the Adirondack region attracted hordes of painters and photographers. No shutterbug could match the range and detail of

Stoddard's vision of this changing landscape with its log drives and rough-hewn towns on the one hand, its posh lakeside resorts and scenery-seeking swells on the other. Scrutinize Stoddard's photographs at the Chapman and you come away with a fair idea of the industrial and cultural currents that helped sweep Glens Falls into its age of prosperity and growth.

Crandall Public Library (518-792-6508; www.crandalllibrary.org; 251 Glen Street) is a true anchor for downtown, with excellent book, DVDs, and periodical selections; a helpful staff; and a full roster of events, from film to lectures. Folklorist Todd DeGarmo curates exhibitions in a vest-pocket gallery at Crandall. Sample exhibits have explored the drawings of Navajo children, the photographs of Alan Lomax, and crafts of the colonial era. At the museum the Center for Folklife, History and Cultural Programs (518-792-3360), an archival resource for regional historians, is open Monday through Saturday, and also hosts great readings, workshops, and performances.

The Hyde Collection Art Museum (518-792-1761; www.hydecollection.org; 161 Warren Street) is the city's pride and joy. It features a fine collection of old and modern masters—works by Rembrandt, Homer, Leonardo, Degas, Eakins, Rubens, Van Gogh—in its lovingly furnished and newly restored 1912 Italian palazzo home and adjoining arts complex. Recent temporary exhibitions include *The Last of the Mohicans,*" a first edition of James Fenimore

The Hyde features a fine collection of old and modern masters.
Courtesy of the Hyde Collection Art Museum

Cooper's American literary classic on view; "European Works on Paper," including Picassos from the museum's permanent collection; and "Degas and Music," a collection of impressionist Edgar Degas's work. In 2013, the museum will feature the Lake George paintings of Georgia O'Keeffe, who summered in the Adirondacks with her photographer husband, Alfred Stieglitz. The Hyde's Helen Froehlich Auditorium hosts lectures and performances; studios and classrooms provide space for art workshops for adults and children. It is also backdrop for the de Blasiis series—chamber music that includes such groups as the Biava String Quartet, with performances inside the house in an enclosed patio with soaring windows and tile floors.

Lower Adirondack Regional Arts Council (518-798-1144; www.larac.org; 7 Lapham Place) features Adirondack artisans and artists in this organization's gallery. LARAC offers workshops, plus its summer craft fair in the city park by Crandall Library.

The Shirt Factory (518-793-9309 or 518-824-1290; www.shirtfactorygf.com; Lawrence and Cooper Streets) is an arts and healing center in a former clothing manufacturing facility. The historic four-story brick structure's renovated, light-filled studios are leased by more than 50 artists and a dozen healing-related businesses.

MUSIC AND THEATER

Adirondack Theatre Festival (518-798-7479; www.atfestival.org; Charles R. Wood Theater, 207 Glen Street) was launched almost two decades ago. Founders of the company were involved with the original production of the Broadway hit *Rent,* and bring real sophistication to their shows, performed in a theater that was converted from an old Woolworth department store (see listing below). The season begins in June, with five or six shows, children's workshops, and new play readings.

Charles R. Wood Theater (518-798-9663; www.woodtheater.org; 207 Glen Street) has 30,000 square feet of space for performances, rehearsals, meetings, and receptions. The place's namesake, the late Charles R. Wood, was the founder of Storytown, now The Great Escape, and a driving force in funding community-based projects and organizations—he played a heavy hand in shaping an old Woolworth's into this modern theater. You'll see it all here: the Adirondack Theater Festival in summer, and an assortment of acts, troupes, and galas throughout the rest of the year.

Glens Falls Community Theatre (518-792-1740; www.gfcommunitytheatre.org) is an old-fashioned family-friendly theater that serves up hearty rations of drawing-room mysteries, vintage dramas, musicals, and revues—community-supported and community-staffed all the way.

Glens Falls Symphony Orchestra (518-792-1348; www.fgso.org; 7 Lapham Place) performs a repertoire that ranges from Bach's *St. Matthew's Passion* to commissioned pieces by the resident composer at Union College. A high-school chorus augments offerings during the holiday season, and every Fourth of July, the orchestra gives a free performance at City Park; fireworks follow. The symphony plays at a variety of venues in the area, including the First Presbyterian Church and Christ Church United Methodist, in Glens Falls; and Queensbury High School, Hudson Falls High School, and Maple Street Middle School, in Saratoga Springs.

SEASONAL EVENTS AND FESTIVALS

Adirondack Balloon Festival (518-761-6366; www.adirondackballoonfest.org) is a famed four-day hot-air balloon event in mid-September that attracts folks from all over the world. This is a big draw and if you aim to catch it up close and personal, make your way to the Warren County Airport by dawn's early light.

Taste of the North Country (www.glensfallstaste.com), a downtown food fair that draws 40-plus restaurateurs of every description, happens every September in City Park.

The Chronicle Book Fair (518-792-1126; Queensbury Hotel, 88 Ridge Street, Glens Falls) is a gathering of dozens of authors, publishers, and members of nonprofit groups who sign books, discuss writing, and give various workshops and kids' activities.

Recreation
Adventures in and around Glens Falls

Runners, dog walkers, and bicyclists can get a blast of fresh air, New York–engineering history, and a 7-mile workout on a graded path that runs the length of the Feeder Canal Park, from the feeder dam 2 miles southwest of Glens Falls to five massive combines in Fort Edward. In 1822, a canal was dug from the Hudson River to "feed" the Champlain Canal some miles off. The surviving locks at the Five Combines Historic Lock Area in Fort Edward are the only ones in New York State that date from the time of the Erie Canal. Kayakers and canoeists can put in at small launch areas at either end of the canal—it's a mellow, easy ride for little kids.

The Feeder Canal Park also marks the southern tip of a 12-mile Warren County Bikeway that traces a scenic stretch of the old Delaware & Hudson line to fetch up in Lake George's Battlefield Park. Bikers should figure on a one- to two-hour ride each way. Rick's Bike Shop (518-793-8986; www.ricksbikeshop.com; 368 Ridge Road, Queensbury) offers a great selection of sports equipment and information, catering to road cyclists, backcountry bikers, and even winter bikers who install spikes on their tires.

For scenic flights, if you want to float on air, call Adirondack Balloon Flights (518-793-6342; www.adkballoonflights.com).

Typical of perhaps a half dozen Adirondack towns, Glens Falls has a ski slope of its own: West Mountain Ski Center (518-793-6606; www.skiwestmountain.com; 59 West Mountain Road). It's small, family-operated, mere minutes from downtown, and with more than 20 trails there's a slope for every skier and snowboarder's speed and style. Another just source of civic pride are the Crandall Park International Ski Trails (518-761-3813): 7 groomed kilometers of wooded trails lighted for night skiing and free to all, right within the city's limits. Fall Line Ski Shop (518-793-3203; www.falllineskishop.com; 366 Quaker Road, Queensbury) rents and sells downhill and cross-country skis. The Inside Edge (518-793-5676; www.insideedgeskiandbike.com; 624 Upper Glen Street, Queensbury) provides downhill and cross-country ski sales and rentals; it's the best local source for racing supplies.

There are plenty of golf courses in Glens Falls and the surrounding area, including the Glens Falls Country Club (518-792-1186; www.glensfallscountryclub.com; 211 Round Pond Road, Queensbury), Sunnyside Par 3 Golf Course (518-792-0148; 168 Sunnyside Road, Glens Falls), and Bay Meadows Golf Club (518-792-1650; 31 Cronin Road, Queensbury), to name a few.

For more family fun, Glens Falls is within a few minutes' drive of many outdoor amusement parks and roadside attractions. Six Flags The Great Escape & Splashwater Kingdom (518-792-3500; www.sixflags.com/greatEscape), in Queensbury—more than 100 rides strong—is the biggest fun park of its kind in northern New York State. It's open spring through fall, but if you're looking for year-round fun, check out the new adjoining Six Flags Great Escape Lodge and Indoor Water Park (1-888-708-2684; www.sixflagsgreatecapelodge.com), a great place for you and the kids to chase away the winter blahs.

Shopping

Stores, boutiques, and antiques in Glens Falls

Antique hounds might want to sample 200 Glen Antique Marketplace (518-792-0323; 200 Glen Street, Glens Falls) or Glenwood Manor Antiques (518-798-4747; 60 Glenwood Avenue, Queensbury).

Fine home furnishings, luxury bed and bath linens, and other designer gifts can be found at Sterling & Company (518-745-6808; www.shopsterlingandco.com; 203 Glen Street, Glens Falls). Crafts and upscale gifts are a big draw at a local favorite, Sutton's Market Place (518-798-1188; www.suttonsmarketplace.com), just north of town on US 9 in Queensbury before The Great Escape. Sutton's is a sprawling complex with a nice gourmet shop, gifts, and interesting women's clothing. Off the same parking lot is a furniture store, with gorgeous leather couches, and chairs, some twig pieces, rugs, bookshelves, and accessories for town or country homes. The Toy Cottage at Sutton's is another popular standby.

Aviation Mall (518-793-8818; www.shopaviationmall.com; 578 Aviation Road, Queensbury), also off Exit 19, has T.J. Maxx, the Bon-Ton, Target, and other shops. But the big shopping experience is toward Lake George, at the "Million Dollar Half Mile" (The Factory Outlets of Lake George; www.factoryoutletsoflakegeorge.com), with brand-name factory outlet stores. Traffic can be snarly, but snag a good spot and walk from plaza to plaza, then park on the other side of the road and do likewise.

2

Central and Southwestern Adirondacks

OLD FORGE'S FULTON CHAIN is a family-friendly natural waterpark, Blue Mountain Lake has the venerable Adirondack Museum, and North Creek draws white-water rafters part of the year and skiers the other. Yet this region is still one of the most tangled, untrammeled chunks of the Adirondack Park. For those looking to get lost, tracts such as the Moose River Plains mean a getaway with just you and, well, the moose.

Pick Your Spot

Lodging in the Central & Southwestern Adirondacks

Highlights for this region, particularly its iconic rustic lodges, follow, but this is housekeeping cabin central. Meaning, from Memorial Day through Columbus Day, affordable little waterside cottages with kitchenettes abound—perfect backdrops for an Adirondack vacation. Most need to be booked way ahead and don't accept credit cards. But all offer a quintessential Adirondack vacation.

Big Moose Lake

Big Moose Inn (315-357-2042; www .bigmooseinn.com; 1510 Big Moose Road, Eagle Bay), a turn-of-the-century backwoods lodge, ranks tops among spots locals recommend to visiting friends and family, plus the food is fine (see page 65). The place is rustic, but comfy. Twelve of its 16 rooms have water views. Unlike other accommodations around here, the inn is an all-season draw: In late spring you can paddle and fish on Big Moose Lake; in summertime you can hike around Pigeon Lake Wilderness Area or visit nearby towns Inlet and Old Forge; in fall you can see foliage or hunt; and when snow comes, there's snowmobiling or cross-country skiing practically right to the front door. Closed in March and November.

Covewood Lodge (315-357-3041; www.covewoodlodge.com; 120 Covewood Lodge Road, Eagle Bay), one of the all-time great woodsy Adirondack

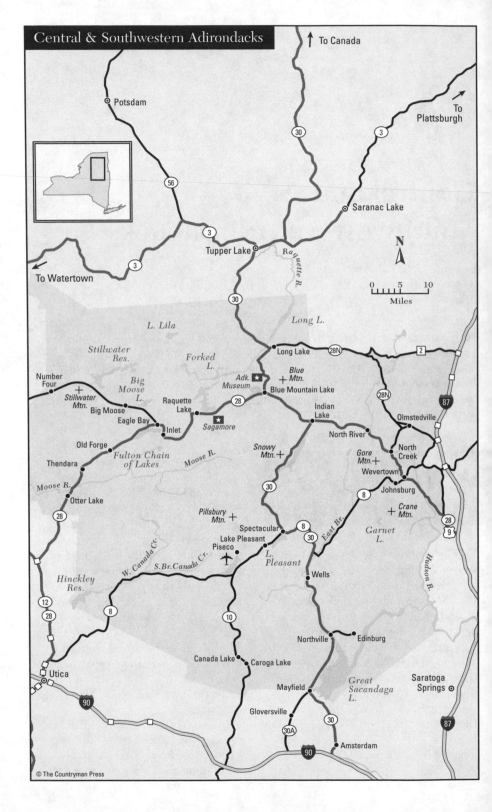

Central & Southwestern Adirondacks

To Canada

Potsdam

To Plattsburgh

56

30

3

Saranac Lake

3

Tupper Lake

To Watertown

3

30

Raquette R.

N

0   5   10
Miles

L. Lila

Long L.

Stillwater Res.

Forked L.

Long Lake

28N

2

87

Number Four

Big Moose L.

Raquette Lake

Adk. Museum

Blue Mtn.

28N

Stillwater Mtn.

Big Moose

28

Blue Mountain Lake

Eagle Bay

Inlet

Sagamore

Indian Lake

Olmstedville

Old Forge

Fulton Chain of Lakes

Moose R.

Snowy Mtn.

North River

Gore Mtn.

North Creek

Thendara

Wevertown

Moose R.

30

Johnsburg

28

Otter Lake

Pillsbury Mtn.

8

Crane Mtn.

9

Spectacular

8

28

Hinckley Res.

W. Canada Cr.

S.Br.Canada Cr.

Lake Pleasant

Piseco

30

East Br.

Garnet L.

L. Pleasant

Hudson R.

12
28

8

10

Wells

Northville

Edinburg

Utica

Canada Lake

Caroga Lake

Great Sacandaga L.

Saratoga Springs

Mayfield

90

Gloversville

30A

30

87

90

Amsterdam

© The Countryman Press

retreats, was built as a hotel back in the days when guests stayed all summer long. Along the shoreline and in the trees are 18 housekeeping cottages. Big Moose Laker Earl Covey built the 1924 rustic lodge and iconic stone fireplace (his charming chapel just down the road is a must-see). There's no cell coverage here, and you won't find TVs on the property, but Covewood offers sailboat, kayak, canoe, and motorboat rentals. The popular Covewood Kids' Program provides daily activities for young guests. Because families return year after year, book at least six months ahead. Open May through October. No credit cards.

The Waldheim (315-357-2353; www.thewaldheim.com; 502 Martin Road, Eagle Bay), built in 1904 by E. J. Martin from trees cut on the property, has run for more than a century by generations of the same family. The Waldheim's 15 cabins, some constructed of vertical half logs and twiggy accents, have names such as "Cozy," "Comfort" and "Heart's Content," and each has a fireplace. Guests can hike, canoe, swim, and fish; arrangements can be made to have a seaplane pick you up at the dock for a scenic flight. The 300-acre property is adjacent to state land so the location is secluded. Rates include three full meals a day, which are served in a gracious dining room. No credit cards.

Blue Mountain Lake

The Hedges (518-352-7325; www.the hedges.com; 1 Hedges Road) was built in the early 1880s by Colonel Hiram Duryea, a Civil War veteran and millionaire industrialist. The main house, with four guest rooms all with private baths, has a wraparound porch. The Stone Lodge, built about 1890, has a two-bedroom suite with fireplace on the first floor, and six rooms with private baths upstairs. There are nine one- to three-bedroom sleeping cabins along the lakeshore (and several more

Wordswoman

Anne LaBastille, 1935–2011, was best known for her 1976 book *Woodswoman*, about roughing it solo in the Adirondack wilds. The young divorcee lived in a handmade cabin on Twitchell Lake, near Big Moose, and wrote as breezily about swinging an ax as she did skinny-dipping—she made woodcraft sexy during a time when Boy Scouts and lumberjacks dominated the scene. LaBastille, who was a wildlife ecologist and Adirondack advocate, empowered women who wanted to ditch their traditional roles, and she went on to pen many more books and articles for publications such as *National Geographic*, *Adirondack Life*, and *Backpacker*.

nearby). Guests have use of canoes, kayaks, rowboats, a clay tennis court, and the library; the Birch Room, with museum-quality rustic detail, is worth a visit. Meals are served in the dining room lodge, where there's a full bar. Open May through October. Book a stay at least a year in advance. No credit cards.

The Hedges, in Blue Mountain Lake, is classic 19th-century Adirondack lodging.

Courtesy of Ted Comstock, Saranac Lake

Hemlock Hall (518-352-7706; www .hemlockhall.com; Maple Lodge Road), another old-school Adirondack hostelry, was carefully restored in the 1950s. The woodwork in the main lodge still gleams. The stone fireplace has hearths on two sides, opening onto part of the living room and a wing of the dining room. There's even a fireplace in an upstairs hallway. There are guest rooms in the lodge with shared baths, plus motel units, and two- or three-bedroom cottages. The tower suite in the main lodge has its own screen porch; several of the lodge rooms have lake views; and you can rent the top floor of the boathouse. Breakfast and dinner are included in the room charges. The dining room serves one entrée each evening in a family-style arrangement. Folks are seated at different tables each night so they get to mingle with the other visitors; alcoholic beverages, which might make all this mingling a bit easier, are not permitted in the dining room. Open mid-May through mid-October. No credit cards.

Indian Lake/Sabael

Timberlock (518-648-5494; www.timber lock.com; Route 30) hasn't changed much since it welcomed its first guests in 1898. The common buildings and the guests' log cabins are still equipped with gaslights and woodstoves. The atmosphere here is rustic and relaxed, yet the resort offers a variety of activities and amenities, such as two Har-Tru tennis courts and two clay courts; horses for guided trail rides; a sandy beach; boats to sail, paddle, or row on Indian Lake; and trails on the property for hiking and birding. Sixteen "family cottages" have full baths, screen porches, and lake views, and there are some small cabins without baths. Rates include three meals a day (the dining hall has canvas walls) and use of all the facilities and activities except horseback riding. There are no neighbors within miles, and your

wake-up call in the morning may well be a loon's yodel from the lake. Open mid-June through mid-September. No credit cards.

Inlet

The Woods Inn (315-357-5300; www .thewoodsinn.com; 148 Route 28), one of the few around here that's open year-round, was built by Fred Hess in 1894 and four years later purchased by Philo Wood, who renamed it the Wood Hotel. Much has changed in more than a century, but thanks to a massive restoration by the current owners, this place, which was ready to topple to the ground, has been saved, and is operating as the grand inn it once was. Guests can choose between 20 rooms in the inn, all with private baths, some with balconies, Jacuzzis, and mountain and lake views; two nearby cottages, both with kitchens; or several Adirondack Guide Tents, throwbacks to 19th- and early-20th-century luxury platform tents. The tents are beautifully furnished and have electric lights and woodstoves. The adjacent bathhouse is heated and has a double shower for two. Breakfast is included in the cost of a night's stay. A restaurant and tavern are also on site.

North Creek

The Alpine Lodge (518-251-2451; www .adirondackalpinelodge.com; 264 Main Street) is a relatively recent add to North Creek's Main Street and it's done wonders for the neighborhood—one local says he'd cross the road to get past what was once a derelict rooming house. Today the charming Alpine Lodge, with its 14 Adirondack-style guest rooms and four kitchen suites, accommodates folks in an equally charming downtown. Restaurants, bars, and boutiques are out the front door, and a shuttle can get you to Gore Mountain Ski Area or to the Hudson for a white-water adventure.

The Copperfield Inn Resort (518-251-2200; www.copperfieldinn.com; 307

Weddings: Where to Say I Do

Lean-tos, islands, lakes, and ponds are postcard-perfect backdrops, but more traditional houses of worship include the quaint **Big Moose Community Chapel** (315-357-2622) and historical **St. Williams on Long Point** (315-354-4265; www.stwilliamsonlongpoint .org), on Raquette Lake. Or go traditional Adirondack-style at a Great Camp: **Sagamore** (315-354-5311; www.greatcampsagamore.org), in Raquette Lake, was once the Vander- bilts' getaway. Old Forge's artsy **View** (315-369-6411; www.viewarts.org) makes for a modern setting, and North Creek's **Copperfield Inn** (518-251-2200; www.copperfield inn.com) hosts grand celebrations, as does nearby **Gore Mountain** (518-251-2411; www.goremountain.com)—ride the gondola up in warm weather or cold for high- altitude nuptials. There's a gazebo behind the **Alpine Lodge** (518-251-2451; www .adirondackalpinelodge.com) that allows for nice, intimate nuptials. In Long Lake a gath- ering at **Donnelly's Sunset Point** (518-624-6551) is an option for a low-key family-style affair. For a nautical wedding, board **Old Forge Lake Cruises'** *Clearwater* (315-369- 6473; www.oldforgelakecruises.com) or Raquette Lake Navigation Company's elegant *W. W. Durant* (315-354-5532; www.raquettelakenavigation.com), named after the 19th- century Great Camp builder. At the sprawling **Lapland Lake Nordic Vacation Center** (518-863-4974; www.laplandlake.com), in Benson, guests can stay in *tupas*, and hike, bike, and ski.

Main Street), shuttered for years, is now revived and has been upgraded into an elegant, tasteful inn with all the ameni- ties you'd expect at a real ski resort—31 big rooms; outdoor pool; health and fit- ness center; sauna; tennis court; confer- ence facilities; pub and dining room; and shuttle bus to the slopes. Unlike most Adirondack hotels, there's nothing rustic about the Copperfield's rooms and shared spaces; the décor evokes something gracious out of the South, with high ceilings and fancy draperies on tall windows. The place is popular for weddings, too, with a parquet- floored ballroom and space for 170 guests. Plus it's right in the center of town and a one-minute walk from the train station.

North River

Garnet Hill Lodge (518-251-2444; www .garnet-hill.com; 39 Garnet Hill Road), on Thirteenth Lake, is the place back from the brink and locals are doing back flips. The rustic compound has changed hands several times and is now a really spotless, renovated, nice place to go.

The main log house with its garnet stone fireplace has 16 rooms; outbuild- ings the Birches and the Tea House have more rooms and accommodate families and larger groups. There's a restaurant and pub on site (see page 67) and, big-time bonus: the resort's ski center and network of almost 40 miles of marked cross-country-ski trails are now getting the attention they deserve.

Old Forge/Thendara

Van Auken's Inne (315-369-3033; www .vanaukensinne.com; 108 Forge Street) was a year old when the Adirondack branch of the New York Central made its first stop in Thendara station in 1892. Since then, the trains have come and gone (and are back again for scenic excursions from Thendara), while Van Auken's has remained a constant pres- ence across the way. The second floor— where 20 bedrooms used to share two baths—now has 12 guest rooms, each with private bath. Original details and antique furniture have been incorpo- rated into these modern accommoda-

Cottage Country

Vacationing at these cute colonies is a trend stretching back to the 1920s, when visitors could drive to the Adirondacks. Descendants of the very first cottagers are keeping the tradition alive.

Housekeeping cottages generally have kitchens, a beach on a nice lake, a dock, porches, room to play horseshoes or volleyball or just sit under a huge pine in an Adirondack chair. And most are open seasonally and do not accept credit cards. Most cost between $800 and $1,500 a week, though it depends on size, condition, and proximity to water. Following are some of the lakeside highlights in this part of the park:

In Blue Mountain Lake you'll find the charming barn-red **Curry's Cottages** (518-352-7355); photographs of the chorus line of white Adirondack chairs along the beach have appeared in numerous national magazines. Also, **Prospect Point** (518-352-7378; www.prospectpt.com) has two-dozen cabins—some that are winterized—that line the curving shore. PP's breakfasts for guests are something special.

Binder's Cabins (518-648-5500) are open year-round in Indian Lake. These have been a mainstay of local lodging for more than five decades, popular with rafters, anglers, hikers, hunters, boaters, and cross-country skiers. Also in Indian Lake is **Camp Driftwood** (518-648-5111; www.goodcabins.com) and its 10 cabins—a good base from which to plan day trips or simply to relax.

Inlet's **The Crosswinds** (315-357-4500), on Fourth Lake, includes five two-bedroom cabins. **Deer Meadows** (315-357-3274; www.deermeadowsmotel.com), on Seventh Lake, is open year-round.

Long Lake has **Donnelly's Sunset Point** (518-624-6551), a 1920s restored hotel plus housekeeping cabins on a surprisingly private point of the lake. The **Shamrock** (518-624-3861; www.shamrockmotellonglake.com) has a motel and newly renovated neat-as-a-pin cottages.

Waterfront seclusion is what you'll find at **Morningside Camps and Cottages** (518-251-2694; www.morningsidecamps.com), in Minerva. There are 15 camps—a combo of log cabins and chalets, all of which have complete kitchens, bathrooms, stone fireplace or woodstove, and decks or screen porches.

All seven of **Sunderland Cottages** (518-585-3520; www.sunderlandcottages.com), in Paradox, are on a quiet cove of Paradox Lake.

tions, and some rooms open onto the second-floor veranda. The public areas downstairs, such as the taproom and the lobby, have polished wood floors and stamped-tin ceilings. Van Auken's restaurant is open for lunch and dinner (see page 65).

Speculator

Bearhurst Lakeside Cottages (978-424-1931; www.bearhurst.com) isn't what comes to mind when you think of the Great Camps on Raquette or the Saint Regis Lakes, but in other parts of the park there are some smaller estates that are of equal architectural interest.

One of these is Bearhurst, which was built in 1894 by Herman Meyrowitz (fashionable optical shops in Paris, Geneva, and Milan still carry his name), and it occupies a quarter-mile of shoreline on Lake Pleasant. Guests stay in five of the original outbuildings, including the icehouse, pump house, summer kitchen, and boathouse, all of which have been converted into modern accommodations while still maintaining historical charm. There's a private beach, dock space for guests' boats, and a pretty, rustic gazebo for watching the sunset over the lake. No credit cards.

Stillwater

Stillwater Hotel (315-376-6470; www
.stillwateradirondacks.com; 2591 Stillwater Road, Stillwater) is on Stillwater
Reservoir, which is several miles back
from the main highways via a winding
gravel road, with 117 miles of shoreline,
45 islands, and thousands of acres of
public land for you to discover. There are
more loons here than any other lake in
the Adirondacks, and the fishing's not too
bad, either. Stillwater is understandably
popular with snowmobilers because the
snow cover is excellent and several trail
systems are accessible from the property.
There are seven winterized motel rooms,
plus a good restaurant and a friendly
bar—the only accommodations that you
can drive to on the reservoir.

Wevertown

Dillon Hill Inn (518-251-2912;
www.dillonhill.com; 58 Dillon Hill
Road) has an Adirondack-country vibe.
The centerpiece is a lovely mid-19th-
century farmhouse with five guestrooms
and private baths. The cabins on the
property are rustic basic, but fine bases
for launching hiking or whitewater-
rafting adventures. Dillon Hill's 6-acre
property also makes a pretty backdrop
for a family reunion or wedding.

Local Flavors

Where to eat in the Central &
Southwestern Adirondacks

Calling ahead is a necessity in this
region—imagine driving 50 minutes
from Blue to Big Moose to find the
lights out. But if you plan ahead there
are some sweet spots in these hamlets,
and not just places that open in summer.
Following are highlights.

Big Moose

Big Moose Inn (315-357-2042; www.big
mooseinn.com; 1510 Big Moose Road),
overlooking Big Moose Lake, is an old-
time lodge and a favorite destination
for year-round residents who want to
go someplace special on birthdays and
anniversaries; some people even arrive
by seaplane. In summer, eating on the
lakeside deck is a treat. The menu
includes fine-dining choices: lobster
tail, roasted duckling, rack of lamb, the
"house favorite" prime rib, and the list
goes on. Closed in April, November,
and part of December.

Big Moose Station (315-357-3525;
www.bigmoosestation.com; 2138
Big Moose Road), an attractively

An American Tragedy

In July 1906, 20-year-old pregnant factory worker Grace Brown and her 22-
year-old boyfriend Chester Gillette
rented a boat from the Glenmore
Hotel on Big Moose Lake. Brown
was later discovered beneath the
water, allegedly killed by Gillette with
a tennis racket. Gillette's sensational
trial—and subsequent death by electric chair—put this Herkimer County
hamlet on the map, as did Theodore
Dreiser's acclaimed 1925 novel based
on the case, An American Tragedy,
and the 1951 movie starring Elizabeth
Taylor, A Place in the Sun. The Glenmore burned to the ground in 1950.

Courtesy of Ted Comstock, Saranac Lake

Big Moose's Glenmore Hotel.

CENTRAL AND SOUTHWESTERN ADIRONDACKS

The Middle of Nowhere

Beaver River on Stillwater Reservoir is one of the toughest settlements to reach in the Adirondacks—you can't drive there, though you can hike, cross-country ski, snowmobile, or paddle in.

In the late 1800s the place was a stop along the Mohawk & Malone line, and hunters rushed here by rail, the hamlet's surrounding state-owned wilderness a big-game–apalooza. Boardinghouses and hotels sprang up, then, in 1924, the hamlet's namesake river was dammed for hydropower. The resulting Stillwater Reservoir socked in the train-access-only community, giving it a last frontier vibe. The train stopped chugging here in 1965, further disconnecting this remote community.

In the 19th century, Beaver River was big-game Shangri-La.

Courtesy of Ted Comstock, Saranac Lake

Today most of the outpost's year-round population of 20 or so, as well as its summer residents, embrace its remoteness, even its lack of electricity (power comes from generators). For visitors who want to explore this spit of land, particularly snowmobilers drawn by seemingly endless trails and plenty of white stuff, the **Norridgewock Lodge** (315-376-6200; www.beaverriver.com) is open year-round; the **Beaver River Hotel** (315-376-3010) closes in winter.

restored depot, is a fine après-adventure destination—its hog wild wings are pork shanks you can eat like a caveman (or -woman). The down-home fare is delicious, presented in ample portions, and the setting is charming.

Inlet

Seventh Lake House (315-357-6028; www.seventhlakehouse.com; 479 NY 28) has been operated by chef-owner Jim Holt since 1989, and his varied seasonal menus continue to offer innovative dishes made from the best ingredients. The place, which serves dinner only, is elegantly simple, with white tablecloths, an imposing fireplace, and lots of picture windows facing the lake. There's a comfortable bar and a canopied deck stretching across the back. Seventh Lake House is child-friendly, especially in the summer, when the deck is open. Appetizers are delicious, including

shrimp focaccia, Thai marinated chicken strips, and crab cakes. Soups are heavenly, especially the crab bisque. Entrées run the gamut of fresh seafood on angel hair pasta to triple meat loaf made with beef, veal, and pork—a combination that trumps all other recipes. The Long Island duck is scrumptious. Desserts made on the premises include the Adirondack, a warm pastry made with fresh Granny Smith apples, walnuts, and maple syrup. Closed in November.

The Woods Inn (315-357-5300; www.thewoodsinn.com; 148 NY 28) is really something to see as you're paddling past on Fourth Lake, and it's dining room serves comfort food that includes popular dishes such as home-style meat loaf, lamb shank, and chicken potpie. There's also lighter fare—the beet salad's good—and the inn's Laughing Loons Tavern has pub grub such as burgers, Saranac Black & Tan beef stew, and salads.

Long Lake

Long Lake Diner (518-624-3941; NY 30), a spotless, bright lakeside restaurant, is hard to beat. The staff is friendly and fast, and it's tough to find a clunker on the menu. Go for the eggs Benedict or Belgian waffles with real maple syrup; at lunch, homemade potato chips and homemade soups, chargrilled burgers, the fish sandwich, and huge Caesar salads are all good. The clam basket is tasty. Wednesday is prime rib and chicken night; on Friday you can get good fish fry in the diner's bar, referred to as the Owl's Head Pub.

The new place in Long Lake is Flavor (518-624-6657; 1142 Main Street behind Hoss's), opened in 2011 by caterer Susan Rohrey. You can eat a tasty lunch of mesclun greens and homemade soup on the deck or take a gourmet dinner back to your cabin. She even delivers meals to boat-access-only camps on Long Lake.

Mayfield

Lanzi's on the Lake (518-661-7711; www.lanzisonthelake.net; 1751 NY 30), on the western shore of Great Sacandaga Lake, is a deservedly popular restaurant. Ample docks and a long outdoor deck invite boaters in summer, and skiers dine by the stone fireplace in winter. Dinner portions are large and often provide leftovers for meals the next day. Fresh fish and quality steaks are carefully prepared; vegetables, salads, and desserts are tasty, too. Lanzi's can become crowded on weekends, so reservations are recommended.

North Creek

BarVino (518-251-0199; www.barvino .net; 272 Main Street) is a chic family-owned and -operated sweet spot on North Creek's Main Street. The décor is hip, the wine and beer lists lengthy, and menus, which change constantly, are mostly funky small plates with delectables such as curried chickpea fritters with red onion *rita* or Prince Edward Island mussels served in your choice of sauce combo: white wine, parsley, and garlic; Abbey Ale, spinach, and bacon; or green curry, lime, and cilantro. Live music each week is another draw.

Basil & Wicks (518-251-3100; www .basilandwicks.com; Route 28) is back as a beacon by the side of the road. The bar has a nice fireplace and music many weekends, and families can head for a casual dining room. The menu goes from excellent burgers and fried eggplant strips to real dinner fare for hungry skiers, white-water rafters, and hikers, as well as anyone looking for a comfortable spot with good service, nice ambience, and reasonable prices.

North River

Garnet Hill Lodge (518-251-2444; www .garnet-hill.com; 39 Garnet Hill Road) is a fitting destination after hiking in Siamese Ponds Wilderness, fly-fishing on the Hudson, or paddling the nearby lake. The lodge is up high in North River, where there's a million-dollar view of Thirteenth Lake from the pub, the deck, or blackfly-proof screened porch. Mindy Piper and Don Preuninger rescued the venerable log inn from a downhill slide late last year, making delicious, hearty fare a priority. Among the dinners are ratatouille, wild mushroom ragout, glazed duck breast, and grilled trout. Don't overlook the breadbasket—it's all homemade—and save room for awesome pie. Another plus: You don't have to spend a fortune here since prices for apps (onion pie a must) and entrées are very reasonable.

Old Forge

Five Corners Café (315-369-2255; 3067 NY 28) is a funky little space on Old Forge's main drag. The place, owned and operated by Kathy and Paul Rivet, had been open seasonally, serving up scrumptious breakfasts and lunches. But

Sacandaga Saga

Cities downstream of Adirondack rivers, fed up with destructive flooding, celebrated on March 27, 1930, when the gates of the new Conklingville Dam were shut, and 283 billion gallons of water swallowed the valley. Schools, farms, homes, stores, and businesses were lost to the rising waters of the reservoir. Between 1928 and 1930, almost 4,000 graves from 22 cemeteries in the valley were relocated.

Today, the resulting Great Sacandaga Lake, a 29-mile-long reservoir with 125 miles of shoreline, is a summertime draw for swimmers, anglers, and boaters. But old-timers recall their once-vibrant farmland communities underneath all that water. Sometimes in October, when the reservoir's levels dip low, stumps, stone fences, foundations, and roads emerge.

The Sacandaga Valley was flooded to create Great Sacandaga Lake, a 29-mile-long reservoir that ended destructive downstate flooding.

Courtesy of Johnathan Esper, www.wildernessphotographs.com

as of spring 2012, the Rivets, who used to run Van Auken's Inne in Thendara, launched a new look, new hours—they hope to stay open year-round—and a new menu. Kathy says they're offering a neighborhood restaurant vibe with simple bistro fare, "using great ingredients and preparing them well." (Everything is moderately priced, from $8 to $20.) Paul, a Culinary Institute of America graduate, developed a big- and small-plate menu with beef short ribs, spicy chicken hash, and an apple fennel goat cheese crepe, among others, that'll change throughout the summer. All bread and desserts are homemade, including the Rivets' cookies, hot commodities at the area farmers' market. A wine and beer bar with high tables plus a patio accommodate those waiting for a seat at this living room–size café.

Sisters Bistro (315-369-1053; www.sistersbistro.com; 3046 Main Street) has a pretty Victorian mansion and eclectic décor as backdrop for its gourmet fare. Foodies all over the park are talking about Sisters' artful presentations and

flavors—for example, an appetizer, or "flora" of herbed goat cheese flan with figs, hazelnuts and salad; an entrée, or "fauna," of pomegranate and black pepper chicken breast with stuffing waffle and vegetable; and a "fini" of Pavlova with lemon curd and berry compote—all listed with a suggested wine pairing. Not to mention, where else in these parts can you order a maple bourbon Manhattan?

Speculator

Logan's Bar & Grill (518-548-3287; www.logans921.com; Route 8) is former Anthony Bourdain–sous chef Steve Tempel's low-key restaurant in the heart of the park. Tempel, who has also been a contestant on various Food Network cook-offs, named the place after his son, and, according to locals, has created an Adirondack-family-style joint right down to the moose cutout on his restaurant's façade. The menu has the mainstream standbys, such as Italian and Mexican fare and burgers and wings, but there's also crab fondue, salade Niçoise, and herb-crusted filet mignon with wild mushrooms.

Melody Lodge (518-548-6562; www.melodylodge.com; NY 30) feels almost like an Adirondack Great Camp, with its antiques, massive stone fireplaces, and view down Page Hill toward Lake Pleasant. The rambling inn (upstairs are guest rooms named after musical instruments) was built in 1912 as a singing school for young girls, and became a restaurant and hotel in 1937. The lodge's menu is interesting, with unexpected choices, such as an awesome seafood jamboree with scallops, shrimp, and mussels in a smoked salmon sauce, and trout stuffed with artichokes and sun-dried tomatoes. Closed Monday and Tuesday in winter.

MORE MEALS

Blue Canoe (518-352-7744; Route 30), in Blue Mountain Lake, can't be missed—there's a blue canoe full of flowers and the building is blue too. Expect delicious homemade ice-cream sandwiches, maple soft-serve, plus hard ice cream. Open Memorial Day through Labor Day.

Would you believe there's gelato in Inlet, and that the pistachio is divine? A trip to Northern Lights Creamery (315-357-6294; Route 28) is a must. Also in Inlet, the Red Dog Tavern (315-357-5502; www.reddogtavern.com; 2682 South Shore Road) has good ribs and bar food, including chicken wings, quesadillas, and bruschetta.

In Northville Klippel's Kozy Korner Café & Deli (518-863-8550; 221 Bridge Street) serves breakfast in the summer, and lunch and dinner year-round. Timeless Tavern and Inn (518-863-4635; 162 South Main Street) is where insiders go for dinner to celebrate special occasions.

Café Sarah (518-251-5959; 260 Main Street) is an institution on North Creek's Main Street. Sarah makes excellent sandwiches—fresh mozzarella, pesto, and tomato hot from the panini press; roast beef with caramelized onions and cheese; curried smoked chicken salad. And then there are the delish baked goods. This is a local hot spot, so it bustles year-round.

In Old Forge, Tony Harper's Pizza & Clam Shack (315-369-3777; www.tony harperspizzaandclamshack.com; 3062 Main Street) has good stuff, plus it's open late. The best burger in Old Forge—and the nachos and guac are good, too—can be found at Slickers (315-369-3002; NY 28, near the covered bridge).

In Olmstedville, the Owl at Twilight (518-251-4696; 1322 CTY 29) is one of the best restaurants around. It's a moving target, you never know if it's open or closed.

In Speculator, King of the Frosties (518-548-3881; NY 30) has soft-serve ice cream, as well as good burgers, salads, and excellent Filipino noodle soup. Open breakfast, lunch, and dinner.

The Lake House Grille (518-924-2424; www.lakehousegrille.com; NY 30), in Wells, has an eclectic menu and live music on Saturday evenings in summer.

To Do

Attractions and activities in the Central & Southwestern Adirondacks

Lakes and woods define the central Adirondacks, and the same elements shape iconic architecture in Great Camps, such as Sagamore, as well as the lively cultural scene. Community arts centers such as View and Adirondack Lakes Center for the Arts are bustling in every season with professional theater, classes, exhibitions, and concerts. Tannery Pond Community Center and Indian Lake Theater schedule both films and live performances. In summer Long Lake's

Sagamore Great Camp (315-354-5311; www.sagamore.org; Sagamore Road, off NY 28, Raquette Lake), a massive rustic lodge, along the lines of a Swiss chalet, was built by Adirondack entrepreneur William West Durant in 1897, and then sold to Alfred G. Vanderbilt Sr. in 1901. Even though the Vanderbilts spent much of their time elsewhere, Sagamore was a self-sufficient village in the heart of the wilderness, with its own farm and a crew of craftsmen to supply furniture, hardware, and boats. Today, the millionaires' complex—main lodge, dining hall, rustic guest cottages, casino/playhouse, open-air bowling alley, and boathouse—and the artisans' barns, carriage house, workshops, and blacksmith shop are open to the public. Two-hour tours are presented by college interns and other volunteers; a highlight is sending a vintage bowling ball down the lane toward the pins to demonstrate the loop-de-loop ball return.

Sagamore is a National Historic Landmark in a gorgeous setting on Sagamore Lake, 4 miles off the main state highway on a rough dirt road. Besides tours, the Great Camp sponsors workshops and conferences; is available for overnight accommodations; has a small gift shop and café; and can be hired for special events such as wedding receptions and family reunions. The Sagamore was the backdrop for scenes from director Robert DeNiro's 2006 film *The Good Shepherd,* starring Angelina Jolie and Matt Damon, and often appears as the iconic Great Camp in mainstream publications.

Call ahead for walking tour schedule. Admission: $14 adults, $13 seniors, $7 school-aged children; preschoolers are free. Open Memorial Day through October.

Mount Sabbatis Park is the venue for musicians such as Martin Sexton and Shonen Knife. And no visit is complete without a day at the Adirondack Museum, which celebrates the region's roots in 22 buildings.

ARCHITECTURE AND HISTORIC BUILDINGS

The heart of the Adirondacks has few pre–Civil War buildings, but it is home to a vernacular architectural style that honors French Canadian and Yankee traditions in steep-roofed, simple homes. Olmstedville, off NY 28N, has a cluster of Greek Revival storefronts and houses from the 1840s. Farther south, on NY 30, Wells has nicely restored Victorian-era homes along the Sacandaga River. For rustic architecture, a boat tour of Raquette Lake on the *W. W. Durant* (315-354-5532; www .raquettelakenavigation.com), a replica of an old steamboat, allows glimpses of Great Camps such as Pine Knot (the first rustic camp designed by William West Durant), Camp Echo, and Bluff Point (the former Collier estate). Great Camp Sagamore (315-354-5301; www.sagamore.org) occasionally offers tours of nearby rustic estates, as does Adirondack Architectural Heritage (518-834-9328; www.aarch.org).

ARTS CENTERS

Adirondack Lakes Center for the Arts (518-352-7715; www.adirondackarts.org; NY 28, next to the post office, Blue Mountain Lake), a multiarts center, has brought a full palette of programs to Blue Mountain Lake, population 150 (give or take) for more than four decades. The center is a former garage, where hundreds of performers, including the Tokyo String Quartet, Doc Watson, Tony Trischka, Odetta, and more, have taken the stage. New to the center has been an emphasis on theater: It offers professional theater in summer—even a popular traveling Shakespeare in the Park production—and community theater in fall, spring, and winter. Its galleries exhibit contemporary paintings, sculpture, photography, and crafts; Adirondack furniture; children's art; and traveling shows. Complementing the shows are intensive workshops for adults on weekends in fall and winter and weekdays in summer. Programs for adults have been sand mandala workshops and skit-writing classes. For kids and families: crafts, dance, and music workshops to presentations of storytelling, New Vaudeville, and magic.

Fulton Chain of Lakes Performing Arts Council, Inc. (315-357-3799; Inlet) has brought professional musicians to small central Adirondack communities that may never have seen the likes of a piccolo or timpani. Each summer—always the last Friday in July—the council has sponsored a concert featuring the Syracuse Symphony Orchestra in a tent overlooking Fourth Lake. (The symphony disbanded in 2011; at press time it's unclear who will play the council's summer concert.)

Sacandaga Valley Arts Network (518-321-3468; www.svanarts.org; Northville), serving those in the Sacandaga River watershed in the south-central Adirondacks since 1997, spreads its knowledge and philosophy through programs ranging from group shows of internationally acclaimed artists to drum circles to quilt and film clubs to watercolor and photography classes. A coffeehouse series brings music to the region in winter; in summer, alfresco performances at Northville Park provide audiences with a variety of music—gospel, bluegrass, country, folk, and rock. SVAN also sponsors a classical music series at the Batchellerville Presbyterian Church, in Edinburg.

Tannery Pond Community Center (518-251-2505; www.tpcca.org; 228 Main Street, North Creek) is the state-of-the-art home to North Creek's cultural scene. It hosts chamber music players and theater groups, and houses a gallery that features work by regional artists. The facility has four multipurpose meeting rooms, a caterer's kitchen, and a 150-seat auditorium. Tannery Pond is base for Upper Hudson Musical Arts (www.upperhudsonmusicalarts.org), which brings fine music, dance, and theater to the Adirondacks. In summer, kids can enroll in the center's Art and Nature Camp, where they take fieldtrips to collect natural pigments for painting, learn to make raku pottery, create shadow puppets, build floating boat sculpture, and participate in other wilderness-inspired projects.

View (315-369-6411; www.viewarts.org; NY 28, Old Forge) was once the Arts Center/Old Forge, but it's still the oldest community-arts organization in the region, and the organization continues to grow, change, and pursue new directions. Its brand-spanking new 28,000-square-foot LEED-certified facility—already a model for other art centers—gives Old Forge a cultural wow factor. View has a state-of-the-art performance hall, slick gallery spaces, and workshop studios. Annual events include the Adirondacks National Exhibition of Watercolors (August–September) and Old Forge Plein Air Paint Out, among others. View hosts visiting theater troupe productions; classical concerts as well as bluegrass, folk, and jazz programs are staples in a packed performance schedule.

In summer, there are local history outings and lectures and presentations

View, Old Forge's stunning new arts center.
Courtesy of View

by artists, naturalists, and writers. Throughout the year, View shows contemporary American and foreign films and offers workshops for adults and children, from boat building to basketry, jewelry making to the photography, plus yoga and self-defense classes.

CINEMA

The community-run Indian Lake Theater (518-648-5950; www.indian laketheater.org) brings mainstream and indie films, but it also presents opera, and performances by musicians such as Dar Williams. In Old Forge, the Strand Theatre (315-369-2792; www.strandold forge.com; NY 28) is a beautiful vintage cinema with three screens. And Inlet's Tamarack Café & Movie House (315-357-2001; NY 28) shows recent films five nights a week, though it closes for a month in fall and a month in spring. You can get breakfast and lunch here, too.

LIBRARIES

Libraries are popular for free wireless in communities where cell phones are just baubles. In North Creek there's the Johnsburg Library (518-251-4343; 219 Main Street); farther south is Northville Public Library (518-863-6922; www.northville.mvls.info; 341 South Third Street). Old Forge Library (315-369-6008; www.oldforgelibrary.org; 220 Crosby Boulevard) has an Adirondack collection, lecture series, writers' workshops, and other events.

The Adirondack Museum, in Blue Mountain Lake, is a must-see for all park visitors.

Courtesy of the Adirondack Museum, Blue Mountain Lake

Adirondack Photography Institute

Adirondack photography graces coffee-table books, wall calendars, screen savers, and the pages of popular regional magazines such as *Adirondack Life*. The Adirondack Park is such a photography mecca that photographer John Radigan established the Adirondack Photography Institute (518-478-8592; www.adkpi .org), which provides often sold-out workshops on a range of topics in the Adirondack Park. Workshops happen at various venues within the Blue Line and are taught by an A-list staff of expert Adirondack photographers, such as Radigan, Mark Bowie, Joe LeFevre, and Eric Dresser. Guest instructors have included all-stars Carl Heilman II, Nancy Rotenberg, Johnathan Esper, and George DeWolfe.

The Raquette Lake Free Library (315-354-4005; 1 Dillon Road) and Town of Indian Lake Library (518-648-5444; indianlakelibrary.wordpress.com; Pelon Road) also accommodate the region.

MUSEUMS

The Adirondack Museum (518-352-7311; www.adkmuseum.org; NY 28 and 30, Blue Mountain Lake) is a cultural icon. Simply put, no visit to the Adirondacks is complete without visiting the place. Perched on the side of Blue Mountain and overlooking the island-studded lake, this is a major outdoor museum that is user-friendly, scholarly, beautiful, amusing, and superlative in every way. Not surprisingly, the place has been described by the *New York*

Adirondack Poet

Poet Jeanne Robert Foster, born Julia Elizabeth Oliver, grew up in grinding poverty in Johnsburg and went on to be an editor of the *Transatlantic Review*. Her circle of friends included Ezra Pound, T. S. Eliot, and John Butler Yeats, father of the Irish poet. Her poetry-and-prose memories of her youth were published in *Adirondack Portraits: A Piece of Time*. Foster is buried in Chestertown.

Times as "the best museum of its kind in the world."

The museum's theme is interpreting man's relationship to the Adirondacks, and it does so in 20-plus exhibit buildings. Adjacent to the entrance is a theater showing *The Adirondacks: The Lives and Times of an American Wilderness*, an award-winning film. In the galleries of the main building, there are changing exhibits of paintings; in 2012 special exhibitions included historical regional quilts and comforters, and 19th-century painter A. F. Tait's Adirondack scenes.

There are scores of wooden boats, including fine Adirondack guideboats and a Gold Cup racer; there are dozens of carriages, sleighs, and wagons. You can glide through August Belmont's private railroad car and imagine yourself en route to your very own Great Camp, or you can picture the other extreme of Adirondack life, in displays covering agriculture and logging. In "Woods and Waters: Outdoor Recreation in the Adirondacks," you'll find hunting and fishing gear. On Merwin Hill, Bull Cottage—a nice example of everyday rustic architecture—showcases rooms of rustic furniture.

The museum is a great place for children who can read and understand historical ideas; there are multi-media stations that add depth to the displays. "The Great Outdoors" is an exhibit building devoted entirely to interactive sections for kids: snowshoes to try on fake snow, a tent to scramble into, a climbing wall to scale, fishing poles with magnets to catch (and release) your own faux brook trout or bass. There's a rustic "tot lot" with swings and a log cabin to play in, and inside Rising Schoolhouse—moved to the site from 80 miles away—are slates, vintage maps, and an old-school teacher.

The museum comes alive with craft demonstrations, music, and storytelling on selected days. The "Dog Days of Summer" features agility contests, best-selling dog book authors (in 2012 *Marley and Me*'s John Grogan was a featured speaker), sheepherding demonstrations, dogs at work—and guests can even bring their own dogs for this special event. The Rustic Furniture Fair in September showcases 50-plus builders so that visitors can decide how to begin their own Adirondack collections.

It's probably a natural response to plan a visit to the Adirondack Museum on a rainy day, but thousands of other folks think along the same lines, and the place can get crowded. Far better to pick a gorgeous day when you can savor the view and the many outdoor displays, and see the exhibits without having to jockey for position.

Open daily, Memorial Day through mid-October 15, though workshops and lectures continue year-round. Admission is $18 adults; $12 teens, $6 ages 6–12; discounts available for seniors.

The Riley House—next door to Riley's Tavern—in Piseco, is home to the Piseco Lake Historical Society (518-548-4812; Old Piseco Road), a collection of antiques and ephemera open 1 to 4 on weekends in summer.

In Edinburg, the Nellie Tyrell Museum (518-863-2034; www.edinburg-hist-soc.org; County Road 4) is an old schoolhouse with displays showing life before the creation of the Great Sacandaga Reservoir in the 1930s.

Vintage Watercraft

In 1843, John Todd visited the lonely settlers in Long Lake and wrote, "Their little boats were their horses, and the lake their only path." Traditional wooden boats, especially the guideboat, performed a major role in nineteenth-century work and play. At several affairs across the park, you can get a taste of this era, and enjoy beautifully restored guideboats, canoes, sailboats, and even classic powerboats.

In July the Fulton Chain Rendezvous of the **Antique and Classic Boat Society** (315-369-6983; www.oldforgeny.com) welcomes exhibitors and members, with a dockside show at the Old Forge waterfront, and a grand parade—everything from old Fay & Bowens and Chris-Crafts, to HackerCrafts and Gar Woods—through the channel that marks the beginning of the eight lakes.

Guideboats played a major role in 19th-century work and play. Courtesy of Ted Comstock, Saranac Lake

Northville has two museums right on South Main Street: the Gifford Valley Schoolhouse, behind the municipal offices, and the Paul Bradt Museum (518-863-4040 ext. 22), which is filled with North American taxidermied wildlife and housed inside the village office complex. The outdoor museum complex near Caroga Lake, the Caroga Historical Museum (www.carogamuseum.org; London Bridge Road), re-creates pioneer life in the southern Adirondacks in a farmstead, schoolhouse, and country store.

In Olmstedville, the Minerva Historical Society (518-251-2229; Main Street) is open July through Columbus Day; displays honor artists who visited the area, such as Winslow Homer. In Old Forge, the Town of Webb Historical Association (315-369-3838; Main Street) has exhibits on railroads, resorts, rustic furniture, and early industries in its Goodsell Museum, which is open year-round. On the edge of town is the Forest Industries Exhibit Hall (315-369-3078; 3311 NY 28), with displays on forest management, logging history, and dioramas, open Memorial Day through Columbus Day.

MUST-SEE ANNUAL EVENTS

Long Lake Winter Carnival (518-354-1510; www.mylonglake.com), in January, has a snowmobile parade, cardboard box derby race, snowball golf, and fireworks.

Indian Lake Winter Festival (518-648-5112; www.indian-lake.com), on Presidents' Weekend in February, mixes local history programs with outdoor events such as cross-country-ski treks, downhill races at the town ski area, snowmobile poker runs, and snowshoe events throughout Indian Lake and Blue Mountain Lake. There's music and sometimes square dancing in the evenings, plus community suppers.

Polkafest USA (www.polkafestusa.com; Hiltebrant Recreation Center, North Street), in Old Forge, in May, has polka bands, and Polish food and drink.

Olde Home Days and Carnival (518-548-4521), in Wells, held in August, with a parade featuring horse-drawn wagons, antique cars, floats, and marching bands. Expect all kinds of music, plus a carnival and a craft fair.

Adirondack Authors' Fair at Hoss's Country Corner (518-624-2451; www.hosss countrycorner.com), in Long Lake, is a great opportunity to meet and greet regional writers, held under a huge tent in mid-August.

Antiques Show & Sale at the Adirondack Museum (518-352-7311; www.adk museum.org), in August, draws dealers and buyers from all over.

Upper Hudson Bluegrass Festival (518-251-2240; www.upperhudsonbluegrass .com), in August, brings fine bluegrass acts to North Creek.

Teddy Roosevelt Weekend (518-582-3211; www.newcombny.com), in Newcomb, Minerva, and North Creek, celebrates Teddy Roosevelt's wild ride to the presidency with historical programs, train rides, and sports contests, in early September.

Great Adirondack Moose Festival (518-648-5636 or 518-648-5112; www.indian -lake.com), in Indian Lake, is a September weekend of music, guided hikes, lectures, logging demos, and much more.

Rustic Furniture Fair (518-352-7311; www.adkmuseum.org), in September, at the Adirondack Museum, in Blue Mountain Lake, features the work of talented craftsmen from across the Adirondacks and beyond. Also, demonstrations, rustic designs sale, music, and food.

THEATER

North Creek's amateur Our Town Theatre Group (518-251-2938 or 518-494-5280; www.ottg.org; Tannery Pond Community Center, 228 Main Street) is headquartered at Tannery Pond Community Center, and occasionally takes its shows on the road. All who are involved in this community-based organization—actors, costumers, stagehands, and ushers—are volunteers.

Recreation

Adventures around the Central & Southwestern Adirondacks

The central Adirondacks is defined by water, with interconnected lakes and swift rivers. It's also defined by snow, with the most impressive cover in places like Old Forge, North River, and Long Lake. Mountain snobs may look down their noses at the peaks here, though some—like Snowy—are higher than some of the vaunted 46 High Peaks. In every season there are challenging adventures, such as white-water rafting or backcountry skiing and trout fishing on pristine ponds. Every outdoorsperson has a favorite spot, from the fire tower on Pillsbury Mountain to the lean-to on Cascade Pond. And there's more public land in this part of the Adirondack Park than in any other.

ADIRONDACK GUIDES

For all your hiking, biking, climbing, hunting, paddling, skiing, you-name-it needs, there's a guide for that. See the New York State Outdoor Guides Association's website, www.nysoga.org, for a list of licensed Adirondack guides who can show you the adventure of a lifetime.

BIKING

As mountain biking continues to grow in popularity, the Inlet–Old Forge area has emerged as a center for the sport. (Just a reminder: all-terrain bicycles are barred from wilderness and primitive areas in the Adirondack Park.) Old Forge welcomes pedalers to explore its extensive snowmobile trails; contact the Central

Mountain Bike Rules of the Trail

- Ride on open trails only. Respect trail and road closures and avoid trespassing on private lands. Wilderness areas are closed to cycling.
- Leave no trace. Even on open trails, you should not ride under conditions where you will leave evidence of your passing. Practice low-impact cycling by staying on the trail and not creating any new ones. Pack out at least as much as you pack in.
- Control your bicycle. There is no excuse for excessive speed.
- Always yield the trail to hikers and others. Make your approach known well in advance; a friendly greeting or a bell works well.
- Never spook animals. Give them extra room and time to adjust to your presence; use special care when passing horseback riders.
- Plan ahead. Know your equipment, your ability, and the area in which you are riding, and prepare accordingly. Be self-sufficient; carry the necessary supplies and tools you may need.

—From the International Mountain Bicycling Association

Adirondack Association (315-369-6983; www.visitmyadirondacks.com; Main Street, Old Forge) for a map. Inlet is perched on the edge of the Moose River Recreation Area, which is laced with old logging roads and fantastic trails. Check out www.inletny.com for a list of loops of varying difficulty.

Lift-serviced biking is available at New York State–owned ski area Gore Mountain (518-251-2441; www.goremountain.com; Peaceful Valley Road, North Creek). Some ski trails—as you'd suspect—are gnarly, scary, bumpy rides, but there are traverse routes and woods roads, too. A favorite of Neil Auty's, of the Bike Works (518-762-1342), just outside the Blue Line in Johnstown, is the intermediate 5-or-so-mile loop alongside Nine Corner Lake, north of Route 29A near Canada Lake. Ted Christodaro, of bike and flower shop combo Pedals & Petals (315-357-3281; www.pedalsandpetals.com; 176 Route 28), in Inlet, recommends the area's surrounding snowmobile network that doubles as mountain-bike trails, but also the quiet dirt Uncas Road from Eagle Bay to Raquette Lake with a side trip to Sucker Brook. Read about bike-route conditions or add your input at Pedals & Petals's message board, inlettrails.com. And the second Saturday in June hard-core bikers can compete in the Black Fly Challenge (www.blackflychallenge.com), a grueling 40-mile mountain-bike race through the Moose River Plains, between Inlet and Indian Lake.

Road cyclists will discover that many state highways have wide, smooth shoulders. You won't have to contend with much traffic in May and June or September and October, except on weekends, but main roads become busy with log trucks, sightseeing buses, and RVs throughout the summer. Some folks combine rides on the Adirondack Scenic Railroad (1-877-508-6728; www.adirondackrr.com), in Thendara, to get to starting points. The Speculator Loop (518-548-4521; www.adrkmts.com) is popular, too.

See chapter 8 for road-bike and mountain-bike guidebooks and regional magazines that offer ideas for bike trips. Check www.bikeadirondacks.org for an online atlas. Beaver Brook Outfitters (518-251-3394; www.beaverbrook.net; 2349 NY 28, Wevertown) and Garnet Hill Lodge (518-251-2444; www.garnet-hill.com; Thirteenth Lake Road, North River) are also good resources.

Be prepared for any long trips: Check topographical as well as highway maps for significant hills on your proposed route. Always carry plenty of water, a compass, and a good tool kit. Remember, there's no cell-phone service here. *And wear a helmet!*

The Narrows between Third and Fourth Lakes. Courtesy of Ted Comstock, Saranac Lake

BOATING

Many Adirondack lakes have public launches for motor- and sailboats. Most are free, operated by the New York State Department of Environmental Conservation or villages; individual businesses may charge a nominal fee. You'll find these launch sites marked on regional road maps. State campgrounds often have boat ramps. If you have a reserved campsite, there's no extra charge to launch a boat, and if you'd like to make a short visit to Eighth Lake, for example, you pay the day-use fee.

Marinas and boat liveries offer another chance for folks with trailers to get their boats in the water. Many more options are open to canoeists and kayakers who can portage their boats a short distance. The *New York State Boater's Guide* (www.nysparks.com) contains the rules and regulations for inland waters, and is available from offices of the New York Department of Transportation. See page 211 for statewide laws for pleasure craft.

See page 212 for information about invasive species and regulations on cleaning watercraft.

BOAT TOURS

If you'd prefer not to be your own helmsman, board a cruise vessel. Prices vary widely depending on the length of the tour, and what kind of frills come with it—music, dancing, and champagne. Most boats can be chartered for special events; some captains are licensed to perform weddings. The season generally runs from early May through October; always call ahead for a reservation. Blue Mountain Lake Boat Livery (518-352-7351; www.boatlivery.com; NY 28, Blue Mountain Lake) provides narrated rides through the Eckford Chain of Lakes aboard three restored wooden launches: the *Neenykin,* the *Toowaloondah,* and the *Osprey.*

Dunn's Boat Service (315-357-3532; www.dunnsboats.com; 1500 Big Moose Road, Big Moose Lake) gives tours of the setting of *An American Tragedy* aboard *Grace,* a beautiful inboard.

Norridgewock III (315-376-6200; www.beaverriver.com; 150 Norridgewock Lake Road, Eagle Bay) takes visitors on tours and offers water-taxi service on Stillwater Reservoir, which allows access to remote Beaver River.

Old Forge Lake Cruises (315-369-6473; www.oldforgecruises.com; NY 28, Main Street, Old Forge) has a narrated 28-mile cruise on the Fulton Chain of Lakes aboard the *Uncas* or the *Clearwater,* plus weekend shuttles to Inlet from Old Forge. Passengers can ride on the *President Harrison,* a 20-foot vessel used to deliver letters and packages on the longest running freshwater mail boat route in the country.

Raquette Lake Navigation Co. (315-354-5532; www.raquettelakenavigation.com; Pier I, Raquette Lake) does lunch, brunch, and dinner cruises—by reservation only—aboard the posh *W. W. Durant.*

CAMPING

Camping is allowed year-round on state land, but you need a permit to stay more than three days in one backcountry spot or if you are camping with a group of more than six people. You may camp in the backcountry provided you pitch your tent at least 150 feet from any trail, stream, lake, or other water body. (See "low-impact camping," page 146.)

From Memorial Day through Labor Day, the Department of Environmental Conservation (518-402-9428; www.dec .ny.gov) operates public campgrounds. Facilities at state campgrounds include a picnic table and grill at each site, water spigots for every 10 sites or so, and lavatories. DEC public campgrounds do not supply water, electric, or sewer hookups for recreational vehicles. If you require

Lewey Lake. Courtesy of Ted Comstock, Saranac Lake

these amenities, there are privately owned campgrounds in many communities. Along the Northville–Lake Placid Trail and on popular canoe routes you'll find lean-tos for camping. These three-sided log structures are an Adirondack icon.

Reservations can be made for a site in the state campgrounds by contacting Reserve America (1-800-456-CAMP; www.reserveamerica). Its website includes details about every state campground, as does the DEC's campsite listings on its site, so you can see for yourself if site #4 at Lake Durant is on the water. (It is.) Or contact the campground itself. DEC campgrounds will take you on a first-come, first-served basis if space is available. Camping fees listed in the following Central and Southwestern Adirondacks' campgrounds are for 2012:

Alger Island (315-369-3224; 303 Petrie Road, Old Forge), on Fourth Lake. Access by boat, lean-tos, tents only. $18 camping fee.

Brown Tract Pond (315-354-4412; Uncas Road, Raquette Lake). Canoe to Raquette Lake or Fulton Chain. Swimming, canoe or rowboat rentals, no powerboats allowed. $18 camping fee.

Caroga Lake (518-835-4241; 3043 NY 29A, Gloversville). Swimming, showers, boat launch. $20 camping fee.

Eighth Lake (315-354-4120; NY 28, between Raquette Lake and Inlet). Swimming, showers, canoe or rowboat rentals, boat launch. $22 camping fee.

Forked Lake (518-624-6646; 381 Forked Lake Campsite Lane, Long Lake). Primitive walk-in or canoe-in sites, launch for cartop boats. $18 camping fee.

Golden Beach (315-354-4230; NY 28, Raquette Lake). On Raquette Lake. Swimming, showers, boat or canoe rentals, boat launch. $20 camping fee.

Indian Lake Islands (518-648-5300; off NY 30, Sabael). Access by boat, tents only, boat launch. $20 camping fee.

Lake Durant (518-352-7797; NY 28 and 30, Blue Mountain Lake). Swimming, showers, canoe rentals, boat launch; handicapped-accessible campsite. Access to Blue Ridge Wilderness and Northville–Lake Placid Trail. $20 camping fee.

Lake Eaton (518-624-2641; NY 30, Long Lake). Swimming, showers, canoe or rowboat rentals, boat launch. $20 camping fee.

Lewey Lake (518-648-5266; NY 30, Sabael). Swimming, showers, canoe or rowboat rentals, boat launch. $20 camping fee.

Limekiln Lake (315-357-4401; Limekiln Lake Road, Inlet). Swimming, showers, canoe or rowboat rentals, boat launch. Access to Moose River Recreation Area. $20 camping fee.

Little Sand Point (518-548-7585; Old Piseco Road, Piseco). On Piseco Lake. Swimming, canoe or rowboat rentals, boat launch. $20 camping fee.

Moffit Beach (518-548-7102; Page Street, Speculator). On Sacandaga Lake. Swimming, showers, canoe or rowboat rentals, boat launch. $22 camping fee.

Nicks Lake (315-369-3314; 278 Bisby Road, Old Forge). Remote lakeside location. Swimming, trout fishing, nearby hiking trails, no motorboats. $22 camping fee.

Northampton Beach (518-863-6000; 328 Houseman Street, Mayfield). On Great Sacandaga Lake. Swimming, showers, canoe or rowboat rentals, boat launch. $22 camping fee.

Point Comfort (518-548-7586; Old Piseco Road, Piseco). On Piseco Lake. Swimming, showers, canoe or rowboat rentals, boat launch. $16 camping fee.

Poplar Point (518-548-8031; Old Piseco Road, Piseco). On Piseco Lake. Swimming, canoe or rowboat rentals, boat launch. $20 camping fee.

Sacandaga (518-924-4121; NY 30, Northville). On Sacandaga River. Swimming, showers, no powerboats. $20 camping fee.

Tioga Point (315-354-4230; NY 28, Raquette Lake). On Raquette Lake. Access by boat; some lean-tos, although it's best to bring a tent. Beautiful spot. $18 camping fee.

CAMPS

Famous folks spent their summers at Adirondack kids' camps: Arlo Guthrie and his mother, a dance instructor, enjoyed many seasons at Raquette Lake Camp (315-354-4382; www.raquettelakecamp.com); Demi Moore and Bruce Willis enrolled their kids at Long Lake Camp for the Arts (1-800-767-7111; www.longlakecamp.com). Another popular one in this region is Adirondack Woodcraft Camps (1-800-374-4840; www.awcl.com), in Old Forge.

If you're in the Adirondacks during July or August, and would like to visit a particular camp with your prospective happy camper, call ahead. Or check out www.acacamps.org for camps accredited by the American Camping Association.

CANOEING AND KAYAKING

The Adirondack Park offers some of the best canoeing and kayaking in the Northeast. For thrill seekers, there's serious white water (with rapids up to Class V) on the Upper Hudson, the Moose, portions of the Schroon, and other rivers; for flatwater fans, there are long trips linking lakes, such as the 44-mile route from Long Lake to Tupper Lake; the 35-mile trip from Old Forge to Blue Mountain Lake; the 25-mile trip from Osgood Pond to Lake Kushaqua; or the Old Forge to Lake Champlain stretch of the 740-mile Northern Forest Canoe Trail, which begins in Old Forge and ends in northern Maine. There's even a three-day race, the Adirondack Canoe Classic, or "90-Miler," which covers 90 miles of water in a long diagonal from the Fulton Chain of Lakes to Saranac Lake village

Check out guidebooks in chapter 8 for specific paddling routes. *The Adirondack Paddler's Map*, a waterproof and tear-proof guide for multiday trips with enough details for navigating, includes trailheads, portages, and white-water ratings across the region.

The Department of Environmental Conservation (518-891-1200; www.dec.ny .gov) has pamphlets that describe canoe routes; ask for *Adirondack Canoe Routes* or the "official map and guide" of the area you wish to paddle. The excellent 24-four-page booklet *Adirondack Waterways Guide* is available at www.visitadirondacks.com.

When you're planning any trip, allow an extra day in case the weather doesn't cooperate. Remember that you're required to carry a life jacket for each person in the boat; lash an extra paddle in your canoe, too. Bring plenty of food and fuel, a backpacker stove, and rain gear. A poncho makes a good coverall for hiking, but you're far better off with rain jacket and pants in a canoe, as a poncho can become tangled if you should dump the canoe. Always sign in at the trailhead registers when you begin your trip.

And if you're eager to try canoeing but just aren't sure of your abilities, there are plenty of places where you can get lessons in flatwater or white-water techniques. Old Forge's Paddlefest (315-357-6672; www.mountainmanoutdoors.com), in mid-May, has demonstrations and more than 100 different boats to try. Blue Mountain Outfitters (518-352-7306; www.laprairiecottages.com/bmo.html; 144 Main Street, Blue Mountain Lake) offers demo days. For lessons, hire a guide for one-on-one sessions or check with your local Red Cross office for water safety courses and basic canoe instruction. Other good resources are Beaver Brook Outfitters (1-888-454-8433; www.beaverbrook.net; 2349 NY 28, Wevertown); Haderondah Company (315-369-3868; www.haderondah.com; 3011 Main Street, Old Forge); Mountainman Outdoor Supply Company (315-369-6672; www.mountainmanoutdoors.com; NY 28 Old Forge); and Tickner's Moose River Canoe Outfitters (315-369-6286; www .ticknerscanoe.com; Riverside Drive, Old Forge).

CLIMBING

The High Peaks isn't the only great place to rock climb. Challenging routes abound in this region of the park, and the Southern Adirondacks Rock Climbers Festival is an annual outlet for climbers to explore them. Among the sweet spots are Shanty Cliffs, Crane Mountain; newly developed crags near Caroga Lake, such as McMartin, Lost T, and the Annex; plus classics including Nine Corner Lake—a mega-bouldering area—and Good Luck Mountain, home of Mystery Achievement, Deck of Cards, and Medicine Man. Check out www.mtnsideview.com/sadkrock .html to learn more, and see chapter 8 for climbing guidebooks.

FAMILY FUN

Looking for something that doesn't involve hiking boots or paddles? You won't have to break a sweat to do the following:

Adirondack Scenic Railroad (315-369-6290; www.adirondackrr.com; NY 28, Thendara) runs excursions from Thendara to Minnehaha or Carter Station, about 4 and 6 miles, respectively. Inquire about bike and rail or canoe and rail combinations. Scheduled are train robberies, Halloween rides, Thomas the Tank Engine, and other special events. Open May through November.

Enchanted Forest/Water Safari, New York's largest water theme park, is an Old Forge institution. Courtesy of Ted Comstock, Saranac Lake

Rooms with a View

There were once 57 **fire towers** within the borders of what we know as the park today. The very first was made of logs and was established on Mount Morris in Franklin County, in 1909; within a decade the total number of strategically placed fire lookouts had swelled to 52. It was the arrival of the light plane, coupled with rising costs to man the structures that initiated the decline and eventual demise of the active fire towers. Many of these towers still stand today. And while a few of the mountains require the climb to the towers' cab for a superior vantage point above the surrounding trees, there are plenty with open and sprawling summits equally satisfying for those with a fear of heights.

Want to find them all and get a patch for your effort? The **Fire Tower Challenge**, dreamed up about 15 years ago, has simple rules: Climb 18 of the 23 designated summits with fire towers in the Adirondacks (and all five in the Catskills). Learn more about the challenge and read descriptions of the qualifying summits in *Views from on High: Fire Tower Trails in the Adirondacks and Catskills* by John Freeman (518-668-4447; www.adk.org). A sampling of the mountains in the Central and Southwestern region of the Adirondacks where you can find towers are: Bald (Rondaxe), Snowy, Blue, Hadley, Owl, Wakely, Pillsbury, Goodnow, and Gore.

—Gary VanRiper, coauthor of The Adirondack Kids series (www.adirondack kids.com), from "The Fire Tower Challenge," Adirondack Life.

Barton Garnet Mine Tours (518-251-2706; www.garnetminetours.com; Barton Mines Road, North River) happen in garnet central. Take a tour of Barton's open-pit mines, collect rocks, then browse the specimens in the mineral shop. Open June through Columbus Day.

Calypso's Cove (315-369-6145; www.calypsoscove.com; 3183 NY 28, Old Forge) has an arcade, bumper boats, batting cages, driving range, mini golf, and go-karts—plenty of entertainment for the entire family. Open Memorial Day through Columbus Day.

Enchanted Forest/Water Safari (315-369-6145; www.watersafari.com; 3183 NY 28, Old Forge), New York's largest water theme park, is a blast for teenagers and younger kids. Open daily Memorial Day through Labor Day.

Gore Mountain Northwoods Gondola Skyrides (518-251-2411; www.gore mountain.com; Peaceful Valley Road, North Creek) take you up high for primo foliage viewing. Open fall weekends.

McCauley Mountain Scenic Chairlift Ride (315-369-3225; www.mccauleyny .com; McCauley Mountain Road, Old Forge) is open daily June 25 through Labor Day; weekends Memorial Day through June 24.

Natural Stone Bridge and Caves (518-494-2283); www.stonebridgeandcaves .com; 535 Stone Bridge Road, Pottersville), a 1,000-acre property, is a stunning, natural attraction: Walk into three caves, peer into others, or follow trails through the woods. Open late-May through Columbus Day.

Saratoga & North Creek Railway (1-877-726-7245; www.sncrr.com; 3 Railroad Place, North Creek) revives a route that had been abandoned for a century by connecting the Spa City to North Creek with stops at Corinth, Hadley/Luzerne, Stony Creek, Thurman, the Glen, and Riparius. Trains run all year, including snow trains that deliver skiers to North Creek.

FISHING

This region's interior waters harbor bass, northern pike, muskie, trout, landlocked salmon, among other species. The *New York State Freshwater Fishing Regulations Guide*, available at sporting goods stores, tourist information centers, and www.dec .ny.gov, details all the seasons and limits for various species. Everyone 16 and older who fishes in the Adirondacks must have a New York fishing license, which can be purchased on the DEC's website or at sporting goods stores and town offices. Non-residents can get special five-day licenses; state residents 70 and older may get free licenses.

For information on special regulations and mercury levels consult the Department of Environmental Conservation's www.dec.ny.gov/outdoor/7917.html. *Adirondack Fishing: An Angler's Guide to Adirondack Lakes, Ponds, Rivers and Streams*, from the Adirondack Regional Tourism Council, has maps, gamefish descriptions, advice on techniques and is available in print or at http://visitadirondacks .com. Check out I Love New York's www.fishadk.com, and see chapter 8 for Adirondack fishing guidebooks.

GOLF

Savor the green rolling hills, craggy peaks, deep blue lakes, and bracing air—the Adirondacks does recall Scotland's landscape just a wee bit. Once upon a time, there were even more golf tracks than are open today, links that were attached to grand hotels and exclusive private clubs. The courses in this region include:

Brantingham Golf Course (315-348-8861; Brantingham Road, Brantingham Lake). Eighteen holes; par-71; 5,300 yards.

Cedar River Golf Course (518-648-5906; www.cedarrivergolf.com; 180 West Main Street, Indian Lake). Nine holes; par-36; 2,700 yards.

Buzz Off

Springtime in the Adirondacks can be lovely, but this earthly paradise has a squadron of tiny, persistent insects to keep humans from overwhelming the countryside. Blackflies. Bug season is usually late May through June, although its duration depends on the weather. If you're planning an extended hike, golf outing, streamside fishing trip, or similar activity, you'll want to apply insect repellent, wear light-color clothing (blue, especially dark blue, seems to attract blackflies), and tuck in your pant legs and shirt. Avoid using perfume, shampoo, or scented hairspray—these products broadcast "free lunch!" to hungry little buggers.

There's a pharmacy of lotions and sprays that use varying amounts of DEET (diethyl-meta-toluamide) as the active ingredient, but note that products containing more than 25 percent DEET should not be applied to children's skin. DEET should not be used at all on infants.

Some people love Avon's Skin So Soft bath oil for confounding insects. Fabric softener sheets, such as Bounce, can be tucked into your hatband to keep flies away from your face. Some Adirondackers prefer pine-tar based bug dopes, such as Ole Woodsman, that also have the lasting aroma of authenticity; after a good dose of Ole Woodsman, your pillows and sheets will be scented, too. Lots of Adirondack shops sell homemade concoctions, including Bye Bye Black Fly made by Vermontviller Marge Glowa. If these fail, there are bug jackets and pants, veils, and even crusher-type hats with lightweight netting attached.

Inlet Golf Course and Country Club (315-357-3503; NY 28, Inlet). Eighteen holes; par-72; 6,000 yards.

Lake Pleasant Golf Course (518-548-7071; NY 8, Lake Pleasant). Nine holes; par-35; 2,900 yards.

Nick Stoner Golf Course (518-835-4211; 1803 NY 10, Caroga Lake). Eighteen holes; par-70; 5,800 yards.

Sacandaga Golf Club (518-863-4887; NY 30, Sacandaga Park, Northville). Nine holes; par-36; 3,000 yards.

Thendara Golf Club, Inc. (315-369-3136; www.thendaragolfclub.com; off NY 28, Thendara). Eighteen holes; par-72; 6,000 yards.

HIKING AND BACKPACKING

Whether it's up a peak with a fire tower—Bald Mountain near Inlet is nice—or along the epic 133-mile Northville–Lake Placid Trail, or a major trek up Snowy, deciding just where to go in this vast region might be as challenging as the actual trek. But no worries, there are plenty of guidebooks and other resources in chapter 8 to help. A reminder: Trails can be steep and treacherous; weather is downright changeable. Wherever you choose to go, be prepared. Your pack should contain a flashlight, matches, extra food and water, map, compass, GPS, and extra clothes (wool or fleece for warmth; leave the cotton at home). Your cell phone won't work around here. Always sign in at trailheads. And in the unlikely event that you get lost, the information about when you started, where you were planning to go, and who you were with would be helpful to the search team.

An Epic Trek

Parts of the **Northville–Lake Placid Trail** (NPT) are many miles from the nearest road; passing through the West Canada Lakes or Cold River areas, you might go several days with just the cry of the loon or howl of the coyote for company. Going end-to-end on this long trail requires a minimum of 10 days (unless you're ultra trail runner Drew Haas, who in 2009 completed the NPT alone and unassisted in 60.5 hours). You also need a solid amount of backcountry knowledge, but you can pick shorter sections for three-day junkets. The Adirondack Mountain Club (www.adk.org) publishes a guidebook devoted to this popular route.

Turkeys are now common in the central Adirondacks' mixed hardwood forest.

Courtesy of Eric Dresser, www.ecdphoto.addr.com

HUNTING

There are seasons for deer, black bear, snowshoe hare, coyote, bobcat, and other small mammals, plus ruffed grouse, woodcock, wild turkey, and waterfowl. The booklets outlining game seasons is available at the Department of Environmental Conservation (www.dec.ny.gov) or by writing for them; licenses can be purchased online, from sporting goods stores, town offices, or the DEC. Nonresidents may purchase five-day licenses. If you have never had a New York State hunting license, you must show proof that you have attended a hunter education course. Turkey hunting requires a special stamp from the DEC; waterfowl hunters must possess a Federal Migratory Bird Hunting Stamp.

In general, big-game seasons begin with early bear (mid-September through mid-October); archery for deer or bear (late September through mid-October); muzzleloading for deer or bear (one week in mid-October); and regular big-game season (third Saturday in October through the beginning of December). Bow and black-powder hunters may take antlerless deer; during regular season, it's bucks only in the Adirondack Park.

Wild turkeys, brought back to habitat in the southeastern Adirondacks, have been very successful moving into new territory such as mixed hardwood forest in the central Adirondacks. Toms are sought after in spring and fall seasons, but these birds are very wary and tough to track.

Wilderness, primitive, and wild forest areas are all open to hunting. Hunters—even if they have a brand-new, state-of-the-art GPS unit—should be proficient with map and compass. Global-positioning units don't always work well in thick forest, and batteries do wear out. And there's no cell-phone service here.

ICE SKATING

Many towns offer lighted rinks with warming huts; check with tourist offices for hours. Long Lake's Geiger Arena Adirondack Skating Rink (518-627-3031) is one of the better ones, and it's conveniently located on NY 30. At Indian Lake, the town has built a great rink (518-648-5828) at the foot of the ski hill, off NY 30. There's free indoor skating at the Fern Park Pavilion, in Inlet (1-866-464-6538); Old Forge has ice-skating at the intersection of Joy Tract and Railroad Avenue at the site of the old town highway garage.

RACES AND SEASONAL SPORTING EVENTS

Raquette Lake Winter Carnival (518-624-3077; www.mylonglake.com) has a ladies' fry-pan toss, plus crosscut and chain-saw competitions, in February.

Snowflake Derby (315-369-6983; www.oldforgeny.com; Old Forge) is a weekend carnival of races, parades, and fireworks, in February.

Hudson River Whitewater Derby (518-251-2612; www.whitewaterderby.com), sponsored by North Creek Chamber of Commerce, includes a slalom race and Chuck Severance Memorial Downriver Race for canoes and kayaks on Saturday; Whitewater Derby Downriver race from North Creek to Riparius on the Hudson on Sunday; first weekend in May.

Adirondack Paddlefest (315-369-6672; www.adirondackpaddlefest.com) is a popular canoe and kayak weekend with instruction, boats to try, and clinics, mid-May, in Old Forge.

Speculator Seaplane Fly-in (518-548-4521; www.speculatorchamber.com) is a seaplane extravaganza held in June, on Lake Pleasant.

Black Fly Challenge (www.blackflychallenge.com), in June, is a 40-mile mountain-bike race through the Moose River Plains.

Adirondack Birding Festival (518-548-3076; www.adirondackbirds.com; at venues across Hamilton County) includes birding hikes and paddles, lectures, and other events, in June.

Damn Wakely Dam Ultra (www.wakelydamultra.com) begins in Piseco and ends 32.6 miles later at the Wakely Dam campground near Indian Lake, in July.

Piseco Lake Triathlon (518-548-4521; www.adrkmts.com; Speculator) is a half-mile swim, 11.5-mile bike, and 3-mile run, in July.

Race the Train (www.adirondackrunners.org; Riparius), in August, is a run along the Upper Hudson River Railroad.

Mark 7 Road Races (www.campmark7.org; Old Forge) include 5- and 10 kilometer runs, in August.

Adirondack Canoe Classic (www.macscanoe.com), sponsored by the Saranac Lake Chamber of Commerce, is a 90-mile three-day canoe race from Old Forge to Saranac Lake village, in early September.

Moose River Festival (www.mountainmanoutdoors.com; Old Forge) features an extreme race for kayaks and closed canoes through Class IV and V rapids, in October.

SEAPLANES

Seaplane services are equipped to take canoeists, fishermen, and hunters into ponds and lakes. Among the few fixed-wheel and seaplane private charters in this region are Bird's Seaplane Service (315-357-3631; 275 NY 28, Inlet); Helms Aero Service (518-624-3931; helmsaeroservice.com; Town Beach, Long Lake); and Payne's Air Service (315-357-3971; Seventh Lake, Inlet). Always call ahead for a reservation.

SKIING, CROSS-COUNTRY

Many of the designated wilderness and wild forest areas offer great ski touring on marked but ungroomed trails. State campgrounds—closed to vehicles from November through May—offer quiet, woodsy, snow-covered roads with gentle grades; Lake Durant, near Blue Mountain Lake, and Lake Eaton, near Long Lake, are popular with local skiers and usually have set tracks. Locals also love the work of the Siamese Pond Trail Improvement Society, which has revived seemingly endless miles of a spectacular cross-country-ski-trail network in the 114,000-acre Siamese Ponds Wilderness Area.

Before setting out on any of these wilderness excursions, prepare your pack with quick-energy food; a thermos filled with hot tea or cocoa; extra hat, socks, and gloves; topo map and compass; matches; flashlight; and space blanket. Dress in layers of wool, polypropylene, or synthetic pile. Don't travel alone. Sign in at the trailhead register. Let friends know your destination and when you plan to return. Cell phones don't work in this part of the park.

Beside wilderness trails and informal town ski trails, there are some excellent cross-country-ski areas with meticulously groomed tracks and rental equipment: Adirondack Woodcraft Ski Touring Center (315-369-6031; Rondaxe Road, Old Forge). Fifteen kilometers of groomed trails; night skiing; rentals; ski shop.

Fern Park Recreation Area (315-357-5501; Loomis Road, Inlet). Twenty-two kilometers of groomed trails; night skiing.

Garnet Hill Ski Center (518-251-2444; www.garnet-hill.com; Thirteenth Lake Road, North River). Fifty kilome-

Groomed cross-country-ski trails can be found across this region—at Gore, Lapland Lake, and Garnet Hill. Courtesy of ORDA/Dave Schmidt

ters of groomed trails; connects with trails in Siamese Ponds Wilderness Area; rentals; lessons; ski shop; food; lodging.

Gore Mountain (518-251-2411; www.goremountain.com; Peaceful Valley Road, North Creek). Eleven kilometers of groomed trails; rentals; lessons; ski shop; food.

Lapland Lake Nordic Vacation Center (518-863-4974; www.laplandlake.com; 139 Lapland Lake Road, Benson). Founded and operated by former 1960 Olympic cross-country-ski member Olavi Hirvonen. Forty kilometers of groomed trails; rentals; lessons; ski shop; food; lodging.

McCauley Mountain (315-369-3225; www.mccauleyny.com; McCauley Mountain Road, Old Forge). Twenty kilometers of groomed trails at downhill area plus skiing at Thendara Golf Club; rentals; lessons; food.

Speculator Trails (518-548-4521). Check out www.adrkmts.com for a variety of free, southern Adirondack trails.

SKIING: DOWNHILL AND SNOWBOARDING

Skiing has been a part of Adirondack life since the 1930s. Weekend ski trains brought thousands of folks to Old Forge and North Creek. In North Creek they could "ride up and slide down." The "ride up" was in school buses equipped with wooden ski racks mounted on the outside, and the "slide down" was on twisty trails carved out of the forest near Barton Mines, across from the present-day slopes on Gore Mountain.

Today there's once again a snow train that chugs from Saratoga to North Creek (www.sncrr.com), delivering skiers to the Olympic Regional Development Authority–run Gore Mountain. Also in this region is nice little McCauley, where the emphasis is on family fun rather than on the trendiest gear. Indian Lake runs a free downhill area for residents and guests. Of course, you won't find human-made snow there, and you'll have to remember dormant skills for managing a Poma lift or a rope tow, but you can have a blast with the kids and beat the crowds.

Gore Mountain Ski Resort (518-251-2411; www.goremountain.com; 711 Peaceful Valley Road, off NY 28, North Creek), near North Creek, is the cradle of North Country alpine skiing and the home of state-owned Gore Mountain, which opened in 1964. Since 1984, Gore has been managed by the Olympic Regional Development Authority, as is Whiteface Mountain.

Gore, with its 2,537-foot vertical drop, 95 trails, five freestyle areas, and 21 glades—the longest ones in the East—has trails for all levels of skiers and riders: wide-open cruising runs, but also double-black diamonds such as The Rumor and

Old Forge ski hill and tow.

Courtesy of Ted Comstock, Saranac Lake

Lies. The high-speed eight-passenger gondola is a godsend on frigid days, while another nine chairs and three surface lifts deliver people up the slopes. In 2012, 160 tower guns for snowmaking—using water from the Hudson River—were added, allowing fine skiing during a lackluster winter.

North Creek's original Ski Bowl has been revitalized, offering family-friendly slopes, a terrain park with half-pipe, and lift-serviced tubing day and night. Most recently, Gore Mountain's Interconnect was completed to link the Ski Bowl to Gore Mountain proper, dramatically expanding Gore onto four peaks, including Bear, Burnt Ridge, and Little Gore. The mountain has four lodges—a remodeled Tannery Pub & Restaurant and an expanded deck—and excellent snow sports instruction, and day care. A free ski shuttle runs from Main Street, North Creek's depot, and other locations. Weekend lift tickets are $75 adults, $59 teens, $40 kids; ages 6 and under are free daily.

McCauley Mountain (315-369-3225; www.mccauleyny.com; McCauley Mountain Road, off Bisby Road, Old Forge) is where Hank Kashiwa, the international racing star and ski designer, learned his first snowplow turns; his brilliant career is something folks in Old Forge still talk about. Actually, the Town of Webb school has produced three U.S. Olympic ski-team members, thanks to good coaches and the welcoming intermediate slopes at the local hill.

This little mountain has 21 trails, two lifts and two tows—plus a new terrain park for snowboarders—and heaps of natural snow, due to a microclimate that can produce 200 inches or more in winter. Helmers and Olympic, both of which have snowmaking, are the most difficult runs. Intermediates can sample Upper God's Land, a ridge trail; Sky Ride, a wide route serviced by the double chair; or the gentle, sweeping Challenger. You'll find all the amenities at McCauley: a ski school, rentals, food, and drink. Weekend lift tickets: $30 adults, $15 kids, $25 students and seniors.

SNOWMOBILING

A hub of snowmobile activity is Old Forge, which provides 500-plus miles of groomed, packed trails and issues more than 14,000 snowmobile permits each winter. Folks around here like calling it the "Snowmobile Capital of the East." Trails in Old Forge spread out like a river with numerous tributaries. You can connect with the Inlet trails to the east, or the Independence River Wild Forest and Big Moose trails to the north, and Forestport and Boonville routes to the south. These trails meet still other trails, so that you can continue farther east from Inlet to Indian Lake or Speculator, and then from Speculator to Wells, or

Old Forge is often called the "Snowmobile Capital of the East." Courtesy of Nancie Battaglia

you can go from Inlet to Raquette Lake, and then on to Long Lake and Newcomb. Confused? Permits, safety course information, events, clubs, trail maps, trail conditions, dealers and rentals, and everything else you need to know can be found at www.snowmobileoldforgny.com.

Beside the Old Forge–Inlet area, many trail networks throughout the park cross private timberlands as well as the state forest preserve. Public lands designated as wild forest areas are open to snowmobiling; wilderness areas are not. The DEC's www.dec.ny.gov has rules and regulations and links to sites with Adirondack snowmobile trails. For maps of local trails, contact Long Lake Parks, Recreation and Tourism Department (518-624-3077; www.longlake-ny.com); Indian Lake Chamber of Commerce (518-648-5112; www.indian-lake.com); Inlet Information Office (315-557-5501; www.inletny.com); and Adirondacks Speculator Region Chamber of Commerce (518-548-4521; www.speculatorchamber.com). For Indian Lake trail conditions, go to www.ilsnow.com.

As with any winter pursuit, planning and preparation help make a successful outing. Know your machine; carry an emergency repair kit and understand how to use it. Be sure you have plenty of gas. Travel with friends in case of a breakdown or other surprise situations. Never ride at night unless you're familiar with the trail or are following an experienced leader. Avoid crossing frozen lakes and streams unless you are absolutely certain the ice is safe. Some town or county roads are designated trails; while on such a highway, keep right, observe the posted snowmobile speed limit—there are numerous fatalities each year due to excessive speed—and travel in single file.

Your basic pack should contain a topographic map and compass as well as a local trail map; survival kit with matches, flashlight, rope, space blanket, quick-energy food, and something warm to drink; extra hat, socks, and mittens. Although a sip of brandy may give the illusion of warming you up, alcohol impairs circulation and can hasten hypothermia. And an arrest for snowmobiling under the influence carries with it severe penalties.

WATERFALLS

Some of the park's cascades are spectacularly high, including T-Lake, which is taller than Niagara; others, such as Buttermilk Falls, near Long Lake, are just a quick walk from the car. You can also visit Auger Falls on the Sacandaga River in Wells; Buttermilk Falls on the Raquette River in Long Lake; Cascade Lake Inlet falls in Bog Moose; Falls Brook in Minerva; OK Slip Falls in Indian Lake, with the highest vertical drop in the Adirondacks; and remote, steep, and dangerous T-Lake Falls in Piseco. See chapter 8 for an Adirondack waterfalls guidebooks.

WHITE-WATER RAFTING

The wild, remote Upper Hudson River provides some of the East's most exhilarating white water: nearly 17 miles of continuous Class III to IV+ rapids. From 1860 to 1950, river drivers sent logs downstream every spring to sawmills and pulp mills, and they followed along behind the churning, tumbling timber in rowboats to pry logjams loose. Since the mid-1970s, the Hudson's power has been rediscovered for recreational purposes, with numerous rafting companies making the trip from Indian River, just south of Indian Lake, to North River.

Reliable water levels are provided by a dam release below Lake Abanakee, courtesy of the town of Indian Lake. Releases begin about April 1 and last through fall.

Although you don't need white-water paddling experience to enjoy a trip down the Hudson, you do need to be in good physical condition, and a competent swimmer. (Nobody under age 18 is permitted to raft when the water is at its highest—or on Class V waters such as the Moose River.) The outfitters supply you with wetsuit, paddle, life jacket, and helmet; they also shuttle you to the put-in, give on-shore instructions in safety and paddling techniques, and most serve lunch. Rafters should bring polypropylene underwear to wear under the suits; wool hats, gloves, and socks; sneakers; and dry, warm clothing for after the trip. (Springtime Adirondack air can be chilly, and the water temperature is truly frigid.)

A licensed guide steers each raft and directs the crew. It's a good idea to research Adirondack rafting companies before booking a trip. Recent troubles on the river—unlicensed guides, among other problems—have spotlighted this sport's dangers. This trip is not for passive passengers; you're expected to paddle—sometimes hard and fast—as the guide instructs. The trip is only hard and strenuous in spring or during high water from, for example, a tropical storm. The Hudson Gorge is an all-day

The Big Blowdown

Sixteen-year-old Richard "Bud" Brownell was scoping the woods around Russian Lake, near Big Moose Lake, on the last day of hunting season, November 25, 1950. He had split from a hunting party, when a hurricane crashed in "from the east around noon, felling huge trees that had survived for centuries," according to *Big Moose Lake in the Adirondacks: the Story of the Lake, the Land and the People.* Brownell crouched "alone under a large tree for what seemed like an eternity while the (100-mile-per-hour) wind howled and trees all around were snapping like matchsticks, flying through the air." Later that day the young hunter was reunited with his party, though it took them hours to negotiate through the jumbled trees to safety. Scenes like this played out from the High Peaks to Herkimer County, some hunters and hikers barricaded for days behind the blowdown.

Networks of roads were impassable, fire towers had fallen, telephone and power lines were wiped out, dozens of public campsites and private residences were destroyed. And the forest was ravaged: Barbara McMartin, in *The Great Forest of the Adirondacks,* reported that the blowdown "affected 420,000 acres and was said to have caused a loss that ranged from a quarter of the trees to the entire forest cover. The loss was estimated at two million cords of softwood and 40 million board feet of hardwood. The Cold River country between Seward and Santanoni experienced the greatest destruction, followed closely by the Moose River Plains," and private lands of more than a quarter-million acres were also wrecked.

Hikers would have to wait five years until trails could be cleared to scale more than a half dozen High Peaks. Even Article XIV of the state constitution, which protects the Forest Preserve, had to be circumvented to allow lumberjacks in to clean up the mess. Otherwise the fallen timber posed a fire hazard: One spark and the entire park could be torched. Most of the cleanup was finished by 1956, though you can still find blow-down across the region.

adventure, containing four to five hours of strenuous exercise, with the 2012 price, depending on the season, of about $80 per person.

Several rafting companies also offer short, fun trips on the Sacandaga River near Lake Luzerne. These junkets float 3.5 miles and last, from start to finish, about two hours. Dam releases make the stream navigable all summer, and the cost is about $25 per person. On the other end of the spectrum is the Moose River from McKeever to Fowlerville Falls; this is a 14-mile beast absolutely for experienced white-water paddlers only. The Moose is runnable after spring ice-out, and the charge is about $120 per person.

Among the Adirondack white-water rafting companies are: Adirondac Rafting Company (518-523-1635; www.lakeplacidrafting.com; 7 Patch Lane, Lake Placid); Adirondack Adventures (1-877-963-RAFT; www.adkadventures.com; 4659 Route 28, North River); Adirondack River Outfitters Adventures (1-800-525-RAFT; www.aroadventures.com; Box 649, Old Forge); Adventure Sports Rafting Company (1-800-441-RAFT; www.adventuresportsrafting.com; Main Street, Indian Lake); Beaver Brook Outfitters (1-888-454-8433; www.beaverbrook.net; 2349 Route 28, Wevertown); Middle Earth Expeditions (518-523-7172; www.adirondackrafting .com; 4529 Cascade Road, Lake Placid); North Creek Rafting Company (1-800-989-RAFT; www.northcreekrafting.com; 9 Ordway Lane, North Creek); Sacandaga Outdoor Center (1-866-696-RAFT; www.4soc.com; 1 Whitewater Way, Hadley); White Water Challengers (1-800-443-RAFT; www.whitewaterchallengers.com;

Route 28, North River); and Wild Waters Outdoor Center (518-494-4984; www.wildwaters.net; 11333 Route 28, The Glen).

WILDERNESS AREAS

These portions of the Forest Preserve are 10,000 acres or larger and contain little evidence of modern times. Wilderness areas are open to hiking, cross-country skiing, hunting, fishing, and other similar pursuits, but seaplanes may not land on wilderness ponds, nor are motorized vehicles welcome. Following are Adirondack wilderness areas in the Central and Southwestern region:

Blue Ridge. 46,000 acres; south of Blue Mountain Lake. Contains several miles of the Northville–Lake Placid Trail for hiking and cross-country skiing; Cascade, Stephens, Wilson, Mitchell, and other trout ponds.

Five Ponds. 101,000 acres; between Cranberry Lake and Stillwater Reservoir. Numerous ponds, canoeing on the Oswegatchie River, many acres of old-growth forest, some hiking trails. This area receives little use.

Ha De Ron Dah. 27,000 acres; west of Old Forge. Small ponds and lakes, hiking and cross-country-ski trails around Big Otter Lake. This area receives little use.

Hoffman Notch. 36,000 acres; between Minerva and the Blue Ridge Road. Ponds and trout streams, a few hiking trails. This area is used mostly by fishermen and hunters.

Nehasane Primitive Area. 6,000 acres; lovely Lake Lila, near Long Lake.

Pepperbox. 15,000 acres; north of Stillwater Reservoir. Few trails, difficult access, mostly wetlands, excellent wildlife habitat.

Pigeon Lake. 50,000 acres; northeast of Big Moose Lake. Numerous lakes, ponds, and streams; trails for hiking and cross-country skiing.

Siamese Ponds. 114,000 acres; between North River and Speculator. Canoeing on Thirteenth Lake; Sacandaga River and numerous trout ponds; trails for hiking and cross-country skiing.

Silver Lake. 105,000 acres; between Piseco and Wells. Silver, Mud, and Rock Lakes; southern end of the Northville–Lake Placid Trail. This area receives little use.

West Canada Lakes. 157,000 acres; west of Speculator. Cedar, Spruce, West Canada Lakes, and 160 other bodies of water; portions of the Northville–Lake Placid Trail and other hiking trails. One of the largest roadless areas in the Northeast.

William C. Whitney. 15,000 acres, between Long and Tupper Lakes. Little Tupper Lake and Rock Pond for excellent paddling and camping, miles of woods roads for cross-country skiing, several remote ponds.

WILD FOREST AREAS

Wild forest areas are open to snowmobile travel, mountain biking, and other recreation. In this region they're:

Black River. Between Otter Lake and Wilmurt. Ponds and streams.

Blue Mountain. Northeast of Blue Mountain Lake. Contains part of the Northville–Lake Placid Trail; Tirrell Pond; views from Blue Mountain.

Ferris Lake. Between Piseco and Stratford. Dirt roads for mountain biking and driving through by car; numerous ponds and streams.

Independence River. South of Stillwater Reservoir. Dirt roads; Independence River; snowmobile trails; beaver ponds.

Jessup River. Between the south end of Indian Lake and Speculator. Miami and Jessup Rivers, and Lewey Lake; views from Pillsbury Mountain; trails for snowmobiling, hiking, and mountain biking.

Adirondack Hermit

Noah John Rondeau, the "Mayor of Cold River," as he called himself, lived near a tributary of Long Lake in the 1930s and '40s. Noah John was popular among hikers, who trekked deep in the woods for an audience with the eccentric hermit at his handmade "village," which included two semi-log cabins with hard-packed floors—one dubbed "Town Hall"—and three teepeelike stacks of tree-length firewood. After the great blowdown of 1950 destroyed his camp, Rondeau didn't return to the woods. But the charismatic character—hardly hermitlike—soaked up the spotlight as a featured exhibit at the 1947 National Sportsmens Show in New York City, and as part of the Saranac Lake Winter Carnival parade, waving to the crowd as he rode a farm sleigh pulled by a tractor. Today you can see his Town Hall on display at the Adirondack Museum, in Blue Mountain Lake.

Famous hermit and "Mayor of Cold River City" Noah John Rondeau.

Courtesy of Holly Wolff

Moose River Plains. Between Indian Lake and Inlet. Dirt roads; numerous ponds and streams; Cedar River and Cedar River Flow; primitive car-camping sites; snowmobile trails. If you want to see moose, this is the place.

Sargent Ponds. Between Raquette Lake and Long Lake. Trout ponds; hiking trails; canoe route between Raquette Lake and Blue Mountain Lake.

Shaker Mountain. East of Canada Lake. Dirt roads; hiking, cross-country skiing and mountain-biking routes.

Vanderwhacker Mountain. Northwest of Minerva. Fishing on the Boreas River; views from Vanderwhacker Mountain.

WILDLIFE

Many interior lakes and ponds are home to kingfishers, ducks, herons, and loons; listen and watch for that great northern diver in the early morning and at dusk. In the evening, listen for owls: the barred owl, known by its call, "Who cooks for you, who cooks for you," is quite common. In the fall, look up to see thousands of migrating Canada and snow geese. Wild turkeys—absent from the Adirondacks until the 1990s—are positively ubiquitous, especially along roadsides in the central Adirondacks.

The Adirondack Birding Festival (518-548-3076; www.adirondackbirds.com), in June, happens in venues across Hamilton County, and involves birding hikes and paddles, lectures, and other events.

In June, Hamilton County's Adirondack Birding Festival attracts birders from afar.

Courtesy of Jeff Nadler, www.jnphoto.net

Small mammals are numerous: varying hares, weasels, mink, raccoons, fisher, pine martens, otters, bobcats, porcupines, and red and gray foxes. Coyotes, with rich coats in shades of black, rust, and gray, can be seen in fall, winter, and spring, and their yips and yowls on a summer night can be thrilling to the backcountry campers' ears. White-tailed deer are seemingly everywhere, especially in the early spring before the fawns are born. In Old Forge, even in front yards facing busy Main Street, does are as common as squirrels.

About 800 moose live here now, definitely restocking themselves and raising calves in the central Adirondacks and northwest lakes as well as other logged forests in the park. The best place to see moose is—no surprise—Moose River Recreation Area, where bulls can be seen in fall from woods roads. If you encounter one of these draft-horse size guys, do not approach! They tend to be very cranky during rutting season.

Shopping

Adirondackana and more in the Central & Southwestern Adirondacks

Want The Gap, J. Crew, or Eddie Bauer? Then head to Lake George or Lake Placid. In this, the heart of the park, it's all Adirondackana, antiques, artwork, books, and furniture.

ADIRONDACKANA

The word defines all kinds of material things that complement the countryside and evoke textures: bark, wood grain; smells: balsam, cedar; tastes: maple, apple; forest colors: deep green, gold, sienna. In Blue Mountain Lake there's the Adirondack Museum Store (518-352-7311; www.adkmuseum.org; NY 30), open Memorial Day Weekend through Columbus Day; in Northville, the Adirondack Country Store (518-863-6056; www.adirondackcountrystore.com; 252 N. Main Street); in North Creek, Hudson River Trading Co. (518-251-4461; www.hudsonrivertradingco.com; 292 Main Street); in Old Forge, Moose River Trading Company (315-369-6091; www.mooserivertrading.com; NY 28, Thendara); and in Wells, Mountain Memories (518-924-7778; www.mountainmem.com; NY 30).

ANTIQUES

The best fair is unquestionably the Adirondack Antiques Show & Sale, at the Adirondack Museum, in Blue Mountain Lake—call the museum at 518-352-7311 or see www.adkmuseum.org for details.

The following shops are among the handful in this region: Airdville Antiques & Clock Repair (518-548-5390; NY 8, Lake Pleasant); Mountain Niche Antiques (518-251-2566; NY 28N, 2 miles north of Minerva post office); the Red Barn (518-863-4828; 202 S. Main Street, Northville); Board 'n' Batten Antiques (518-251-2507; 1447 County 29, Olmstedville); and Stagecoach (518-494-3192; US 9, Pottersville).

In September, the Adirondack Museum's annual rustic show is a regional highlight.

Courtesy of Nancie Battaglia

The best 19th-century American painters came to the Adirondacks to interpret wild scenery on paper and canvas, and many artists still rely on the great outdoors for inspiration, no matter what the medium. Always call artists ahead, as some require appointments.

Painter Constance Dodge's Dodge House Lakeside Gallery (518-863-2201; 936 S. Shore Road) is in Edinburg. Indian Lake is where you'll find Kathy Larkin and Jane Zilka's Abanakee Studios (518-648-5013; www.abanakeestudios.com; NY 28). Photographer and painter Elizabeth Mangle's Lake Pleasant studio is Cabin in the Woods Adirondack Creations (315-826-3172; www.adirondackcabincreations.com; P.O. Box 790). In Northville, the Stinky Art Company (518-863-7051; www.stinky dog.com; 142 N Main Street) is a sensation. In Old Forge there's Dragonfly Cottage (2972 Main Street), mixed-media artist Tina Snow's warm-weather gallery; the fine arts Gallery 3040 (315-369-1059; 3040 NY 28); and Starving Artist Gallery (315-369-1060; 3071 NY 28), a co-op of 40 artists. Riparius is home to potter Lisa Steres's Scenic Outlook Studios (518-494-5367; www.scenicoutlookstudios.com; 440 Riverside Station Road). In Thurman is the studio of assemblage artist Diane Golden (www.dianegolden.com). Sculptor John Van Alstine and his 8-acre Adirondack River Sculpture Park are in Wells (518-924-9204; www.johnvanalstine.com); Van Alstine's wife, Caroline Ramsdorfer (www.carolineramsdorfer.at), is an internationally recognized sculptor.

BOAT BUILDERS

Mason Smith, of Long Lake's Adirondack Goodboat (518-624-6398; www .adirondackgoodboat.com), makes fine wooden boats that are car-toppable and multipurpose (row, sail, or motor). In Olmstedville, Peter Hornbeck builds popular, lightweight Hornbeck Boats (518-251-2764; www.hornbeckboats.com; 131 Trout Brook Road).

BOOKS

You'll find independently owned bookstores in this region, most with extensive collections of Adirondack titles, including the Adirondack Museum Shop (518-352-7311; www.adkmuseum.org; NY 28/30), in Blue Mountain Lake, open daily late May through Columbus Day; the Adirondack Reader (315-357-2665; 156 Main Street), in Inlet, open Memorial Day through Columbus Day; Hoss's Country Corner (518-624-2481; www.hossscountrycorner.com; 247 Lake Street), in Long Lake; Hudson River Trading Co. (518-251-4461; www.hudsonrivertradingco.com; 292 Main Street), in North Creek; Old Forge Hardware (315-369-6100; www.oldforge hardware.com; 104 Fulton Street); and Charlie Johns Store (518-548-7451; www .charliejohns.com; The Four Corners), in Speculator.

An Adirondack Lifer

Adirondack Life magazine creative director Elizabeth Folwell, who first wrote this guidebook in 1992, is a Blue Mountain Lake resident—year-round population 150ish. Check out her essays in *Short Carries*, published by *Adirondack Life* (www.adirondack life.com), to understand mountain living in all its grizzle and glory. Folwell is the real deal and her anthology of almost four decades of Adirondack writing is a must-read.

CLOTHING

The following have classic woolens, practical sportswear, footwear, and high-tech outer gear:

Blue Mountain Outfitters (518-352-7306; 144 Main Street), in Blue Mountain Lake; French Louie ADK Sports (315-357-2441; www.frenchlouieadk.com; 156 Main Street), in Inlet; Holly Woodworking (315-369-3757; www.hollywoodworkingold forge.com; 3286 NY 28), in Old Forge; Mountainman Outdoor Supply Company (315-369-6672; www.mountainmanoutdoors.com; 2855 NY 28), in Old Forge; and Speculator Department Store (518-548-6123; speculatordepartmentstore.com; NY 8).

CRAFT SHOPS

Many of these highlighted craft shops/studios are in private homes, so call ahead.

Blacksmith shop Bear Paw Forge (518-648-0155; NY 28) is in Indian Lake. Get handmade snowshoes at Havlick Snowshoe Company (518-661-6447; www.havlick snowshoe.com; NY 30), in Mayfield. Holly Woodworking (315-369-3757; www.holly woodworkingoldforge.com; 3286 NY 28), in Old Forge, sells rustic furniture.

FURNITURE

Regional woodworkers create furniture in a variety of styles, from Shaker-inspired designs, to rugged sculptural pieces, to the straightforward Adirondack chairs that now come in an infinite range of permutations. For an overview, check out www .adirondackwood.com.

In the driveway to Backwoods Furnishings (518-251-3327; NY 28), in Indian Lake, is a Paul Bunyan–size log chair. Backwoods creates and sells twig, birch-bark, and cedar beds, tables, sideboards, settees, and rockers.

In Long Lake, Cold River Gallery & Woodwork (518-624-3581; P.O. Box 606, Deerland Road) offers painted arch-top trunks; carved furniture, mirrors and frames with wildlife designs; custom doors and signs. North Country Images and Accents (518-624-4811; PO Box 211) has rustic furniture and frames.

Mayfield's Sampson Bog Studio and Art Funk and Junk (518-661-6563; 171 Paradise Point Road) is home to Barney Bellinger's twig mosaic and birch-bark tables, desks, wall shelves, benches with fine hand-painted details and graceful lines, plus his new projects that incorporate vintage cars and tramp art.

Peter Winter's Rustic Studio (518-863-6555; 132 Division Street), in Northville, features rustic furniture and accessories, open daily in summer. Russ Gleaves and Bill Coffey's Fine Handcrafted Rustic Furniture (518-863-4602; 322 North Third Street) includes armoires, vanities, cabinets, beds, and more.

Otter Lake Rustics (315-369-

Artist Barney Bellinger, of Sampson Bog Studio, in Mayfield, is a master craftsman.

Bellinger desk photo courtesy of Sampson Bog Studio

6530; www.otterlakerustics.com; 13977 NY 28) creates rustic furniture, carved doors, and other Adirondack-style décor in Otter Lake.

And in Speculator, Jerry's Wood Shop (518-548-5041; www.jerryswoodshop.com; Box 116 NY 30) has Adirondack chairs and settees that fold for storage, picnic tables, and lawn furniture.

GENERAL STORES

At a general store, chances are you'll find odd things like nail pullers and chick-feeding troughs alongside the glass percolator tops and sugar shakers, an aisle over from the suspenders and boot socks, around the corner from the chips and salsa. If you can't find it at one of these stores, you can probably live without it:

Pine's Country Store (518-648-5212; www.pinescs.com; 1 Main Street, NY 28), in Indian Lake. Hoss's Country Corner (518-624-2481; www.hossscountrycorner .com; corner 247 Lake Street), in Long Lake. Murdie's General Store (518-251-2076; 1688 NY 28N), in Minerva. Old Forge Hardware (315-369-6100; www.old forgehardware.com; 104 Fulton Street), in Old Forge, of course. Raquette Lake Supply (315-354-4301; Main Street), in Raquette Lake. The Lake Store (518-648-5222; NY 30), in Sabael. And the Stillwater Shop (315-376-2110; 2590 Stillwater Road at the boat launch), in Stillwater.

Garnet, embedded in the Adirondack Mountains, is the regional stone of choice.

Courtesy of Melody Thomas, www.melodythomasphoto.com

JEWELRY AND GEM SHOPS

Garnet's the stone of choice in this region—it's embedded in these mountains, plus in beautiful bling that you can buy at the following:

Minerals Unlimited (518-624-5825; 965 NY 28/30), in Long Lake. In North River: Gore Mountain Mineral Shop (518-251-2706; www.garnetminestours .com; Barton Mines Road); J and J Brown Garnet Studio (518-251-3368; www.garnetstudio.net; 68 Casterline Road); and Jasco Minerals (518-251-3196; NY 28). In Old Forge, Allen's offers fine jewelry (315-369-6660; 3017 Main Street), as does South Bay Jewelers (315-354-5481; www.southbay jewelry.com; P.O. Box 35), in Raquette Lake. South Bay's Mary Blanchard once made a special piece for Neil Diamond.

3

Northwest Lakes

WANT REMOTE? The Adirondacks' Northwest Lakes region is wild, woodsy country, with teensy hamlets that emerge like rustic oases. This is also paddler Shangri-La: It would take weeks to navigate all the waters of the Saint Regis Canoe Area, a pristine, motorless network of lakes and ponds. All this is a fitting backdrop for hidden hunting lodges, one of the most exclusive resorts in the Northeast, plus a ranger school, black bears, moose and eagles, and the park's Natural History Museum, a.k.a. "the Wild Center," in Tupper, a must-see for all visitors.

Pick Your Spot

Lodging in the Northwest Lakes

In the 19th century, Paul Smith built his wilderness resort for adventurous sports, hosting guests such as Theodore Roosevelt, Charles Dickens, and P. T. Barnum. His famous hospitality skills launched today's Paul Smith's College, in Paul Smiths, but also an enduring trend of backwoods lodging in these parts—you won't find cookie-cutter hotels or franchises around here. Following are the region's highlights.

Lake Clear

Hohmeyer's Lake Clear Lodge and Retreat (518-891-1489; www.lodgeon lakeclear.com; 6319 NY 30) is acclaimed for home-style German cuisine, and overnight guests have enjoyed the family's gracious hospitality for more than four decades. On 25 secluded lakeshore acres, accommodations here combine modern conveniences with Old World charm. Four guest rooms in the 1886 lodge each have a private bath; three winterized chalets with fireplaces provide woodsy privacy; and three lakeside cottages cater to larger groups—perfect for weddings or retreats. Guests may use canoes, rowboats, a picnic area, and beach; sleigh rides are popular in winter; and Cathy and Ernest Hohmeyer are happy to arrange mountain-bike rentals, guide service, or overnight canoe trips for visitors. They've started a culinary program, too—Cathy is a chef who specializes in what she calls "culinary naturopathy." The lodge allows pets in chalets and vacation rentals and offers

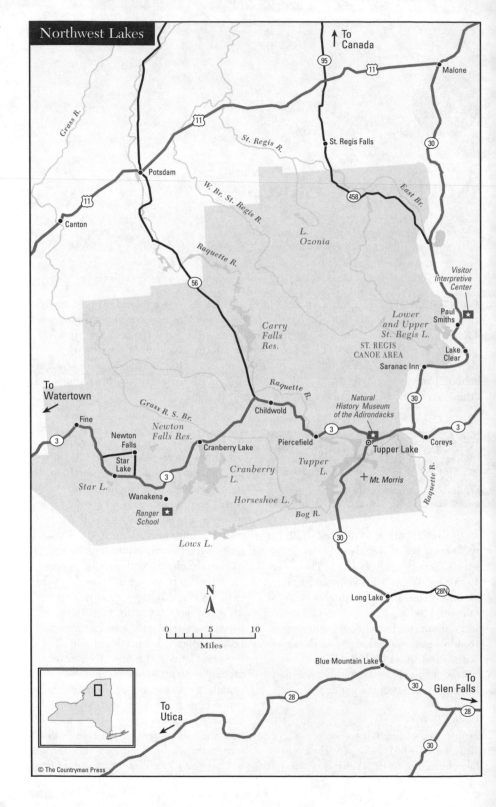

Northwest Lakes

To Canada

Malone

St. Regis Falls

Potsdam

Canton

Grass R.

St. Regis R.

W. Br. St. Regis R.

Raquette R.

East Br.

L. Ozonia

Visitor Interpretive Center

Lower and Upper St. Regis L.

Paul Smiths

ST. REGIS CANOE AREA

Lake Clear

Carry Falls Res.

Saranac Inn

To Watertown

Grass R. S. Br.

Raquette R.

Childwold

Natural History Museum of the Adirondacks

Fine

Newton Falls

Newton Falls Res.

Cranberry Lake

Piercefield

Tupper Lake

Coreys

Star Lake

Star L.

Wanakena

Ranger School

Cranberry L.

Tupper L.

Mt. Morris

Raquette R.

Horseshoe L.

Bog R.

Lows L.

N

0   5   10
Miles

Long Lake

28N

Blue Mountain Lake

To Glen Falls

To Utica

© The Countryman Press

packages ranging from wellness weekends to romantic getaways.

Paul Smiths

White Pine Camp (518-327-3030; www.whitepinecamp.com; White Pine Road), a real Great Camp, was once the summer White House of President Coolidge. Four of the cabins along Osgood Lake are available to guests by the week in July and August and for shorter visits in spring and fall; a couple of units are available for winter rentals as well. All 13 cabins—furnished with an eclectic assortment of rustic and Mission-style antiques—have porches, kitchens, separate bedrooms that accommodate two to eight people, and some either fieldstone fireplaces or woodstoves. Guests can use the beach, boathouse, Japanese teahouse, croquet lawn, bowling alley, canoes, rowboats, and kayaks. Pine Camp also operates as a historic site; Adirondack Architectural Heritage gives tours on Saturdays in July and August. In spring 2012, L.L. Bean used White Pine as a backdrop for its latest catalog's photo shoot.

Saranac Inn

Sunday Pond Bed & Breakfast (518-891-1531; www.sundaypond.com; 5544 NY 30) is perfect for paddlers or hikers who want to explore the Saint Regis Canoe Area with its dozens of lakes and ponds, but hate the thought of camping out. Adventures can be started right from Sunday Pond's front door. The Lyons' home—one of a very few in this corner of the park—is nice, with a long porch, skylights, a fireplace, and a big family room. Guests can choose from three rooms or spacious sleeping loft, all with private baths. Breakfasts are ample and healthy; hearty trail lunches and dinners are available by request.

Tupper Lake

Three Pillars (518-359-3093; winter 914-948-1650; www.tupper-lake.com /1280/three-pillars; 1361 NY 30), with about a quarter-mile of shoreline on Big Tupper Lake, is secluded cabins with great views, open mid-June through mid-September. The location, close to Bog River Falls, is one of the best you'll find on this large lake. There are three pine-paneled, comfortably furnished housekeeping cottages with complete kitchens, fireplaces, and screen porches, plus a three-bedroom apartment above the boathouse that gives the wonderful sensation of being right on the water. There's a nice sandy beach and a long dock for guests' boats. Ask about where to find the walleyes. No credit cards.

Wilderness Weddings

Just about anyplace in this region—even a lone lean-to—would be a lovely backdrop for an Adirondack wedding, but if you're seeking a traditional house of worship consider the stone chapel **Saint John's in the Wilderness Episcopal Church** (518-891-3605), in Paul Smiths; Tupper Lake's historical **Beth Joseph Synagogue** (518-359-3580); or **Island Chapel** (chapelisland.org) on Upper Saranac Lake, a dreamy spot that requires watercraft to deliver you to the altar. Reception sites that often accommodate receptions are the **Wild Center** (518-359-7800; www.wildcenter.org), Tupper Lake's slick natural history museum; President Calvin Coolidge's summer White House, **White Pine Camp** (518-327-3030; www.whitepinecamp.com), in Paul Smiths; and the **Lake Clear Lodge and Retreat** (518-891-1489; www.lodgeonlakeclear.com). And brides looking for exclusive, top-shelf luxury should consider **The Point** (518-891-5674; www.thepoint resort.com), on Upper Saranac Lake.

Upper Saranac Lake

The Point (518-891-5674 or 1-800-255-3530; www.thepointresort.com; P.O. Box 1327) was William Avery Rockefeller's drop-dead gorgeous Great Camp Wonundra, built in the 1930s, on an Upper Saranac Lake peninsula. If you've read any recent articles about the Adirondacks, chances are you've seen The Point, now a Relais et Châteaux property. The 11 rooms, in four different buildings, each have vast beds, lake views, and fireplaces, and are filled with an astutely planned mixture of antiques, Adirondack furniture, Oriental rugs, old prints, and stuffed beasts. The Boathouse is Adirondack classic, with its own private dining alcove and wraparound balcony, but all the rooms are divine. In the main lodge, there's a great hall; fireplaces of astonishing proportions blaze away. The atmosphere here is that of a truly elegant house party, with black tie suggested for dinner. The food warrants that treatment, too, with menus deftly combining native bounty, fine herbs, exquisite seafood, and imported ingredients in an imaginative kaleidoscope of flavors. The wine list is unsurpassed, and the bar is always open.

All this elegance and hedonism comes at a price, with one night for a couple at The Point costing more than a week for two at most other resorts. But *Forbes* magazine summed it up well: "There are no telephones, no newspapers, and no menu choice. You partake of what is prepared each day and sit down to dine at the appointed hour. If you don't like the hosts, the food, the guests or the digs, tough luck . . . [yet] for those in search of sybaritic creature comforts, there is only one destination—The Point."

Wanakena

Packbasket Adventures Lodge (315-848-3488; www.packbasketadventures.com; 12 South Shore Road) is Wanakena Ranger School graduate and

The Rockefellers' Upper Saranac Lake Great Camp is now a luxury resort. Courtesy of The Point

Adirondack guide Rick Kovacs's dream come true. Rick spent time in Vermont as a back-to-the-lander, but the Green State's surge in development was a turn off for him and his wife, Angie Oliver. Remote Wanakena had everything they hoped for, so they established Packbasket Adventures Lodge and Guide Service so other folks could enjoy it, too. Expect comfortable Adirondack rustic-style accommodations—log furniture, wrought-iron accoutrements—in their four-bedroom, four-bath lodge and adjacent cozy log cabin. Guests are loyal repeat customers, often sportsmen hunting or angling in the region, many who also hire Rick for fly-fishing instruction. Meals are provided, and Rick will even set up picnic lunches in nearby lean-tos. Visitors can also rent snowshoes, canoes, kayaks, you name it through Packbasket, as Rick and Angie also operate the Wanakena General Store (www.wanakenageneralstore.com).

Local Flavors
Where to eat in the Northwest Lakes

In these parts lumberjack flapjacks and camp-stove meals come to mind, though there are a handful of indoor spots where you can find a fine meal. As with most Adirondack ventures, be sure to call these restaurants ahead since hours of operation can change like the weather.

Cranberry Lake
Windfall Bar & Grill (315-848-3559; www.windfallbarandgrill.com; 550 Tooley Pond Road) is a backwoods bistro where you can find simple and fresh fare, but you really do have to look for this place, even drive a couple of miles down a winding back road, to get to it. The one-story roadhouse itself isn't the draw, it's John Dragun's consistently good food that stands out in a forest of the same-old-thing-deep-fried plates of most local restaurants. Dragun is a Culinary Institute of America graduate, and he and his wife, Roz, are committed to using local bounty for their seasonal menus, though don't expect anything too over-the-top: mostly Italian standbys, fish dishes, chicken wings, and burgers. The Windfall's wine list favors New York State labels, and John's homemade root beer is popular with kids. There's a pub and a low-key dining room that draws fly-fishermen, backpackers, snowmobilers, and folks willing to go out of their way for a delicious meal.

Cranberry Lake postcard courtesy of Ted Comstock, Saranac Lake

The Great Windfall

On September 20, 1845, almost half a century before the Adirondack Park was formed, what's been described as a tornado leveled everything in its 275-mile-or-so path, from Watertown, across Lake Champlain—even sucking up the steamer *Burlington*'s deck planks—into Vermont. Thousands upon thousands of acres of timber were toppled.

An excerpt from the 1892 *Annual Report of the Forest Commission of the State of New York* describes the "most marked destruction" by the Great Windfall "occurring about 6 miles north of Lake Massawepie. . . . The path of the cyclone is still to be seen here, extending for 25 miles in length and varying from a half to over a mile in width.

"Not a single tree was left standing," wrote Frederick J. Seaver in *Historical Sketches of Franklin County and its Several Towns*. "All were snapped off or uprooted, with a result a tangle of trunks and limbs and tops that was impenetrable."

Old maps depict the scarred swath as a stripe that runs from Newton Falls to present-day Windfall Pond, north of Tupper Lake. Writer Paul Jamieson commented in his guidebook *Adirondack Canoe Waters: North Flow* that the storm's course can be traced by names such as the "Windfall Road . . . three Windfall Brooks, and two Windfall Ponds." Post–Civil War pioneers, drawn to the windfall's clearing, settled in Franklin County. Today there's barely evidence of the destruction, though it's believed that Route 3 from Cranberry Lake to Tupper Lake follows the storm's path.

Far Out in Cranberry Lake

The psychedelic revolution came to Cranberry Lake in 1965 when Arthur Kleps opened his Morning Glory Lodge on the water's east shore. The camp became headquarters for the former North Country school psychologist's Neo-American Church, founded on the catechism that "psychedelic substances such as LSD are sacraments in that they encourage enlightenment, which is the realization that life is a dream." Among Morning Glory Lodge visitors were LSD guru Timothy Leary, plus guests—"and a few hippies"—from around the country, including undercover federal agents, as Kleps documented in his 1975 book *Millbrook*. Morning Glory Lodge is long gone, but Kleps's church still exists at okneoac.com.

—From "Far Out" by Mary Thill, Adirondack Life

Lake Clear

Hohmeyer's Lake Clear Lodge (518-891-1489; www.lodgeonlakeclear.com; 6319 NY 30), a charming 1880s Adirondack inn, was the town's first post office and an early stagecoach stop; the décor today is a pleasant European/Adirondack fusion. Bring a small group of friends for dinner so you can sample many of the interesting appetizers (marinated herring, smoked oysters, and pâté, for example) and homemade desserts. Soups, especially oxtail, are wonderful. All meals come with a combination of German potato pancakes, wild rice, potato dumplings, fresh vegetables, and a bowl of sweet red cabbage and green apples. Entrée choices are heirloom German recipes that showcase farm-raised venison, rabbit, duckling, pork, and veal in traditional sauces, plus sauerbraten, roulades, and schnitzels. Desserts can include delicious blueberry strudel (right from the oven if your timing's good). After dinner, take your party down to the Bierkeller to sit by the fire or play pool, Ping-Pong, or backgammon. There's an extensive variety of beers (some 125 kinds from around the world) and a good list of German, French, and California wines.

Paul Smiths

Saint Regis Café (518-327-6355; www.paulsmiths.edu; Routes 86 and 30) may be a training restaurant for the culinary students at Paul Smith's College, but don't assume anything less than fine food. Wannabe chefs work beside faculty in a nice dining room with views of Lower Saint Regis Lake in the Joan Weill Student Center. Lunches include staples such as burgers and Reubens; dinners range from crispy salmon with fondant potatoes, roasted fennel, charred red onion, herbs and lemon, to grilled flatiron steak with Dauphinoise potatoes, wilted spinach, and smoked tomato chutney.

Tupper Lake

P-2's Irish Pub (518-359-9980; www.p2sirishpub.com; 31 Main Street), former Al's Lounge, a four-decade mainstay in Tupper, is now a bustling little joint that draws locals, plus Wild Center employees thirsty for a postwork Guinness. There's often live music here, the vibe is friendly, and someone just might share the location of a nearby fishing honey hole. Open Wednesday through Sunday, 4 PM on.

Wanakena

The Pine Cone (315-848-2121; www.pinecone-wanakena.com; 68 Ranger School Road), a classic North Woods tavern with respectable fare, is worth a visit—if you're nearby—to check out the ceiling, plastered with about a thousand baseball caps of all descriptions. Come by boat from Cranberry Lake for one of the pig roasts or barbecues. The Friday fish fry (beer-battered had-dock) is fine, and try the prime rib, which is quite popular. You'll find the service to be quick and friendly. No credit cards.

To Do
Attractions and activities in the Northwest Lakes

To the wealthy industrialists of far northern New York in cities such as Watertown, Ogdensburg, Potsdam, and Canton, the Oswegatchie wilds were the Great South Woods, full of tall trees, huge bucks, and wily brook trout. Native son and artist Frederic Remington painted fishermen, logging camps, and humble guides' cabins, while writers such as Irving Bacheller documented the dialect and tales of manly men. His *Eben Holden: A Tale of the North Country* was among the first American best-sellers. While the High Peaks and central Adirondacks attracted numerous Hudson River School painters, Marc Chagall spent time near Star Lake in the 1940s. Finding an Adirondack-influenced Chagall is difficult, perhaps because his wife, Bella, was very ill at the time. She died in the hospital in Tupper Lake in 1944.

ARCHITECTURE AND HISTORIC BUILDINGS

White Pine Camp (518-327-3030; www.whitepinecamp.com), the summer White House of President Calvin Coolidge, in Paul Smiths, on Osgood Pond, is a Great Camp you can visit. For boathouse fans, Upper Saint Regis Lake, near Paul Smiths, has many lovely waterfront buildings, in high rustic, cobblestone, and shingle style. You'll need a boat to make this tour, and you'll have to paddle several miles from the public put-in on Keese Mill Road, west of Paul Smith's College. Also, a reminder—respect landowners' privacy by staying away from docks and shore.

Beth Joseph Synagogue (518-359-3580; Lake Street, Tupper Lake), built in 1905, is an elegant structure made of simple pine boards and tall arched windows. Beth Joseph once served an active congregation, but after the 1930s, attendance declined. In 1959, the synagogue closed and stood vacant for 25 years. Community interest in the historic building was rekindled by a summer resident who encouraged former temple members to get the structure listed on the National Register of Historic Places and begin restoration work. Local people of all religions pitched in with donated labor, materials, and funds; the ornate embroidered velvet Torah covers were painstakingly restored by a local weaver. Today the facility, which is open in July and August, hosts art exhibitions, concerts, lectures, and other events.

Sadly, the popular Wawbeek Resort, with its fine restaurant and cozy rooms, on Upper Saranac Lake, was razed to make room for a new private home, but Spitfire and other lakes in the Saint Regis chain have architectural gems,

A traditional Adirondack lean-to courtesy of Ted Comstock, Saranac Lake

though much of the fine architecture you see in coffee table books exists behind locked gates so best to tour vicariously. Going around the west short of Upper Saranac Lake via boat can mean fine views of amazing compounds, including Wenonah Lodge, Prospect Point, and Eagle Island—all true 19th-century Great Camps.

LIBRARIES

Tupper Lake's Goff Nelson Memorial Library (518-359-9421; 41 Lake Street) has a good Adirondack collection available to readers. Paul Smith's College's Joan Weill Adirondack Library (518-327-6211; Paul Smith's College, NY 86 and NY 30) is an impressive college library with all the high-tech wizardry and a coffee shop, also open to the public.

MUSEUMS AND NATURE CENTERS

The Wild Center, a.k.a. Natural History Museum of the Adirondacks (518-359-7800; www.wildcenter.org; 45 Museum Drive, Tupper Lake), is a slick, state-of-the-art facility that's a must-see for every visitor who's interested in the Adirondacks and its natural world. Think adorable otters somersaulting in a glass tank, plus more than 900 other live critters, some that scurry, slither, and swim in and out of the museum via a reflective pond. Exhibits tell the story of this park's natural history— who doesn't love touching a glacier (there's a freezy chunk that mimics the ice sheet that coated this place just 10,000 years ago)? A theater shows a variety of movies, among them *A Matter of Degrees,* narrated by Long Lake summer resident Sigourney Weaver. The museum's schedule is packed with lectures, workshops, and performances; museum staffers stroll about with porcupines and raptors, and lead guided treks on the museum's network of trails. Kids love the natural playground, roots, twigs, and all. The

The Wild Center is a slick natural history museum in Tupper Lake. Courtesy of the Wild Center

place hosts climate conferences, private parties and weddings, an area farmers' market (June through September), plus eco-friendly-living festivals, among them one where local growers and green advocates gather to swap ideas. The science-based Wild Center is, after all, the first LEED-certified museum in New York State. Admission: $15 adults, $9 ages 4–14, discounts available for seniors and groups. Open seven days in summer, Friday through Sunday in winter, plus Presidents' Week and Martin Luther King Day; closed in April.

Paul Smith's College Visitor Interpretive Center (518-327-3000; www.adirondack vic.org; Route 30, Paul Smiths), the former state-funded Paul Smiths Visitor Interpretive Center (VIC), is now operated by the college and the Adirondack Park Institute. The facility explains the region's natural history through exhibits, guided hikes, workshops for kids and adults, and it has miles of interpretive and backcountry trails open year-round for hiking, snowshoeing, and cross-country skiing. Dogs are allowed on trails, but they must be leashed. In summer it has a wonderful butterfly house with flowers, plants, and indigenous insects, and also sponsors the Great Adirondack

Paul Smith's College's VIC hosts the Great Adirondack Birding Celebration, which includes treks to Whiteface to search for the elusive Bicknell's thrush.

Courtesy of Jeff Nadler, www.jnphoto.net

Birding Celebration in June (see page 114).

WRITERS' PROGRAMS

The Adirondack Center for Writing (518-327-6278; www.adirondackcenter forwriting.org; Paul Smith's VIC, Paul Smiths) schedules workshops, readings, book signings, literary contests; hosts children's literature seminars, in-school programs, publishing conferences, lectures by authors including Andrea Barrett and Terry Tempest Williams; sponsors a prison-writing program; and has a comprehensive listing of opportunities for writers for the Adirondacks and beyond.

Woodswork: An Adirondack Education

Appropriately, **Paul Smith's College** (1-800-421-2605; www.paulsmiths.edu), in Paul Smiths, and the **State University of New York–Environmental Science and Forestry Ranger School** (315-470-6500; www.esf.edu/rangerschool), in Wanakena, are based in this region of the Adirondack Park. Paul Smith's, on the shores of Lower Saint Regis Lake, offers four-year programs in hospitality, culinary arts, forestry, recreation, fish and wildlife, or liberal arts. The Ranger School uses its wilderness digs to give students training for an associate's degree in environmental conservation, forest technology, or land surveying.

Paul Smith's hosts the hot new, intensive **Adirondack Woodsmen's School** (518-327-6990; www.adirondackwoodsmenschool.com), a three-session summertime college-credit program that teaches proficiency in speed chopping, ax flinging, log rolling, sawing, and other woodsmen's skills.

See the finest lumber skills at the annual **Woodsmen's Days** (518-359-9444; www .woodsmendays.com), in Tupper Lake. This event underlines the importance of logging in the Adirondack economy today. There's a parade with sparkling log trucks hauling the year's biggest, best logs; contests for men and women (chainsaw carving, ax tossing), beast (skidding logs with draft horses), and heavy equipment (precision drills for skidders and loaders); and games for kids. It's all on the second weekend in July, in the municipal park on the lakefront in Tupper Lake.

Paul Smith's Hotel was a 19th-century North Woods destination. Today Paul Smith's College has a thriving forestry program, plus the Adirondack Woodsmen's Camp.

Courtesy of Ted Comstock, Saranac Lake

Recreation

Adventures in the
Northwest Lakes

To find a guide to lead your hiking,
camping, hunting, fishing, or other outdoor activity in the Northwest Lakes
region, check out the New York State
Outdoor Guides Association's site,
www.nysoga.com.

BICYCLING

Mountain-biking at the Peavine Swamp
trail, accessible from Route 3 in Cranberry Lake or from the northeast at the
end of the Ranger School campus, in
Wanakena, is incredible in late summer
and early fall. This well-marked system in the Cranberry Lake Wild Forest has three
loops of about 10 miles of intermediate-to-difficult riding. You'll roll through old-
growth forest and encounter hills, roots, and rocks. But there are lots more routes for
fat tires, and long stretches of woodsy highways for skinny ones. Free guides provide
more riding options: Franklin County Tourism (518-483-9470; www.adirondack
lakes.com; 10 Elm Street, Malone) publishes a brochure describing off-the-beaten-
path treks that's available at the office and online. Check www.bikeadirondacks.org
or the guidebooks in chapter 8 for other ideas.

BOATING

Lots of lovely Adirondack lakes have public launches for motor- and sailboats. Many
are free, operated by the New York State Department of Environmental Conservation or villages; individual businesses may charge a nominal fee. You'll find these

An Insider's Guide to the Oswegatchie

Rick Kovacs, of Adirondack Packbasket Adventures Guide Service, in
Wanakena, guides many fly-fishing
and paddling excursions. He offers
the following as some of the region's
wild hot spots:
Favorite trip: High Falls on the
Oswegatchie River and beyond in the
Five Ponds Wilderness.
Favorite campsite: Any of the sites
along Round Hill Rapids on the Oswegatchie River.
Favorite place: Cage Lake springhole
lean-to on the Oswegatchie on a fall
evening.

The Northwest Lakes' Saint Regis Canoe Area is paddlers' heaven. Courtesy of Mark Bowie, www.markbowie.com

You Give Me Fever

The cool, clear water may seem like the ideal thirst quencher, but please resist the temptation to drink freely from Adirondack lakes, rivers, ponds, and streams. Sadly, due to careless campers and occasional animal pollution, these wild waters may harbor a microscopic parasite known as *Giardia lamblia,* which can cause bloating, diarrhea, cramping, and vomiting. Giardiasis—also known as beaver fever—is easily diagnosed (with a stool sample) and treated (with quinacrine or Flagyl), but it's better to avoid the ailment in the first place. Practice good campsite sanitation. Treat all drinking water by boiling for 10 minutes, by using a specially designed *Giardia*-proof filter, or with chlorine or iodine tablets.

launch sites marked on regional road maps. Many state campgrounds have boat ramps. If you have a reserved campsite, there's no extra charge to launch a boat, and if you'd like to make a short visit to Cranberry Lake, or Fish Creek Pond, for example, you pay the day-use fee. The *New York State Boater's Guide* (nysparks.com /recreation/boating/documents/NYSBoatersGuide.pdf) contains the rules and regs for inland waters, and is available from offices of the New York Department of Transportation.

CAMPING

Camping is allowed year-round on state land, but you need a permit to stay more than three days in one backcountry spot or if you are camping with a group of more than six people. These permits are available from forest rangers. Some locations such as Lows Lake, Little Tupper Lake, or Lake Lila have designated primitive camping spots with fire rings and/or privies. You may camp in the backcountry provided you pitch your tent at least 150 feet from any trail, stream, lake, or other water body. (See "low-impact camping," page 146.) Campground fees below are for 2012.

Fish Creek is a classic Adirondack campground. Courtesy of Ted Comstock, Saranac Lake

From Memorial Day through Labor Day the Department of Environmental Conservation (518-402-9428; www.dec.ny.gov) operates the following public campgrounds in the Northwest Lakes region:

Cranberry Lake (315-848-2315; 243 Lone Pine Road, Cranberry Lake. Beach for swimming, showers, rowboat or canoe rentals, the trailhead to easy but pretty Bear Mountain. $20 camping fee.

Fish Creek Pond (518-891-4560; 4523 NY 30, Saranac Lake). A quintessential Adirondack campground with swimming beaches, showers, canoe or rowboat rentals, boat launch, nature and beginner camper programs. $20 camping fee.

Rollins Pond (518-891-3239; NY 30, near Fish Creek Pond campsite), Showers, canoe or rowboat rentals, boat launch. $20 camping fee.

A reminder: Camping fees listed are for 2012. Also, DEC public campgrounds

Tear Up the Adirondacks

For a weekend each June teardrop trailer enthusiasts from across the United States and Canada come to Fish Creek Pond campground for the **ADK Spring TearUp** (www.taruptheadk.com). During the gathering, impromptu groups paddle the nearby waterways, hike the peaks, have potlucks, and kick back by fires. And most important, ramble campsite to campsite, checking out all the teardrops.

Popular after World War II, when the military's excess aluminum was used to build them, teardrops trailers—traditionally 4 by 8 feet—with their funky stand-up rear-galley kitchens and overall cute-as-a-button appeal, have made a comeback. They can be pulled behind any vehicle, even a motorcycle.

The Fish Creek event lures teardrop lovers who tow fancy stainless-steel, air-conditioned, souped-up trailers with sound systems and satellite radio and television. But also hobbyists who restore vintage model or build them from scratch.

do not supply water, electric, or sewer hookups for recreational vehicles. Reservations for a single night or as long as three weeks can be made for a site in the state campgrounds by contacting Reserve America (1-800-456-CAMP; www.reserve america.com). DEC campgrounds will cheerfully take you on a first-come, first-served basis if space is available; before July 4 and after September 1, it's usually easy to find a nice site without a reservation.

CANOEING AND KAYAKING

For flatwater fans, there are long trips linking lakes, such as the 44-mile route from Long Lake to Tupper Lake. In the Saint Regis Canoe Area it's possible to paddle for weeks on end and visit a different pond or lake each day.

Options have improved considerably with New York State's acquisition of beautiful, motorless Little Tupper Lake and Rock Pond, and the myriad white-water rivers that formerly belonged to Champion International Company. More lakes opened to paddlers, such as Round Lake, adjacent to Little Tupper Lake. Four-mile-long Little Tupper Lake offers gorgeous paddling, swimming, and loon-watching, with several primitive campsites you can reserve from the registration box at the parking lot. The Department of Environmental Conservation's Northville office (518-863-4545) has an excellent guide to the William C. Whitney Area, which encompasses Little Tupper Lake.

The DEC's Ray Brook office (518-891-1200; www.dec.ny.gov; NY 86, Ray Brook 12970) has pamphlets that describe canoe routes, including the Bog River area near Tupper Lake; ask for *Adirondack Canoe Routes* or the "official map and guide" of the area you wish to paddle. The excellent booklet *Guide to Paddling Adirondack Waterways* is available at visitadirondacks.com or by calling 1-800-487-6867. Some tourist information offices, such as the

Osgood Pond is a serene place for a paddle.

Courtesy of John DiGiacomo, www.placidtimesphotography.com

Saranac Lake Chamber of Commerce (518-891-1990; www.saranaclake.com), have useful brochures and maps; ask for Canoe Franklin County. Always consult U.S. Geological Survey topographic maps for the area you're traveling through.

When you're planning any trip, allow an extra day in case the weather doesn't cooperate. Remember that you're required to carry a life jacket for each person in the boat; lash an extra paddle in your canoe, too. Bring plenty of food and fuel, a backpacker stove, and rain gear. A poncho makes a good coverall for hiking, but you're far better off with rain jacket and pants in a canoe—a poncho can become tangled if you should dump your boat. Sign in at the trailhead registers when you begin your trip.

If you're still overwhelmed by making a decision about where to go, consult one of the following outfitters: Mac's Canoe Livery (518-891-1176; www.macscanoe.com; 5859 NY 30, Lake Clear), a complete year-round outfitter and guide service that also offers wilderness education; scheduled trips and races; sales and rentals. Raquette River Outfitters (518-359-3228; www.raquetteriveroutfitters.com; 1754 NY 30, Tupper Lake), a complete trip outfitter that also does canoe repairs, guided treks, and car shuttles. Saint Regis Canoe Outfitters (518-891-1838; www.canoeoutfitters.com; Floodwood Road, Lake Clear), a trip outfitter in the heart of the Saint Regis Canoe Area that offers guided adventures, canoe instruction, and car shuttles.

FISHING

Lake trout in Star Lake, landlocked salmon in Lake Ozonia, bass in Lake Lila, walleye in Tupper Lake, and brook trout near Cranberry Lake and interior ponds—these are just a sampling of the fish native to waters in this corner of the Adirondack Park. With preparation—such as reading a guidebook or calling one of the hotlines or spending a day with a guide on remote waters—you may be able to tell the story about the big one that *didn't* get away.

Begin your fishing education with the *New York State Freshwater Fishing Regulations Guide*, published by the Department of Environmental Conservation and available at DEC offices or its www.dec.ny.gov, sporting goods stores, and tourist information centers. The free booklet details all the seasons and limits for various species. Everyone 16 and older who fishes in the Adirondacks must have a New York fishing license, which can be purchased at sporting goods stores and town offices. Nonresidents can get special five-day licenses; state residents 70 and older may get free licenses.

The DEC site also has helpful hotlines for anglers, describing the top fishing spots and what's hitting where on which kind of bait. Plus, there's information about the toxic buildup of mercury in fish. The site lists certain fish species in the Adirondacks that should not be consumed by children or pregnant women.

If you'd like to read about fishing, see I Love New York's comprehensive *Adirondack Fishing* guide at www.fishadk.com. Chapter 8 has a list of Adirondack fishing guidebooks. To get in the proper frame of mind for fishing, nothing beats a trip to a local fish hatchery. In the Northwest Lakes, the Adirondack Fish Hatchery (518-891-3358; NY 30, Saranac Inn) specializes in raising landlocked salmon for stocking lakes.

GOLF

Golf courses in this area include the Clifton-Fine Golf Course (315-848-3570; 4173 Main Street, Star Lake), which has nine holes, is par-36 with 2,800 yards; and Tupper Lake Golf & Country Club (518-359-3701; Country Club Road), with its 18 holes, par-71, 6,200 yards.

Saint Regis Canoe Area

State Route 30 is the main road to the **Saint Regis Canoe Area**, west of Saranac Lake and northeast of Tupper Lake. Off Route 30 the DEC's Fish Hatchery Road, near Lake Clear, has two put-ins, and Floodwood Road, near Saranac Inn, has three parking areas near canoe access points. Floodwood is also a launching place for ponds in the Saranac Lakes Wild Forest to the south. Canoe area itineraries can be extended into this region, and a "Quiet Waters" campaign is advocating making 13 of the wild forest's ponds off-limits to gas-powered motorboats and Jet-Skis.

Several maps and guidebooks offer canoe area information. Though dated, a reliable source is Paul Jamieson and Don Morris's *Adirondack Canoe Waters: North Flow* (1994). *Adirondack Paddler's Guide: Finding Your Way by Canoe and Kayak in the Adirondack Park* (2008) by Paddlesports Press is more recent. The canoe area is covered by the Saint Regis Mountain and Upper Saranac Lake USGS topographic maps as well as by the 2008 Paddlesports Press "Adirondack Paddlers' Map" and the "Adirondack Canoe Map" (1987, Plinth, Quoin & Cornice Associates). However, no map is entirely accurate; trails and campsites have been moved or mismarked, so be prepared to change plans accordingly.

The **Department of Environmental Conservation Unit Management Plan** for the canoe area contains lots of information on usage and natural history: www.dec.ny.gov /docs/lands_forests_pdf/srcafinal.pdf.

Signature routes include the **Seven Carries**, originally a way to travel between Prospect House on Upper Saranac Lake and Paul Smith's Hotel, on Lower Saint Regis Lake. Today it's a popular day-trip or overnight; pond and put-in options vary—there aren't always seven carries, but the name endures.

The **Nine Carries** can start on Little Clear Pond, Hoel Pond, or Upper Saint Regis Lake and follow a variety of pond-hop itineraries ranging from 13 to 18 miles (including 1.5 to 2.5 miles of carries). Consult maps and guidebooks to design your own route.

A hike up **Long Pond Mountain** (about 1.5 miles, 900 feet ascent) adds variety to outings in the Long Pond–to–Hoel Pond area. The trail is gorgeous, rerouted about a decade ago by the DEC; the take-out on a northern lobe of Long Pond is well marked and also leads to Mountain Pond.

Saint Regis Mountain's 3.4-mile trail is north of most of the ponds, but its unbroken views of the waters below attract nearly as much traffic as the rest of the canoe area combined. There's a preserved 1918 fire tower at the summit.

Nearby outfitters offer boats and gear for rental or purchase as well as guided trips: **Saint Regis Canoe Outfitters** (518-891-8040; www.canoeoutfitters.com), on Floodwood Road at the Long Pond portage, with its couch and woodstove, is as much woodland lounge as shop. **Mac's Canoe Livery** (518-891-1176; www.macscanoe.com), at the edge of the canoe area, 5859 State Route 30, in Lake Clear, is close to the Fish Hatchery Road put-ins. **Raquette River Outfitters** (518-359-3228; www.raquetteriver outfitters.com), on Route 30, in Tupper Lake, is also a fine source of information.

—*Mary Thill, from "Carry On,"* Adirondack Life

HIKING AND BACKPACKING

In some parts of the park, you can leave the trailhead and not see another person until you return to your car and look in the rearview mirror. The Five Ponds Wilderness Area, between Stillwater Reservoir and Cranberry Lake, is especially remote. You might go several days without seeing a soul.

Wherever you choose to go, be prepared. Your pack should contain a flashlight, matches, extra food and water, map, compass, GPS—chances are slim you'll get cell service—and extra clothes (wool or fleece for warmth; leave the cotton at home). At most trailheads, there's a register for signing in. Forest rangers rely on this data to estimate how much use a particular area receives; and, in the unlikely event that you get lost, the information about when you started, where you were planning to go, and who you were with would be helpful to the search team.

The Cranberry Lake 50, a collection of trails that forms a 50-mile loop around the Adirondacks' third-largest body of water, offers hikers a variety of stretches, from easy logging road rambles to pond hopping. The trail goes beyond its namesake water's shoreline, extending into the Five Ponds Wilderness and the Cranberry Lake Wild Forest. On this network you'll find lean-tos and lovely ponds, particularly Curis and Cowhorn Ponds, but most important is what you'll find at www.cranberrylake50 .org, which covers everything you need to know about the 50.

The Tupper Lake Irregulars (518-891-8433) is a crew of adventurers, ages eight to 80, from all points in the park and beyond. Tag along with these folks on Mondays and Thursdays in summer for some of the best, but lesser-known, treks and paddles in the Adirondacks. Or if you want to go it alone, see chapter 7 for a list of guidebooks and other resources with further ideas for hiking this region; a licensed guide to lead you can be found at www.nysoga.com.

HUNTING

Native Americans, colonial scouts, and 19th-century travelers regarded the Adirondacks as happy hunting grounds. The Northwest Lakes was once a hotbed of hunting clubs for blue-collar locals as well as the wealthy who trained in from metropolises for sporting getaways.

Today, wilderness, primitive, and wild forest areas are all open to hunting. And deer are still the main target, with snowshoe hares popular prey in winter. Hunters— even if they have a brand-new, state-of-the-art GPS unit—should be proficient with map and compass. Cell phone service is spotty in the backwoods; global-positioning units don't always work well in thick forest, and batteries do wear out.

See the Department of Environmental Conservation's webpage, www.dec.ny .gov, for hunting seasons and Adirondack regulations.

SKIING: CROSS-COUNTRY AND SNOWSHOEING

Although 2012 was a bust, most winters there's plenty of snow, upward of 100 inches. Many of the marked hiking trails on state land are not only suitable for cross-country skiing or snowshoeing, they're actually better for winter recreation because swampy areas are frozen, and ice-bound ponds and lakes can be easily crossed.

Designated wilderness and wild forest areas offer great ski touring on marked but ungroomed trails. State campgrounds—closed to vehicles from November through May—offer quiet, woodsy, snow-covered roads with gentle grades. Another option for exploring the wild wintry woods is to hire a licensed guide (see www.nysoga.org).

Before setting out on a wilderness excursions, prepare your pack with quick-energy food; a thermos filled with hot tea or cocoa; extra hat, socks, and gloves; topo map, compass, and GPS; matches; flashlight; and space blanket. Dress in layers of wool, polypropylene, or synthetic pile. Don't travel alone. Sign in at the trailhead register. Let friends know your destination and when you plan to return.

Many towns maintain cross-country-ski trails, and the Paul Smith's College Visitor Interpretive Center (518-327-3000; www.adkvic.org) has miles of paths. There's also the Cranberry Lake Trail (315-386-4000; NY 3, Cranberry Lake) and the 15-kilometer backcountry Deer Pond Loop (518-359-3328; NY 30, Tupper Lake). The Saranac Inn Horse Trail System, off NY 30 near Saranac Inn, has several short trails in the Saint Regis Canoe Area and an 11-mile round-trip on the Fish Pond Truck Trail—excellent for cross-country skiing.

The Jackrabbit Trail is a superb resource, some 35 miles of groomed trails connecting Paul Smiths with Keene. The trail combines old logging roads and abandoned rail lines. Dogs aren't welcome on groomed portions of this trail.

SKIING: DOWNHILL AND SNOWBOARDING

Big Tupper Ski Area (518-359-3730; www.skibigtupper.org; Ski Tow Road, Tupper Lake) is a hometown hero, if ever a mountain can be. Big Tupper was shuttered for years until local volunteers, in an attempt to revive Tupper's sleepy economy, opened the locally popular ski area. There's no snowmaking here, just a no-frills, two-chair, 25-plus-trail mom-and-pop-type operation that's affordable and fine for skiing and snowboarding. Day passes are $25 (seniors and children under the age of 6 are free).

SNOWMOBILING

Beside the Old Forge–Inlet area, there are more than 400 miles of snowmobile trails in the Tupper Lake–Saranac Lake–Lake Placid area, and near Cranberry Lake, there are miles and miles of trails. Many trail networks throughout the park cross private timberlands as well as the state forest preserve. Public lands designated as wild forest areas are open to snowmobiling; wilderness areas are not. The Department of Environmental Conservation is a clearinghouse for snowmobile rules and regulations in the park, and offers snowmobile trail maps; www.dec.ny.gov has links to sites with Adirondack snowmobile trails. Also, check out www.visitadirondacks.com for snowmobile info, plus local meteorologist and sled head Darrin Harr keeps tabs on area conditions and all things snowmobile at his www.ilsnow.com.

As with any winter pursuit, planning and preparation help make a successful outing. Know your machine; carry an emergency repair kit and understand how to use it. Be sure you have plenty of gas. Travel with friends in case of a breakdown or other surprise situations. Never ride at night unless you're familiar with the trail or are following an experienced leader. Avoid crossing frozen lakes and streams unless you are absolutely certain the ice is safe. Some town or county roads are designated trails; while on such a highway, keep right, observe the posted snowmobile speed limit, and travel in single file.

Your basic pack should contain a topographic map, compass, and GPS, as well as a local trail map; survival kit with matches, flashlight, rope, space blanket, quick-energy food, and something warm to drink; extra hat, socks, and mittens. Although a sip of brandy may give the illusion of warming you up, alcohol impairs circulation and can hasten hypothermia. And an arrest for snowmobiling under the influence carries with it severe penalties.

TRIATHLONS

Lake Placid's Ironman (www.ironmanlakeplacid.com) is a grueling test—it's even ultra-competitive just to get to the starting line (entry slots have been known to sell out in minutes). Which is why Tupper Lake's Tinman Triathlon (518-359-7571; www.tupper-lake.com), a USA Triathlon-sanctioned event that is half the length of Ironman, is a draw for amateur athletes looking to test their mettle, as well as professionals preparing for the real deal. Competitors converge late-June on Tupper Lake's Municipal Park and swim 1.2 miles in Raquette Pond, bike 56 miles past Cranberry

The Darkest Skies

At press time the **Adirondack Public Observatory** (www.apobservatory.org), in Tupper Lake, was in phase one of its plans to construct a roll-off roof structure to house its telescopes. But the nonprofit organization is more than a place for stargazing: it's a club of amateur and expert astronomers who present lectures, activities, and public awareness to the Adirondack community.

Its Tupper Lake base is a fitting place for an astronomy group. Minus brightly lit correctional facilities in some nearby towns, Tupper and most of the Adirondack Park is free of the light pollution that blots out the night sky and disrupts the reproduction and migration cycles of many species.

That's why Adirondack photographer **Mark Bowie** uses this region for much of his night-sky shooting. His guidebook *The Light of Midnight: Photographing the Landscape at Night* is available at 413-442-9125 or www.markbowie.com; his photography workshops—often affiliated with the Adirondack Photography Institute (www.api.com)—usually sell out. Check out dates for his workshops and photo tours at his website.

Lake, then run 13.1 miles along Route 3; the footrace has earned a reputation as "mosquito alley."

WATERFALLS

In this region is Bog River Falls, a two-tier falls at Big Tupper Lake, in Tupper Lake. It's visible from County Road 421. Also, High Falls is on a remote stretch of the Oswegatchie River, in Cranberry Lake. And Raquette Falls, on the Raquette River, in Tupper Lake.

WILDERNESS AREAS

These portions of the Forest Preserve are 10,000 acres or larger and contain little evidence of modern times. Wilderness areas are open to hiking, cross-country skiing, hunting, fishing, and other similar pursuits, but seaplanes may not land on wilderness ponds, nor are motorized vehicles welcome.

In the Northwest Lakes region is the Saint Regis Canoe Area, with 20,000 acres, west of Paul Smiths. Its 58 lakes and ponds are the ultimate for paddling; the views are postcardlike from Saint Regis and other mountains, and there's a trail network for hiking and cross-country skiing.

WILD FOREST AREAS

More than a million acres of public land in the park are designated as wild forest, which are open to snowmobile travel, mountain biking, and other recreation.

In this region is Cranberry Lake Wild Forest, between Cranberry Lake and Piercefield, with snowmobile and hiking trails and trout ponds. Also, 9,837-acre White Hill Wild Forest, near Parishville. Its 35-acre Clear Pond is the tract's centerpiece, though other pretty ponds and wetlands draw adventurers and bald eagles.

WILDLIFE

In late spring, warblers in all colors of the rainbow arrive, and the best places to watch for them is along edges where habitats meet, such as woods on the border of a wetland, or along a brushy field. A variety of songbirds, including kingbirds, flycatchers, grosbeaks, waxwings, thrushes, wrens, and sparrows, all nest here. Many interior lakes and ponds are home to kingfishers, ducks, herons, and loons; listen and watch for that great northern diver in the early morning and at dusk. Bald eagles, absent from the park for much of the 20th century, have been reintroduced. You should be able to spot one near Tupper Lake or Meacham Lake.

Small mammals are numerous: varying hares, weasels, mink, raccoons, fisher, pine martens, otters, bobcats, porcupines, and red and gray foxes. Coyotes, with rich coats in shades of black, rust, and gray, can be seen in fall, winter, and spring, and their yips and yowls on a summer night can be thrilling to the backcountry campers' ears. White-tailed deer are everywhere, especially in the early spring before the fawns are born, and you might see a moose.

Great Adirondack Birding Festival

Birders can participate in the **Great Adirondack Birding Festival**, at Paul Smith's College's Visitor Interpretive Center (518-327-3000), in Paul Smiths, in June. It's a birding extravaganza with workshops, lectures from top ornithologists, and expeditions with an emphasis on boreal species.

Shopping

Adirondackana and more in the Northwest Lakes

Obviously, this isn't the area to shop for a cocktail dress. But you can find Adirondack art, handmade boats, and supplies for your Adirondack adventure.

ART GALLERIES AND PAINTERS' STUDIOS

In Cranberry Lake, Jean Reynolds, of End of the Pier Studio (315-848-2900), paints watercolors of Cranberry Lake and Adirondack vistas. Her work can be seen at Cranberry Lake Lodge (www.cranberrylakelodge.com).

Diane Leifheit (518-327-3473; www.dianeleifheit.com), of Gabriels, works en plein air in a variety of mediums.

Snow Line Design (315-262-3150; www.snowlinedesign.com) is Suzanne Langelier Lebeda's South Colton studio, where she paints, draws, and creates graphic design work.

In Tupper Lake, Casagrain Gallery (518-359-2595; 68 Park Street) is where artist Gary Casagrain exhibits his paintings. Also in Tupper is photographer Burdette Parks's Round Lake Studios (518-359-9324; www.roundlakestudios.com).

BOAT BUILDERS

In Lake Clear, James Cameron, of Boathouse Woodworks (www.adkguideboat.com; 518-327-3470; P.O. Box 317), crafts traditional wooden Adirondack guideboats built to order. In Tupper Lake, Rob Frenette, of Spruce Knee Boatbuilding (518-359-3228; NY 30 near Moody Bridge), makes Rushton-design wooden canoes and rowboats, guideboats, and sailboats all built to order. He also does wooden boat repairs and seat caning.

CRAFT SHOPS

In Childwold, Tom Amoroso's Leather Artisan (518-359-3102; www.leatherartisan.com, NY 3) has been making and selling classic leather handbags, wallets, belts,

Shania Twain's Adirondacks

In 1890, Orrando Dexter had his Dexter Lake Camp, a four-story mansion in Santa Clara, built to replicate renaissance man Albrecht Dürer's home in Nuremburg, Germany. After Dexter was shot and killed on his property—some believe by a disgruntled neighbor, as his restrictions on his vast North Country holdings weren't popular with locals—his estate fell to various hands, and was restored in the early 1990s.

Country singer Shania Twain and her then-husband, Robert "Mutt" Lange," purchased the camp and its surrounding acreage in 1994, demolishing the historical structure and constructing a home and recording studio on the property. For a time the celebrities were spotted around Saint Regis Falls, including the Riverside Bar, but a year or so later they put their off-the-beaten track getaway on the market.

briefcases, backpacks, and gorgeous made-to-order leather golf bags for decades. Paul Smiths is where David Woodward creates hand-forged ornamental elements and décor, such as wrought-iron fireplace screens with wildlife silhouette designs and iron lighting fixtures through his Train Brook Forge (518-327-3747; www.trainbrook forge.com; 243 NY 86).

FURNITURE

Need a rustic gate or archway over the entrance of your Great Camp? Jay Major Dawson (518-891-5075; www.majorpieces.com; off NY 30), in Lake Clear, is your guy. He'll also make custom railings, built-in furniture, and lawn pieces.

Michael Trivieri (518-359-7151; Moody Road), of Tupper Lake, creates burl bowls and tables; woodcarvings; mantels; custom railings and rustic trim work. And Thomas Phillips Rustic Furniture (518-359-9648; 681 Bartlett Carry Road) does ash-splint baskets with sculptural branch handles; twig-style and birch-bark chairs, tables, benches, and beds; cedar outdoor furniture; and rustic furniture restoration.

Most of these artisans are available by appointment only, so call ahead.

GENERAL STORES

Fortunately more entertaining than a mall, the old-school general store is pretty much it in the way of shopping in the backcountry. Stores really take the word *general* to heart, so that you can pick out a nice gift as well as the fixings for an afternoon picnic, including sunglasses, bug dope, and sustenance.

Cranberry Lake's Emporium (315-848-2140; NY 3) is a tiny place crammed with souvenirs, maps, fishing tackle, and canned goods, but there's even more—it's a marina with gas pumps, water taxi, and a big, long weathered wooden dock. Lakeside General Store (315-848-2501; 7140 NY 3), also in Cranberry Lake, is open May through October. It's a liquor store, Laundromat, and it has campground, gas pumps, plus just about any supplies you need, but is only open May through October.

Open year-round is Wanakena General Store (315-848-3008; www.wanakena generalstore.com, 6 Hamele Street), the go-to place for venturing out in the Five Ponds Wilderness or Cranberry 50. This is one-stop wilderness shopping: you can arrange a boat or car shuttle, hire a guide service, buy a bear canister, fly-fishing lesson, food, and, for free, get lots of advice and a rundown of the region's highlights. Not at all what you can expect at the Nice N' Easy up the road.

4

High Peaks and Northern Adirondacks

THE HIGH PEAKS are all about drama, whether it's craggy mountains, Olympic glory, or even arts centers. There's a critical mass to the hubs of this region that means competition for good lodging and meals, interesting galleries, cool events, even primo fly-fishing spots along celebrated stretches of the Ausable. Sure, Lake Placid's Main Street is a draw, but there's way more to this region if you know where to look.

Pick Your Spot

Lodging in the High Peaks & Northern Adirondacks

Of all the regions in this book, this is where you'll find year-round lodging and places suited to conferences and other gatherings. Not to mention all sorts of choices—motels, hotels, hostels, bed & breakfasts, backwoods cabins, luxury lodges, lean-tos. The following have character that can only enhance your Adirondack getaway.

Elk Lake

Elk Lake Lodge (518-532-7616; www .elklakelodge.com, 1106 Elk Lake Road) is the quintessential Adirondack lodge. Set on a private lake ringed by the High Peaks, in the midst of a

12,000-acre preserve, the place offers everything an outdoorsperson could ask for: great fishing, unlimited wilderness hiking, and canoeing on an island-studded lake that's off limits to motor-boats. Of course, if just hanging out, listening to the loons and admiring the view are your kinds of recreation, there's that, too. There are a half-dozen rooms in the turn-of-the-century lodge, all with private baths. Around the lakeshore are seven cottages, some that that can accommodate 12. Several of the cabins are equipped with kitchens and fire-places or have decks overlooking the lake. The price of a stay at Elk Lake includes all meals, which are served in the dining room, where huge picture windows reveal the mountains and lake. Canoes and rowboats are available for guests. Open seasonally. No credit cards.

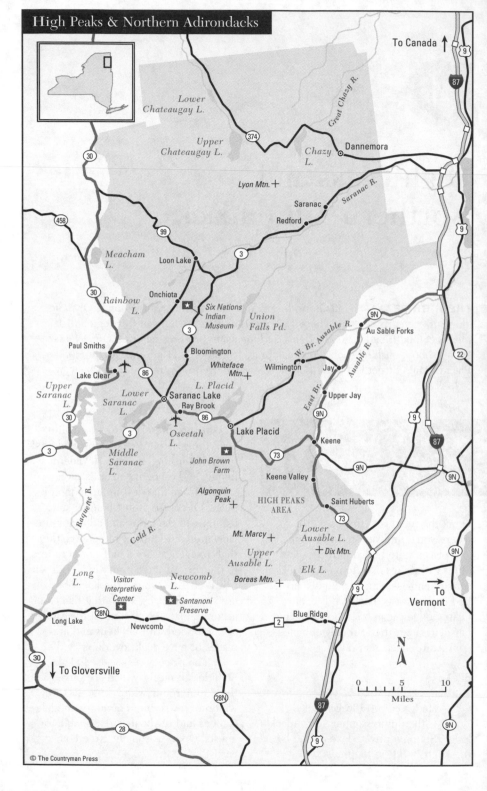

High Peaks & Northern Adirondacks

To Canada ↑

Lower Chateaugay L.

Upper Chateaugay L.

Chazy L.

Dannemora

Lyon Mtn.

Saranac

Redford

Saranac R.

Great Chazy R.

Meacham L.

Loon Lake

Onchiota

Rainbow L.

Six Nations Indian Museum

Union Falls Pd.

Au Sable Forks

Paul Smiths

Bloomington

Lake Clear

Upper Saranac L.

Lower Saranac L.

Whiteface Mtn.

Wilmington

Jay

W. Br. Ausable R.

Ausable R.

Saranac Lake

L. Placid

Ray Brook

Upper Jay

Oseetah L.

Lake Placid

Keene

East Br.

Middle Saranac L.

John Brown Farm

Raquette R.

Algonquin Peak

HIGH PEAKS AREA

Keene Valley

Saint Huberts

Cold R.

Mt. Marcy

Lower Ausable L.

Dix Mtn.

Upper Ausable L.

Elk L.

Long L.

Visitor Interpretive Center

Newcomb L.

Boreas Mtn.

Santanoni Preserve

Long Lake

Newcomb

Blue Ridge

To Vermont

To Gloversville

N

0   5   10
Miles

© The Countryman Press

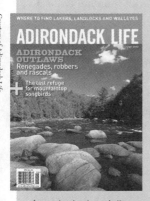

Award-winning *Adirondack Life* magazine has covered the Adirondacks for more than four decades.

Adirondack Life

Published since 1970, *Adirondack Life* (www.adirondacklife .com) has earned numerous national awards for the quality of its photography and design and the depth of its editorial content; most recently it was named 2011 Regional Magazine of the Year by the International Regional Magazine Association. The magazine covers New York's 6-million-acre Adirondack Park, which has more wild country than Yellowstone, Yosemite, and Glacier National Parks combined. Within six bimonthly and two special-focus issues, the magazine, based in Jay, explores the region's people, places, wildlife, history, and public issues, and gives readers insider tips on outdoor recreation, from hiking and canoeing to ice-climbing and backcountry skiing. In late spring, the *Annual Guide to the Great Outdoors* is devoted entirely to outdoor pursuits; in fall, *At Home in the Adirondacks* features architecture, interior design, gardening, and home products reflecting the region's signature style.

Jay

The Book and Blanket (518-946-8323; www.bookandblanket.com; 12914 NY 9N), in a restored Greek Revival home, has rooms named for authors: The Jack London chamber has a north-woods ambience, queen-size bed, and private bath with a whirlpool tub; the Jane Austen room has a queen-size bed and a quiet nook for reading; the F. Scott Fitzgerald room has a double bed and shares a bath. All of them—upstairs and down—have lots of books, and guests are encouraged to browse and borrow at will. Or they can kick back in front of the living room fireplace.

KEENE

Dartbrook Lodge (518-576-9080; www .dartbrooklodge.com; 2835 Route 73, at the intersection with 9N), a relatively new, rehabbed compound of seven well-appointed Great Camp–style cabins, most with kitchenettes—plus a three-cabin complex with private entrance and a dreamy mountaintop retreat—is a welcome addition to drowsy Keene. Dartbrook offers travelers rustic luxury—think chic twiggy and bark

Since 1846, a structure—in a handful of incarnations thanks to floods, ice jams, logging rigs, and a runaway soda delivery truck—has connected the banks of the Ausable River in Jay. Today's pedestrian-only 175-foot-long stretch still has timbers from one of its 19th-century predecessors, drawing covered-bridge buffs. Beneath this centerpiece of the historic hamlet is a popular swimming hole, and folks come here to picnic, bike, or stroll around the surrounding park.

The Jay covered bridge, shown here before its facelift, has anchored this drowsy hamlet since 1857.

accoutrements, details such as balsam soap, and proximity to High Peaks adventures. On site there's also the delicious ADK Café (see page 127) as well as Dartbrook Rustic Goods (see page 159), where you can purchase pieces like the ones you'll covet in Dartbrook's cabins.

Keene Valley

Keene Valley Lodge (518-576-2003; www.keenevalleylodge.com; 1834 NY 73), from 1929 to 1949, was known as Beede Cottage; now it's a cozy inn with all the modern comforts in nine guest rooms. On the first floor of this big Italianate home, there's a suite with queen-size bed, full bath, and its own entrance. Most of the second-floor rooms have private baths and king-size beds, and all are furnished with antiques and hand-stitched quilts. A breakfast buffet is included in the rate.

Mountain Meadows Bed & Breakfast (518-576-4771; 1756 NY 73) is a haven for hikers, cross-country skiers, and rock climbers. The East Branch of the Ausable River curls through this property and the pointy

peak of Noonmark Mountain looms to the west. The bed & breakfast is actually two comfortable Adirondack-style houses that share a sunny deck. The bedroom wing has three large rooms that share two baths, with king-size beds that convert to twins. There's another chamber with private bath and a southern exposure. No credit cards.

Rooster Comb Inn (518-576-9916; www.roostercombinn.com; 3 Market Street), a lovely, colorful place, may be relatively new to the High Peaks, but the 19th-century home was one of the earliest boardinghouses around, taking in travelers when this area—in the late-1800s called Keene Flats—started attracting visitors. The inn, named after the peak just up the road, has a half-dozen rooms and is affordable and dog-friendly. Steve Bowers's Bald Mountain Rustics, very funky Adirondack-style furniture, is located on the premises.

Trail's End Inn (518-576-9860 or 1-800-281-9860; www.trailsendinn.com; 62 Trail's End Way), a gambrel-roofed house with eyebrow windows on a quiet road, calls itself a hikers' lodge, implying that the accommodations aren't so

Old Mountain Phelps

Legendary guide Orson Schofield Phelps, a.k.a. Old Mountain Phelps, named Skylight, Basin, Saddleback, Haystack, and Dial. He slashed the first trail up Mount Marcy 150 years ago, made plenty of first ascents and paths over Great Range peaks, and led an esteemed crew of 19th-century intellectuals above the forests, into the clouds. Winslow Homer captured Phelps and another guide in his 1875 oil *Two Guides*, now hanging at the Sterling and Francine Clark Art Institute, in Williamstown, Massachusetts, and the eccentric elfin guide was immortalized by writer Charles Dudley Warner in his 1878 *Atlantic Monthly* essay "The Primitive Man."

Courtesy of Keene Valley Library

Weddings: Adirondack Love

This is a popular region of the park to tie the knot. The sky—if you count mountain summits—is the limit: **Whiteface Mountain** (518-523-1655; www.whiteface.com) has a gondola that'll carry a wedding party into the clouds, and the High Peaks, depending on the size of your crew, make fine backdrops. **Heart Lake**, by Adirondak Loj (518-523-3441; www.adk.org), is a romantic spot; **Chapel Pond** in Keene is naturally beautiful; and some folks park their boats beneath Lake Placid's **Pulpit Rock**. There's also Jay's **covered bridge**; the **Mountain House** (www.mountainhouseadirondacks.com) on Keene's East Hill—with dramatic views of High Peaks; and **Great Camp Santanoni**, in Newcomb, though that historic place comes with a 10-mile round-trip trek on foot, horse, or bike. For more traditional venues that can accommodate hundreds of guests, Lake Placid's **Crowne Plaza Golf Club** (518-523-2556; www.lakeplacidcp.com) has super views, **Lake Placid Lodge** (518-523-2700; www.lakeplacidlodge.com) is posh, **Mirror Lake Inn Resort & Spa** (518-523-2544; www.mirrorlakeinn.com; 77 Mirror Lake Drive) is classy, **Whiteface Club & Resort** (518-523-2551; www.whitefaceclubresort.com) has lakeside charm, and **Whiteface Lodge** (518-523-0500; www.thewhitefacelodge.com) has every amenity you could ask for, including a bowling alley and movie theater.

The High Peaks is a popular wedding destination.

Courtesy of Mark Kurtz, www.markkurtzphotography.com

---

fancy that you need to worry about blow-drying your hair before you come to breakfast. Some guest rooms upstairs have fireplaces, private porches, and whirlpool tubs. There are four double rooms that share baths, plus a two-bedroom cottage—with kitchen and washer/dryer—that accommodates up to six guests and even a pet. Hiking clubs or family groups can take over the entire place, which holds about 40 comfortably. The bus stops every day at the Noon Mark Diner (see page 128), a five-minute walk away, and from the inn, there's easy access to Roostercomb and other peaks.

Lake Placid

The Haus (518-523-3005; www.thehauslp.com; 2439 Main Street), an "eco-chic boutique lodging" hidden along Lake Placid's Main Street, is more apartment rental than hotel. There's no elevator, no parking, no beach, no bar, spa, or restaurant, but no worries: The place is smack in the middle of the action with Mirror Lake out back, and eateries, shopping, and everything you could possibly need just out the door. Those who appreciate aesthetics, particularly a fresh take on Adirondack style, will dig this place. Nine elegantly designed suites offer various views, stainless-steel kitchens, hardwood floors, and can sleep from two to four people.

The Interlaken Inn (518-523-3180; www.theinterlakeninn.com; 15 Interlaken Avenue, around the corner from Mirror Lake Inn) has walnut-paneled walls, tin ceilings, a polished garnet fireplace, a winding staircase, and antiques that make it a true oasis. Built in 1912 by one of the founders of the Bank of Lake Placid, the secluded, high-end spot has been operated as an inn for most of its existence. There are seven lovely guest rooms, two suites, and a carriage house, most with queen-size beds, all with private baths—some with Jacuzzis or a clawfoot tub. Downstairs, the dining room is elegant yet casual. Off the living room is the cozy bar, where there's a pub menu and an extensive wine list. The inn makes an elegant backdrop for small weddings and other gatherings. Closed in April.

Lake Placid Lodge (518-523-2700; www.lakeplacidlodge.com; Whiteface Inn Road) was originally built as a summer home at the turn of the last century. The place opened as a hotel in 1946, and more than six decades—and a devastating fire—later, it's one of the most stylish, exclusive places in the region. The luxurious lodge's rooms, suites, cottages, and cabins are decked out in Adirondack Great Camp style, with handcrafted rustic furniture, crackling stone fireplaces, rich fabrics, and over-the-top accoutrements, and its pub and restaurant are among the best in the park. And then there's the lakeside pinch-me view. Guests can lounge on the property's sandy beach; help themselves to canoes, sailboards, pedal boats, and bicycles; or stroll to the beautiful, challenging 18-hole Whiteface Inn golf course.

Mirror Lake Inn Resort & Spa, in Lake Placid, is classy colonial. Courtesy of Mirror Lake Inn Resort & Spa

Mirror Lake Inn Resort & Spa (518-523-2544; www.mirrorlakeinn.com; 77 Mirror Lake Drive), on a hillside overlooking Mirror Lake, is a lovely hotel in the heart of town. The resort has five lodging buildings—three across the street from Mirror Lake and the other two by a small, private beach. All rooms are upscale, with mountain or lakeside views and fireplaces; suites are also available to accommodate families. The Colonial House Ultimate Suites on Mirror Lake are sensational, with fine furniture, Oriental rugs, cathedral ceilings, enormous living quarters, and marble tubs. Onsite is a nice restaurant, a cozy pub, and various nooks and crannies for guests to kick back in. And there's a spa: If your interest is relaxing, improving your skin, or launching a healthier lifestyle, the staff can help. The resort now hosts wedding receptions, and is an exceptional facility for conferences, with plenty of attractive meeting rooms for large or small groups.

Paradox Lodge (518-523-9078; www.paradoxlodge.com; 2169 Saranac Avenue) reopened as a cozy inn a century after Paradox Lodge was built, in 1899. Although the place has been scrubbed, rewired, replumbed, painted, and decorated with an eclectic jumble of antiques and art, the house's underlying character is handsomely intact. Four rooms, all with private baths, are upstairs. The Cedar Lodge has four elegantly rustic upscale rooms, each with

A Geography Lesson

The village of Lake Placid is on tiny Mirror Lake; the lake named Placid is slightly west of downtown and it's a big body of water with a trio of islands and gorgeous views.

The Epicurean Adirondacks

With a name that means "those who eat bark" in the Mohawk language, the Adirondacks might not seem a promising destination for gourmands. A smorgasbord of annual foodie events in the park proves otherwise.

At the high end is a pair of shoulder-season festivals sponsored by two of Lake Placid's finest hotels. In April, the AAA-rated four-diamond Mirror Lake Inn Resort & Spa (518-523-2544; www.mirrorlakeinn.com) uncorks its **Adirondack Festival of Food and Wine**: three days of seminars, interactive cooking demonstrations, and innovative tasting menus with guest chefs and sommeliers. The posh and cozy Lake Placid Lodge (518-523-2700; www.lakeplacidlodge.com) hosts a **Gastronomic Getaway** one weekend each October or November, and some years, in May. Expect champagne on arrival, face time in the kitchen with the chefs, and extravagant multicourse dinners.

Summer is the season for casual, family-friendly fare. Lake Placid's **I Love Barbecue Festival** (www.ilbbqf.com) is a three-day celebration of smoking, grilling, and music that attracts big players on the competitive barbecue circuit the first weekend in July.

Meanwhile, two events at Tupper Lake's Wild Center (518-359-7800; www.wildcenter.org) make the connection between what we eat and the natural world. At July's **BuzzFest**, insects are on the menu—intrepid eaters can sample creepy-crawly delicacies like fried scorpions and waxworm cookies. **FlavorFest**, in August, puts the focus on local, sustainable ingredients, with sampling stations, cooking demonstrations and live music, plus children's activities, such as making—and tasting—hand-cranked ice cream. (Read more about the Wild Center on page 104.)

—Lisa Bramen, from "The Epicurean Adirondacks," Adirondack Life

king-size bed, Jacuzzi tub, deck, gas fireplace, robes, and refrigerator. All rooms have air-conditioning and guests have access to Paradox Bay and the inn's watercraft. Downstairs are two cozy dining rooms. If you stay at Paradox, do not miss the opportunity to eat here—some would argue Chef Moses "Red" LaFountain makes the most fabulous food in the North Country (and his wife, Nan, who presents his creations, is extraordinarily nice). Closed in April and November.

The Stagecoach Inn (518-523-9698; www.lakeplacidstagecoachinn.com; 3 Stagecoach Way), built in 1833, is probably the oldest but loveliest spot in all of Lake Placid. The current owners rescued this historical stop along what was a well-traveled stagecoach route that brought abolitionists to John

Lake Placid's Stagecoach Inn has old-school charm. Courtesy of Nancie Battaglia

Brown's nearby North Elba farm. Today, the place is gorgeous with its polished dark woodwork, eclectic with his varied antiques and accoutrements, and charming with its fireplaces, narrow hallways, and stairwells. Four suites sleep anywhere from two to four people; a fine, complimentary breakfast is offered; and the inn's proximity to the Lake Placid Horse Show Grounds make this a sought-after—and recommended—getaway.

Van Hoevenberg Lodge and Cabins (518-523-9572; www.adklodging.com; 4529 Cascade Road) are owned and operated by Wayne Failing, a fantastic and respected New York State–licensed guide, who, if you hire him, will take you on the rafting trip, hiking trek, or fishing or hunting adventure of your life. Eight cabins and three guest rooms in the lodge would make accommodations appealing in any Adirondack setting, but the attraction at Failing's spread is its proximity to excellent cross-country skiing, hiking, and mountain biking—and pets are welcome. The cabins and lodge are next to the more than 50 kilometers of groomed tracks at the Olympic cross-country complex and connects with the Cascade Ski-Touring Center and Jackrabbit Trails. You can head into the High Peaks Wilderness Area without parking your car at a trailhead and afterward enjoy an invigorating wood-fired sauna.

The Whiteface Lodge (1-800-903-4045; www.thewhitefacelodge.com; 7 Whiteface Inn Lake) is a luxury resort that's appeared in all sorts of travel magazines, and in 2012 was included on *Condé Nast Traveler*'s Gold List, under "The World's Best Places to Stay." Although it isn't on waterfront or at the base of a mountain, there are nice views and the lodge itself is over-the-top in Adirondack-style detail and décor. The lodge has the feel of an elegant 19th-century Adirondack Great Camp, but with all the comforts of the modern

A well-appointed room at the Whiteface Lodge in Lake Placid. *Courtesy of The Whiteface Lodge*

world. It's also an extraordinary place for families with kids, with so many amenities and activities "on campus." Evening s'mores gatherings are a hit. The Whiteface Lodge operates as a resort hotel and private residence club—folks can buy full and partial ownership. Rooms are spacious and incredible—nothing has been overlooked here—and the resort includes a state-of-the-art spa, an outdoor boating club on Lake Placid, indoor and outdoor swimming pools, an outdoor skating rink, movie theater, bowling alley, bocce and tennis courts, and a separate facility with massive porch and banquet hall that makes a perfect backdrop for wedding receptions or other gatherings. The onsite bar and its fireplaces and couches are perfect for cocktails and conversation; the lodge's elegant Kanu restaurant is recommended for a romantic meal or special occasion.

Saranac Lake

Fogarty's Bed and Breakfast (518-891-3755 or 1-800-525-3755; www.adirondacks.com/fogarty; 74 Kiwassa Road) was built in 1910 as a cure cottage for tuberculosis patients. This attractive home overlooking Lake Flower has handsome woodwork, leaded-glass windows, wonderful porches, and five bedrooms. Although Fogarty's is a quick walk from Saranac Lake's business district and restaurants, it's in a peaceful

High Peaks Hostels

Save a night in a tent or lean-to, there are other affordable places to sleep in this region: **Adirondak Loj** (518-523-3441; www.adk.org; 1002 Adirondak Loj Road), in Lake Placid, has a sweeping panorama of Mount Marcy and Indian Pass, and the drive in sets you up for a visit to the Adirondack Mountain Club's (ADK) wilderness retreat. On Heart Lake in the midst of the High Peaks, the 1920s-era lodge is a rustic, comfortable place. In the living room, you can rock in an Old Hickory chair in front of the vast stone fireplace and choose from the shelves practically any book that's ever been written on the Adirondacks. Breakfast—the wake-up bell rings bright and early—is served buffet style, as is dinner, at picnic tables in an adjoining room. Bag lunches are available, and plain, home-cooked dinners are served when the lodge is busy. There are four private rooms, four bunkrooms, and a huge coed loft. The bunkrooms, which have four built-in log beds, are snug and cozy, like cabins on a ship; the loft can be a hard place to get a good night's sleep if there are any snorers in the crowd. You don't need to be a member of ADK to stay at the Loj, but you must make advance reservations. On Heart Lake are two cabins that accommodate four to 16 people during the fall, winter, and spring. For the intrepid traveler, ADK has three excellent backcountry cabins that are accessible by foot—all are a 3.5-mile hike in from Keene Valley: **Johns Brook Lodge**, which is open Memorial Day through Columbus Day (in July and August you can get two hot meals and bag lunches here); and **Grace Camp** and **Camp Peggy O'Brien**, which are open year-round and have tiers of bunks, gas lights, and propane heat; they're excellent bases for hiking, snowshoe, or ski weekends.

Mount Marcy.
Courtesy of Ted Comstock, Saranac Lake

High Peaks Hostel (518-523-4951; www.highpeakshostel.com; 5956 Sentinel Road), also in Lake Placid, offers clean, convenient lodging at its off-the-main-tourist-drag headquarters. For $40 you get a bed (with sheets), towels, and breakfast (the cost includes tax). Be sure to make a reservation in advance to save a bunk, as the place is popular with outing clubs, scout troops, college crews, and other groups. At press time the place is for sale, but the owners have booked visitors through the fall and hope a buyer will continue operating the hostel.

Again in Lake Placid, though away from the village on Route 73, is **TMax-n-Topo's Hostel** (518-523-0123; www.tmax-n-topo.com; 5046 Cascade Road), en route to Keene, where you can get a bunk for $28, plus tax, per night. Four bunkrooms can accommodate up to 33 people, and, upstairs are private rooms. The owners know just about everything about recreation in this parts.

Keene Valley Hostel (518-576-2030; www.keenevalleyhostel.com; 1755 Route 73) is a great spot in the middle of the High Peaks action. It's $25 for a night in the bunkhouse (linens and towels provided), and you can book a shuttle that'll deliver you to Adirondak Loj, the Garden parking lot, Newcomb, or beyond.

neighborhood and has a dock on the lake for swimmers and boaters. Winter guests note that cross-country skiing at Dewey Mountain is about a mile away, and in early February, when the winter carnival is in full swing, you can look over to the fabulous ice palace on the opposite shore of the lake. An important Fogarty's feature: Because the house is set on a steep hillside, you've got to climb a lot of steps—73 to be exact—to get to the entrance. No credit cards.

The Porcupine (518-891-5160; www.theporcupine.com; 350 Park Avenue), designed by architect William Coulter, was built for Thomas Bailey Aldrich, *Atlantic Monthly* editor, author of *The Story of a Bad Boy,* and friend of Mark Twain. The name "Porcupine" isn't some cute modern affectation: This massive six-gabled, gambrel-roofed house acquired that title in the early 1900s because "it had so many good points and because it was occupied by a quill driver"—the quill driver being author Aldrich. He brought his wife and sons to Saranac Lake not on some vacation whim but because one of his twin sons had tuberculosis, and the family hoped that the fresh mountain air and good doctors at nearby Trudeau Sanatorium could cure him. Sadly, the young man died. Nowadays, a happier chapter has unfolded for this grand home. With plenty of elbow grease and lots of enthusiasm, the place opened as a bed & breakfast. Downstairs is a comfortable living room with fireplace, as well as a billiards room and wine bar. Five spacious guest rooms are on the second floor, up the beautiful Jacobean-style staircase. All have private baths; most have glassed-in "cure porches," an architectural element dating back to the days when TB patients were made to sleep in unheated rooms, swaddled in blankets. Breakfast is served in a big, bright dining area. An outdoor hot tub allows for soaking and relaxing in all weather.

Saranac Lake Inn, a.k.a. Gauthier's (518-891-1950; www.saranaclakeinn .com; 488 Lake Flower Avenue), is a green success story. That is, new owners took a tired Depression-era lakefront motel and turned it into eco-conscious lodging. Among their practices: Only nontoxic, biodegradable cleaners are used in rooms; guests are offered organic Fair Trade coffee and tea purchased from local vendors; low-flow showerheads and compact fluorescent light bulbs have been installed; the pool is solar heated; and no pesticides and chemicals are used on the grounds, which are landscaped with native plants. Gauthier's is right on Lake Flower, which means guests can take its canoes or paddleboats for a spin.

Wilmington

Willkommen Hof Bed & Breakfast (518-946-SNOW or 1-800-541-9119; www.willkommenhof.com; 5367 NY 86) is a European-style guesthouse within a one-minute walk of the Ausable River's spectacular flume. The B&B has three rooms with private baths, a three-room suite, and three rooms that share baths, to house a maximum of 24 guests. Full breakfasts and after-ski treats are included in the room rate; hearty dinners may be arranged. World-famous trout waters are nearby, as are numerous state-marked trails for cross-country skiing, mountain biking, and hiking. (The innkeepers Heike and Bert Yost can suggest trips off the beaten path on foot or by bike, or guests can book Bert, a licensed guide, for an outdoor excursion.) Willkommen Hof is popular with Whiteface Mountain downhill skiers because it's just minutes away from the slopes. After all that exertion, guests can wind down in either the outdoor hot tub or indoor sauna. Closed April 15 through May 15; October 15 through November 15.

MORE LODGING

In Lake Placid, in the center of town, the Adirondack Inn by the Lake (518-523-2424; www.adirondack-inn.com; 2625 Main Street) has a heated indoor pool; whirlpool; sauna; and exercise room. Golden Arrow Lakeside Resort (518-523-3353; www.golden-arrow.com; 2559 Main Street) is an eco-friendly modern motor inn along Main Street on the lakefront with a health club, a heated pool, a private beach, and all nonsmoking rooms. Comfort Inn (518-523-9555; www.comfortinn.com; 2125 Saranac Avenue) is a pet-friendly hotel across the street from the delicious Saranac Sourdough; a half-mile or so walk away from downtown Lake Placid; and close to Peninsula hiking/skiing trails. Crowne Plaza Resort & Golf Club (518-523-2556; www.lakeplacidcp .com; 101 Olympic Drive) overlooks the Olympic Arena and Mirror Lake; has a heated pool, sauna, and whirlpool; access to Jackrabbit cross-country-ski trails; two championship golf courses; a health club; a lake view; a restaurant and lounge. The historic Northwoods Inn (518-523-1818; www.northwoodsinn .com; 2520 Main Street) anchors downtown and has an on-site restaurant and bar. Prague Motor Inn (518-523-3410; www.praguemotorinn.net; 6048 Sentinel Road) is a quiet, folksy mom-and-pop, pet-friendly place with a Queen Anne–style house in front of the motel units.

In North Hudson the Blue Ridge Falls Campground (518-532-7863; www.blueridgefallscampsite.com; 3493 Blue Ridge Road), closed in winter, is inexpensive, has a pool, and is a quick walk to waterfalls.

Ray Brook has the Sherwood Forest Motor Inn (518-891-4400; www.sher woodforestmotorinn.com; 15 Knotingham Road), not a motel at all but nice one- and two-bedroom housekeeping cabins, just off the busy highway and by the Tail O' the Pup restaurant (see page 130). Most cabins have wood-burning fireplaces and views of a pretty little pond.

Saranac Lake's the Lake Flower Inn (518-891-2310; www.lakeflowerinn .com; 234 Lake Flower Avenue) is a clean, tidy motel with pleasant grounds, boat dockage, a swimming pool, and a picnic area; pets are welcome with a fee.

Wilmington's Hungry Trout Resort (518-946-2217; www.hungrytrout.com; 5239 NY 86) is a motel with great views and close proximity to Whiteface Mountain, a nice restaurant, and R. F. McDougal's Tavern. There's onsite guide service that offers fly-fishing lessons, and a tackle shop, plus the resort owns a super stretch of the Ausable River.

Local Flavors

Where to eat in the High Peaks & Northern Adirondacks

If you like your meal seasoned with a stunning view, you've come to the right place. This part of the park doesn't lack for options, but it helps to know which ones don't reach for the Sysco cans or freezer bags when it comes time to prep your feast. The following are picked for quality of eats as well as ambience.

Keene

The ADK Café (518-576-9111; www.the adkcafe.com; 2835 Route 73), a new addition to Keene, is part of the Dartbrook compound at the intersection of Routes 9N and 73 that includes Great Camp–style cabins and the Adirondackana showroom Dartbrook Rustic Goods. ADK stands for "A Delicious Kitchen," an apt description for this one-room roadside restaurant and outdoor deck, with its mouth-watering meals and baked goods. Co-owner Fiona Burns calls it simple, fresh, from-scratch food. Breakfasts are hearty; sweet potato chili and Reuben or white-bean-spread sandwiches are popular lunches; and Guinness beef stew, chicken potpie, and meat loaf are recommended dinners. A vegan Earth Plate—beans, grains, and veggies—is always on the menu; hand-stretched flatbread pizzas, "flatizzas," can be ordered to go. Ingredients are sourced locally: pasture-raised meat from Kilcoyne Farms, just outside of the Blue Line; vegetables from area growers.

Baxter Mountain Tavern (518-576-9990; www.baxtermountaintavern.com; 10050 NY 9N) is casual and comfortable, with an overstuffed couch facing a stone fireplace, a bar, and a simple dining room with a view of Hurricane Mountain. Settle in with a beer after hiking Baxter Mountain, whose trailhead is just down the road. Every day there's a ravioli special. Save room for dessert, which is always made on the premises.

Cedar Run Bakery and Market (518-576-9929; www.cedarrunbakery.com; 2 Gristmill Lane), a local hot spot open 7 to 7 every day, is a delicious and convenient option in this teensy mountain town. Although there are a couple of café tables inside and outside, most folks grab their muffins, scones, bagels, soup, and sandwiches to go. Everything here is fresh and tasty. This is where you can buy gourmet chips or chocolate, local artisan cheeses, or a fine cup of coffee; the market's coolers are stocked with scrumptious take-and-bake meals and desserts. And the attached wine and spirits shop has a good selection.

Keene Valley

Noon Mark Diner (518-576-4499; www.noonmarkdiner.com; NY 73/Main Street) accommodates High Peaks backpackers to investment bankers to kids on bikes who come to stoke up on homemade baked goods, soups, French fries, and whatever else is on the menu. You can order breakfast any time, if you're not up for the chili or a cheeseburger. Dinners lean toward frozen things popped into the deep fryer, such as clams or shrimp, but soup, salad, and potatoes or rice come with any choice. After a long day in the outdoors, try the lasagna or broccoli quiche, and then order some homemade pie (worth a visit for coconut cream alone, though Noon Mark does have a mail-order pie busi-

ness). An ice-cream stand is off to one side of the huge front porch (open seasonally), if you want some walk-around dessert. This diner can be jammed on summer weekends, with a half-hour wait for a table and another half hour before your meal is served.

Lake Placid

Caffè Rustica (518-523-7511; www.caffe rustica.com; 1936 Saranac Avenue, in the Price Chopper Plaza) may be a pocket-size place in the Price Chopper plaza, but there are delicious rustic Italian/Mediterranean meals to be had in this little café, prepared by the capable hands of Kevin Gregg. Try the *fungi misti* pizza (mushrooms, Taleggio, mixed greens, rosemary, truffle oil, and garlic) or the *gnocchi alla rustica* (lemon basil pesto, sun-dried tomatoes, wilted greens, and feta cheese). You just can't go wrong here. This isn't the place to go if you're hoping for a private dinner—tables are close together, like at crammed-in city restaurants. But this is where you go for a fine lunch or dinner. Gregg and his team are also popular local caterers. Or you can arrange to have a private shindig in the café's backroom.

Chair 6 (518-523-3630; www.chair6 .com; 5993 Sentinel Road) is the sort of place that makes you feel, once you find it, like a Placid insider. All the meals are super—roasted quail, pumpkin risotto, the smoked trout quesadilla, quinoa and golden beet salad, or braised pork shank—either to go or served in the teensy dining room. The fare is always fresh, and it changes seasonally with the local ingredients the chefs incorporate. The Why Not Wednesday dinners are a staple among area gourmands: For $20 you choose an app, a main plate, a dessert, and a glass of wine. Why not?

The Cowboy (518-837-5069; www .placidcowboy.com; 2226 Saranac Avenue) is the chef-owned offspring of the Caribbean Cowboy, which recently closed its cramped Saranac Avenue space, streamlined its name, and moved up the road. The funky Caribbean vibe is pretty much gone, but you can still get tasty cocktails—try the rum-infused Painkiller—plus jerk chicken and other delicious dinners, even sushi—from the creative kitchen. The freshly made Key lime pie is sublime.

Interlaken Inn (1-800-428-4369; www.theinterlakeninn.com; 39 Interlaken Avenue) is a grand old small hotel tucked into a peaceful downtown neighborhood. This place has fantastic food for the classy dining room and the informal pub (in the latter there's a stamped-tin ceiling and an elegant bas relief of trees—not many restaurants or inns would do this kind of detail in a public space, kind of like the detail put into the food itself). In the pub, try the crab cakes with orange basic beurre blanc; or the pulled pork sandwich with maple barbecue sauce and *pommes frites*. There's an excellent wine and beer list, too. In the dining room, entrées, depending on the season, include grilled Kilcoyne Farm steak with sweet potato purée, garlic baguette, and wild mushroom veal jus; or black mustard seed–crusted diver scallops with roasted beets and herb vinaigrette. Desserts, such as the rosemary phyllo-wrapped crème brûlée, are scrumptious.

Lake Placid Lodge (518-523-2700; www.lakeplacidlodge.com; Whiteface Inn Road) is one of finest, most elegant restaurants in the Adirondacks. The décor is Great Camp posh, the view stunning, and dining here means the chance to be at a Relais & Châteaux property without busting the bank. In Maggie's Pub, try the poached scallops or cheese and charcuterie plate. Entrées in the lodge's Artisans restaurant range from sumac-dusted beef strip loin, with smoked potato, glazed beets, pickled scallion, and foie gras demi; to grilled quail with braised endive, root vegetable, salted potato and port jus; or acorn squash *agnolotti* with Brussels sprouts, brown butter, and crème fraîche.

Liquids and Solids at the Handlebar (518-837-5012; www.liquidsand solids.com; 6115 Sentinel Road), a relatively new farm-to-fork gastropub, attracts foodies from afar. The vibe is hip and happening and the place is pretty small, so you might have to wait a while for a table or a spot at the bar, where mixologist Keegan concocts funky cocktails like her cilantro daiquiri, Balsamic Fizz, or guava margarita. The fried Brussels sprouts are amazing, and there's always a *poutine* special. Fresh, seasonal food is featured on the Smalls and Bigs menus, such as smoked pig belly in a blanket, or saffron cavatelli, or salt cod fritters, or steak tartare. Chances are good kids won't appreciate what's served here; don't come if you're looking for quick, traditional fare.

Lisa G's (518-523-2093; www.lisags .com; 6125 Sentinel Road) advertises "Comfort food with a modern twist." That's not the only reason diners love this place: There's its proprietor's friendliness (Lisa G. is usually greeting, chatting, serving); its off–Main Street former opera-house digs; and its roomy deck out back along the Chubb River. Meals can be pizza, like one with fried green tomatoes or topped with garlic, oyster mushrooms, rosemary, fontina cheese, and truffle oil. Four kinds of chicken wings include Greek-style or atomic hot, and there's a daily burger special. The dining room will accommodate an entire outing club, while the bar has smaller tables and comfy couches. Closed Tuesdays.

Veranda (518-523-3339; 1 Olympic Drive across from the Crowne Plaza hotel), a grand restaurant in a gracious old home, features Chef Claude Gaucher's delicious and classically prepared dinners. This place is worth a special trip, and eating on the deck is heavenly. A stunning panorama of the Sentinel Range marches across your

Courtesy of Lake Placid Pub & Brewery

Lake Placid Pub & Brewery (518-523-3813; www.ubuale.com; 813 Mirror Lake Drive), also known as P.J.'s, is home to good fare, from ribs to quesadillas to specialty burgers. But the draw here is the brews—a half dozen ales and beers on tap at all times, some brewed in the back of the restaurant, including the very popular Ubu Ale and Lake Placid IPA. Demand for these suds has increased so much that the Ubu you buy at the supermarket is now crafted in Utica.

field of view, with a bit of Mirror Lake in the foreground. Menu choices are tried-and-true examples of French country cuisine. Appetizers are all delectable, with excellent escargot and jumbo shrimp amandine. The many entrées include duck breast, broiled sea bass, grilled rosemary lamb, aged steaks, and, in summer, superb bouillabaisse. Desserts, such as apple tart and Paris-Brest (puff paste with hazelnut cream), are all made in the Veranda's kitchen. The wine list is extensive. Closed Mondays.

Ray Brook

Tail O' the Pup (518-891-0777; www .tailofthepupbbq.com; NY 86) has served happy travelers with its winning combination of good, cheap food, and come-as-you-are atmosphere for more than eight decades. You can eat at a picnic table beneath a huge tent or inside at a booth. Bring the kids—they'll love it here. The ribs and chicken are good,

as are the waffle fries, baked beans, corn on the cob, and a minuscule dab of pretty good coleslaw. You can also get steamed clams or whole lobster for bargain prices, plus hot dogs, of course, for which this landmark is named. Onion rings are just the way they should be, crunchy and sweet. About half a dozen good imported and domestic beers are on tap. Open mid-May through mid-October.

Saranac Lake

Blue Moon Café (518-891-1310; blue mooncafe-adk.com; 46 Main Street) at breakfast means homemade bread and English muffins accompanying Greek omelets (with feta and spinach) and home fries. Regulars dig into bowls of steel-cut oats with a side of blueberries. At lunch, soups, burgers, and sandwiches are all made fresh; dinners, including Asian-influenced rice or noodle bowls with fresh vegetables, are reasonably priced and delicious. There's a small bar in the back dining room, and a friendly neighborhood vibe.

Eat-N-Meet Grill & Larder (518-891-3149; www.eatnmeet.com; 139 Broadway), on Upper Broadway, is an unexpected surprise, though if you're driving past you can't miss the place, with its life-size plastic Elvis posing on the front sidewalk. Inside is a busy meal counter where you place your order and pick it up; three or so modest tables; and a larder with walls of exotic condiments, like mega-jars of saffron. Proprietors John (who is also the chef) and Colleen Vargo subscribe to the slow-food movement, which means a constantly changing menu of fresh local seasonal fare cooked long, carefully, and to perfection. Dishes range from gyros to Jamaican curried goat stew to Chesapeake oyster stew to tacos to huge salads to pork schnitzel sandwiches to fresh fish cooked as you choose. Slow food also translates to . . . well, slow food, so if you're ravenous, call in your order

Eat-N-Meet Grill & Larder, in Saranac Lake, is an offbeat and exceptional place for great food. Courtesy of Nancie Battaglia

ahead or, once you're there, play a complimentary round or two of mini golf at Eat-N-Meet's adjacent nine-hole course while you wait. And the place is BYOB. There's no industrial-size dishwasher in the tiny kitchen, so all meals are served in take-out containers with plastic eating utensils.

The Left Bank Café (518-354-8166; www.leftbankcafe36.com; 34 Broadway) brings back a delicious French vibe to Saranac Lake. (Some four decades ago, this was a bakery of the same name, run by the father of Kenneth Weissberg, who now operates this place. The Weissbergs also own the Maison des Adirondacks bed & breakfast in Entrains-Sur-Nohain, France.) Breakfasts are croissants and crepes; lunches are panini and soups and salads; dinner may be tapas with wine; and there's always fine coffee to be sipped and savored in this rich, earthy space with dark polish wood—or skinny deck overlooking the Saranac River. The cuisine may be international, but the vibe is all community: The work of local painters, jewelry makers, and musicians is often featured here.

Little Italy Pizzeria (518-891-9000; 23 Main Street) appears to be a simple pizza joint, but is much more. Venture beyond the front counter and booths in this Saranac institution—this is, after all,

the town's number one take-out/delivery pizza place—and you'll find yourself in a spacious dining room with Old Country décor and tables that accommodate parties from two to 20. What you'll get here is straight-up Italian fare—no pretension, no nonsense. Just ziti, manicotti, lasagna, chicken Parmesan, spaghetti with meatballs, gnocchi, ravioli, fettuccine Alfredo—all the standards. No credit cards.

Wilmington

The Hungry Trout (518-946-2217; www.hungrytrout.com; 5239 NY 86) is perched along a mile-long section of the legendary West Branch of the Ausable River. This motel/restaurant/fly shop complex has fine views of Whiteface Mountain and a foaming waterfall can be seen from the dining room—the view upstages the food. The menu is extensive, with numerous trout (farm-raised) dishes, plus quality lamb, steaks, pasta, chicken, and salmon. If you'd like to sample this spot but prefer not to spend a bundle, try the tavern on the ground floor, R. F. McDougall's (as in Rat Face McDougall, a trout fly). It's casual, with antique woodsy/sporty décor, a long bar, comfortable booths, a lighter menu (excellent charbroiled burgers), and lots of good beers on hand. Sometimes closed in March and April.

MORE MEALS

Asgaard Farm & Dairy (www.asgaard farm.com; 74 Asgaard Way), in Au Sable Forks, makes absolutely delectable caramels and award-winning farmstead cheeses. In Lake Placid, the Taste Bistro at Mirror Lake Inn Resort & Spa (518-302-3000; www.mirrorlakeinn.com; 77 Mirror Lake Drive) is comfy and classy—you can order a fine glass of wine or microbrew with *pommes frites*, teriyaki prawns, or a Black Angus burger. (The resort's Cottage, across the road, is a lively spot with a nice outdoor deck, but the kitchen is limited, so it's best just for a cocktail and sandwich or salad.) The Breakfast Club, Etc. (518-523-0007; 2490 Main Street) isn't some greasy spoon but a place for imaginative, delicious breakfasts—and all sorts of Bloody Marys and mimosas—all day long. Brown Dog Deli & Wine Bar (518-523-3036; 3 Main Street) offers sophisticated bare-table bistro lunch and dinner options. Downtown Diner (518-523-3709; 2728 Main Street) has good breakfasts (and doesn't take credit cards), the wait staff appears to be part of a *Girl with the Dragon Tattoo* casting call, and Bruce Springsteen has been known to pop in. Open May through November, the Lake Placid Club Boathouse (518-523-4822), on Mirror Lake, has good meals and gorgeous scenery. Nicola's on Main Mediterranean Cuisine & Grill 211 (518-523-5853; www.nicolasandgrill211.com; 211 Main Street) is the massive restaurant across from the Olympic Center. The food is good here, and Nicola's makes its own mozzarella and other cheese. Nicola's Mediterranean Cuisine is served in the dining room on the left; Grill 211, which is pricier, is on the right. Saranac Sourdough (518-523-4897; 2126 Saranac Avenue, across from Howard Johnson's) has delicious deli-style sandwiches and subs; soups and salads; and baked goods. Simply Gourmet (518-523-3111; www.simplygourmetlakeplacid.com; 1983 Saranac Avenue) is simply delicious for an upscale breakfast or deli lunch—as is its sister site, Big Mountain Deli & Creperie (518-523-3222; 2475 Main), by the library on Main Street. Villa Vespa (518-523-9789; www.villavespa.net; 2250 Saranac Avenue) carries homemade Italian sauces, frozen and dried pastas, and ready-to-heat entrées that generally include chicken cacciatore, sole, and a meat-based special. The ravioli—about 3 inches in diameter—are wonderful.

In Saranac Lake, the Adirondack Bean-To (518-891-2932; 12 Shepard Avenue) has the best coffee drinks; its Hammer Down blend is organic and Fair Trade. Donnelly's, open Memorial Day through Labor Day, is, without a doubt, the place for soft-service ice cream (518-891-1404; intersection of NY 86 and 186). Lakeview Deli (518-891-2101; www.lakeviewdeli.com; 137 River Street) is where to go for a quick lunch in the Adirondacks' All-America City. In summer, boaters crisscross Lake Flower for the soft ice cream at Mountain Mist Custard (518-891-000; 260 Lake Flower Avenue). Nori's Village Market (518-891-6079; www.norisvillagemarket.com; 68 Main Street) has a natural foods deli with daily lunch specials and excellent salads, plus all you'd expect from a good health food store.

Paul Johnson's Bakery at Standard Falls Iris Gardens (518-578-1676), in Upper Jay, is an idyllic country setting along the Ausable River, with delicious baked goods, lunches, and dinners. Dine in or take out and always call ahead to check days and hours.

In Wilmington, At the River's Edge Emporium (518-586-1718; www.theriversedgeemporium.com; 1179 Haselton Road) has tasty, healthful sandwiches and soups and other natural and organic foods. The bartender at the Wilderness Inn II (518-946-2391; www.wildernessinnadk.com; 5481 NY 86)—the place along NY 86 bedecked year-round in holiday lights—knows how to make a fine mixed drink; light fare ordered in the bar, such as the chicken and fish sandwiches, is recommended, but if you want traditional meat and potatoes, hunker down in the dining room in front of the fireplace.

Several area farmers' markets are exceptional places to find local produce, as well as crafts and other items. In Au Sable Forks, the market happens Fridays from June through August in Riverside Park. In Keene, it's Sundays from June through October on Marcy Field, between Keene and Keene Valley. Lake Placid's market is Wednesdays, June through October, at the Lake Placid Center for the Arts. Saranac Lake's is Saturdays, from June through October, at Riverside Park. Learn more about these farmers' markets as well as other ones in the Adirondacks at www.adirondackharvest.com.

To Do

Attractions and activities in the High Peaks & Northern Adirondacks

Winslow Homer painted woodsmen in Keene Valley. Harold Weston, who lived most of his life in Keene Valley, made bold, burly oils of the High Peaks that were exhibited widely from the 1920s to the 1970s, and now reside in major collections throughout the world. Rockwell Kent spent his last decades at his farm in Au Sable Forks, painting the Ausable River Valley and designing houses for friends. Composers Charles Ives and Béla Bartók both spent extended periods working in the Adirondacks. Ives created the "Concord" Sonata while visiting Elk Lake, and began the "Universe" Symphony, one of his last major works, while at the summer home of his wife's family, in Keene Valley. Bartók wrote the Concerto for Orchestra at a modest cottage in Saranac Lake, where he was taking the cure for tuberculosis. And Robert Louis Stevenson worked on his *The Master of Ballantrae,* among other pieces, while taking the cure at a Saranac Lake cottage. These hills are still alive with artists—musicians, dancers, writers, painters, actors—and cultural centers that support their work and encourage others to appreciate it.

ARCHITECTURE

Rustic lodges and boathouses in all their twiggy glory are mainly on remote lakeshores, but you can visit Great Camp Santanoni Preserve near Newcomb. It requires a 10-mile round trip without a car, but it's well worth the effort. You can reach the impressive rustic complex by walking, cross-country skiing, snowshoeing, biking, or riding a horse-drawn wagon.

The Ausable River Valley holds many historic buildings that are visible along roadways. South of Keene Valley, it's worth a quick detour off NY 73 at Saint Hubert's to see the massive Victorian inn, the Ausable Club. It is "members

The architecture of Great Camp Santanoni, in Newcomb, is classic Adirondack.
Courtesy of Nancie Battaglia

only" inside the building, but you can get a rare glimpse of the kind of hostelry that visitors once enjoyed throughout the Adirondacks. North on US 9, between Upper Jay, Jay, and Au Sable Forks, there are fine Federal-style stone and brick houses and churches; in Jay, the sole remaining covered bridge in the Adirondacks, built in 1857, was dismantled in 1997 and rebuilt with an adjacent park (John Fountain Road, ½ mile off NY 9N).

The Olympic Village—Lake Placid, that is—has only a few buildings left from its earliest days, when the settlement of North Elba, near the ski jumps, was an iron-mining center: One that's easy to spot on Old Military Road is the Stagecoach Inn. Another, off Old Military, is John Brown's Farm (518-523-3900; 115 John Brown Road). In 1849, abolitionist John Brown came to North Elba to help Gerrit Smith foster a self-sufficient enclave for free black citizens. Smith owned more than 100,000 acres across northern New York, and his plan was to give 40 acres to each would-be African American homesteader. The idea may have been doomed from the start since the families—many of them from northern cities—were not prepared to farm in the harsh climate or work the rugged, unprepared ground. Most of the residents of "Timbuctoo," as it became known, left within a few years of their

Abolitionist John Brown's farm in North Elba.
Courtesy of John DiGiacomo, www.placidtimesphotography.com

arrival. Brown lived only a few years at the farm, leaving his family for months at a time to pursue a failing wool business and work on antislavery concerns. After his final adventure in Harpers Ferry, Virginia (modern-day West Virginia), Brown was executed on December 2, 1859. In 1870, the property was acquired by a group of the abolitionist's admirers. Today the farmhouse and outbuildings, managed by New York as a state historic site, contain exhibits related to John Brown's life, and his "body lies a-mouldering in the grave" nearby. Brown's birthday, May 1, brings a major gathering of people to the site sponsored by the Westport-based group John Brown Lives! (www.johnbrownlives.org).

In Saranac Lake, which was incorporated in 1892, the tuberculosis industry inspired its own architecture, manifested in "cure porches" and "cure cottages." The group Historic Saranac Lake (518-891-4606; www.historicsaranaclake.org) sponsors lectures, concerts, and tours from time to time, highlighting buildings of note; ongoing restoration projects include the cure cottage used by composer Béla Bartók and the 1894 laboratory of tuberculosis pioneer Dr. E. L. Trudeau.

Saranac Lake is also where you can see the Robert Louis Stevenson Memorial Cottage and Museum (518-891-1462; www.robertlouisstevensonmemorialcottage .org; 44 Stevenson Lane). Robert Louis Stevenson took the cure for TB here from 1887 to 1888. He slept in an unheated porch all winter and took in plenty of fresh air while hiking and skating. During his Adirondack stint, Stevenson wrote a dozen essays for *Scribner's Monthly,* started *The Master of Ballantrae,* and worked on *The Wrong Box,* a collaborative effort with Lloyd Osbourne. In a letter to Henry James, the Scotsman described his tiny cottage: "Our house . . . is on a hill, and has sight of a stream turning a corner in the valley—bless the face of running water!—and sees some hills too, and the paganly prosaic roofs of Saranac itself; the Lake it does not see, nor do I regret that; I like water (fresh water, I mean) either running swiftly among stones, or else largely qualified with whiskey." The Stevenson Society was founded in 1916 to commemorate the writer's life and works; one of the group's original projects was to interest Gutzon Borglum, the sculptor best known for creating Mount Rushmore, in designing a bronze bas-relief depicting Stevenson—now displayed next to the cottage's front door. The society still manages the property and museum, which has displays of Stevenson letters, photographs, memorabilia, and first editions, and sponsors readings and lectures. It's open July 1 through Columbus Day, Tuesday through Sunday, 9:30–noon, 1–4, or year-round by appointment; admission is $5.

North of Newcomb on County Road 25, en route to the Upper Works trailhead for the High Peaks, is the Adirondack Iron and Steel Company's blast furnace, an immense stone monolith built in 1854 that produced high-quality iron. Continuing on the road, you'll pass a faded white farmhouse that was the office of an early iron-mining concern. (The other deserted buildings nearby belonged to the 1890s Tahawus Club.)

ARTS CENTERS AND ARTS COUNCILS

Bluseed Studios (518-891-3799; www.bluseedstudios.org; 24 Cedar Street, Saranac Lake) has been home to a bustling arts scene for a decade. This 7,000-square-foot 1930s train warehouse is an oasis for artists and the community. Between its must-see exhibitions, studio space, weekend and one-day workshops—everything from printmaking and letterpress to ceramics and photography—and eclectic music series that features regional and national performers, such as Eliza Gilkyson, the Honey Dewdrops, and Martin Sexton, and every musical genre you can think of, the place is hopping all year. Bluseed's popular "open-minded" mic nights draw all sorts of entertainers.

Lake Placid Center for the Arts (518-523-2512; www.lakeplacidarts.org; 17 Algonquin Drive, Lake Placid) is a multiarts center with a community focus, and the facility is topnotch. It boasts a theater that seats about 300; well-equipped studios; and a bright, airy gallery. Exhibitions are slated throughout the year, including juried shows for regional artists and craftspeople. Presentations include visiting theater groups; contemporary American and foreign films; folk, blues, and Zydeco music; dance-company residencies; gala programs by soloists of the New York City Ballet; and excellent classical and chamber performances. The Lake Placid Sinfonietta plays here on Sunday evenings in July and August. The LPCA also is home to the Community Theatre Players, who offer three or four shows annually. For kids, in July and August, there's the free "Young and Fun" performance series on weekday mornings.

Upper Jay Art Center (518-946-8315; www.upperjayartcenter.com; Recovery Lounge, Upper Jay Upholstery, NY 9N, Upper Jay) was, at first, an underground scene—locals gathering at brothers Scott and Byron Renderer's Upper Jay Upholstery

Lady in the Lake

In 1963, a group of divers, exploring caves more than 100 feet below the surface of Lake Placid, discovered the body of 56-year-old Mabel Smith Douglass, founder and former dean of the New Jersey College for Women at New Brunswick. Douglass, who had disappeared from her Camp Onondoga on the west shore of the lake 30 years earlier for reasons that are still a mystery—though most sources allege she had committed suicide—was found remarkably intact, probably because of the depth and extreme coldness of her resting place. At press time, the movie *Dancehall*, written and directed by Tennyson Bardwell and starring Ellen Burstyn and Stephen Lang—based on Bernard F. Conners's novel of the same name, loosely inspired by the lady in the lake—was filming around Lake Placid.

to hear the Renderers' band Monsterbuck and their friends play music. But nowadays, the shop's 1920s former Model-T factory headquarters, just across the Ausable River from what was the Land of Makebelieve theme park, is a thriving nonprofit arts organization drawing culture seekers. The Renderers turned their funky, cavernous space, called the Recovery Lounge in the hours they aren't upholstering furniture, into an arts center. There are impromptu performances by regional and national acts as well as Arts Nights, drawing hundreds of people to see paintings, sculpture, and films, often by local artists, some of whom are nationally recognized, such as photographer Nathan Farb and painters Harold Weston and Paul Matthews. Recent theater productions at the Recovery Lounge include Michael Hollinger's *Opus*, Patrick Meyers's *K2*, and Sam Shepard's *True West*. On Sunday afternoons in January locals bring their fiddles, guitars, or whatever and jam the winter blues away.

CINEMA

In 1941, Alfred Hitchcock's only comedy, *Mr. and Mrs. Smith,* was set at the Lake Placid Club. A few years later, *Lake Placid Serenade,* which featured dizzying reels of figure skating and Roy Rogers as king of the Placid winter carnival, was a commercial success. In 1958, scenes of *Marjorie Morningstar* were shot in Schroon Lake; local extras were paid the princely sum of $125 per day.

Today, there are many places where you can catch foreign, classic, and first-run films. Several vintage theaters have been lovingly restored in recent years. The Lake Placid Film Forum (518-523-3456; www.lakeplacidfilmforum.com) runs a silent-film series using the Palace Theater and its magnificent Robert Morton theater organ. The Film Forum, held in early June each year, also has screenings, panel discussions, and workshops in various Lake Placid venues led by critics, screenwriters, actors, and directors. Participants have included Steve Buscemi, Kyra Sedgwick, Martin Scorsese, Russell Banks, among others.

Hollywood Theatre (518-647-5953; Main Street, Au Sable Forks) is a restored two-screen art deco theater that shows recent releases and independent films.

Lake Placid Center for the Arts (518-523-2512; www.lakeplacidarts.org; Saranac Avenue, Lake Placid) presents foreign and contemporary American film series in fall, winter, and spring.

Palace Theater (518-523-9271; Main Street, Lake Placid) runs current American releases on four screens.

DANCE

In the fall, the sensual and athletic Elisa Monte Dance (www.elisamontedance.org) spends three weeks in residence at the Lake Placid Center for the Arts. The arts center also presents modern dance concerts, including stars of the New York City Ballet, throughout the year.

In 2011, contemporary dance ensemble Rebecca Kelly Ballet (www.rebecca kellyballet.com) made Au Sable Forks its summer base—NYC's Soho is its home the rest of the year—when it renovated and opened Tahawus Lodge, a former Masonic Temple, for classes and workshops. The lodge, with its first-floor gallery space, is a cultural light in an old mill town.

LIBRARIES

Keene Valley Library (518-576-4335; www.kvvi.net; 1796 NY 73) has an excellent local history and mountaineering collection with monographs, maps, photographs, and rare books.

Lake Placid Library (518-523-3200; www.lakeplacidlibrary.org; 67 Main Street) has story hours for children and a good general collection.

Saranac Lake Free Library (518-891-4190; www.saranaclakelibrary.org; 100 Main Street) has an extensive Adirondack collection in the William Chapman White Room, which is open by appointment. It also hosts a lecture series, has a gallery featuring local artists, and is the home of the Charles Dickert Memorial Wildlife Museum.

MUSEUMS

Six Nations Indian Museum (518-891-2299; www.sixnationsindianmuseum.com; 1462 County Route 60, Onchiota) reflects this region's indigenous roots. Native peoples traveled to the Adirondacks for spring fishing, summer gathering, and fall hunting; the mountains, forests, and lakes offered abundant resources. At many local institutions, this information is overshadowed by all the other stories those museums have to tell, but at Six Nations, the kaleidoscopic collection of baskets, beadwork, quill work, tools, weapons, paintings, drums, cradle boards, hats, pottery, and clothing all celebrate the lives and times of the Haudenosaunee (Iroquois). Artifacts fill cases, line the walls, hang from the ceilings. Open July through August, 10–5, or by appointment. Closed Mondays.

In Lake Placid, the depot for the Adirondack Scenic Railroad is home to the Lake Placid–North Elba Historical Society Museum (518-523-1608; 242 Station Street). There's a nostalgic country store display, sporting gear and memorabilia from the 1932 Olympics, and a music room honoring famous former residents Victor Herbert and Kate Smith. Open Memorial Day through mid-October, 10–4. Closed Mondays and Tuesdays.

In the Olympic Center is the Lake Placid Winter Olympic Museum (518-302-5326; www.whiteface.com), open daily year-round. Photographs, vintage films, equipment, trophies, clothing, and memorabilia illustrate the two sets of Olympic competitions that have come to town. In the works is an International Sliding Sports Museum—dedicated to bobsledders, lugers, and skeleton riders—at Lake Placid's Olympic Sports Complex at Mount Van Hoevenberg.

Tucked away in the basement of the Saranac Lake Free Library, the Charles Dickert Memorial Wildlife Museum (518-891-4190; www.dickertmuseum.org; 100 Main Street) is open when the library is, with displays of hundreds of stuffed mammals, birds, and fish native to the Adirondacks.

Beyond the Blue Line: North of the park, in Chazy, is the quirky Alice T. Miner Museum (518-846-7336; www.minermuseum.org; 9618 US 9). Located in a three-story mansion, it houses a fine textile collection, china and glass, rare books, colonial furniture, and strange curiosities from around the world. The Alice is open Tuesday through Saturdays, 10–4. In Plattsburgh, the Kent-DeLord House Museum (518-561-1035; www.kentdelordhouse.org; 17 Cumberland Avenue) is a nicely restored late-18th-century home. Also in Platt, on the old air-force base, is the Champlain Valley Transportation Museum & Kids' Station (518-566-7575; cvtmuseum.com; 12 Museum Way). It was originally planned as a Lozier museum, but expanded to include the history of handmade watercraft, steam ferries, rail cars, and all forms of military transportation—plus interactive exhibitions for little ones. Near Malone is the Wilder Homestead (518-483-1207; www.almanzowilderfarm .com; 177 Stacy Road), the setting for the novel *Farmer Boy* by Laura Ingalls Wilder. The farmstead was the home of the author's husband, Almanzo Wilder, in the mid-1800s.

The Adirondacks' Bluegrass Brothers

The Gibson Brothers, from Ellenburg, in the most northern reaches of the Adirondacks, are award-winning bluegrass stars. Siblings Eric and Leigh Gibson, who grew up on their family farm, most recently won Album of the Year and Vocal Group of the Year at the 2011 International Bluegrass Music Association awards, held in Nashville. They often play big-time shows and festivals, such as Mountain Stage and Grey Fox, but it's not unusual to see them perform in the North Country, usually to support regional causes; check www.gibsonbrothers.com for tour information.

Award-winning bluegrass stars Leigh and Eric Gibson. Courtesy of the Gibson Brothers

MUSIC

Nearly every town with a summer tourist draw presents outdoor or indoor musical programs. A few examples: If you're traveling to the High Peaks, in Jay, the Jay Entertainment and Music Society (518-946-7362; www.jemsgroup.com) presents music and other programs, on Saturday evenings at the village green. (It also puts on a winter coffeehouse series and other events as its Amos & Julia Ward Theater on the green, a 130-plus-seat structure to support concerts, art exhibitions, workshops, and other community events.) Saranac Lake has music on Friday nights at Riverside Park, on Lake Flower (518-891-1990; www.saranaclake.com). Arts centers Bluseed Studios (www.bluseedstudios.org), Lake Placid (www.lakeplacidarts.org), and Upper Jay (www.upperjayartcenterorg) also host regular performances by local and national performers. Lake Placid's summertime Songs at Mirror Lake Series (www.songsat mirrorlake.com) features local bands as well as regional ones, and happens at Mids Park on Main Street at 7 PM on Tuesdays.

Hill and Hollow Music (518-293-7613; www.hillandhollowmusic.com; 550 Number 37 Road, Saranac) hosts fine, mostly classical, music in an off-the-beaten-path corner of the Adirondacks. The organization also sponsors retreats, community dance programs, and coordinates special events that weave dance with food and historical reenactment.

Lake Placid Institute for Arts and Humanities (518-523-1312; www.lakeplacid institute.org; various locations, Lake Placid) provides an adult chamber music seminar, giving string players and pianists a chance to perform and study with world-class faculty in various local venues. There are also residencies for cutting-edge playwrights, poetry and nonfiction events for kids, an artists' roundtable, ongoing workshops in ethics, and an annual children's literature conference.

Lake Placid Sinfonietta (518-523-2051; www.lakeplacidsinfonietta.org; various locations, Lake Placid) was established almost a century ago as the house orchestra at the Lake Placid Club (the exclusive resort of Melvil Dewey, of the Dewey decimal system), playing for the guests. Now the summertime chamber orchestra is a valued community resource, presenting free Wednesday night Pops in the Park concerts in the Paul White Memorial Shell in Mids Park, overlooking Mirror Lake in the center of town (7 PM; bring a lawn chair), children's programs at the Lake Placid Center for the Arts, and concerts on stages across the Adirondack Park. On Sunday nights, the Sinfonietta performs its Symphony Series at the Lake Placid Center for the Arts.

Loon Lake Live (518-891-0757; www.loonlakelive.org) presents small classical ensembles in cozy spaces such as Loon Lake's Jewish Center, the Saranac Lake Free Library, and Harrietstown Hall, in Saranac Lake. Each concert, played in summer by fine, professional musicians, is preceded by a master class with the performers; programs are delightfully informal.

SEASONAL EVENTS

The following events (in chronological order) emphasize history, music, storytelling, crafts, and skills, or a combination of the arts.

Saranac Lake Winter Carnival (518-891-1990; www.saranaclake.com), in February, is reputedly the oldest winter carnival in the country. On the shore of Lake Flower, there's an awesome ice palace, dramatically lit by colored spotlights each evening; events include ski races, a parade, concerts, theater, and kids' activities.

Round the Mountain Festival (518-891-1990; www.macscanoe.com), in Saranac Lake, is a spring celebration centered around a canoe race that circles Dewey Mountain, with bluegrass bands and a barbecue, all on the second Saturday in May.

Lake Placid Film Forum (518-523-3456; www.lakeplacidfilmforum.com), early in June, brings directors, screenwriters, and indie film producers together to meet and greet the public each year. Venues throughout Lake Placid, including the Palace Theater, show films from morning to midnight.

I Love Barbecue Festival (www.ilbbqf.com) is a barbecue competition sanctioned by the Kansas City Barbecue Society, with vendors and two full days of music by local bands at Lake Placid's speed skating oval at the beginning of July.

Jay Studio Tour (518-946-2824; www.jaystudiotour.com), in July, involves a dozen artisans in Jay who open their studios to the public for demonstrations.

Adirondack Rust Fest (drive back@aol.com), the second weekend in August, is a gathering of Neil Young fans in Jay. It's a weekend of all things Young: jams at bar 20 Main, in Au Sable Forks, as well as an off-site deep-woods stage; Name That Neil Tune games; raffles to benefit the star's Bridge School; and more.

Hobofest (www.hobofest.com), organized by local arts organizations at Saranac Lake's depot, is a hip,

Saranac Lake's Hobofest is a popular new music event. *Courtesy of Shaun Ondak, www.shaunondak.com*

daylong September event that brings talented musicians and the community together—even during a Carhartt fashion show.

Oktoberfest (518-946-2223; www.whiteface.com), at the end of September, draws Bavarian culture lovers to Whiteface Mountain, in Wilmington, for oompah-pah and gemütlichkeit. There's live music and German-style dancing, a crafts fair, ethnic food and beer booths, children's activities, and rides on the ski area's chairlift to view the fall foliage.

THEATER

Community Theatre Players, Inc. (518-523-2512; Lake Placid Center for the Arts, 17 Algonquin Drive, Lake Placid) is an amateur group founded in 1972, CTP mounts three or four shows a year at the Lake Placid Center for the Arts and other venues, and sponsors workshops.

Pendragon Theatre (518-891-1854; www.pendragontheatre.com; 15 Brandy-brook Avenue, Saranac Lake), a highly successful local troupe, was awarded the prestigious Governor's Art Award, and has received acclaim for performances at the Edinburgh International Arts Festival, the Dublin Theatre Festival, and in Stockholm at the English-Speaking Theater. During the summer and fall, Pendragon puts on three or four shows in repertory format. During the school year and in winter, actors tour local classrooms and perform in regional venues.

Recreation
Adventures in the High Peaks & Northern Adirondacks

In this part of the park you can find backcountry solitude, extreme adventure, and everything in between when it comes to muscle-powered activity. Deep snow draws alpine and cross-country skiers; fast water appeals to fly-fishers and paddlers. Trails go up steep peaks, skirt tranquil ponds and even link communities. Bicyclists can head for single-track routes or cruise country roads. In all five seasons (the extra one is "mud season"), there's somewhere to go and something to do if sitting isn't your idea of fun.

Fly-fishing along the Ausable River.
Courtesy of Drew Haas, www.adkbcski.com

ADIRONDACK GUIDES

There are several hundred guides who are members of a select group within the DEC-licensees: the New York State Outdoor Guides Association (www.nysoga .com). These folks make a point of preserving wild resources as well as helping clients find the right places for hunting, fishing, camping, climbing—whatever your adventure.

BICYCLING

Chapter 8 lists biking guidebooks, but for this region Essex County Visitors Bureau (518-523-2445; www.lakeplacid.com; Olympic Center, Lake Placid) also has a selection of backcountry bike trips of varying difficulty on its website. The Whiteface Regional Visitors Bureau (518-946-2255; www.whitefaceregion.com), in Wilmington, has a new brochure with area mountain bike trails. In fact, Wilmington's the hot new mountain-biking spot in the North Country, with a new trail system on state land around town, plus more and more offerings around Whiteface Mountain (518-946-2233; www.whiteface .com; NY 86, Wilmington). Barkeater Trails Alliance (www.barkeatertrails.org), a volunteer crew of mountain-bike-loving trail-builders and -maintainers, have every-thing to do with booming fat-tire scene at Hardy Road and the flume, in Wilmington,

Mountain biking at Whiteface Mountain.
Courtesy of Drew Haas, www.adkbcski.com

plus Henry's Woods, in Lake Placid. Also, Mount Van Ho, in Lake Placid, has great bike trails (and a mountain-bike center, with rentals, run by High Peaks Cyclery), but unlike riding on state trails, it requires paying a use fee.

A reminder: All-terrain bicycles are barred from wilderness and primitive areas in the Adirondack Park. In the state-land areas designated as wild forest, you'll find old logging roads that make excellent bike routes, and in most of these places, you'll find far fewer people.

As far as skinny wheels: in much of the northern Adirondacks road cyclists appear in spring, training for the Lake Placid Ironman so locals, like it or not, are used to cyclists zooming along roadways. Always carry plenty of water and a good tool kit. *Wear a helmet!* For bike repairs, rentals, and sales, visit High Peaks Cyclery (518-523-3764; www.highpeakscyclery.com; 2733 Main Street, Lake Placid) also, LeepOff Cycles (518-576-9581; 23 Market Street, Keene Valley); Maui North (518-523-7245; www.mauinorth.net; 134 Main Street, Lake Placid); or Placid Planet (518-523-4128; www.placidplanetbicycles.com; 2242 Saranac Avenue, Lake Placid).

BOATING

The *New York State Boater's Guide* contains the rules and regulations for inland waters, and is available from offices of the New York Department of Transportation. See statewide laws for pleasure craft on page 183. And see page 212 for a list of regional invasive species and practices for cleaning your watercraft.

BOAT TOURS

Sadly, Lake Placid Marina & Boat Tours (518-523-9704; www.lakeplacidmarina .com; 24 George and Bliss Road) retired its classic wooden boat *Doris II*, but it still offers scenic narrated (don't believe everything they tell you) trips on Lake Placid. These days, an enclosed pontoon boat will chug you around.

Trouble Bruin

As humans have become comfortable sleeping out in the wilds, some wild animals have learned to recognize coolers, packs, tents, and even car trunks as potential food sources. Hungry black bears or pesky raccoons may not be in evidence when you set up camp, but it's best to take all precautions. If your site has a metal locker for food storage, use it. Otherwise, stash your supplies and cooking gear well away from your tent: Put it in a pack or strong plastic bags and suspend it between two trees with a sturdy rope at least 20 feet off the ground. Tie it off by wrapping several times around one tree and tie a complicated knot; bears have been known to swat down food stashes within their reach, climb saplings, and even bite through ropes. Don't try to outsmart bruin by putting your food in an anchored boat away from shore; bears swim well. In some places, the campsite caretaker can give you an update on the bear situation. Also, special poles for bear bags can be found in some High Peaks Wilderness campsites. Bear-proof canisters for food can be rented at places such as EMS, in Lake Placid; however, there are reports that some bears have learned how to rip tops off these sturdy tubes. As soon as humans think they have outsmarted the bears, the wild ones come up with creative solutions.

Avoid uninvited guests to your campsite by using bear canisters and stashing supplies and cooking gear well away from your tent. Courtesy of Eric Dresser, www.ecdphoto.addr.com

If a bear does visit your camp, loud noises (yelling, banging on pots, loud whistles) usually discourage it. Attacks are extremely rare in the Adirondacks; keep your dog under control in the event of a close encounter of the ursine kind.

CAMPING

The Department of Environmental Conservation (518-402-9428; www.dec.ny.gov) operates public campgrounds across the park, open from Memorial Day through Labor Day, though some can vary.

Facilities at state campgrounds include a picnic table and grill at each site, water spigots for every 10 sites or so, and lavatories. Not every campground has showers. Many facilities have sites for mobility-impaired campers, with hard-surface areas, water spigots at wheelchair height, and ramps to restrooms. Most campgrounds have fishing docks for wheelchairs.

DEC public campgrounds do not supply water, electric, or sewer hookups for recreational vehicles. If you require these amenities, there are privately owned campgrounds in many communities.

Camping is allowed year-round on state land, but you need a permit to stay more than three days in one backcountry spot or if you are camping with a group of more than six people. Special regulations apply in the High Peaks Wilderness Area. These permits are available from forest rangers. You may camp in the backcountry provided you pitch your tent at least 150 feet from any trail, stream, lake, or other water body. (See "Low-Impact Camping," which follows.) Along the Northville–Lake Placid Trail and on popular canoe routes you'll find lean-tos—three-sided Adirondack icons—for camping.

HIGH PEAKS AND NORTHERN ADIRONDACKS

Learn about particular campsites by visiting the DEC's website; reservations can be made for a site in the state campgrounds by contacting Reserve America (1-800-456-CAMP; www.reserveamerica). Some campgrounds will take you on a first-come, first-served basis if space is available; before July 4 and after September 1, it's usually easy to find a nice site without a reservation. The following are public campgrounds in this region; camping fees listed are for 2012:

Buck Pond (518-891-3449; 1339 County Route 60, Onchiota). Swimming, showers, canoe or rowboat rental, boat launch. $20 camping fee.

Lake Harris (518-582-2503; 291 Campsite Road, Newcomb). Swimming, showers, boat launch. Near Adirondack Visitor Interpretive Center nature trails. $18 camping fee.

Meacham Lake (518-483-5116; 119 State Campsite Road, Duane). Swimming, showers, horse trails and barn, some primitive sites accessible by foot only, boat launch. Good place to see bald eagles in summer. $20 camping fee.

Meadowbrook (518-891-4351; 1174 NY 86, Ray Brook). Showers, no swimming. Closest campground to downtown Lake Placid. $20 camping fee.

Saranac Lake Islands (518-891-3170; 58 Bayside Drive, Saranac Lake). Access by boat, tents only. Beautiful sites. $22 camping fee.

Taylor Pond (518-647-5250; 1865 Silver Lake Road, Au Sable Forks). Boat launch. $16 camping fee.

Wilmington Notch (518-946-7172; 4953 NY 86, Wilmington). On the West Branch of the Ausable River. Great area for fly-fishing; fairly close to Lake Placid. $18 camping fee.

CANOEING AND KAYAKING

The Adirondack Canoe Map shows several routes (518-576-9861; www.adirondack maps.com). Adirondack Paddler's Map, a waterproof and tear-proof guide for multi-day trips with enough details for navigating, includes trailheads, portages, and white-water ratings across the region. It's available at Saint Regis Canoe Outfitters, in Saranac Lake (1-888-775-2925), or at www.canoeoutfitters.com.

The Department of Environmental Conservation (518-891-1200; www.dec.ny .gov; NY 86, Ray Brook NY 12970) has pamphlets that describe canoe routes; ask for "Adirondack Canoe Routes" or the "official map and guide" of the area you wish to paddle. The excellent 24-page booklet "Guide to Paddling Adirondack Waterways" is available by calling 1-800-487-6867. Some tourist information offices, such as the Saranac Lake Chamber of Commerce (518-891-1990; www.saranaclake.com), offer useful brochures and maps; ask for "Canoe Franklin County." Always consult U.S. Geological Survey topographic maps for the area you're traveling through.

When you're planning any trip, allow an extra day in case the weather doesn't cooperate. Remember that you're required to carry a life jacket for each person in the boat; lash an extra paddle in your canoe, too. Bring plenty of food and fuel, a backpacker stove, and rain gear. A poncho makes a good coverall for hiking, but you're better off with rain jacket and pants in a canoe, as a poncho can become tangled if you should dump the canoe. Sign in at the trailhead registers when you begin your trip.

If you're still overwhelmed by making a decision about where to go, or need a primer on paddling technique, hire a guide (see www.nysoga.org) or consult one of the following outfitters: Adirondack Lakes and Trails Outfitters (518-891-7450;

www.adirondackoutfitters.com; 541 Lake Flower Avenue, Saranac Lake); Adirondack Rock and River Guide Service (518-576-2041; www.rockandriver.com; Alstead Hill Lane, Keene); Cloud-splitter Outfitters (518-582-2583; NY 28, Newcomb); High Peaks Mountain Adventures (518-523-3764; www.highpeaksma.com; High Peaks Cyclery, 331 Main Street, Lake Placid); Jones Outfitters Ltd. (518-523-3468; www .jonesoutfitters.com; 331 Main Street, Lake Placid); Saint Regis Canoe Outfitters (518-891-1838; www.canoeoutfitters.com; 73 Dorsey Street, Saranac Lake); or Tahawus Guide Service (518-891-4334; Lake Placid).

FAMILY FUN

Santa's Workshop (518-946-2212; www.northpoleny.com; NY 431, Wilmington), near Whiteface Mountain, is touted as the oldest theme park in the world, dating back to 1946, and it's the place to mail your Christmas cards, as the postmark reads "North Pole, NY." Don't expect something slick like Disney World—this place suits the nostalgic set with small children: You'll find Santa and his lap; reindeer (arrive early enough so your kids can feed them before the animals' belly is too full); gentle rides for children; and corny singing and dancing.

On the other end of the spectrum, the Olympic Regional Development Authority (518-523-1655; www.orda.org) offers an Olympic Sites Passport ($32 in 2012), which provides VIP entry to all Lake Placid region Olympic venues: the gondola up Whiteface; the Whiteface Veterans Memorial Highway that you can drive to the summit; the Lake Placid Olympic Museum; the Olympic Speed Skating Oval; the Olympic Sports Complex with its bobsled, luge and skeleton track; and the 120-meter jump tower's elevator at the Olympic Jumping Complex. Also popular are bobsled rides, with a professional driver and brakeman, though these cost $80 a pop for adults, $75 ages 13–19, and $70 ages 12 and under.

If sliding down a frozen chute is something your family wants to try but the bobsled price tag is a bit much, Lake Placid's toboggan run, near the Mirror Lake beach, is a cheap thrill. It's open winter weekends, weather permitting; check with the North Elba Parks Department (518-523-2591).

Brand new in spring 2012 is Saranac Lake's Adirondack Carousel (www .adirondackcarousel.org; 6 Depot Street in the William Morris Park), made of 18 hand-carved critters indigenous to the Adirondack Park: a blackfly, moose, brook trout, moose, and toad among them. At press time, the cost for a ride was $2; hours for operation were still being determined.

The Adirondack Interpretive Center in Newcomb (518-582-2000; 5922 State Route 28N) is a great place for hiking well-marked trails, with lots of workshops and programs for kids and adults. Open daily except Thanksgiving, Christmas, and New Year's Day; no admission charge for trails or exhibits.

Adirondack Scenic Railroad (518-891-3238; www.adirondackrr.com; 19 Depot Street, Saranac Lake) provides a 10-mile trip from Saranac Lake to Lake Placid from Memorial Day through Columbus Day. Trains are a thrill for little ones and older folks too, but be warned: onboard it's loud—the whistle's toots as well as the clackety-clacks.

High Falls Gorge (518-946-2278; www.highfallsgorge.com; NY 86, Wilmington) has waterfalls and trails on the Ausable River. Open July and August, and in winter for spectacular snowshoeing.

Tucker Farm's Autumn Corn Maze (518-327-5054; www.tuckertater.com; 112 Hobart Road, Gabriels), with its varying themes, is open August through early November.

No-Kill Fishing

Angling for fun rather than for the frying pan is catching on across the country, especially in trout waters. If you'd like to match wits with a wild piscine and then send it back to live another day, here are some tips for catch-and-release fishing:

• Use a barbless hook or take a barbed hook and bend down the barb with a pair of pliers.

• Be gentle landing your fish; some anglers line their nets with a soft cotton bag. When removing the hook, it's best not to handle the fish at all, as you can disturb the protective coating on the skin.

• If you have to touch the fish, wet your hands first, don't squeeze the body, and don't touch the gills.

• If you can, extract the hook without touching the fish: Hold the hook's shank upside down and remove it. Usually, the creature will swim happily away.

• If your fish is tired, you can cradle it gently, facing upstream so that water flows through the gills, or if you're in a lake, move it back and forth slowly as a kind of artificial respiration.

A 5-mile-long section of the West Branch of the Ausable River between Lake Placid and Wilmington is designated for catch-and-release fishing only. With the no-kill rules in effect for more than a decade, the action on the river has been transformed; the fly-fishing here can be the stuff dreams are made of.

Whiteface Mountain Cloudsplitter Gondola Ride (518-946-2223; www.white face.com; NY 86, Wilmington) is recommended for fall foliage. Open late June through Columbus Day.

FISHING

The Department of Environmental Conservation (www.dec.ny.gov) is the place to go for everything you need to know: the top fishing spots and what's hitting where on which kind of bait; how and where to get a license (everyone 16 and older who fishes in the Adirondacks must have a New York fishing license); where to find outfitters and guides; the latest on the toxic buildup of mercury in fish (some species in the Adirondacks should not be consumed by children or pregnant woman); and fishing seasons. The I Love NY *Adirondack Fishing* guide (www.fishadk.com) is also indispensable.

A sampling of regional outfitters includes Blue Line Sports, LLC (518-891-4680; 81 Main Street, Saranac Lake); the Hungry Trout (518-946-2217; www.hungrytrout .com; NY 86, Wilmington); Jones Outfitters (518-523-3468; www.jonesoutfitters .com; 2733 Main Street, Lake Placid); and the Mountaineer (518-576-2281; www .mountaineer.com; NY 73, Keene Valley).

GOLF

Adirondack golf courses range from informal, inexpensive, converted cow pastures to challenging, busy, championship links. This region's courses include:

Ausable Club (518-576-4411; www.ausableclub.org; 137 Ausable Road, St. Huberts). Nine holes; Scottish links-type course. Open to nonmembers in September only, Monday through Thursday.

Ausable Valley Country Club (518-647-8666; www.avgolfcourse.com; 58 Golf Course Road, Au Sable Forks). Nine holes; par-34; 2,700 yards.

Craig Wood Golf Course (518-523-9811; www.craigwoodgolfclub.com; Cascade Road, Lake Placid). Eighteen holes; par-72; 6,500 yards. Named after Lake Placid native Craig Wood, who won both the U.S. Open and Masters in 1941.

Crowne Plaza Resort & Golf Club (518-523-2556; www.lakeplacidcp.com; Mirror Lake Drive, Lake Placid). Two 18-hole courses: the Mountain course, and the Links course.

High Peaks Golf Course (518-582-2300; Santanoni Drive, Newcomb). Nine holes; par-33; 2,600 yards; magnificent High Peaks views.

Saranac Inn Golf & Country Club (518-891-1402; www.saranacinn.com; 125 County Route 46, Saranac Inn). Eighteen holes; par-2; 6,600 yards; beautifully maintained course.

Saranac Lake Golf Club (518-891-2675; NY 86, Ray Brook). Nine holes; par-36; 3,000 yards.

Whiteface Club Golf Course (518-523-2551; 373 Whiteface Inn Lane, Lake Placid). Eighteen holes; par-72; 6,500 yards; challenging course with beautiful views.

HIKING AND BACKPACKING

There are trails leading to pristine ponds, roaring waterfalls, spectacular peaks, and hidden gorges; perhaps the toughest choice for an Adirondack visitor is selecting where to go. Chapter 8 lists the best guidebooks to help you make that decision.

Low-Impact Camping

Wilderness camping in the old days relied on techniques such as digging deep trenches around tents, cutting balsam boughs for backwoods beds, sawing armloads of firewood, and burying garbage and cans. For camp cleanup, we used to think nothing of washing dishes in the lake or scrubbing ourselves vigorously with soap as we cavorted in the shallows. All of these activities left a lasting mark on the woods and waters; today it's important to leave no trace of your visit.

Low-impact camping is perhaps easier than old-fashioned methods once you grasp the basics. Most of the skills are simply common sense: Think of the cumulative effects of your actions when you set up camp, and you're on your way to becoming a responsible wilderness trekker.

Choose a site at least 150 feet away from the nearest hiking trail or water source, and try to select a place that will recover quickly after you leave. Separate your tent from your cooking area to avoid attracting animals and to distribute the impact of your stay. When you leave, tidy up. Be sure the spot is absolutely clean of any trash—even stuff we commonly regard as biodegradable, such as banana peels—and spread dirt or dead leaves around any trampled areas.

Use a portable stove for backcountry cooking rather than a campfire. (Use only dead and down wood in the Forest Preserve; cutting trees on state land is prohibited.) Plan your meals so that you don't have extra cooked food; if no one in the party can assume the role of "master of the Clean Plate Club," then pack out all of your leftovers. Wash your dishes and your body well away from streams and lakes, using a mild vegetable-based soap.

How to sh-t in the woods is something to consider; nothing kills that "Gee, isn't it terrific out here in the wilderness" feeling more than finding unmistakable evidence of other humans. Bring a shovel or trowel and bury that hazardous waste at least 6 inches down and 150 feet from the nearest water. Lean-tos and some backcountry campsites have privies; use them.

In some parts of the park, you can leave the trailhead and not see another person until you return to your car and look in the rearview mirror. Parts of the Northville–Lake Placid Trail are many miles from the nearest road; going end-to-end on this long trail requires a minimum of 10 days and a solid amount of backcountry knowledge, but you can pick shorter sections for three-day junkets. Parts of the High Peaks—especially from southern access points—offer similar overnights. It's possible to find solitude even in the middle of the busy summer season if you select the right destination. There are also plenty of easy hikes of 2 to 5 miles that traverse beautiful terrain throughout the park.

Don't assume that just because the Adirondacks doesn't reach the height of the Rockies, it's all easy strolling; trails can be steep and treacherous and weather is downright changeable. Wherever you choose to go, be prepared. Your pack should contain a flashlight, matches, extra food and water, map, compass, and extra clothes (wool or fleece for warmth; leave the cotton at home). At most trailheads, there's a register for signing in. Forest rangers rely on this data to estimate how much use a particular area receives; and, in the unlikely event that you get lost, the information about when you started, where you were planning to go, and whom you were with would be helpful to the search team.

For neophyte hikers, the trails at the Adirondack Interpretive Center at Newcomb (518-582-2000) is ingeniously designed to offer a wide range of nature in a relatively short distance, and you won't be too far from the building no matter how long you travel. You can join a guided trip to learn about wildflowers, mushrooms, trees, or birds.

The Adirondack Mountain Club (518-523-3441; www.adk.org), based in the High Peaks at the Heart Lake Program Center at Adirondak Loj, in Lake Placid, leads trips and gives map-and-compass, woodcraft, and low-impact-camping workshops.

HORSEBACK RIDING AND WAGON TRIPS

New York's North Country may not have the wide, open spaces of the Wild West, but there are hundreds of miles of wilderness horse trails to explore, and plenty of outfitters to put you on a reliable mount. The possibilities range from hour-long rides to overnight guided backcountry forays; if you have your own horse, the Department of Environmental Conservation (www.dec.ny.gov) has trail networks across the park, and even operates campgrounds that accommodate man and beast. One rule applies for bringing in out-of-state horses: proof of a negative Coggins test is necessary. If you plan to camp more than three nights in the Forest Preserve, or in a group of six or more, you'll need a permit from the local forest ranger. Public horse trails in this region are:

Cold River Horse Trails. Six miles east of Tupper Lake off NY 3, very difficult 13- and 32-mile-loop dirt trails; lean-tos and corral. Connects with easier Moose Pond and Santanoni trails.

Meacham Lake. Three and a half miles north of Paul Smiths, off NY 30; 10 miles of trails, although they include two separate dead-end routes; lean-tos and barn.

Moose Pond Trail. Starts at Santanoni trailhead just north of Newcomb off NY 28N; 10 miles.

Raquette Falls Horse Trail. Branches off Cold River Trail; 1.6 miles.

Santanoni Trail. North of Newcomb off NY 28N; 10-mile round-trip. Hitching trails and two wagon teams that transport people.

Lake Placid Horse Shows

If you enjoy just watching horses, there are two excellent annual horse shows in Lake Placid, located a canter away from the Olympic ski jumps: the **Lake Placid Horse Show** in late June and the **I Love NY Horse Show** (518-523-9625; www.lakeplacidhorseshow .com; 514 Cascade Road, Lake Placid) immediately afterward. The shows attract about 800 horses, their riders and trainers, plus grooms, farriers, veterinarians, vendors, and sponsors. Competitions begin at 8 AM each day and happen in four different rings so spectators can watch a variety of action. In "model" classes, nearly naked animals are paraded before judges to show off their conformation, scrutinized for their perfect looks; equitation is all about the rider's posture, hands, and way of handling his or her well-matched mount. The hunter division is for horses that approach the ideal in a foxhunting creature, one that moves with exceptional fluidity and intelligence, with beautiful proportions from head to hock. Jumpers can be homely with mismatched parts; this group is about speed, confidence, and accuracy when faced with obstacles placed only a few giant strides apart.

The Lake Placid Horse Shows attract about 800 horses, their riders and trainers, plus grooms, farriers, veterinarians, vendors, and sponsors   Courtesy of John DiGiacomo, www.placidtimesphotography.com

Jumping events feature 15 to 20 obstacles arranged in the ring, with low, simple rails for juniors and double or triple jumps as high as 5 feet for the Grand Prix. Horses in this championship turn are covering the ground at about 12 miles per hour, but excess speed can result in knocking down an obstacle, a fall, or a balk—all of which are faults that affect the overall score. Riders get the chance to walk the course, which coils around the ring in different patterns, and the order for competing can give later contestants the advantage of seeing how others handle the route.

Although horse shows have the aura of a closed society, Lake Placid's events are family friendly and welcoming to the novice. Leashed dogs are also welcome. Tickets for a full day are only $2 on weekdays and $5 on weekends for adults, with kids under 12 free. You can bring a picnic, grab a burger, ask for an autograph on your program, and zero in on the contests that catch your interest.

Ranches and stables that give lessons, guide trips, and board horses include: Circle 7 (518-582-4191; NY 28N, Newcomb), which offers wagon trips to Santanoni Preserve by reservation only, plus hunting and fishing pack trips. Emerald Springs Ranch (518-891-3727; www.emerald-springs.com; 651 NY 186, Saranac Lake) has horseback riding and equestrian classes. At High Peaks Stables (518-582-2260; 5788 NY 28N, Newcomb) there's horseback riding and horse boarding; wagon trips to Santanoni Preserve; sleigh rides; and hunting trips to Moose Pond. The Ranch (518-891-5684; www.childrenscamps.com; Forest Home Road, Lake Clear) is an equestrian camp for girls. Sentinel View Stables (518-891-3008; Harrietstown Road, Saranac Lake) gives English and Western lessons, plus jumping instruction.

Hunting is a popular, regulated pursuit each fall in many Adirondack counties. There are seasons for deer, black bear (some years, the bear take for the Adirondack Park is around 550), snowshoe hare, coyote, bobcat, and other small mammals, plus ruffed grouse, woodcock, wild turkey, and waterfowl. The booklets outlining game seasons are available from the Department of Environmental Conservation (www.dec.ny.gov; DEC, 625 Broadway, Albany, New York 12233); licenses can be purchased from sporting goods stores, town offices, or the DEC. Nonresidents may purchase five-day licenses. If you have never had a New York State hunting license, you must show proof that you have attended a hunter education course. Turkey hunting requires a special stamp from the DEC; waterfowl hunters must possess a Federal Migratory Bird Hunting Stamp.

Wilderness, primitive, and wild forest areas are all open to hunting. Hunters— even if they have a brand-new, state-of-the-art GPS unit—should be proficient with map and compass. Global-positioning units don't always work well in thick forest, and batteries do wear out.

There are many Adirondack hunting guides, who can be found at the New York State Outdoor Guides Association's site, www.nysoga.org.

ICE SKATING

The modern sport of speed skating was launched in Saranac Lake and Lake Placid: In the early 1900s, more world records were set—and broken—by local bladesmen than at any other wintry place. Nowadays, there's backcountry skating on remote lakes and ponds or skating on plowed rinks in the towns and even indoor figure skating or hockey on Zamboni-maintained ice sheets.

If you'd like to try wilderness skating, wait until January. Cold, clear, still weather produces the most consistent surface. Ice that's 2 inches thick will support one person on skates, but it's better to wait for at least 3 inches to form, as currents and springs can create weak spots. Ice is thinner near shore, and be sure to steer clear of inlets, outlets, and other tributaries. Ponds in the High Peaks are often good for skating by New Year's Day, especially if there's been little snow. You can scout Chapel Pond, off NY 73 south of Keene Valley, or the Cascade Lakes, on the same road, north of Keene, or Heart Lake, at the end of the Adirondak Loj Road.

In Lake Placid, you can enjoy terrific ice outdoors most evenings at the Olympic Speed Skating Oval (the James B. Sheffield Olympic Skating Rink), on Main Street, or you can skate in the Olympic Arena (518-523-1655; www.white face.com; 2634 Main Street) at scheduled times for a small charge. If you want to try speed skating, you can get rental skates, a lesson, and ice time in Lake Placid. You can also try curling with the Lake Placid Club (518-327-3223). Lake Placid's Olympic ice gets lots of attention in annual Can-Am Hockey tournaments, camps, and clinics. Hockey fans can check out www.whiteface.com, for schedules. Tupper Lake (518-359-2531; McLaughlin Street) maintains rinks for hockey and skating; Saranac Lake's Civic Center (518-891-3800) has good ice indoors and an active youth hockey program. Some seasons there's even a little volunteer-made rink behind Keene's community center, though you'll have to ask around town about its hours and availability.

Dimon Sports (518-523-1729; www.dimonsports.com; 6197 Sentinel Road, Suite 1, Lake Placid) specializes in hockey and speed and figure skates, outfits, and equipment. You can rent skates here or at the speed skating oval. Many of the sporting-goods stores throughout the region stock skates for children and adults.

Lake Placid is the only place in North America that has hosted two Winter Olympic Games, in 1932 and 1980. During the '32 Games, the American team won the bobsledding events; took silver and bronze medals in speed skating, hockey, figure skating, and bobsledding; and was therefore regarded as the unofficial Olympic champion. In 1980, Eric Heiden garnered five gold medals in speed skating, and the U.S. hockey team won the tournament following a stunning upset over the Russians in the semifinal round. The legacy of Olympic glory lives on here, at the Olympic Training Center on Old Military Road, where hundreds of athletes eat, sleep, and work out in a high-tech setting, and in several specialized sports facilities in and around Lake Placid. Every season, competitors come to town for coaching and practice.

Courtesy of ORDA

High Peaks Olympic venues.
Courtesy of ORDA/Dave Schmidt

There's just one place in the Northeast where you, too, can ride a real bobsled on an Olympic run: the Olympic Sports Complex at Mount Van Hoevenberg, a few miles from downtown Lake Placid. This thrill does not come cheap; in 2012 it was $70–$80, depending on the season, for the longest minute you'll ever spend. (Note that the sleds are piloted by professional drivers.) Rides are available around Christmas through early March, depending on the track conditions. There's also a bobsled with wheels that shoots down the track when there's no ice on it. Call for details (518-523-1655; www.whiteface.com; Olympic Center, Lake Placid).

Watching international luge, skeleton, and bobsled competitions is almost as exciting as trying it yourself, and perhaps easier on the cardiovascular system. Races are held nearly every winter weekend. Dress warmly for spectating; you'll want to walk up and down the mile-long track to see and hear the sleds zoom through. At some vantage points, sliders fly by nearly upside down, and the racket of the runners is a lesson in the Doppler effect. You'll definitely want to see several push starts, where track stars have a decided advantage.

In the Olympic Arena, at the center of Lake Placid, you can watch youth and collegiate ice hockey tournaments, exhibition NHL games, indoor short-track speedskating, figure-skating competitions, and skating exhibitions such as "Stars on Ice," year-round. Since 1993, stars such as Kristy Yamaguchi, Scott Hamilton, Sasha Cohen, and Kurt Browning have come to Lake Placid either to practice for national touring or to perform.

Ski jumping on the 90- and 120-meter jumps is thrilling; seeing people fly through the air is far more impressive in person than the sport appears on television.

If watching from the bleachers, dress warmly. The 120-meter jump tower has a sky deck accessible by elevator and chairlift that provides the perfect spot to watch jumpers and surrounding mountains from above. In spring 2012, the elevator was $11 (the chairlift closes this time of year); in summer, the chairlift and elevator was $15 on event days. Annual favorite competitions are the Fourth of July Ski Jump and October Flaming Leaves Festival (with blues, brews, and BBQ); these are Lake Placid spectator events where you will avoid hypothermia. Also, at the jumping complex, you can watch the U.S. freestyle skiers training in warm weather. The skiers go off jumps, tumble through the air, and land in a huge aerated pool of 750,000 gallons of water with their skis still attached.

At Whiteface Mountain you can see occasional international freestyle and down-hill and slalom races, as well as snowboard cross and parallel giant slalom races. Or you can try riding the slopes yourself.

RACES AND SEASONAL SPORTING EVENTS

Events are listed in chronological order:

Adirondack International Mountainfest (518-576-2281; www.mountaineer.com; the Mountaineer, Keene Valley) includes clinics, slide shows, and lectures by renowned ice and rock climbers, in mid-January.

Lake Placid Loppet (518-523-1655; www.orda.org; Olympic Regional Development Authority, Lake Placid), popular 25- and 50-kilometer citizens' races at Mount Van Hoevenberg, is supposed to happen in late January, though in 2012 there wasn't enough snow.

Empire State Winter Games (518-523-1655; ORDA, Lake Placid) brings competitors in figure skating, luge, bobsled, speed skating, ski jumping, cross-country skiing, and other events, in Lake Placid, in early March.

Pond Skimming (518-946-2223; www.whiteface.com; Whiteface Mountain, Wilmington), a goofy display at Whiteface, challenges skiers and snowboarders to jump across a pool of freezing water, in April.

'Round the Mountain Canoe Race (518-891-1990; Saranac Lake Chamber of Commerce, Saranac Lake), a 10-mile canoe race on Lower Saranac Lake and the Saranac River, happens in early May.

Whiteface Mountain Uphill Bike Race (518-946-2255; www.whiteface race.com; Wilmington) is a race up the Whiteface Mountain Veterans Memorial Highway, in June.

Willard Hanmer Guideboat and Canoe Races (518-891-1990; Saranac Lake Chamber of Commerce, Saranac Lake) take over Lake Flower for guideboats, canoes, rowing shells, war canoes, and kayaks, in early July.

Lake Placid Ironman (www.iron manlakeplacid.com; Lake Placid) is an epic competition that includes a 2-plus-mile swim in Mirror Lake; 112-mile bike race from Lake Placid to Keene and back, twice; followed by a marathon, in late July.

The Longest Day

Ironman Lake Placid (www.ironman lakeplacid.com) is the real deal: a grueling 2-plus-mile swim in Mirror Lake; 112-mile bike race from Lake Placid to Keene and back, twice; followed by a marathon. During this annual July event, international competitors give it their all in the High Peaks for a spot at Kona. As far as skinny wheels: In much of the northern Adirondacks road cyclists appear in spring, training for the Lake Placid Ironman, so locals are used to cyclists zooming along roadways.

Can-Am Rugby Tournament (518-891-1990; www.canamrugby.com; Saranac Lake Chamber of Commerce, Saranac Lake), North America's largest rugby meet, attracts more than 100 teams competing in fields throughout Lake Placid and Saranac Lake, in early August.

Olga Memorial Footrace (518-891-0375; www.saranaclake.com; Saranac Lake), five- and 10-kilometer runs in Riverside Park, happen in August.

Summit Lacrosse Tournament (518-441-8228; www.lakeplacidlax.com) includes teams of kids, old-timers, men, and women competing at the North Elba Horse Show Grounds, in mid-August.

Whiteface Mountain Uphill Footrace (518-946-2255; www.whitefacerace.com; Wilmington) is a race up the Whiteface Mountain Veterans Memorial Highway, in September.

ROCK AND ICE CLIMBING

The Adirondacks is a hot destination for ice climbers. Courtesy of Drew Haas, www.adkbcski.com

Plenty of steep, arduous rock walls can be found in the High Peaks. Possibilities for rock and ice climbers abound, from nontechnical scrambles up broad, smooth slides to gnarly 700-foot pitches in the 5.11+ difficulty range. Adirondack climbers—from wannabes to folks with permanently chalky palms—all depend on a thick green guidebook, *Climbing in the Adirondacks: A Guide to Rock and Ice Routes,* by Don Mellor. This book is indispensable as the approaches to many of the best climbs involve a hike or bushwhack to the base. It also outlines hundreds of climbs and explains the local ethic on clean wilderness climbing: Leave as little trace as possible and place a minimum of bolts. Also helpful is Jim Lawyer and Jeremy Haas's *Adirondack Rock,* a guide to new climbing routes and a remapping of old ones.

Climbers can get tips in a few places. The Mountaineer (518-576-2281; www.mountaineer.com; NY 73, Keene Valley) sells climbing gear, topo maps, and guidebooks; advice is free. Many climbers' questions can be answered at the Adirondack International Mountaineering Festival each January, sponsored by the Mountaineer. Hardware, and software for climbing can also be found in Lake Placid at Eastern Mountain Sports (518-523-2505; www.ems.com; 2453 Main Street) and High Peaks Cyclery (518-523-3764; www.highpeakscyclery.com; 2733 Main Street), which has an indoor-climbing wall.

To learn the basics of climbing or to polish your skills if you've had some experience, a handful of guide services specialize in helping you climb higher, such as Adirondack Alpine Adventures, Keene (518-576-9881; www.alpineadven.com); Adirondack Mountain Guides, Keene (518-576-9556; www.adirondackmountain guides.com); Adirondack Rock & River Guide Service, Keene (518-576-2041; www.rockandriver.com); Cloudsplitter Mountain Guides, Keene (518-569-8910;

The High Peaks

Dozens of mountaintops rise 4,000 feet or more above sea level in the Adirondack Park. You don't need to be a technical climber to enjoy the views, but you should be an experienced, well-prepared hiker capable of putting in at least a 12-mile round trip. For trail descriptions and access points, consult the *Adirondack Mountain Club's High Peaks Region* guidebook. The following "Forty-Six" are in the area bounded by Newcomb on the south, Elizabethtown on the east, Wilmington on the north, and the Franklin County line on the west.

Peak	Elevation (in feet)	Peak	Elevation (in feet)
1. Mount Marcy	5,344	24. Mount Marshall	4,380
2. Algonquin Peak	5,115	25. Seward Mountain	4,347
3. Mount Haystack	4,961	26. Allen Mountain	4,347
4. Mount Skylight	4,924	27. Big Slide Mountain	4,249
5. Whiteface Mountain	4,866	28. Esther Mountain	4,239
6. Dix Mountain	4,839	29. Upper Wolf Jaw	4,185
7. Gray Peak	4,830	30. Lower Wolf Jaw	4,173
8. Iroquois Peak	4,830	31. Phelps Mountain	4,161
9. Basin Mountain	4,826	32. Street Mountain	4,150
10. Gothics Mountain	4,734	33. Sawteeth Mountain	4,150
11. Mount Colden	4,734	34. Mount Donaldson	4,140
12. Giant Mountain	4,626	35. Cascade Mountain	4,098
13. Nippletop Mountain	4,610	36. Seymour Mountain	4,091
14. Santanoni Peak	4,606	37. Porter Mountain	4,085
15. Mount Redfield	4,606	38. Mount Colvin	4,085
16. Wright Peak	4,580	39. South Dix Mountain	4,060
17. Saddleback Mountain	4,528	40. Mount Emmons	4,040
18. Panther Peak	4,442	41. Dial Mountain	4,020
19. Table Top Mountain	4,413	42. East Dix Mountain	4,006
20. Rocky Peak Ridge	4,410	43. Blake Peak	3,986
21. Hough Peak	4,409	44. Cliff Mountain	3,944
22. Macomb Mountain	4,390	45. Nye Mountain	3,944
23. Armstrong Mountain	4,390	46. Cousachraga Peak	3,820

(Elevations from *Of the Summits, Of the Forests, Adirondack Forty-Sixers*)

The **Adirondack Forty-Sixers** is an organization dedicated to these High Peaks. To earn its member's patch, you must have climbed all of the mountains listed above. The group performs trail work and education projects; for information, visit www.adk46r.org.

www.cloudsplitterguides.com); Redline Mountain Guides, Lake Placid (518-524-3328); Don Mellor (mellord@northwoodschool.com); and Royce Van Evera, Lake Placid (518-524-1105). Some climbers like to brush up on technique at the Crux (518-963-4646) indoor-climbing center, in Willsboro.

SCENIC FLIGHTS

A 15- to 20-minute flight covering about 50 miles of territory costs less than the average evening out. You can make arrangements for longer flights, but in 2012 a typical short trip cost about $40 per person. Adirondack Flying Service (518-523-2473;

www.flyanywhere.com; 73 Cascade Road, Lake Placid) will bring you over the High Peaks, the Olympic venues, or the lakes of this region.

SCENIC HIGHWAYS

Most Adirondack byways are pretty darn scenic: Even Interstate 87—the Northway —won an award as "America's Most Beautiful Highway" the year it was completed. Not too far from Lake Placid, Whiteface Mountain Veterans Memorial Highway (518-946-2223; www.whiteface.com; off NY 431, Wilmington) has a great view, too, looking down on other summits and silvery lakes. It's a state-operated toll road open daily from late May through the fall.

SKIING: CROSS-COUNTRY AND SNOWSHOEING

The Adirondack Park is paradise for cross-country skiers. Most winters there's plenty of snow, upward of 100 inches, especially in the higher elevations. A wide range of destinations entices skiers, from rugged expeditions in the High Peaks to gentle groomed paths suitable for novices, plus hundreds of miles of intermediate trails. Many of the marked hiking trails on state land are not only suitable for cross-country skiing or snowshoeing, they're actually better for winter recreation, as swampy areas are frozen, and ice-bound ponds and lakes can be easily crossed.

For suggestions on backcountry ski trails, see chapter 8 for a list of helpful guide-books.

Designated wilderness and wild forest areas offer great ski touring on marked but ungroomed trails. Another option for exploring the wild wintry woods is to hire a licensed guide.

Before setting out on any of these wilderness excursions, prepare your pack with quick-energy food; a thermos filled with hot tea or cocoa; extra hat, socks, and gloves; topo map and compass; matches; flashlight; and space blanket. Dress in layers of wool, polypropylene, or synthetic pile. Don't travel alone. Sign in at the trailhead register. Let friends know your destination and when you plan to return.

At the Adirondack Interpretive Center in Newcomb (518-528-2000), the trails are not quite so great for skiing, but you can try snowshoeing at no charge. The Jackrabbit Trail (518-523-1365; 301 Main Street, Lake Placid) is a superb resource, some 35 miles of groomed trails connecting Keene with Lake Placid, Saranac Lake, and Paul Smiths. The trail combines old logging roads, abandoned rail lines, and trails and is named for Herman "Jackrabbit" Johannsen, who laid out many ski routes in the 1920s. From some of the hotels in downtown Placid, you can strap on your skis and just head for the woods. The Jackrabbit Trail joins with many of the commercial ski-touring areas and traverses the McKenzie Mountain Wilderness Area between Whiteface Inn and Saranac Lake. Dogs are not welcome on groomed portions of the Jackrabbit Trail, nor at the privately owned ski centers, though Mount Van Hoevenberg (518-523-8824; www .adirondacksikidog.com), in Lake Placid, has skijoring clinics, where you can learn to cross-country ski with your dog.

Skiing the High Peaks backcountry.
Courtesy of Drew Haas, www.adkbcski.com

Adirondak Loj (518-523-3441; www.adk.org; Adirondack Loj Road, Lake Placid) has 12 kilometers of backcountry trails that connect with numerous challenging wilderness trails, guided tours, lessons, food, and lodging.

Cascade Ski Touring Center (518-523-9605; www.cascadeski.com; NY 73, Lake Placid) grooms 20 kilometers of trails and connects with the Jackrabbit Trail, offers night skiing (ask about its full-moon parties), rentals, lessons, and a ski shop.

Dewey Mountain Recreation Center (518-891-2697; www.deweyskicenter.com; NY 30, Saranac Lake) maintains 20 kilometers of groomed trails, has night skiing, lessons, guided tours, and is great for snowshoeing, too.

Olympic Sports Complex at Mount Van Hoevenberg (518-523-2811; www.white face.com; NY 73, Lake Placid) is a 50-kilometer groomed Olympic trail system that connects with the Jackrabbit Trail; it also has rentals, lessons, and a ski shop.

Cross-country sales, rentals, maps, and other gear can be found at Blue Line Sports, LLC (518-891-4680; 81 Main Street, Saranac Lake); Eastern Mountain Sports (518-523-2505; www.ems.com; 2453 Main Street, Lake Placid); High Peaks Cyclery (518-523-3764; www.highpeakscyclery.com; 2733 Main Street, Lake Placid); Maui North (518-523-7245; www.mauinorth.net; 134 Main Street, Lake Placid); and the Mountaineer (518-576-2281; www.mountaineer.com; NY 73, Keene Valley).

SKIING: DOWNHILL AND SNOWBOARDING

Naturally, downhill season in the Adirondacks depends on the weather. Often, snowmaking begins in early November, and some trails may open by Thanksgiving, but it can be Christmas week before the snow is reliable throughout an entire ski area. Many skiers prefer spring conditions when there's corn snow and bright sunshine. Whatever the weather, it's not a bad idea to call ahead for the ski conditions before you go.

Compared to ski areas in Vermont or the Rockies, the Adirondack ones seem undeveloped. The emphasis at the hills is on skiing and snowboarding, not on hot-tub lounging, nightlife, or après-ski ambience. At the base of a mountain, you won't find condos or designer restaurants for fancy meals and lodging, you have to go to town. Following are some downhill ski areas within the Adirondack Park:

The Cloudsplitter gondola delivers skiers above the clouds on Whiteface Mountain.
Courtesy of ORDA/Dave Schmidt

Mount Pisgah (518-891-0970; Mount Pisgah Road, off Trudeau Road, Saranac Lake) was mentioned in *The Bell Jar*. Sylvia Plath skied there in the 1950s and chronicled her spectacular tumble in the book. The mountain today, with its brand-new T-bar and slopes geared to beginner and intermediate skiers, is still very much a family ski area, with a friendly atmosphere. Tubing is also a big deal here. There's snowmaking for most of the hill, and a ski school, patrol, and a cozy base lodge with

Cold, Cold, Cold

In the old days, folks caught unprepared in the wilds occasionally died of "exposure." Today, we call that same condition *hypothermia* (literally, "low temperature"), and it remains a serious concern in cool, moist climates year-round. Even on a summer's day, a lightly clad hiker can suffer from hypothermia after getting caught in the rain. In winter, unaccustomed strenuous exercise, coupled with the wrong kind of clothing, can lead to hypothermia.

Hypothermia is caused when the body loses warmth faster than it can produce heat. The normal body-core temperature of 98.6 degrees Fahrenheit decreases to a dangerous level, which happens when the body is inadequately insulated by clothing. Precipitating events can be a dunking in cold water or soaking in steady drizzle. To compensate for heat loss, the body tries to produce more warmth, which burns up energy. As energy reserves dwindle and muscles become exhausted, hypothermia sets in.

Signs of hypothermia arrive in stages: First, the person feels and acts cold. He or she may shiver, have trouble with manual dexterity, or show bluish skin color. Next, shaking becomes uncontrollable, and the person starts to behave erratically, acting sluggish, apathetic, or cranky. The victim may stagger or seem off balance. Some folks refer to the "Umble Rule"—watch out when a companion begins to stumble, mumble, grumble, and fumble.

The final stage of hypothermia is a true medical emergency. The skin feels cold to the touch; shivering has stopped; limbs may be frostbitten. The victim may seem uncaring about survival. The treatment of all stages of hypothermia is basically the same—add heat. Warm the person with your hands, body-to-body contact, or a fire. Provide hot liquids: tea, soup, cocoa, or any nonalcoholic beverage. For a person in severe hypothermia, prevent additional heat loss and get the victim to a medical facility quickly.

A few ounces of prevention go a long way in avoiding hypothermia. Dress in layers, especially clothing made of wool, polypropylene, or synthetic pile, all of which insulate when wet. ("Cotton kills," forest rangers say.) Bring spare hats, mittens, socks, overpants, and a Windbreaker. Pack plenty of high-energy food and warm liquids. Put an "instant heat" packet in a pocket. Watch out for your friends and be honest about your abilities. Know when to turn back.

Frostbite and its cousin, frostnip, are not hypothermia. The terms refer to flesh's actually freezing, and it's usually fingers, toes, ears, nose, or chin that are affected. Frostbite can occur quickly; look for skin appearing waxy. One test for frostbite is to pinch the affected part gently and watch for the color to change. Unaffected flesh will revert to its normal color, but frozen parts remain whitish and feel hard and cold.

At the first sign of frostbite, warm the affected part at body temperature. You can warm your hands by sticking fingers in your mouth, by placing them in an armpit or between your legs; ears and cheeks can be warmed with a dry hand; feet can be warmed up with the help of a buddy's body. Do not rub a frostbitten part; you can cause severe tissue damage as there are actual ice crystals in the cells. Don't use temperatures above 110 degrees Fahrenheit for warming, as excessive heat can cause greater damage. (Be very careful using a pocket hand warmer.) Avoid refreezing frostbitten parts.

Deep frostbite should not be thawed. It sounds grim, but it's better to walk out on frozen feet than it is to thaw them and then try to shuffle along. Severe frostbite is a medical emergency that will need evacuation and lengthy hospitalization to repair circulatory damage.

a snack bar. Pisgah is one of the few places left in the Adirondacks where you can enjoy night skiing; local residents often hit the slopes after work. Open Tuesday through Sunday.

Whiteface Mountain (518-946-2233; www.whiteface.com; 5021 NY 86, Wilmington), at 3,430 feet, has the longest vertical drop in the East. New York governor Averill Harriman dedicated Whiteface Mountain, a state-owned facility, in 1958; the event was marred slightly when the chairlift he was riding came to a dead halt and Harriman had to be rescued by ladder from his lofty perch. On its 86 trails there's lots of intense, expert skiing. Tackling the mountain's double black-diamond slides when they're open is a real adventure. The mountain is big enough—but not a place you can get lost in—to accommodate scads of skiers without building up long lift lines. Eight chairlifts, plus a high-speed gondola, propel skiers up the slopes. There's an excellent Kids Kampus—play-and-ski program for tots—and a first-rate ski school. Whiteface is constantly expanding offerings for snowboarders, including a quality half-pipe and terrain parks. World Cup snowboard athletes compete here. Other races, on boards and skis, happen during the season—check www.whiteface.com for a calendar of events. Three lodges supply food, drink, and a place to discuss the slopes, plus a full ski shop with rentals. Although in 2012 a weekend adult ticket was more than $80, there are sizable midweek discounts, special promotions, and ladies' days.

Catching air on Whiteface's slopes.
Courtesy of ORDA

SNOWMOBILING

More than 400 miles of snowmobile trails weave through the Tupper Lake–Saranac Lake–Lake Placid area. Many trail networks throughout the park cross private timberlands as well as the state forest preserve. Public lands designated as wild forest areas are open to snowmobiling; wilderness areas are not. The Department of Environmental Conservation is a clearinghouse for snowmobile rules and regulations in the park, with snowmobile trail maps and links at www.dec.ny.gov.

Know your machine; carry an emergency repair kit and understand how to use it. Be sure you have plenty of gas. Travel with friends in case of a breakdown or other surprise situations. Never ride at night unless you're familiar with the trail or are following an experienced leader. Avoid crossing frozen lakes and streams unless you are absolutely certain the ice is safe. Some town or county roads are designated trails; while on such a highway, keep right, observe the posted snowmobile speed limit, and travel in single file. Your basic pack should contain a topographic map and compass as well as a local trail map; survival kit with matches, flashlight, rope, space blanket, quick-energy food, and something warm to drink; extra hat, socks, and mittens.

For navigating unfamiliar territory during a full day's riding, a knowledgeable leader is a real asset. In Lake Placid, Lake Placid Snowmobiling, Inc. (518-523-3596; www.lakeplacidsnowmobiling.com) gives tours.

SPAS

In Lake Placid, there are state-of-the-art spas at the Mirror Lake Inn Resort & Spa (518-523-2544; www.mirrorlakeinn.com) and the Whiteface Lodge (518-523-0560; www.thewhitefacelodge.com). If time is short, there's the Speedy Spa (518-523-5500; www.lpspeedyspa.com). River Rock Salon (518-523-4400; www.riverrocksalon.com; 2049 Saranac Avenue) offers Reiki, facials, and expert care. In Wilmington, you can get a massage at the Wellness Center, upstairs in At the River's Edge Emporium (518-586-1718; www.theriversedgeemporium; 1179 Haselton Road).

WATERFALLS

Among the cascades in this region are Beaver Meadow Falls in the High Peaks Wilderness Area; Blue Ridge Falls on the Branch in North Hudson; the Flume on the West Branch of the Ausable River in Wilmington; Hanging Spear Falls on the Opalescent River in the High Peaks Wilderness; and Wanika Falls on the Chubb River in Lake Placid. See chapter 8 for a parkwide waterfalls guide.

WILDERNESS AREAS

Wilderness areas are open to hiking, cross-country skiing, hunting, fishing, and other similar pursuits, but seaplanes may not land on wilderness ponds, nor are motorized vehicles welcome.

It's not unusual to hear a loon's moody yodel on Adirondack lakes . Courtesy of John DiGiacomo

Dix Mountain. 45,000 acres; southwest of Keene Valley. Adjacent to High Peaks wilderness; rock climbing at Chapel Pond; views from Noonmark, Dix, and many other mountains.

Giant Mountain. 23,000 acres; between Elizabethtown and Keene. Roaring Brook Falls; extensive hiking trails; views from Rocky Peak Ridge, Giant, and other mountains.

High Peaks. 226,000 acres; between Lake Placid and Newcomb. Excellent trail network; rock climbing at Wallface and other peaks; small lakes and ponds; views from Mount Marcy, Algonquin, and numerous other summits. Some interior destinations (Lake Colden and Marcy Dam) and peaks are very popular, to the point of being overused; more than 12,000 people climb Mount Marcy every year.

Jay Mountain. 7,100 acres; east of Jay. Lengthy ridge trails.

McKenzie Mountain. 38,000 acres; north of Ray Brook. Trails for hiking and cross-country skiing; Saranac River; views from McKenzie and Moose Mountains.

Sentinel Range. 23,000 acres; between Lake Placid and Wilmington. Small ponds for fishing, few hiking trails, views from Pitchoff Mountain. This area is remote and receives little use.

WILD FOREST AREAS

More than a million acres of public land in the park are designated as wild forest, which are open to snowmobile travel, mountain biking, and other recreation.

Debar Mountain. Between Loon Lake and Meacham Lake. Horse trails, hiking, fishing in the Osgood River.

Saranac Lakes. West of Saranac Lake village. Excellent canoeing, island camping.

With marsh and mountain, field and forest to explore, experienced birders might be able to see a hundred different species in day. (Back in the 1870s, young Theodore Roosevelt and a friend compiled and published a bird guide to the northern Adirondacks, listing some 90-plus native birds they had seen.) In late spring, warblers in all colors of the rainbow arrive, and the best places to watch for them is along edges where habitats meet, such as woods on the border of a wetland, or along a brushy field. A variety of songbirds, including kingbirds, flycatchers, grosbeaks, waxwings, thrushes, wrens, and sparrows all nest here. The Adirondacks has the best Bicknell's thrush habitat in the Northeast.

Many interior lakes and ponds are home to kingfishers, ducks, herons, and loons; listen and watch for that great northern diver in the early morning and at dusk. Peregrine falcons and bald eagles, absent from the park for much of the 20th century, have been reintroduced. Cliffs in the High Peaks are now peregrine falcon eyries, and you should be able to spot a bald eagle or two near Meacham Lake, or Franklin Falls Pond. In the evening, listen for owls: the barred owl, known by its call, "Who cooks for you, who cooks for you," is quite common. In the fall, look up to see thousands of migrating Canada and snow geese.

Small mammals are numerous: varying hares, weasels, mink, raccoons, fishers, pine martens, otters, bobcats, porcupines, red and gray foxes. Coyotes, with rich coats in shades of black, rust, and gray, can be seen in fall, winter, and spring, and their yips and yowls on a summer night can be thrilling to the backcountry campers' ears. About 50 lynx from the Northwest Territories were released in the High Peaks in the 1980s, to restore the big cats to their former range, but it appears now that few survived.

White-tailed deer are seemingly everywhere, especially in the early spring before the fawns are born. Moose live here now, raising calves across the park, though the highest population of these creatures can be found near Upper Chateaugay Lake, and sightings aren't uncommon in North Elba.

YOGA

Inquire about classes at Inner Quest Yoga & Wellness Center (518-891-9944; www.innerquestyoga.net; 238 Broadway, Saranac Lake); the Keene Valley Fitness Center (518-576-2500; www.keenefitness.com; 1771 NYS Route 73); Lake Placid Hot Yoga (518-523-8028; www. www.bikramyogalakeplacid.com; 2049 Saranac Avenue, Lake Placid); and the Wellness Center, upstairs in At the River's Edge Emporium (518-586-1718; www.theriversedgeemporium; 1179 Haselton Road, Wilmington).

Shopping

Adirondackana and more in the High Peaks & Northern Adirondacks

Shopping here ranges from quirky to funky to woodsy, though you can find a Gap on Lake Placid's main drag. But the real finds aren't skinny jeans or some other trend: Look for a piece of Adirondackana; adventurewear or gear for your next excursion; a classic Adirondack chair or some other rustic furniture; or Adirondack art—painted or sculpted or written in these parts.

In Keene, Dartbrook Rustic Goods (518-576-4360; www.dartbrookrustic.com; Routes 73 and 9N) is the place to go for authentic Adirondack rustic furniture and

Great Camp–style accoutrements. You can't come to the High Peaks without a stop at this gorgeous showroom.

The Birch Store (518-576-4561; www.birchstore.com; 1778 Main Street), in Keene Valley, sells hip shoes and apparel, cards, lotions, and interesting jewelry, combined with traditional Adirondack camp furnishings: blankets, birch-bark baskets and frames, chairs, balsam pillows, and wicker ware in a classy vintage storefront.

In Lake Placid, Adirondack Decorative Arts & Crafts (518-523-4545; 2512 Main Street) is a delightful four-story shop with a huge inventory—

Dartbrook Rustic Goods, in Keene, is one of the most stylish showrooms around, with Adirondack rustic furniture and Great Camp accoutrements. *Courtesy of Nancie Battaglia*

everything from birch bark–patterned table linens to one-of-a-kind twig furniture, oiled canvas jackets, bark lampshades, jewelry, Lightfoot's soap, and the best selection of woodsy cabinet hardware. Adirondack Store and Gallery (518-523-2646; www.theadirondackstore.com; 109 Saranac Avenue) is the place that launched the Adirondackana trend decades ago. If you're looking for anything—pottery, wrapping paper, doormats, sweaters, stationery, cutting boards—emblazoned with loon, trout, pinecone, or moose motifs, search no further. There's also an excellent selection of Adirondack prints by Winslow Homer and Frederic Remington; antique baskets and rustic furniture; camp rugs and blankets; and woodsy ornaments for the Christmas tree, including minute Adirondack chairs.

In Ray Brook, the Ray Brook Frog (518-891-3333; www.raybrookfrog.com; NY 86) has everything you could ever need for the rustic home: furniture, lighting, pillows and throws, rugs, signs, clocks, coasters, picture frames, baskets, kitchen stuff, art, birch-bark everything.

Adirondack Trading Company (518-891-6278; 48 Broadway), in Saranac Lake, is a gift shop with plenty to choose from, especially cards, picture frames, and tchotchkes with bear and moose themes.

ANTIQUES

In these parts, antiquing isn't what it was even a decade ago, but if you know where to look you can still find something special, even artifacts from logging and farming days and good-quality mass-produced 19th-century furniture. Redford glass, made in the Saranac River Valley during the early 1800s, is highly prized and hard to find. Vintage rustic furniture, which was discarded willy-nilly in the 1950s as camp owners modernized, is scarce, but Old Hickory pieces have the right look and feel and are widely available. If you're hunting for a pair of snowshoes or antlers to hang at home, you shouldn't have any trouble finding them here. Some shops stock wood engravings and hand-tinted etchings of Adirondack scenes; these prints—many of them by Winslow Homer or Frederic Remington—originally appearing in *Harper's Weekly*, *Every Saturday*, and other magazines—are affordable. Stereoviews of the grand hotels, postcards from 1910 to 1930, and photographs by George Baldwin, H. M. Beach, "Adirondack" Fred Hodges, and others are charming and not too dear. For photographs of the lakes, mountains, and resorts by Seneca Ray Stoddard, a contemporary of William Henry Jackson and Mathew Brady (all three Adirondack born), you can expect to pay more, but the images are exceptional. Another name on the list for ephemera fans is Verplanck Colvin: mountain panoramas, diagrams, and maps from his 1870–90 surveys are meticulous curiosities.

In Bloomingdale, there's Buyer's Paradise (518-891-4242; NY 3), with antiques, used furniture, horse-drawn equipment, and more inside and outside an old road-house. If you're fed up with precious prices and uptight dealers, go here for serious rummaging.

Lake Placid has Alan Pereske Antiques (518-570-6933; 2158 Saranac Avenue), where you shouldn't be deceived by the small roadside storefront; there are rooms and rooms to see with quality oak, pine, and rustic furniture; paintings and prints of local interest; glass; toys; and ephemera. Antediluvian Antiques & Curiosities (518-523-3990; www.antediluvian.biz; 2488 Main Street) has fine art, tramp art, Victorian taxidermy, and lots of other funky stuff. Mark Wilcox's Summer Antiques (518-523-1876; www.summerantiques.com; 2517 Main Street) showcases high-end paintings, Mission and country furniture, camp items, and sporting antiques. If historical preservation interests you, chat with Wilcox, who is an expert on the topic.

In Saranac Lake, the Emporium, a.k.a. Upscale Resale (518-891-4979; 24 Broad-way), has rustic and vintage furniture, old toys, and pottery. And Ted Comstock (518-891-9009; 274 Trudeau Road) has an extraordinary collection—and knowledge—of all things Adirondack: books, prints, photographs; fine small items; paintings; and antique guideboats, Rushton rowboats, and other small craft.

ART GALLERIES AND PAINTERS' STUDIOS

Always call ahead to make an appointment with these artists or gallery owners:

Near North Art is Sue Cassevaugh (518-647-8614; www.nearnorthart.com; 87 Sheldrake Road), of Au Sable Forks, who paints fine flora and fauna watercolors.

In Keene, Bruce and Annette's Heritage Gallery (518-576-2289; www.highpeaks art.com; corner of Spruce Hill and Hurricane Roads) has oil and watercolor paintings of Adirondack and Vermont scenes; and limited-edition wildlife, floral, and landscape prints.

Skylight Fine Art (518-576-9208; www.skylightfineart.com; 1767 NY 73), in Keene Valley, features 19th-century American landscape paintings by artists of the Hudson River School and works by contemporary landscape artists.

In Lake Placid, Cornerstone Gallery (518-569-7992; 2439 Main Street) sells

Adirondack Camera Obscura

The seafoam-green shingled hut on Mark Ellis's Saranac Lake lawn, across from Lake Flower, is one of 50 or so freestanding camera obscuras in the world. First, a little background on how camera obscuras (Latin for "dark chambers") work: When light, which travels in a straight line, passes through a single point, or pinhole, into a dark, enclosed space, it projects an inverted image on the opposite side of the interior sur-face—exactly how the human eye operates. This optical effect has been used for art and entertainment through the ages. Some scholars think it played a part in Paleolithic drawings and there's evidence the Old Masters used camera obscuras. Lenses were eventually incorporated to further focus the light, as well as mirrors added to better direct it. Ellis welcomes artists and photography buffs who want to visit by appoint-ment; see www.adirondackcameraobscura.com or call 518-891-2266.

Adirondack art and furnishings. Also in town are portraitist Nip Rogers (814-577-1821; www.niprogers.com) and painter Peter Seward (518-523-5842; www.peter seward.com).

In Saranac Lake, there's 7444 Gallery (518-524-8207; www.7444gallery.us; 28 Depot Street) with work by regional, national, and international artists. Adirondack Artists Guild (518-891-2615; www.adirondackartistsguild.com; 52 Main Street) is a gallery that features 14 local artists of note, with changing exhibitions. Georgeanne Gaffney (518-524-8603; www.georgeannegaffney.com) is a fine-art and decorative-finishes painter. The Local Fringe (www.thelocalfringe.com; 518-772-3771; 70 Main Street) is a funky, must-see gallery that exhibits the work of local artists such as Peter Seward, Nip Rogers, and Eric Ackerson. Mark Kurtz Photography (518-891-2431; www.markkurtzphotography.com; 41 Broadway) has commercial, special occasions, and fine art. Painter Matt Burnett (518-524-6441; www.mattburnettpaintings.com; 24 Jenkins Street) creates Adirondack scenes and environmental designs. Small Fortune Studio (518-891-1139; www.fortunestudio.com; 76 Main Street) is the venerable and internationally regarded painter Tim Fortune, who creates realistic Adirondack landscapes.

Wilmington is home of Capozio Gallery (518-946-8239; www.capoziogallery.com; Route 86), with its mixed-media works by Joe Capozio; enamel plaques, jewelry, oils, and watercolors by Stevie Capozio; and photography by Jamison.

BOAT BUILDERS

Placid Boatworks (518-524-2949; www.placidboats.com; 263 Station Street), in Lake Placid, is a top-quality carbon/Kevlar canoe-building outfit.

In Saranac Lake, a long line of boat builders has occupied the Woodward Boat Shop (518-891-3961; www.guideboats.com; 9 Algonquin Avenue) on the edge of town, including Willard Hanmer, whose boats are displayed at the Adirondack Museum. Chris Woodward learned the trade from Carl Hathaway, who was taught by Willard himself. He offers traditional wooden Adirondack guideboats with oars and yoke, plus boat repairs. Spencer Boatworks (518-891-5828; www.antiqueand classicboats.com; 956 NY 3, Bloomingdale Road) makes inboard wooden boats built along classic runabout lines, and does inboard-motor repairs.

BOOKS

Along Lake Placid's Main Street, the Bookstore Plus (518-523-2950; www.thebook storeplus.com; 2491 Main Street) really is the place to go for Adirondack titles, not to mention any other book you're looking for. See chapter 8 for a list of guidebooks and must-have Adirondack literary titles. Chances are good the Bookstore Plus has them.

CLOTHING

Around here you'll find classic woolens, practical sportswear, and high-tech outer gear, though there are a handful of mainstream chain store outlets, such as Gap, Bass, and Van Heusen, along Main Street in Lake Placid. Some highlights of places to buy apparel are described here.

Keene Valley's Birch Store (518-576-4561; 1778 Route 73) sells upscale apparel and footwear.

In Lake Placid, Body & Sole (518-523-9398; www.lakeplacidbodyandsole.com; 2439 Main Street) has funky, upscale PJs, lingerie, sweaters, skirts, handbags, belts, and shoes. Eastern Mountain Sports (518-523-2505; 51 Main Street) is the place to go for outdoor clothing and footgear by Woolrich, Patagonia, Merrell, Nike, and EMS, among others. Fallen Arch (518-523-5310; www.thefallenarch.com; 2537 Main Street) has all sorts of athletic shoes. Maui North (518-523-7245; www.mauinorth.net; 2532 Main Street) offers clothing and gear for snowboarding, skiing, and other outdoor pursuits. High Peaks Cyclery (518-523-3764; www.highpeakscyclery.com; 2733 Main Street) is the place for cycling wear. New Vision Lingerie (518-523-1830; www.newvisionlingerie.com; 2477 Main Street) sells elegant lounge- and underwear. Ruthie's Run (518-523-3271; www.ruthiesrun.com; 2415 Main Street) carries Alpaca Imports, Obermeyer, Dale of Norway, and such. Where'd You Get That Hat? (518-523-3101; www.wheredyougetthathat.com; 2569 Main Street) is the question friends back home are bound to ask when you come home with headgear from this boutique.

Saranac Lake's Blue Line Sports (518-891-4680; www.bluelinesportsllc.com; 81 Main Street) sells apparel for all your outdoor pursuits. The Community Store (518-354-8173; www.community-store.org; 97 Main Street), community owned and operated (at press time, 600 people had chipped in an average of $800 each to get the place off the ground), offers various brands of apparel as well as other goods. Eco Living (518-891-1181; 23 Broadway) has apparel made from sustainable fabrics. Major Plowshares (518-891-7214; 19 Broadway) is a surplus store, yes, but also the outlet for locally made children's clothing in woodland prints, corduroys, and denim. Pink (518-891-4042; 5 Broadway) features fun and funky women's clothes, accessories, and shoes. T. F. Finnigan (518-891-1820; 78 Main Street), a venerable department store, sells North Face, Nautica, B.D. Baggies; it also rents formal-wear. Two Horse Trade Company (518-946-7709; www.twohorsetrade.com; 15 Broadway)—for all your buckskin needs.

CRAFT SHOPS

Many of the following are in private homes, so call ahead.

In Keene, North Country Taxidermy (518-576-9549; www.northcountrytaxidermy.com; NY 73) is hard to miss—there's usually a full-size stuffed creature out front. If you'd like to buy a souvenir antler or two, there are boxes full of them; bearskin rugs are a specialty.

Jay is where you can find the Alpaca Shoppe (518-946-7886; www.alpacashoppe.com; 13036 NY 9N), which sells apparel, accessories, blankets, and yarns made from alpacas. Buttons Buttons (518-946-7625; www.buttonsbuttons.com; John Fountain Road, across from the Jay Village Green) is Barbara Smith's shop in a historical home where she sells her pillows, belts, and handbags made from vintage fabrics, ribbon, and buttons.

Adirondack Weaver (www.adirondackweaver.com) Annoel Krider, in Lake Placid, creates exceptional tapestries and naturally inspired rugs. Caribou Trading Co. (518-523-1152; 2364 Saranac Avenue) offers pottery, jewelry, kites and mobiles, woodenware, and handwovens.

Saranac Lake's Moody Tree Farm (518-891-2468; www.adirondackbalsam wreaths.com; 60 County Rte 55) sells balsam pillows and other products, wreaths, centerpieces, and Christmas trees. Smith's Taxidermy (518-891-6289; 108 Lake Flower Avenue) features rustic furniture by Thomas Phillips and the Smith brothers, and antler chandeliers, pottery, baskets.

Four Directions Weaving (www.fourdirectionsweaving.com; 215 Paye Road) is Donna Foley's woven creations for the home, made from eco-friendly and sustainably grown organic cottons, linens, natural dyes, and her naturally raised Lincoln sheep.

FURNITURE

Regional woodworkers create furniture in a variety of styles, from Shaker-inspired designs, to rugged sculptural pieces, to the straightforward Adirondack chairs that now come in an infinite range of permutations. Many studios are in private homes, so don't expect a large ready-made inventory. Check out www.adirondackwood.com, which includes sources for quality hardwood lumber if you wish to build your own furniture or install a rustic railing in your home.

L. Post Rustics (518-647-5114; www.lpostrustics.com; 2056 Route 9N), in Au Sable Forks, is gorgeous, high-end stuff.

In Jay, David Douglas makes mirrors, lamps, shelves, and more made from birch bark and twigs through his Earth Works studio (518-647-1279; www.artofdavid douglas.com). Swallowtail Studio (518-946-7439; www.swallowtailstudio.com; 55 Trumbulls Corners Road) is Wayne Ignatuk's award-winning sculptural furniture with fine dovetailing and mortise and tenon construction. Spencer Reynolds's Twisted Tree Rustics (518-647-5378) is end tables, coffee tables, lamps, and wall art.

Dartbrook Rustic Goods, in Keene, is where you can find the traditional Great Camp–style furniture of George Jaques (518-576-4360; www.dartbrookrustic.com; Routes 73 and 9N).

Bald Mountain Rustics (www.baldmountainrustics.com), at the Rooster Comb Inn, in Keene Valley, is base for Steve Bowers's funky rustic chairs, benches, beds, cabinets, tables, frames, and other items for the home.

Lake Placid is where you'll find Twigs (518-523-5361; 121 Cascade Road), which is a big shop with antiques and rustic furniture by several makers.

The Ray Brook Frog (518-891-3333; www.raybrookfrog.com; NY 86) showcases rustic and fine furniture, plus decorating accessories.

Vermontville's David Daby makes handcrafted home furnishings through his Adirondack Rustic Creations (518-891-2557; 150 Keith Road).

GENERAL STORES

For true North Country culture visit Norman's Wholesale Grocery (518-891-1890; NY 3), in Bloomingdale. Norman's has been in the same family since it began in 1902, and display drawers still have ornate hardware and lettering declaring "Socks and Mittens" or "Silks and Laces." For retail customers, the stock is mainly convenience-store items, but the place still feels very much like the old times when the stagecoach stopped here.

JEWELRY

Susan Camp, of Susan Camp Studio (www.susancampstudio.com), in Lake Clear, creates gorgeous pieces that are really upscale and funky organic looking.

Lake Placid's Arthur Volmrich (518-523-2970; 2413 Main Street) carries amusing earrings and necklaces mixing antique charms, buttons, and stones with modern components; turquoise bracelets and watchbands; and custom rings. Darrah Cooper Jewelers (518-523-2774; www.darrahcooperjewelers.com; 2416 Main Street) has fine jewelry, including sterling silver and gold charms and earrings representing miniature North Country objects: pack baskets, canoe paddles, guideboats, oars, pinecones, and Adirondack chairs. Spruce Mountain Designs (518-523-9212; www .spruce-mountain.com) does Adirondack wildflowers in sterling silver and gold.

Tupper Lake native Rachel King makes her Earth Girl Designs earrings in the Adirondacks (they're available on Etsy.com and local shops such as Eco Living and the Community Store, in Saranac Lake). Winona Studio (518-946-2401;

44 Mulvey Road), in Wilmington, is Jessica Mulvey's porcupine quill jewelry-making headquarters.

POTTERY

Jay Crafts Center (518-946-7824; www.jaycraftcenter.com; NY 9N) is Lee Kazanas and Cheri Cross's showroom, where you can buy their pottery lamps, bowls, vases, and dinnerware. Youngs' Studio and Gallery (518-946-7301; www.adirondackpottery .com; 6588 NY 86) features Sue Young's wonderful pottery (Raku and stoneware) and limited-edition etchings of Adirondack landscapes by her husband, Terry; plus a full range of other local crafts.

Creations by ceramicist Brooke Noble, of Bloomingdale   Courtesy of Brooke Noble

SCULPTURE

Architectural-design elements, folk-art figures, realistic wildlife, and modern concrete sculpture are just a few of the things shaped by Adirondack hands. Brooke Noble, of Bloomingdale, is a ceramicist who sculpts vessels that are interesting and hip (her work can be found at The Local Fringe, in Saranac Lake). And Ralph Prata, of Concrete Abstracts, makes wall reliefs and concrete carvings (518-891-2417; www .ralphprata.com).

Matt Horner, of Matt Horner Stone Work (518-524-0879; www.matthorner stonework.com), in Keene, creates really cool stone vessels and other pieces.

In Lake Placid, PJ LaBarge (518-523-5353; www.pjlabarge.com) makes Bronze sculptures, such as life-size panthers and other wildlife. Robert Scofield (518-572-8126; www.adirondackburlwood sculpture; 20 Strathknoll Way) does Adirondack burl wood sculpture and bowls.

Peter Shrope Studio (518-327-5247; www.shrope.org; 473 County Route 60), in Rainbow Lake, is where Shrope creates sculpture and mixed media. In Upper Jay, Julia Gronski (518-946-7968; 20 Andrus Way) does fine ceramic work.

5

Champlain Valley

THIS CLASSIC CORRIDOR is the right parts pretty, drowsy, and historical. Lake Champlain is a recreational playground in itself, but along its coast is an extensive trail network, meticulously preserved mid-19th-century neighborhoods, agricultural fairs, fascinating forts, and what remains of a thriving iron-ore industry. This terrain may look a world away from the Adirondacks' interior, but it's a special place with a charm all its own.

Pick Your Spot

Lodging in the Champlain Valley

Don't expect many motels and hotels here, but a handful of bed & breakfasts and inns. While some visitors lodge across the lake in Vermont or commute from more-populated spots in the High Peaks region, the finest way to explore and experience the Champlain Valley is to make the Adirondack coast your headquarters. Here are some highlights.

Elizabethtown
Old Mill Bed & Breakfast (518-873-2294; www.adirondackinns.com/oldmill; 136 River Street) was, in the 1930s and '40s, an art school led by landscape painter Wayman Adams. Now it's a lovely bed & breakfast. Four guest

rooms, all with private baths, are in the main house. Breakfast, served on the enclosed patio that has a fountain as its centerpiece, is a highlight.

Stoneleigh Bed & Breakfast (518-873-2669; www.stoneleighbedand breakfast.com; 18 Stoneleigh Way) is an imposing-looking Germanic-looking castle that was built in 1886 for local judge Francis Smith. The house, with babbling Barton Brook in front, has a fine library, as befits a country judge, and several porches and balconies under the tree-shaded, secluded grounds. Downstairs, there's a suite with private bath; upstairs, four spacious rooms share a bath and a half. A separate carriage house with private bath is also available. Ask about the ghost stories.

The Woodruff House Bed & Breakfast (518-873-6788; www.the woodruffhouse.com; 8219 River Street) is an extraordinarily elegant but comfy

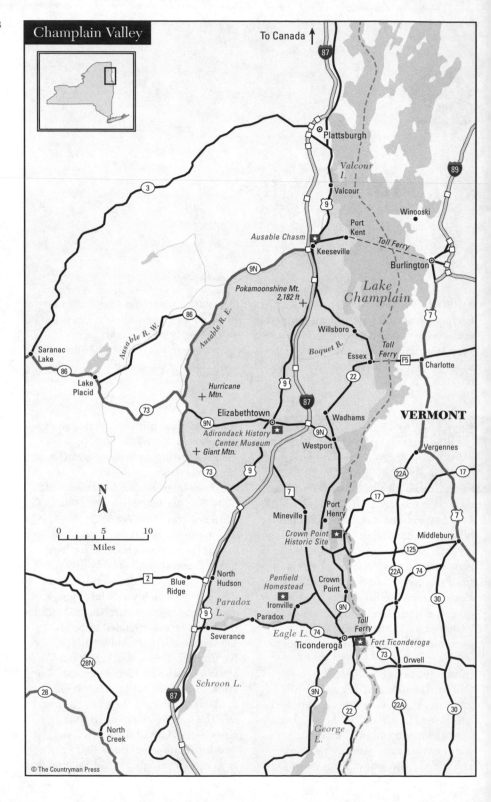

Champlain Valley

To Canada

Plattsburgh

Valcour I.

Valcour

Winooski

Port Kent

Ausable Chasm

Keeseville

Toll Ferry

Burlington

Lake Champlain

Pokamoonshine Mt. 2,182 ft

Willsboro

Boquet R.

Essex

Toll Ferry

Charlotte

Ausable R. W.

Ausable R. E.

Saranac Lake

Lake Placid

Hurricane Mtn.

Elizabethtown

Wadhams

VERMONT

Adirondack History Center Museum

Giant Mtn.

Westport

Vergennes

Port Henry

Mineville

Crown Point Historic Site

Middlebury

N

0   5   10
Miles

Blue Ridge

North Hudson

Penfield Homestead

Crown Point

Paradox L.

Ironville

Severance

Paradox

Eagle L.

Ticonderoga

Fort Ticonderoga

Orwell

Schroon L.

North Creek

George L.

The Woodruff House is a charming 19th-century bed & breakfast in Elizabethtown.
Courtesy of The Woodruff House Bed & Breakfast

Port Henry

The King's Inn (518-546-7633; 42 Hummingbird Way) is a bright spot in Port Henry, though the town is slowly refurbishing neglected buildings from its heyday as an iron-mining center. The inn, an 1893 mansion on a hill overlooking Lake Champlain, has a half-dozen chambers upstairs, all with private baths. Three have working fireplaces; two have views of the lake. The best room in the house has a big sitting area with east-facing windows, and a great big bathroom with a deep porcelain tub. Port Henry's historic sites and waterfront are within walking distance. There's no need to walk very far for a good meal, though: The restaurant on the first floor is fine, and you can enjoy a cocktail while sitting on the wraparound porch.

Westport

All Tucked Inn (518-962-4400; www.alltuckedinn.com; 6455 Main Street), a grand old Dutch Colonial home, occupies a prominent spot on Westport's Main Street. There are nine lovely rooms, all with private baths. A suite on the first floor has its own porch and fireplace. From the inn, you can walk to the Westport Yacht Club, the marina, tennis courts, and even the 18-hole golf course.

The Inn in Westport (518-335-1966; www.innwestport.com; 1234 Stevenson Road), which dates back to 1855, is just across from Westport's quaint Ballard Park. In this recently renovated historical landmark expect peaceful, refined public areas, a café, bookstore, and 10 comfortable rooms—among them William Shakespeare, Ayn Rand, Oscar Wilde . . . you get the idea—each with private baths. An outdoor deck allows views of Lake Champlain and, in summer, the bustle of this Adirondack port community.

Normandie Beach Club (518-962-4750; www.normandiebeachclub.com;

offering on the Boquet River. The home, built in 1868, is getting rave reviews as a B&B. It has two rooms and two baths that can accommodate up to six people, delicious gourmet country breakfasts, and a quaint backyard that's ideal for an intimate wedding.

Essex

The Cupola House (518-963-7494; www.thecupolahouse.com; 2278 Main Street), a prim and proper Greek Revival with wonderful two-story porches, has two handsome apartments that are just two blocks from the ferry to Vermont. Both have complete kitchens and full baths and access to the upstairs porch. A lakeside cottage accommodates two to six people. Guests have access to kayaks, a canoe, and bicycles, and pets are welcome.

Essex Inn (518-963-8821; www.essexinnessex.com; 2297 Main Street) recently underwent a major renovation and is now lovely lodging along Main Street. The inn, which has anchored the most historical hamlet in the park for two centuries, has seven brand-new rooms with new bathrooms. Its Dining Room and Delevan's Tavern are Adirondack rustic, serving meals made with ingredients from local farms. Thursday Community Happy Hours are a hit.

Days of Ore

Approach the Adirondacks from the east—ferrying Lake Champlain from Charlotte, Vermont, to Essex, New York—and you'll see the park's big view of soaring palisades, deep-rooted port towns and ancient metamorphic foothills that undulate beneath dense forests all the way to the High Peaks. Venture south among the iron-rich hills of Westport, Moriah, and Crown Point to find clues that you're in former big-time mining country—ore outcrops visible along lakeside cliffs were clues for 18th-century settlers. In 1776 Benedict Arnold used iron from Moriah to forge hardware for his Revolutionary War fleet on Lake Champlain. After the Champlain Canal opened in 1823, dozens of prospectors shipped ore to ready markets along the Hudson River. Soon local iron was finding its way into everything from transcontinental railroad tracks to cladding for battleships. Eastern Adirondack mines were supplying nearly 9 percent of the nation's iron ore by 1875.

By the early 1900s, most area mines were owned by Port Henry's Witherbee Sherman & Company, which posted agents in New York City to recruit immigrant labor. The company had 1,600 employees by 1917, mined 1.3-million tons that year, and was dispatching 450 railroad cars of ore weekly. Republic Steel took over operations in 1937 but shut down in 1971 when the mines became too deep to compete with open pits in the Midwest. In the end, two centuries of mining tallied 71 million tons of ore—enough to fill a train that could span the continent, and back—leaving an underworld of equivalent volume beneath the foothills of the southeastern Adirondacks. Eleven locomotives and 53 mine cars remain below in the now-flooded system.

Today it's fun to explore communities such as Ironville, Port Henry, Mineville, and Witherbee and watch (from the road) for sealed mineshafts, giant tailings piles, ruins of 19th-century blast furnaces, and European-style mansions built by skilled immigrants for wealthy iron investors. Bring a magnet when you visit lakeside parks—you'll be surprised how much iron you can find in a pail of beach sand.

Patrick Farrell's *Through the Light Hole* (North Country Books, 1996) provides a detailed history of eastern Adirondack iron mining. Visit Port Henry's **Iron Center Museum** (www.townofmoriah.com/localinfo.html) and Ironville's **Penfield Homestead Museum** (www.penfieldmuseum.org) to see exhibits and artifacts.

—Tom Henry

Westport's Ballard Park.   Courtesy of Jo Ann Gardner

96 Furnace Point Lane), open Memorial Day through Columbus Day, had previous incarnations, beginning in 1960, as kids' language and water sports camps. (Allan Sherman's "Hello Muddah, Hello Fadduh" was inspired when his son wrote letters home from here.) Today the Normandie has a variety of lakeside cottages that can be rented by the week. Also, the beach club offers guests waterskiing, sailing, canoeing, tennis, windsurfing, and other activities.

The Westport Hotel (518-962-4501; www.thewestporthotel.com; 6691 Main Street), a spacious clapboard building, has been sheltering travelers since 1876,

The Victorian Lady Bed & Breakfast, on Westport's Main Street, is a historical landmark. Courtesy of Nancie Battaglia

when the railroad came to Westport. Guests can choose from 10 rooms; most have private baths. The onsite Tavern has good meals. People who are traveling without a car should note that there's daily Amtrak service to Westport, and many of the town's charms, from the Essex County Fair and Depot Theatre to the lakefront, are nearby. The hotel's sister property, the Victorian Lady Bed & Breakfast (518-962-2345; www.victorianladybb.com; 6447 Main Street), in a colorful 1850s Greek Revival home, is over-the-top lovely. This historical landmark's gardens are also something to gush about.

The Westport Chair

The Westport chair originated around 1903 in the town of the same name on the shore of Lake Champlain. Summer resident Thomas Lee canted the seat and back at several different angles, gathering family members to test each adjustment until he settled on a tilted 100-degree angle, satisfied he had created a relaxing place to sit. He later gifted the design to Harry Bunnell, a local hunting buddy, who got it patented in 1905 and manufactured chairs of hemlock and basswood until 1930. About this time the Adirondack chair design began its rise, though its origin is a mystery. Westports stamped "Bunnell" can fetch well over $1,000 today.

Courtesy of Nancie Battaglia

—*Mary Thill, from "Angle of Repose,"* Adirondack Life

Local Flavors

Where to eat in the Champlain Valley

Warm-weather lakeside dining is a treat here, though there are exceptional eateries tucked inland. Always call ahead as many of this region's businesses hibernate in winter.

Elizabethtown

Deer's Head Inn (518-873-6514; www.thedeershead.com; 7552 Court Street), a rambling inn, built in 1808 (the guest registry shows that Grover Cleveland and Benjamin Harrison stayed here),

Deer's Head Inn is an Elizabethtown mainstay. Courtesy of Ted Comstock, Saranac Lake

has changed hands through the centuries, but its current owner has transformed it into a special place with creative cuisine. Fresh, locally grown ingredients are used whenever possible, and dishes are surprisingly affordable—the roasted rack of lamb is a customer favorite. The ambience here is old-school elegance—fireplace, walls hung with paintings by regional artists, tables with candles, plus a cozy pub.

Essex

The Old Dock Restaurant (518-963-4232; www.olddockrestaurant.com; Lake Shore Road), like many of the commercial establishments in Champlain Valley villages, is in a handsome stone building dating back to the early 19th century. It was converted to a restaurant in the 1930s and overlooks the landing of the ferry to Vermont. In good weather, everyone sits outdoors to watch the clouds racing above Vermont's Green Mountains. Lunch and dinner offerings, served when the place is open, mid-May through Columbus Day, are varied, although seafood dishes are favorites among diners, particularly the escargot and crab cake appetizers, the fish and chips, and dinner entrées such as the seafood pasta and shore dinner platter. Boat slips are available for customers.

Port Henry

The King's Inn (518-546-7633; 42 Hummingbird Way), a good restaurant

in a town that has lacked such things since the heyday of iron mining ended in the 1960s, has quite a regional following for its healthy-portioned fare, making reservations essential in summer. (Don't be put off by the salad checkmark system.) One big, airy dining room with a stone fireplace occupies the long side of the building; across the front, with windows facing the lake, is a smaller dining room. Between the two rooms is a nice little bar, fine for lingering before dinner in cool weather.

Michigans

Meat as a condiment is all the rage here. A **michigan**, whose nomenclature is spiritedly debated among locals, is, basically, a hot dog with chili—minus the beans or cheese—on top. The following are places where you can get a michigan: **Gene's Michigan Stand** (518-546-7292), in Port Henry; the **Wind-Chill Factory** (518-585-3044), in Ticonderoga; **New Way Lunch** (518-623-2158), in Warrensburg; and **Ethels Dew Drop Inn** (518-963-8389) and **Sportsman's Dinette** (518-963-8399), in Willsboro.

Beyond the Champlain Valley, michigans are sold at **Teddy's Ice Cream** (518-891-0422), in Bloomingdale; **Devin's Deli** (518-946-2235), in Jay; **Skyline Ice Cream & Food** (518-359-7288), in Tupper Lake; and **Whitebrook Dairy Bar** (518-946-7458), in Wilmington.

Courtesy of Mark Kurtz, www.markkurtz.com

Emerald's (518-585-7435; 609 Hague Road, NY 9N, at the Ticonderoga Country Club), inside the clubhouse at Ticonderoga Country Club, serves meals in a sun porch or in a more formal dining room. The golf course is one of the most beautiful in the Adirondacks; the views of the green fairways and nearby mountains from the porch windows are breathtaking. At lunch, very good salads, seafood, and great big sandwiches on crusty French bread are appealing. Dinner includes aged steaks, sauced chicken dishes, quality seafood, and seasonal vegetables. Open May through Columbus Day.

Hot Biscuit Diner (518-585-3483; hotbiscuitdiner.com; 14 Montcalm Street) is a cheery, checked-tablecloth place worth a stop for any meal or if you've got a sudden hankering for hot, made-from-scratch gingerbread dolloped with whipped cream. Everything's homemade, from blueberry muffins to the trademark biscuits. Along with the chow, the place is a mini museum, decorated with old photos, sheet music, tools, advertising art, and local mementos. No credit cards.

Ye Olde Forte View Inn (518-585-7767; 325 NY 22) features dining on an enclosed porch overlooking Lake Champlain and Fort Ticonderoga. The scenery is outstanding, with rock cliffs in the foreground, the lake in middle distance, and the stone walls of the fort beyond. Locals rave about the wings here, and there's an extensive sandwich menu for lunch, with creations named after historical figures who visited Fort Ticonderoga. The General Burgoyne is a lot of turkey piled on a Kaiser roll, topped with a tasty sauce and veggies. Sweet-potato fries or fresh, thick homemade French fries are recommended side orders. Seafood, steaks, and pasta are the featured dinner fare. This is orchard country, with luscious apple pie a fall dessert favorite. No credit cards.

Le Bistro du Lac at the Westport Yacht Club (518-962-8777; www.bistrodulac .com; On Lake Champlain, off NY 22), open seasonally, is probably the finest waterfront setting on either side of Lake Champlain. Guests arrive by car—or they sail right up to the concrete dock that forms the front of the outdoor dining area. Le Bistro is one of the best restaurants in the Adirondacks: simple, fresh ingredients combine in inventive ways. Expect wonderful appetizers such as escargot on puff pastry, *moules marinières* (mussels and shallots in white wine cream sauce), a fine country pâté, or smoked bluefish bruschetta. Then endive salad, or mesclun lettuce topped with Roquefort or goat cheese. The rack of lamb with rosemary and garlic sauce, fillet of beef with béarnaise sauce, and duck with green peppercorns are all winners. Le Bistro may be the only spot between Montreal and Manhattan with true filet mignon tartare on the menu. The bouillabaisse Provençal is highly recommended, and the lovely broth overflows with succulent lobster, mussels, scallops, shrimp, and clams; chicken is prepared in a different way each day. The wine list is excellent, and Continental desserts feature seasonal fruits and top-quality chocolate. Lunch offers an excellent, reasonably priced way to sample the menu and enjoy an alfresco meal in the sun.

Normandie Beach Club (518-962-4750; www.normandiebeachclub.com; 96 Furnace Point Lane), open in warm weather, has two super choices for dining in the Champlain Valley: Furnace Point Grill (named after the blast furnace that stood here in the 1840s)—a fine, but casual establishment—and the more laid-back lunch spot, the Coco Café. The Furnace Point Grill has a big, welcoming bar for cocktails and a dining room that seats about 60. Steaks, seafood, chicken dishes, and salads fill the menu, and homemade bread means

Small Farm Rising

The Champlain Valley, unlike the peak-riddled parkland to its west, is undergoing an agricultural renaissance. And *Small Farm Rising*, a documentary by Ben Stechschulte (www.smallfarmrising .com), has helped spotlight this region's farms—mostly run by first-generation farmers who are implementing sustainable practices and offering Community Supported Agriculture shares to locals. (Locals pay an annual CSA fee and receive, in turn, weekly bounty from the farm.) Most farms sell at area **farmers' markets**—in the Champlain Valley it's behind the Adirondack History Center Museum, in Elizabethtown, on Fridays, 9 AM to 1 PM, May through October.

An agricultural renaissance is underway in the Champlain Valley, with the rise of farms operated by first-generation farmers, such as Fledging Crow Vegetables, in Keeseville.

Courtesy of Ben Stechschulte, www.benstechschulte.com

Essex Farm (www.kristinkimball .com), run by Mark and Kristin Kimball—Kristin's memoir *The Dirty Life* is a hot title—and Keeseville's **Fledging Crow Vegetables** (www.fledgingcrow.com), farmed by Ian Ater and Lucas Christenson, were featured in Stechschulte's film. Other Champlain Valley farms can be found at **Adirondack Harvest**'s website, www.adirondackharvest.com.

delicious sandwiches. The Coco Café includes a stone terrace beside an awninged deck overlooking Lake Champlain, great for a light meal. The menu at both spaces is varied and uniformly good, and in summer there's regular live entertainment. Locals don't miss the Sunday brunch. You can also get a basket lunch to bring on the boat (many diners arrive via water) or the trail.

Wadhams

Dogwood Bread Company (518-962-2280; 2576 County Route 10) is a place folks go out of their way to visit. Bread, sticky buns, scones, cookies—everything is delicious here. Lunches are panini and homemade soup, and Friday pizza nights are popular among locals. Dogwood co-owner Courtney Fair is a master wood-fired-bread maker and a master furniture maker .

Willsboro

Turtle Island Café (518-963-7417; www .turtleislandcafe.com; 3 North Main Street) is in a 127-year-old former pharmacy overlooking the Boquet River. Its chef/owner David Martin grew up in West Chazy, just north of the Adirondack Park, studied at the Culinary Institute of America, cooked in upscale urban eateries, and opened his café a decade ago. Martin hosts plenty of adventurers, often after they've hiked the Champlain Area Trails. He crafts fresh, sustainable meat (from a New England co-op) and vegetables (from Champlain Valley farms Juniper Hill and Fledging Crow) and adds fruit essences, honey, herbs and chiles to signature entrées, such as wild salmon and duck breast. His wine list is extraordinary and constantly evolving, with 180 selections. New is Martin's craft

beer program, with 25 bottles to choose
from.

MORE MEALS

In Crown Point, Crown Point Bread
Company (518-217-8549; www.crown
pointbread.com; 92744 Main Street) is
Yannig Tanguy's artisanal French bakery
that's particularly well-received among
historical re-enactors.

Great breakfasts can be had at Elizabethtown's Arsenal Inn Restaurant
(518-873-6863; 7581 Court Street).

The Dining Room and Delevan's
Tavern at Essex Inn (518-963-4400;
www.essexinnessex.com; 2297 Main
Street) serve fresh, delicious food Tuesday through Saturday in a 200-year-old
hotel. Essex Provisions (518-963-4690;
2270 Main Street), in Essex, of course,
is a coffeeshop/café/market on the lake.

Westport's Galley Restaurant (518-
962-4899; www.westportmarina.com;
20 Washington Street), open in warm

weather, has deck dining, music many
evenings, plus a Lobsterfest in September. Me and My Girls Café & Bakery
(518-962-8588; 6476 Main Street) is a
cheery café popular with locals for
baked goods and some of its dinerlike
breakfasts and lunches, particularly in
winter when the rest of Westport seems
to shut down. The Tavern at the Westport Hotel (518-962-4501; www.thewest
porthotel.com; 6691 Main Street) is
close to the Depot Theatre.

Willsboro is where hometown hero
Sportsman's Dinette (518-963-8399;
www.willsborony.com/sportsmans; 3745
Main Street) offers an unexpected
surprise—a turkey cooked everyday for
fresh sandwiches—among expected
fare. Upper Deck at Willsboro Bay
Marina (518-963-8271; www.upperdeck
restaurant.com; 20 Klein Way, Willsboro
Bay Marina) is pricey but good, open
mid-June through Labor Day, and over-
looks Willsboro Bay and the wooded
cliffs beyond.

To Do
Attractions and activities in the
Champlain Valley

Meticulously preserved 19th-century
neighborhoods, first-rate professional
theater, grand Fort Ticonderoga, and
classy galleries give arts lovers plenty to
appreciate in the Champlain Valley.

ARCHITECTURE/HISTORICAL DISTRICTS

The Champlain Valley is rich in architectural sights. Beginning in the south, the town
of Ticonderoga is a major destination for history lovers. Fort Ticonderoga is about
2.5 miles north of the village on NY 22, but you can find the crumbling walls and
rusting cannons of Fort Mount Hope by exploring near the old cemetery on Burgoyne Street, not far from the village waterworks. At the head of the main drag,
Montcalm Street, is a replica of John Hancock's Boston home, built by Horace
Moses in 1926. Moses made his fortune with the Strathmore Paper Company and
funded many town beautification projects, including the *Liberty Monument*, a
bronze statue by Charles Keck that's in the center of the traffic circle across from
Hancock House. Pride of Ticonderoga (518-585-6366; www.prideofticonderoga.org;
111 Montcalm Street), a nonprofit revitalization organization, offers a walking tour
brochure that highlights Ticonderoga's bustling 19th-century industrial history.

Near today's bridge—a brand-spanking new span—to Vermont, off NY 22, is
Fort Crown Point; there were several fortifications along the lake harkening back to
the French occupation of the Champlain Valley in the 1730s. Crown Point State
Historic Site (518-597-4666; 739 Bridge Road, Crown Point) sits on a thumb-shape

Every Adirondack visitor should go to Fort Ticonderoga, a structure and chunk of land that changed the course of American history. Photograph by Richard Timberlake, courtesy of Fort Ticonderoga

point that parts the waters, with Bulwagga Bay to the west and the long reach of the lake on the east. The sweeping view to the north once provided an ideal spot for guarding the territory. The French built a gargantuan stone octagon here in 1734, Fort St. Frederic, which was attacked repeatedly by the British in 1755 to 1758 and finally captured by them in 1759. Colonial forces launched their assault on the British ships in Lake Champlain from Crown Point in 1775. In 1910, the ruins of the French, British, and colonial forts were given to New York State. There's an excellent visitor center that explains the archaeology and political history of this haunting promontory through exhibits and audiovisual programs, and several miles of interpretive trails winding around stone walls and redoubts. The site is open May through October. Admission: $4 adults, $3 seniors; free for kids 12 and under.

West of Crown Point is Ironville, a well-preserved early-19th-century community, with several white clapboard homes, a lovely church, numerous farm buildings, and peaceful, tree-shaded roads. On the way to Ironville, in Factoryville, you'll see the only octagonal house in the Adirondacks.

Historic markers erected by New York State abound along NY 22 as you approach Port Henry. The original settlement here supplied lumber for the forts at Crown Point and for Benedict Arnold's naval fleet. Later, the discovery of abundant iron ore shaped the town. Evidence of this prosperity appears in an ornate downtown block, elaborate churches, and the exuberant high Victorian Moriah Town Office building, formerly the headquarters of the Witherbee, Sherman & Co. Iron Company. In the carriage house next to the town offices the Iron Center (518-546-3587) is a museum dedicated to local mining and railroads.

The Essex County seat is Elizabethtown, founded in the 1790s. The county courthouse complex is impressive, and about half a mile away are brick buildings built by the illustrious Hand family, which produced a dynasty of civic leaders and attorneys, including Supreme Court Justice Learned Hand. The well-preserved Greek Revival Hand House and the Hands' freestanding law office are on US 9, near the flashing light. About 8 miles east of E'town, along Champlain's shore, is Westport, which was first settled in 1770. Buildings from that era have all disappeared, but a few homes near the lake on Washington Street, off NY 9N and 22, were built in the 1820s. Westport was a vital port, shipping iron, lumber, wool, and other farm products before the Civil War, and a thriving summer community afterward. Following NY 22, you pass Gothic cottages and impressive stone houses overlooking the lake. Between Westport and Essex, on NY 22, is the tiny farm community of Boquet, with its odd little octagonal schoolhouse.

The Adirondack community richest in architectural treasures is undoubtedly Essex. During the brief peaceful period between the French and Indian War and the American Revolution, William Gilliland, an Irish immigrant, bought up huge tracts of land along Lake Champlain. He envisioned a string of prosperous communities, and by 1770, had established Essex. Unfortunately, the town lay smack in the path of General Burgoyne as British troops marched from Canada to Saratoga and, just a decade after the settlers arrived, their town was destroyed. By 1800, Essex was again thriving thanks to iron mining, stone quarrying, a tannery, shipbuilding, and other commerce. By 1850, the population of the town was 2,351, but when railroads came to eastern New York, in the 1870s, fortunes changed for Essex and other lakeside towns. The 1850s marked the peak of the town's prosperity. Thereafter the population dwindled steadily to its current level of about a thousand residents. Because of this decline, and the lack of economic opportunities, there was little need for new housing; old buildings were preserved out of necessity. Today, Essex contains one of the most intact collections of pre–Civil War buildings in the Northeast.

Continuing on NY 22, Willsboro and Keeseville contain many historic buildings. Keeseville has several homes made of buff-pink native sandstone that date back to the 1830s, and buildings in the full range of 19th-century styles from Dutch Colonial to Federal and Greek Revival to Gothic Revival and Romanesque. The Stone Arch Bridge over the Ausable River, built in 1842, is the largest single-span arch bridge in the country. From the bridge you can see the huge factory buildings that made horseshoe nails, an indispensable product of the 19th century. The former AuSable Horse Nail Factory Company offices is now home of Adirondack Architectural Heritage.

Maps with interpretive signs along the route are available through the Champlain Valley Heritage National Partnership (1-866-843-5253; www.champlain valleynhp.org) and highlight historic sites, farmsteads, local industries, and vistas from Keeseville to Ticonderoga.

Adirondack Architectural Heritage (518-834-9328; www.aarch.org; 1745 Main Street, Keeseville) is a parkwide nonprofit organization devoted to historic preservation. Tours of public and private sites in summer and fall, lectures, workshops, and technical assistance to building owners are just a few of the programs and services it offers.

Historic Essex (www.essexny.org), formed in December 1969 as the Essex Community Heritage Organization, has worked for more than four decades to preserve a village that is one of the finest and most intact collections of Federal and Greek Revival architecture in rural New York State. Through

A vintage scene of Keeseville's Main Street.
Courtesy of Ted Comstock, Saranac Lake

education, advocacy, rehabilitation, and economic revitalization initiatives, Historic Essex and its more than 300 members have strived to develop programs that simultaneously preserve the architectural and environmental qualities of the community and create new economic and housing opportunities for residents.

ARTS CENTERS AND ARTS COUNCILS

Adirondack Art Association (518-963-8309; www.adirondackartassociation.com; Schoolhouse Gallery, Essex) is a community gallery, open spring through fall, that showcases regional professional artists in solo and group exhibitions, from quilts to photography and watercolor paintings to designer crafts.

Arts Council for the Northern Adirondacks (518-962-8778; www.artsnorth.org; NY 22, Westport) was launched as an advocacy group for local artists and craftspeople, the Arts Council for the Northern Adirondacks publishes its comprehensive *Annual Arts Directory*, listing exhibitions, lectures, fairs, music, theater, dance performances, and children's programs. In addition, the organization gives grants to working artists, presents traditional and contemporary musicians from the region in different towns, and sponsors traveling juried art shows.

CINEMA

During the silent-film era, the Adirondacks provided a backdrop for popular films, including *The Shooting of Dan McGrew, The Wilderness Woman, Glorious Youth,* and dozens more; the movie industry thrived for more than a decade in unlikely places such as Plattsburgh and Port Henry. Cowboy scenes were staged at Ausable Chasm, "Alaskan" trapper cabins were filmed in Essex County farmyards, and adventures supposedly set in South America, Siberia, and Switzerland took place along the valley. As the cameras rolled, Washington crossed the frozen Delaware—somewhere on the Saranac River. This region again had the spotlight in 2010 when Paul Sorvino, William Sadler, and Nick Wechsler came to the Champlain Valley to film *Mineville*—originally called *Switchback*—about a poor family of Irish immigrants who work in the iron-ore mines of Mineville.

Champlain Valley Film Society (518-963-8662; www.cvfilms.org) is a nonprofit organization that features movies year-round, at venues in Essex, Elizabethtown, Westport, and Willsboro. In August, Ballard Park, in Westport, is backdrop for the society's films.

LIBRARIES

In Ticonderoga, there's Black Watch Memorial Library (518-585-7380; Montcalm Street), designed as a medieval-looking "shrine to literacy" in 1905 and named after the 42nd Highland Regiment that fought at Ticonderoga in 1758.

Paine Memorial Free Library (518-963-4478; 1 School Street), in Willsboro, is a lovely brick building overlooking the Boquet River. The library has numerous summer programs, from art exhibitions to traditional craft demonstrations. Ask a librarian about the library's popular "bridge cam."

Westport Library Association (518-962-8219; 6 Harris Lane, Westport) has a clock tower. This is a great old building with fireplaces, antique woodwork, natural lighting, high ceilings, comfy couches, and several computers.

MUSEUMS

1812 Homestead Farm & Museum (518-963-4071; 112 Reber Road North, Willsboro) is where the past is present. This spread is open 10 AM daily, May through

Courtesy of Fort Ticonderoga

Fort Ticonderoga (518-585-2821; www.fort-ticonderoga.org; 30 Fort Ti Road, off NY 22, Ticonderoga), high above Lake Champlain, is a must-see for Adirondack visitors. In 1755, the French built a fort, Carillon, on the site, and for the next quarter century, the stone fortification was a key location in the struggle to claim North America. The Marquis de Montcalm defended the site against numerous British invaders until 1758, when Lord Jeffery Amherst captured the fort. Ticonderoga was British territory until Ethan Allen and the Green Mountain Boys took the fort "in the name of Jehovah and the great Continental Congress," during the American Revolution. In the early 1800s, the Pell family acquired the ruins and fields where the soldiers once camped. Work was begun in 1908 to rebuild the barracks and parade grounds, making Fort Ticonderoga the nation's first restored historic site (in contrast, Colonial Williamsburg's restoration dates back to the 1930s). In more recent years, the Mars family, and today, a dynamic board of directors have given the fort a makeover, adding a slick conference center, redesigning exhibits, rebuilding parts of the fortification, rehabbing the Pavilion (an 1830s hotel) at the King's Garden, and focusing on the art of creating historically accurate clothing, shoes, musical instruments, and other areas of 18th- and 19th-century military life, popular with a burgeoning reenactment crowd.

Inside the barracks are exhibits on the French and Indian War and the American Revolution, from intricately inscribed powder horns to blunderbusses, cannons, and swords. Below the barracks is the subterranean kitchen, which supplied thousands of loaves of bread every day to the standing army. Beneath the walls, on a broad plain facing the lake, is the King's Garden, a gorgeous spot that's been cultivated for hundreds of years and is open for tours. The walled English-style garden dates back to the 1920s and is one of a handful of American places recognized by the Garden Conservancy. When driving the road to the fortification, stop the car and take a moment to read the monuments, to absorb the battlefield, hallowed ground where thousands of soldiers fell. The fort is set in a spectacular spot with a magnificent view of the lake, but don't end your visit there. It's worth a side trip up Mount Defiance, near town, to get an even higher perspective. From the top of that hill, a show of British cannons so intimidated the officers at Ticonderoga and Fort Independence, a fort across the lake in Vermont, that colonial troops fled both strongholds. (Shots were never fired.) Bring a pair of binoculars and a picnic lunch.

You can eat a meal at Fort Ti, and there's always action at the fort, from tours from costumed interpreters, demonstrations of black-powder shooting, and cannon firing to fife-and-drum drills (check out the musicians' new uniform and period-appropriate instruments). The **Grand Encampment of the French and Indian War** features hundreds of make-believe French, Scottish, and colonial troops, Native American scouts, and camp followers in authentic costumes, in late June. The fort remains open 9 AM daily, mid-May through mid-October Admission: $17.50 adults, $8 ages 5–12; senior and group discount.

September, with an original homestead, barn, and schoolhouse. Families can try making candles, cooking in an open hearth, or gathering eggs. You can meet the farm's resident oxen, sheep, and pigs. Demonstrations include blacksmithing, spinning, gardening, shingle-making, quilting, and other old-time skills. In season, the farm makes apple cider and maple sugar. Recommended for kids ages six to 12.

Adirondack History Center Museum (518-873-6466; www.adkhistorycenter.org; 7590 Court Street/US 9, Elizabethtown), home to the Essex County Historical Society, can help put all the military skirmishes along Lake Champlain into a geographical and chronological context. The museum, open Memorial Day through Columbus Day, also interprets local pioneer life—mining, farming, trapping, logging—through its permanent exhibits and showcases contemporary local artists during the summer. There's a stagecoach that once carried passengers from Elizabethtown to Keene, a 58-foot fire tower that you don't have to climb a mountain to enjoy, a roomful of dolls, and the wonderful Colonial Garden of perennials and herbs. For Adirondack and genealogical scholars, an excellent library is open by appointment year-round.

Heritage Museum (518-585-2696; www.ticonderogaheritagemuseum.org; Bicentennial Park) and the Hancock House (518-585-7868; www.thehancockhouse.org; Hancock House, 6 Moses Circle), in Ticonderoga, are located in a replica of John Hancock's Boston home. The Heritage Museum depicts 19th-century industries, including paper- and pencil-making, in a Victorian office building, once headquarters of the old Ticonderoga pulp and paper company. (Contact the museum for hours.) Hancock House was the first home of the New York State Historical Association (now in Cooperstown), and the house has several period rooms illustrating social history from the 1700s to the turn of the 20th-century. There's an extensive research library, open by appointment year-round; regular hours are Wednesday through Saturdays, 10–4. When you're in Ticonderoga, pick up the brochure "Marker and Monument Tour Guide" for connect-the-dots historical trivia—you'll learn about such figures as the Jesuit martyr Isaac Jogues (died by torture), Lord George Howe (died by musket ball), and Horace Moses (died a millionaire).

Penfield Homestead Museum (518-597-3804; www.penfieldmuseum.org; Old Furnace Road, off NY 74, Ironville) has a sign in the front yard that makes an astonishing claim: The site purports to be the birthplace of the Electrical Age. In 1831, Allen Penfield used a crude electromagnet to separate iron ore from its base rock, thus testing electricity in an industrial application for the

Courtesy of Nancie Battaglia

Whallonsburg Grange Hall

A couple of years ago, an almost-century-old grange in teensy Whallonsburg finally got the revival it deserved when locals pitched in to embrace it, update it, and use it once again as a hub of the community. Today, the **Whallonsburg Grange Hall** (518-962-4386; www.thegrange hall.org; at the corner of Route 22 and Whallons Bay Road) has a popular Lyceum Series, is backdrop for classes and workshops, shows movies, hosts music and square dances, and can be rented for special events.

first time. Ironville today is a lovely, quiet spot so different from its heyday as the center of a major iron industry in 1830 to 1880, when smoke from the smelters filled the skies and the clatter of rock crushers ceased only after dark. The complex, open June through Columbus Day, is an open-air museum dedicated to the local mines, forges, and old railroads, with an eclectic historical collection in the homestead itself, a white-clapboard Federal building, circa 1826. The other buildings along the lane in town are mainly Greek Revival, in excellent condition; there's a self-guided walking tour of the 550-acre grounds that takes you for a nice hike in the woods to find remnants of the days of iron. In mid-August, the museum sponsors Heritage Day, a festival of traditional crafts and skills, with wagon rides and a chicken barbecue. In October, Penfield's Apple Folkfest is a celebration that includes crafts, music, and every kind of apple dessert imaginable. Admission: $4 adults, $2 children.

MUSIC

The Forest, Field, and Stream Festival, in September, at the Adirondack History Center Museum (518-873-6466; www.adkhistorycenter.org), sponsored by the Arts Council for the Northern Adirondacks, features traditional music. Otis Mountain Music Festival (518-962-8687; www.otismountain.com), held in August, brings a weekend of bluegrass, country, and old-time music, plus mandolin, guitar, and fiddle workshops, to Elizabethtown. Whallonsburg Grange Hall (518-962-4386; www.the grangehall.org; corner of Route 22 and Whallons Bay Road) hosts square dances and concerts. Westport's Thursday-night Ballard Park Concert Series (518-962-8778; www.artsnorth.org), has all types of music, overlooking Lake Champlain.

Meadowmount School of Music (518-873-2063; www.meadowmount.com; Lewis-Wadhams Road, Lewis) was founded by violin great Ivan Galamian. His summer music camp alumni gives a hint of the talent nurtured in the hills of the Boquet Valley: Yo-Yo Ma, Itzhak Perlman, Pinchas Zukerman, Michael Rabin, Lynn Harrell, Jaime Laredo, and Joshua Bell. Distinguished faculty, visiting artists, and promising students—ages 8 through 30—give free concerts at the camp's 500-seat Ed Lee and Jean Campe Memorial Concert Hall at 7:30 PM on Wednesday, Friday, and Sunday; the annual scholarship-benefit concert features world-famous string and piano players. Meadowmount is a rare treasure, and if you're visiting the eastern Adirondacks, the programs are worth the drive.

SEASONAL EVENTS

The events listed below (in chronological order) emphasize history, music, storytelling, crafts and skills, or a combination of the arts.

Old-Time Folkcraft Fair (518-963-4478), on the lawn of the Paine Memorial Library, in Willsboro, is a showcase for local artisans and a chance to learn traditional North Country skills, in late July.

Essex County Fair (518-962-8650; www.essexcountyfair.org), in Westport, has harness racing, livestock and agricultural displays, a midway, educational programs by Cooperative Extension, music, and lots of cotton candy. The fair runs in late July.

Forest, Field, and Stream Festival (518-873-6466; www.adirondackhistory center.org), at the Adirondack History Center Museum, in Elizabethtown, happens during the height of fall color, in September, with a full slate of storytelling, old-time music, craft demos, black-powder shooting, and participatory programs for children.

Apple Folkfest at the Penfield Museum (518-597-3804; www.penfieldmuseum .org), in Ironville, features traditional crafts, music, animals, and activities for children, in early October.

THEATER

Boquet River Theatre Festival (518-572-4193; www.brtf.com) presents original children's theater in August at the Whallonsburg Grange Hall.

Depot Theatre (518-962-4449; www.depottheatre.org; Delaware & Hudson Depot, NY 9N, Westport) has given Westport's Delaware & Hudson depot new vitality as home to a fine professional acting company. The former freight room—with air-conditioning—comes alive with four or five plays each summer: 2012's lineup included *The Hound of the Baskervilles, Careless Love, The Marvelous Wonderettes,* and *Real Women Have Curves.* Local artists display their work in the lobby. Depot Theatre offers matinees for each of its shows—a nice option on a rainy day—but be sure to call ahead for tickets

Depot Theater is a professional summer acting company in Westport's Delaware & Hudson depot.   Courtesy of Depot Theater

Essex Theatre Company (518-524-7708; www.essextheatre.org), originally formed to showcase local talent, just celebrated its 20th year. Productions in 2012, performed at Essex's Masonic Lodge, were *Godspell* and Noel Coward's *Blithe Spirit.*

Shakespeare Festival (518-962-8383; Ballard Park, Westport) happens every Labor Day weekend when the American Studio Theater presents a Shakespeare production at Ballard Park, in Westport. The acting and the scenery are equally fantastic. Among the past productions are *Much Ado About Nothing, Twelfth Night,* and *The Merry Wives of Windsor.*

Recreation

Adventures in the Champlain Valley

Roads with bucolic views for cyclists, a new trail network for hikers, a raging river, challenging rock faces for climbers, a vast lake for every watery or icy pursuits—the Champlain Valley is an all-season playground for outsdoorspeople.

ADIRONDACK GUIDES

Several hundred guides are members of a select group within the DEC licensees: the New York State Outdoor Guides Association (www.nysoga.com). These folks make a point of preserving wild resources as well as helping clients find the right places for hunting, fishing, camping, and climbing; many guides practice low-impact camping and offer outdoor education.

BICYCLING

In April, road bikers might find that the snowbanks are gone, but a slippery residue of sand remains on the road shoulders. Likewise, springtime backcountry cyclists might discover patches of snow in shady stretches of woods or muddy soup on sunnier trails. At the other end of the year, note that big-game season begins in October, and some of the best mountain-biking destinations are also popular hunting spots.

Check out chapter 8 for a list of biking guidebooks, though the most comprehensive for road cyclists is *25 Bicycle Tours in the Adirondacks: Road Adventures in the East's Largest Wilderness* by Bill McKibben, Sue Halpern, Barbara Lemmel, and Mitchell Hay (Backcountry Publications). It describes loop trips in wonderful detail, with an eye toward scenic and historic destinations such as Willsboro Point, a thumb of land sticking into Lake Champlain, with great views coming and going. A must-see is *Bicycling the Scenic Byways of the Adirondack North Country* (www.biketheby ways.org), sponsored by the Adirondack North Country Association. Boquet River Association's *Historic Boquet River Bike Trails* (518-873-3688; www.boquetriver.org; Essex County Government Center, Elizabethtown) outlines excellent road trips with historical stops; Essex County Visitors Bureau (518-523-2445; www.lakeplacid.com; Olympic Center, Lake Placid) promotes a selection of backcountry bike trips of varying difficulty on its website. Also, Lake Champlain Bikeways (802-652-2453; www.champlainbikeways.org; Local Motion, 1 Steele Street #103, Burlington, Vermont) has identified a network of routes around the lake, with interpretive maps available online. For still more trip ideas, ask at regional bike shops; many sponsor guided rides or have their own maps of local favorites. Check www.bikeadirondacks .org for an online atlas. Another popular place to pedal for stunning views: across the new Champlain Bridge, from Crown Point to Addison, Vermont.

Remember: Always carry plenty of water and a good tool kit. *And wear a helmet!*

BOATING

See www.nysparks.com for the *New York State Boater's Guide,* which contains the rules and regulations for park waters, and is available from offices of the New York Department of Transportation. See page 212 for information about invasive species and watercraft cleaning procedures.

Some statewide laws for pleasure craft follow:

- You must carry one personal flotation device for every passenger in your boat. Children under 12 are required to wear life jackets while on board.
- Any boat powered by a motor (even canoes with small motors) and operated mainly in New York State must be registered with the Department of Motor Vehicles.
- When traveling within 100 feet of shore, dock, pier, raft, float, or an anchored boat, the speed limit is 5 mph. (Maximum daytime speed limits are 45 mph, and nighttime, 25 mph, although on many lakes with rocky shoals, or on water bodies that are also popular with nonmotorized craft, lower speeds are prudent.)
- Powerboats give way to canoes, sailboats, rowboats, kayaks, and anchored boats.
- The boat on your right has the right-of-way when being passed.
- Running lights must be used after dark.
- Boaters under 16 must be accompanied by an adult, or, if between 10 and 16 and unaccompanied, they must have a safety certificate from a New York State course.
- Boating under the influence of alcohol carries heavy fines and/or jail sentences.
- Littering and discharging marine-toilet wastes into waterways is prohibited.

BOAT TOURS

The season generally runs from early May through October; call ahead for a reservation.

Carillon Cruises (802-897-5331; www.carilloncruises.com; Fort Ticonderoga, Ticonderoga) gives historic tours on the *Carillon,* which presents narrated tours near Fort Ticonderoga and longer cruises to Whitehall, New York, and Vergennes, Vermont.

Lake Champlain Ferries (802-864-9804; www.ferries.com) shuttles cars between Essex, New York, and Charlotte, Vermont; Port Kent, New York, and Burlington, Vermont; and Plattsburgh, New York, and Grand Isle, Vermont. Passengers without cars are welcome.

Ticonderoga Ferry (802-897-7999; NY 74, Ticonderoga) is an inexpensive scenic trip across Lake Champlain on a small cable-operated car ferry.

CAMPING

Public campgrounds operated by the Department of Environmental Conservation (518-402-9428; www.dec.ny.gov), are open from Memorial Day through Labor Day. Reservations can be made for a site in the state campgrounds by contacting Reserve America (1-800-456-CAMP; www.reserveamerica). Its website includes details about every state campground, as does the DEC's campsite listings on its site. If you can't find what you're looking for on Reserve America's site, contact the campground itself. The camping fees listed for the following Champlain Valley campgrounds are for 2012:

Ausable Point (518-561-7080; 3346 Lake Shoe Road, Peru), on Lake Champlain. Showers, swimming, boat launch, wildlife refuge (a good place to explore by canoe), a great beach for kids. $22 camping fee.

Crown Point (518-597-3603; 784 Bridge Road, Crown Point), on Lake Champlain. Showers, boat launch; across from fort, next to good visitor information center. $18 camping fee.

Lincoln Pond (518-942-5292; 4363 Lincoln Pond Road, Elizabethtown). Swimming, showers, canoe or rowboat rentals; no powerboats allowed. $18 camping fee.

Paradox Lake (518-532-7451; 897 NY 74, Paradox). Swimming, showers, canoe or rowboat rentals, boat launch. $18 camping fee.

Putnam Pond (518-585-7280; 763 Putts Pond Road, Ticonderoga). Swimming, showers, canoe or rowboat rentals, boat launch, access to Pharaoh Wilderness Area. $18 camping fee.

Scaroon Manor (518-623-3671; US 9, Schroon Lake). Relatively new, beautiful property—formerly the site of a classy 1950s resort. Several accessible sites, lovely beaches. $25 camping fee.

Sharp Bridge (518-532-7538; 4390 US 9, North Hudson), on Schroon River. Showers, access to Hammond Pond Wild Forest. $18 camping fee.

CAMPS

Among the kids' camps in this region are: Camp Dudley (518-962-4720; www.camp dudley.org; 126 Dudley Road), in Westport, the oldest continuously running summer camp in America. It began in New Jersey; it was moved to this site in the Champlain Valley in 1908, and its sister facility, Camp Dudley at Kiniya, is across the lake, in Colchester, Vermont. Dudley's grounds total 500 acres and include 2 miles of shoreline, with all shapes and sizes of Adirondack-style buildings. Kids play soccer, tennis, swim and sail the lake, run the 200-meter outdoor track, swing golf clubs on the camp's driving range, and shoot on its rifle range. The late Academy Award–nominee Burgess Meredith, who played Sylvester Stallone's boxing coach, "Mickey," in the first three Rocky movies, is a Dudleyite.

Pok-O-MacCready Camps (1-800-982-3538; www.pokomac.com)—Pok-O-Moonshine for 120 boys; Camp MacCready for about the same number of girls—sit on Long Pond and approximately 350 acres in Willsboro. That's about all the sitting that happens here. Since Pok-O's founding in 1905 and its sister's arrival in 1967, more than 300 of its campers have gone on to become 46ers. The curriculum includes high-adventure canoeing, backpacking, and rock-climbing camps, with emphasis on self-reliance in the wilderness.

CANOEING AND KAYAKING

Paddling along the Adirondack coast is a grand adventure: Lake Champlain is big water, so expect big waves. When you're planning any trip, allow an extra day in case the weather doesn't cooperate. Remember that you're required to carry a life jacket for each person in the boat; lash an extra paddle in your canoe or kayak, too. Bring plenty of food and fuel, a backpacker stove, and rain gear.

For those who want to polish their paddle skills, each summer the State University of New York at Plattsburgh hosts a Lake Champlain Sea Kayak Institute (518-564-5292) that includes workshops, demos, and a race around Valcour Island.

The waterways from Old Forge to Lake Champlain make up a stretch of the 740-mile Northern Forest Canoe Trail (www.northernforestcanoetrail.org), which begins in Old Forge and ends in northern Maine. And the Boquet River allows for serious kayak action, though tackling falls like the ones at Split Rock should be reserved for experts only.

See chapter 8 for a list of paddling guidebooks and other resources.

Lake Champlain is a natural waterpark.   Courtesy of Carl Heilman II, www.carlheilman.com

The End of Bats?

Caves inside the Adirondack Park, particularly in the Champlain Valley and in Hague, in Lake George, were once healthy hibernacula for little brown bats, the most common variety in the Northeast. But in the last decade, tens of thousands of these animals have died because of white nose syndrome. When the bats become infected with this highly contagious fungus, their bodies attack it and slough it off, in the process destroying their wing membranes so they can't fly—or they fly so poorly that they can't feed.

Scientists are frantic to quarantine caves (spelunking in designated Adirondack caves is, at press time, off-limits), to study and understand how to combat the disease. The future for the little brown, among other species, is unclear.

White-nose syndrome is pushing little brown bats to extinction.

Courtesy of Kevin MacKenzie, www.mackenziefamily.com

CLIMBING

Poke-O-Moonshine is an ice- and rock-climbing mecca. See the guidebooks in chapter 8 for climb descriptions and directions. And those who looking to brush up on skills in the off-season—or determine if climbing is right for them—can visit the indoor Crux Champlain Valley Climbing Center (518-963-4646; www.pmoec.org; 56 Rogers Lane), in Willsboro.

DIVING

With all the military action that happened on Champlain in the 18th and 19th centuries there's bound to be remnants of ships and battles on the lake bottom. The Lake Champlain Underwater Historic Preserve, established in public trust for the people of New York and Vermont, allows divers public access to some of Champlain's shipwrecks. The hub of this preserve is the Lake Champlain Maritime Museum, on the Vermont side of the lake. Check out the museum's website, www.lcmm.org or call 802-475-2022, for a list of shipwrecks, a map of the preserve, and diving rules and regulations. Jones' Aqua Sports (518-963-1150; www.divechamplain.com; 71 Klein Drive, Willsboro) is a dive outfitter, training center, and a great resource. The New York State Divers Association (www.scubany.org) also provides scuba diving resources.

FAMILY FUN

In this region of the Adirondacks is a spectacular gorge of carved sandstone cliffs near the park's northeastern corner, and one of the country's oldest tourist destinations, dating back to 1870. At Ausable Chasm (518-834-7454; www.ausablechasm.com; US 9, Ausable Chasm) you can hike through the formations, check out the rim walk, then ride a raft or inner tube down 2 miles of rapids. Open daily mid-May through mid-October, the chasm costs $16 for adults and $9 for ages 5–12.

Begin your fishing education with the *New York State Freshwater Fishing Regulations Guide*, published by the Department of Environmental Conservation and available at www.dec.ny.gov. The free booklet details all the seasons and limits for various species. Everyone 16 and older who fishes in the Adirondacks must have a New York fishing license, which can be purchased at the DEC's website, at sporting goods stores, and town offices. Nonresidents can get special five-day licenses; state residents 70 and older may get free licenses.

The DEC site also has helpful hotlines for anglers, describing the top fishing spots and what's hitting where on which kind of bait. See chapter 8 for a list of fishing guidebooks or check out I Love New York's comprehensive *Adirondack Fishing* guide at www.fishadk.com.

To get in the proper frame of mind for fishing, nothing beats a trip to a local fish hatchery. The Essex County Fish Hatchery (518-597-3844; Creek Road, Crown Point) is also open every day. The only fish ladder in the park is on the Boquet River (School Street, Willsboro); if you time it just right in the fall, you can watch big salmon ascend the watery staircase.

The Rotary International Fishing Classic (518-563-1000), sponsored by Plattsburgh Rotary Club, covers all of Lake Champlain, with weigh stations at Port Henry, Westport, and Willsboro, in late May. Mega ones with big bucks prizes and corporate sponsors, such as LCI Father's Day Derby and the Lake Champlain International Fishing Tournament, are listed on www.mychamplain.net.

There are many fishing guides and schools in the region, including Adirondack-Champlain Guide Service (518-963-7351; www.adirondackchamplainguideservice .com; 46629 NY 22. Long Pond Lodge, Willsboro) and Adventure Guide Service (518-963-4286; www.adventureguideservice.com; 37 Maple Street, Willsboro).

GOLF

Courses in the Champlain Valley are:

Cobble Hill Golf Course (518-873-9974; US 9, Elizabethtown). Nine holes; par-35; 3,000 yards. Completed in 1897; great views of the High Peaks.

Harmony Golf Club, Port Kent Golf Course (518-834-9785; 95 North Street, Port Kent). Nine holes; par-30; 2,000 yards. Close to Vermont ferry.

Moriah Country Club (518-546-9979; Broad Street, Port Henry). Nine 9 holes; par-32; 2,100 yards. Opened in 1900.

Ticonderoga Country Club (518-585-2801; www.ticonderogacountryclub.com; US 9, Ticonderoga). Eighteen holes; par-71; 6,300 yards.

Westport Country Club (518-962-4470; www.westportcountryclub.com; Liberty Street, Westport). Eighteen holes; par-72; 6,200 yards. Challenging; beautiful views.

Willsboro Golf Club (518-963-8989; 140 Point Road, Willsboro). Nine holes; par-35; 2,600 yards.

HIKING AND BACKPACKING

The Adirondack woods are free of many of the natural hazards that you need to worry about in other locales. However, there's some poison ivy in the Champlain Valley region. Eastern timber rattlesnakes are occasionally found here; keep your eyes open when crossing rock outcrops on warm, sunny days. These snakes are quite shy and nonaggressive, but take care not to surprise one. And cases of Lyme disease have been recorded in the Adirondacks; hikers should take precautions against exposing themselves to deer ticks (*Ixodes dammini*) (see page 217.)

Dramatic views and endless ice draw Nordic skaters from both sides of Lake Champlain.
Courtesy of Mark Bowie, www.markbowie.com

For folks who wish to hike in the Champlain Valley, the Champlain Area Trails (CATS) are a new network of well-maintained routes in Essex, Westport, and Willsboro continually being expanded that will eventually connect to other communities in the eastern Adirondacks, as well as in Canada and the Hudson Valley. The CATS have an informative website, www.champlainareatrails.com, with trail descriptions, maps, writing contests, events, and more.

HUNTING

Hunting is a popular, regulated pursuit each fall. There are seasons for deer, black bear, snowshoe hare, coyote, bobcat, and other small mammals, plus ruffed grouse, woodcock, wild turkey, and waterfowl. At press time, a feral hog invasion in the Champlain Valley has opened a hunting season on wild boars. For information about hunting seasons for these and other game, see the Department of Environmental Conservation's online regulations (www.dec.ny.gov). To search for a hunting guide in this region check www.nysoga.org.

ICE SKATING

If you'd like to try wilderness skating, wait until January. Cold, clear, still weather produces the most consistent surface. Ice that's 2 inches thick will support one person on skates, but it's better to wait for at least 3 inches to form, since currents and springs can create weak spots. Ice is thinner near shore, and be sure to steer clear of inlets, outlets, and other tributaries. Webb-Royce Swamp near Westport is a terrific place to skate. Something about gliding beneath the Crown Point bridge on Lake Champlain.

Nordic skating is another sport that's gaining popularity and involves gliding long distances on frozen lakes and rivers on special blades that snap into cross-country-ski boots. Lake Champlain is a Nordic-skating mecca; always check ice conditions before setting out.

RUNNING

LaChute Road Runners (518-585-6619; www.lachute.us), based in Ticonderoga, sponsor a variety of area races, such as the Montcalm Mile Run down Ticonderoga's main street on the Fourth of July.

Plattsburgh's Mayor's Cup Regatta & Festival is a time-honored North Country tradition.
Courtesy of *Adirondack Life*

SAILING

Lake Champlain offers good sailing in the midst of beautiful scenery and has marinas for an evening's dockage or equipment repairs. Sailing on island-studded waters can be tricky, since in the lee of an island you stand a good chance of being becalmed. Wind can whip shallow lakes into white-capped mini oceans, too. A portable weather radio should be included in your basic kit; Adirondack forecasts (out of Burlington, Vermont) can be found at 162.40 megahertz.

You can purchase Coast Guard charts for Lake Champlain. Some USGS topographical maps have troughs and shoals marked, but these maps are of limited use to sailors. Your best bet is to ask at boat liveries for lake maps, or at least find out how to avoid the worst rocks.

For hardware, lines, and other equipment, Westport Marina (518-962-4356; www.westportmarina.com; 20 Washington Street, Westport) has a good selection of sailing supplies and rentals.

Beyond the Blue Line, in Plattsburgh, is the annual July Mayor's Cup Regatta & Festival (www.mayorscup.com), a four-day, time-honored North Country tradition.

WILD FOREST AREAS

More than a million acres of public land in the park are designated as wild forest, which are open to snowmobile travel, mountain biking, and other recreation. In the Champlain Valley is the Hammond Pond Wild Forest between Paradox and Moriah, with old roads for hiking and ponds for fishing.

Shopping

Adirondackana and more in the Champlain Valley

With nary a big-box in sight, antiques or other funky treasures can be found in the Champlain Valley. For starters, Essex has the Neighborhood Nest (518-963-4652; www.weegarden.com), a boutique that carries scenic photographs and cottage country paintings, plus Wee Gardens—teensy cute-as-a-button replications of the real thing. In Westport, Pink Pig (518-962-8833; www.pinkpigwestport .com) has cool clothes, jewelry, furniture, and home décor. This shop's owner is a former Wall Street exec who brought her urban sense of style—with a quaint country cottage twist—to this lakeside community.

ANTIQUES

Among the shops in this region—most, which are open seasonally, so call ahead—are the Summer Shop (518-963-7921; NY 22), open in Essex, with its painted furniture, early pressed glad, 19th-century textiles and coins. And, in Willsboro, Brown House Antiques (518-963-7352; www.brownhouse antiques.com; 3732 Main Street), which has a half-dozen rooms of linens, prints, pine and mahogany furniture, china, toys and dolls, and Adirondack collectibles.

ART GALLERIES, ARTISANS, AND STUDIOS

Listed here is a sampling of local artists in residence as well as fine-arts galleries.

In Essex, Adirondack Art Association (518-963-8309; www.adirondack artassociation.com; 2750 Essex Road) showcases fine art by regional artists. Bailey Forge (518-962-4039; www .baileyforge.com) is Russell Bailey's

Courtesy of Nancie Battaglia

blacksmith shop specializing in forged architectural ornamental ironwork. Cupola House Gallery (518-963-7494; www .thecupolahouse.com; 2278 Main Street) has folk art: paintings, quilts, rugs, and antiques.

Keeseville is base for Ann Pember's Water Edge Studio (518-834-7440; www .annpember.com; 14 Water Edge Road)—watercolor paintings of flowers and nature scenes.

Courtney Fair (518-962-2284; www.courtneyfair.com; the Old Feed Store), in Wadhams, makes rustic three-legged stools and simple, elegant farm tables crafted from salvaged lumber.

Westport's Artifacts and Westport Trading Co. (518-962-4801; 6511 Main Street) is Kip Trienens's bark and twig baskets, pottery, jewelry, contemporary furniture, stained glass, and eclectic crafts. Atea Ring Gallery (518-962-8620; 236 Sam Spears Road), open seasonally, is a modern professional fine-arts gallery like one you'd expect to find in a major city, located instead in an out-of-the-way farmhouse. The gallery features one-person and group exhibitions of paintings, quilts, and prints. Past shows have included works by Harold Weston; realist Paul Matthews; primitive paintings by Edna West Teall (who was the Grandma Moses of Essex County); and Lake Champlain fish decoys.

East Side Studio (518-963-8356; 828 Point Road), in Willsboro, is Patricia

Lake Monster

Champ, the legendary sea monster of Lake Champlain—purported to look something like the Loch Ness Monster—has books, symposiums, T-shirts, festivals, and local businesses celebrating its existence. According to one Champ-camp website, the first recorded sighting took place when Samuel de Champlain explored these waters. Check out Bulwagga Bay's Champ-sightings plaque.

Reynolds's watercolor and oil landscapes of Lake Champlain and the Adirondacks and her lovely flower paintings.

In Ticonderoga, Hancock House Gallery (518-585-7868; www.thehancockhouse .org; 6 Moses Circle) exhibits works by local artists and sells historical souvenir items.

GENERAL STORES

In Crown Point, Champ's General Store (518-597-9779; 694 Bridge Road) is a full-service convenient store, deli, and gift shop. McCabe's General Store (518-597-4475; Middle Road) has food and other supplies.

SPAS AND WELLNESS

Live Well (518-963-4300; www.livewellessexny.com; 2310 Main Street), in Essex, is a collaborative partnership between holistic health practitioners and the Champlain Valley community. Expert instructors offer yoga workshops, physical therapy and massage, personal training, tai chi, and the list goes on.

6

Lake George and Southeastern Adirondacks

IN WINTER, THIS REGION is one big ghost town. In summer it balloons with visitors who jockey for space along Lake George village's touristy Canada Street, or escape the crowds on vast—and gorgeous—Lake George, or scoot north to quaint Chestertown. Whatever your taste in lodging, meals, recreation, and culture—there's Elvis and opera—it's all here.

Pick Your Spot
Lodging in Lake George & the Southeastern Adirondacks

Old-school mom-and-pop motels and housekeeping cabins abound on some stretches of this region and many of them are just fine. But the following are mostly B&Bs—listed here because they're lovely launch pads for whatever your Adirondack adventure.

Bolton Landing
Boathouse Bed & Breakfast (518-644-2554; www.boathousebb.com; 44 Sagamore Road) was once the summer home of Gold Cup–winning speedboat racer George Reis. This extravagant place offers an absolutely perfect backdrop for a relaxing getaway on Lake

Bolton Landing's Sagamore Resort on Lake George. Courtesy of the Sagamore Resort

George, no matter what season. There are four rooms and a suite, which has an enclosed sun porch, in the main house, all with Jacuzzi tubs, mini fridges, and either queen- or king-size beds. The separate carriage house has two suites, both with lake views, king-size beds, and

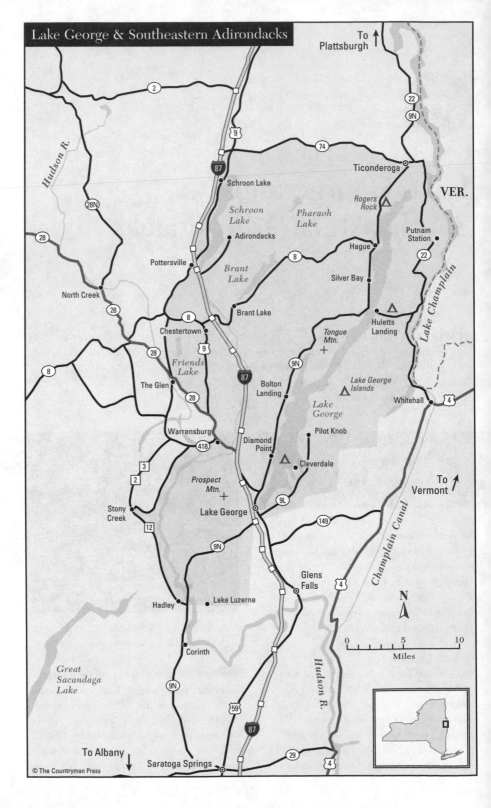

Lake George & Southeastern Adirondacks

To Plattsburgh

Hudson R.

2

9

87

74

Schroon Lake

To VER.

22

9N

Ticonderoga

Rogers Rock

28N

Schroon Lake

Pharaoh Lake

Putnam Station

28

Adirondacks

8

Hague

22

Pottersville

Brant Lake

Silver Bay

North Creek

28

8

Brant Lake

Huletts Landing

Lake Champlain

Chestertown

9

Tongue Mtn.

Friends Lake

8

28

9N

Lake George Islands

The Glen

87

Bolton Landing

Whitehall

4

28

Lake George

Warrensburg

418

Diamond Point

Pilot Knob

Cleverdale

To Vermont

3

2

Prospect Mtn.

Lake George

9L

149

4

Stony Creek

12

Champlain Canal

N

Glens Falls

4

9N

0   5   10
Miles

Hadley

Lake Luzerne

Hudson R.

Corinth

Great Sacandaga Lake

9N

59

87

To Albany

© The Countryman Press

Saratoga Springs

29

4

The Sagamore Resort, first built on this spot in 1883, is still a grand hotel.

Courtesy of the Sagamore Resort

gas fireplaces. Guests can swim the lake, park their boat in the available slips, soak in the hot tub on the dock, and have free access to the fitness center and indoor pool at the nearby Sagamore. Included in the price are family-style three-course hot breakfasts. Open February–October. No children.

The Sagamore Resort (518-644-9400; www.thesagamore.com; 110 Sagamore Road) is the latest incarnation of a grand hotel that has overlooked Lake George here for more than a century. Completed in 1883, the grand lodge has survived two fires and weathered the Depression, but gradually declined during the 1970s. Today the Sagamore is the pride of the community. The elegantly appointed public areas include a conservatory with lake views, six restaurants—everything from fine dining to tapas to pub fare (Mister Brown's Pub is a longtime favorite)—a spa, and a gift shop. Guests have 350 deluxe units to choose from, including suites, hotel bedrooms, lakeside lodges, and executive retreats with lofts. The list of Sagamore amenities is impressive: a huge indoor pool and fitness center, miniature golf, an indoor tennis/racquetball facility, an indoor rock-climbing wall, outdoor tennis courts, playground, a beautiful sandy beach, docks for guests' boats, endless activities and programs

for kids, and a Donald Ross–designed championship golf course 2 miles away. Closed in winter.

Chestertown

The Chester Inn Bed & Breakfast (518-494-4148; www.thechesterinn.com; 6347 Main Street) is one of Chestertown's beautiful homes listed on the National Register of Historic Places—this Greek Revival inn dates back to 1837. Beyond the grand hall, with its mahogany railings and grain-painted woodwork, are four second-floor guest rooms with private baths. Guests are welcome to explore the 13-acre property, which has gardens, a horse barn, smokehouse, and an early cemetery. Nondrivers take note: Chestertown is a regular stop on the Adirondack Trailways bus line, and this inn is just a block from the station. It's also next door to the Main Street Ice Cream Parlor—a great place to eat.

The Fern Lodge (518-494-7238; www.thefernlodge.com; 46 Fiddlehead Bay Road) is an over-the-top spot to get away from it all. All five rooms at the lodge on Friends Lake have king-size

The Fern Lodge, a Friends Lake getaway, offers Adirondack-style luxury.

Courtesy of The Fern Lodge

beds, massive stone fireplaces, lake or mountain views, mini refrigerators for chilling wine or cheese boards, spacious baths with steam showers, Jacuzzi tubs, and elegantly rustic décor. Ramble, cross-country ski, or snowshoe the surrounding 70 acres, stroke the lodge's kayaks out on the lake, hang around the impressive great room, shoot pool, watch movies in the private theater, relax in the sauna, get fit in the exercise room, or browse the fine wine cellar for the perfect vintage. Enjoy an evening boat tour with historic narrative and wine; in the morning linger over an extraordinary multicourse breakfast with homemade breads and pastries. New is an outdoor hot tub and lakeside lean-to.

Friends Lake Inn (518-494-4751; www.friendslake.com; 963 Friends Lake Road) has been a hostelry of one kind or another for about 150 years, although its first tenants, the tannery workers, would marvel to see people rather than cowhides soaking in the enormous wooden hot tub outdoors. Today there are 17 comfortable rooms and small suites—either traditional- or Adirondack-style—all with private baths, some with steam showers and whirlpool tubs, fireplaces, private entrances and balconies, and views of Friends Lake. Truly an inn for all seasons, guests can enjoy cross-country skiing or snowshoeing on 32 kilometers of groomed trails here in the winter; fishing in the spring; swimming and mountain biking in the summer; hiking in the fall.

Landon Hill Bed & Breakfast (518-494-2599; www.bedbreakfast.net; 10 Landon Hill Road), a lovely Victorian home set among rolling hills on a country lane, is peaceful and comfortable. An oak spiral staircase leads you to the four guest rooms upstairs (all with private baths), and downstairs are a handicapped-accessible guest room and bath. Before the sit-down breakfast, have

Lakeside Weddings

Weddings in the Lake George region can mean lakeside affairs, woodsy gatherings, or an intimate gathering in a historical home. Brant Lake's **Jimbo Club at the Point** (518-494-4460; www.jimbos club.com) can host hundreds in its rustic-style lodge. In Bolton Landing, the **Sagamore Resort** (518-644-9400; www.the sagamore.com) is the place for a classy event, with everything—spa, climbing wall, golf course, beach—on campus. Chestertown's luxurious **Fern Lodge** (518-494-7238; www.thefernlodge.com)

Northwest Bay and Tongue Mountain, Lake George. Courtesy of Ted Comstock, Saranac Lake

can accommodate a small group—or elopements, of course. And tying the knot in Lake George can mean a ceremony on board one of the vessels operated by **Lake George Shoreline Cruises** (518-668-4644; www.lakegeorgeshoreline.com) or **Lake George Steamboat Company** (518-668-5777; www.lakegeorgesteamboat.com); an explosive affair (the cannon will blast after you exchange I dos) at **Fort William Henry Resort** (1-800-234-0267; www.fortwilliamhenry.com); a gathering at **Top of the World Golf Resort** with fresh, delicious fare at its Farmhouse restaurant; or a grand party with plenty of pomp and circumstance at the **Inn at Erlowest** (518-668-5928; www.inn aterlowest.com). If none of this says "I love you" in a memorable way, there's always **Elvis** (www.lakegeorgeelvisfest.com), who will officiate with panache.

coffee and homemade muffins by the woodstove; then, after stoking up on quiche and fresh fruit, explore the property's 89 acres, or head for Chestertown's historic district or the nearby Schroon River for fishing and canoeing. Guests can unwind in the outdoor hot tub. Landon Hill is just a mile from I-87, the Northway, so it's a convenient jumping-off spot for further adventures.

Diamond Point

Canoe Island Lodge (518-668-5592; www.canoeislandlodge.com; 3820 Lakeshore Drive) first opened in 1946, after Bill Busch financed the down payment on Canoe Island with a couple hundred bushels of buckwheat. The 21-acre, 25-building complex now offers all kinds of family vacation options from quaint log cabins to modern suites and private chalets. There are clay tennis courts, a sandy beach on Lake George, hiking trails, and numerous boats to sail. Perhaps the best part of a stay here, though, is the chance to enjoy the lodge's very own 3-acre island, about three-quarters of a mile offshore. Shuttle boats take guests to the island where they can swim, snorkel, fish, sunbathe, and explore a beautiful, undeveloped part of the lake. The lodge accommodates about 175 people at peak capacity. Open mid-May–mid-October.

Hague

The Locust Inn (518-543-6934; www.locustinn.com; NY 9N & 8), a graceful homestead built in 1865, packed with antiques and art, and conveniently next to the town beach and boat ramp on Lake George. The three attractively appointed guest suites—all with lake views—have queen beds, private baths and sitting areas. The third-floor suite, under the eaves—which can sleep four and has a sitting room, kitchen, and private bath—is charming. The carriage house is a separate cottage open in summer, located on Hague Brook. Children over 12 welcome.

Ruah Bed & Breakfast (518-543-8816; www.ruahbb.com; 9221 Lakeshore Drive) has amusing legends: This stone mansion was designed by Stanford White; part of the estate was won in a poker game; the Lake George monster—the biggest hoax ever seen in northern New York—was created in the studio of the original owner, artist Harry Watrous. Bing Crosby and Jack Dempsey slept here. Stay at Ruah and you'll have your own stories to tell—about visiting a lovely inn overlooking a beautiful lake. The four guest chambers are upstairs and have private baths. The Queen of the Lakes is spacious, with access to the balcony and views from every window. Common areas downstairs include a vast living room with a fieldstone fireplace and an antique grand piano, a cozy library, and an elegant dining room. To give you an idea of the scale of this inn, the veranda stretches across the front of the house and measures about 80 feet long. Open May through January.

Trout House Village Resort (518-543-6088 or 1-800-368-6088; www.trout house.com; 9117 Lakeshore Drive), one of the few four-season resorts on the quiet northern portion of Lake George, is a handsomely maintained complex of log cabins and chalets. Many of the cabins have fireplaces, decks, and complete kitchen facilities; there are numerous suites and rooms in the main lodge, all with private baths. There are canoes, rowboats, sailboats, kayaks, bikes, and even a nine-hole putting green for guests. Trout House is a short distance from historic sites such as Fort Ticonderoga and Crown Point, while the Ticonderoga Country Club—a challenging 18-hole course—is just up the road. By January, the atmosphere changes from that of an active resort to a quiet country inn, perfect for cold-weather getaways.

Warrensburg

Allyn's Butterfly Inn (518-623-9390; www.alynnsbutterflyinn.com; 69 NY 28) is elegantly appointed, and its huge wraparound porch invites lingering on a summer day to watch real butterflies visiting the garden. All five of the inn's guest chambers are named after native butterflies, and have private baths. A full gourmet breakfast is served daily.

The Glen Lodge & Market (800-867-2335; www.theglenlodge.com; 1123 NY 28) is an eco-friendly bed & breakfast (all its power comes from wind) on the Hudson. Its proprietors run Wild Waters rafting company, so ask about the "Rafting and a Room" package. The place can accommodate up to 16 guests in five nice, simple Adirondack-style rooms.

Ridin'-Hy Ranch (518-494-2742; www.ridinhy.com; 64 Ridin'-Hy Ranch Road), an 800-acre complex on Sherman Lake, is a western-style dude ranch that has everything, from a private intermediate-level downhill ski area to rodeos. There are 50 miles of trails for snowmobiling, cross-country skiing, or horseback riding. In warmer weather, guests can swim, row, or water-ski on Sherman Lake, and fish in Burnt Pond or the Schroon River. The centerpiece of the ranch is an enormous log cabin that contains a cocktail lounge, living room, game room, and dining room. Accommodations include chalets, lodge rooms, and motel units.

Seasons B&B (518-623-3832; www .seasons-bandb.com; 3822 Main Street) has remarkable regional history. James Fenimore Cooper was a guest at this house, which belonged to Peletiah Richards, when he was researching *The Last of the Mohicans*. In those days, the home was among the grandest in town, and later in the 19th century this place became more elaborate still, with the addition of an Italianate tower, a long veranda, and a bay window. Details inside the Seasons include an ornate fireplace in the parlor, a coffered wood ceiling above the staircase, and antiques throughout. There are four guest rooms upstairs, two with private baths and two that share a bath. A section of the house that dates from 1820 has been renovated into a handsome suite with a corner fireplace in the living room, queen-size bed, and spacious bathroom with double whirlpool with separate shower. Guests are treated to a fine, full breakfast.

Local Flavors

Where to eat in Lake George & the Southeastern Adirondacks

Beware of tourist traps that dish out pricey, lousy dinners. The following are among the consistently good restaurants where you can expect a delicious meal, cool ambience, and character.

Bolton Landing

The Algonquin (518-644-9442; www.the algonquin.com; 4770 Lakeshore Drive), on Lake George's Huddle Bay, is a bustling lakeside institution that continues to attract waterfront diners all summer long. Most guests prefer to arrive by boat. Be aware: In high summer, an hour wait is possible for seating on the deck; service upstairs begins at 5 PM, for full entrées only (no burgers or sandwiches). The menu's "beginnings" range from chicken wings and stuffed mushrooms to duchess pâté and baked brie. Dinner entrées include chicken Monterey or cordon bleu, horseradish-encrusted salmon, flat-iron bourbon steak, and veal Oscar. Burgers and club sandwiches are available on the deck and in the downstairs dining room.

The Sexiest Cheese in America

Turns out *Esquire* magazine's pick for "the sexiest cheese in America" is made in this region, in Thurman, by **Nettle Meadow Farm** (518-623-3372; www.nettlemeadow.com). Bring the famous Kunik or the farm's other artisan cheeses home as a delicious Adirondack souvenir.

Open mid-April through Columbus Day.

Cate's Italian Garden Restaurant and Bar (518-644-2041; www.cates italiangarden.com; 4952 Lakeshore Drive) has a spacious covered terrace between the building and the street that hums with the activity of a popular tourist town. Inside, the small dining room is crowded with art posters and Italian bric-a-brac. The pizza here is the best around, or you can get full-course dinners. Specials are consistently delicious—be sure to ask about the lasagna.

Pumpernickel's Restaurant (518-644-2106; www.pumpernickels.com; 4571 Lakeshore) boasts America's largest cuckoo clock, a 10-foot-tall timepiece that was carved in Germany's Black Forest, then hung for many years in Times Square. German cooking has a bad reputation—heavy, greasy, inert. But the wursts and the schnitzels and virtually everything on Pumpernickel's menu tastes vivid, intense, almost light. Don't miss the potato pancakes with applesauce; they're deftly fried, a crisp treat. There's a wide selection of the finest German beers on draft.

Villa Napoli (518-644-9047; www.melodymanor.com; 4610 Lakeshore Drive) is where Naples meets the Adirondacks: Frescos and paintings of quaint towns and Lake Como adorn the dining room. With heavy drapes, Vene-tian plaster walls, and hand-carved marble fireplace, the atmosphere is unmistakably Old Country but the view is pure North Country. Appetizers include sautéed artichoke hearts, steamed mussels and clams, and a large antipasto with Italian meats, vegetables, cheeses, and olives. Traditional pasta, veal, chicken, steak, and fish entrées provide many delicious, bountiful choices. Be sure to leave room for tiramisu, a cannoli, or cappuccino.

Chestertown

Main Street Ice Cream Parlor & Restaurant (518-494-7940; www.main streeticecreamparlor.com; 6339 Main Street) is a family affair: Bruce and Helena Robbins took charge of the popular eatery from Bruce's parents a few years back. Housed in a 99-year-old former high school, the place is chockablock with local antiques and vintage signs; the focal point of the big, bright dining room is an old-school soda fountain dishing out sundaes, floats, malts and fantastic deli sandwiches, homemade soups and burgers. The signature Pack Basket is roast turkey with trimmings and cranberry mayo on a hard roll, and other sandwiches are on Rock Hill Bakehouse bread, the best in the region.

Cleverdale

Sans Souci Restaurant and Bar (518-656-9285; 92 Nathan Road), a busy neighborhood eatery, is family-friendly, noisy, and fun. The bar is partially separated and may or may not be a little quieter as exuberant neighborly greetings and conversation flow. Burgers, pizzas, and a full set of entrées fill the evening menu. Don't miss the daily specials board; the "mom-style" offerings are delicious.

Lake George

Adirondack Brewery & Pub (518-668-0002; www.adkpub.com; 33 Canada Street) has a North Woods atmosphere, with log pillars and twig screens, creating just enough privacy and sense of separation from the bar. Families with children are very much in evidence—not always the case at brewpubs. You may wish to remain at the bar, however, given the tasty assortment of beers brewed on the premises. The kitchen does well with a variety of thick sandwiches and handmade burgers. Take-out—even the beer, in growlers—is available.

Barnsider Smokehouse Restaurant (518-668-5268; www.barnsider.com; 2112 US 9) serves a rack of pork that's as scrumptious as it gets. Owner/chef Ed Pagnotta's parents ran a produce market on this roadside spot, so he comes by his food savvy naturally. The method, he says, is "Memphis style," and involves "a process using dry rub which kind of marinates the ribs, then I throw 'em in a water smoker, and use hickory and oak for wood, which filters up through the oven and heats up the water, which I think keeps a moister flavor." There's barbecued chicken, smoked baked beans, and brisket, too.

Bistro LeRoux (518-798-2982; www.bistroleroux.com; 668 Route 149) is a newish establishment in this part of the Adirondacks. The bistro's earthy space is chef-owned and -operated, serving tasty fare that's a world away from the heavy Italian offerings of other area restaurants: try the toasted goat cheese with cherry Kirsch fondue, or the truffled *pommes frites,* or the coconut curry chicken, or the Guinness and venison chili. There are even vegan dishes on the menu.

The Boathouse (518-668-3332; www.cresthavenlodges.com; 3210 Lake Shore Drive at The Lodges at Cresthaven), during high season (it's closed in winter), often has watercraft lined up, waiting to put in at the restaurant's dock. The food is well worth the wait, whether you arrive by Chris-Craft or car. The main dining room is a mas-

sive post-and-beam boathouse built in the late 1800s, once owned by *New York Times* publisher Adolph Ochs; umbrella-shaded seating is available dockside. The menu is loaded with delicious seafood and steak items, and original sauces and side dishes add enticing twists to traditional plates.

The Farmhouse at the Top of the World (518-668-3000; www.topofthe worldgolfresort.com; 441 Lockhard Mountain Road), on French Mountain, is adjacent to a sustainable farm that grows the majority of the produce that appears, in all sorts of creative combinations, on the menu. Even the cut flowers decorating the restaurant come from the farm. The idea here is to offer fresh, "exciting"—according to Chef Kevin London—dishes made from organically grown ingredients from regional farms in an elegant atmosphere off Lake George's main drag. The views from the Farmhouse's 19th-century dining room are lovely. The restaurant is open seasonally, and the menu changes daily. Examples of London's entrées include Hudson Valley duck with fava, butter, and cannellini beans; and Flying Pigs Farm pork with apple gratin and wild arugula. The lunch and bar menus have lighter fare. Every Thursday, the Farmhouse puts on a seven-course Harvest Dinner, served family style on a community table.

Inn at Erlowest (518-668-5928; www.theinnaterlowest.com; 3178 Lakeshore Drive) is, by far, the fanciest place around. This mansion, more than a century old, is the ultimate for an upscale meal in Lake George. A private residence until 1999, Erlowest is now a four-star bed & breakfast, with several elegant private dining rooms—stunning backdrops for romantic dinners, small receptions, and other affairs. The lake itself isn't visible from the restaurant, but guests can sip premeal cocktails on the mansion's Grand Patio, where there's a gorgeous Lake George view.

Rachael Ray's Adirondack Roots

Celebrity chef and talk show host Rachael Ray grew up in Lake George—she even worked at the local HoJos—and keeps a woodsy and unassuming cabin in Lake Luzerne. Ray's grandfather Emmanuel was a stonemason who emigrated from Sicily to the Adirondacks. "[He and his brothers] worked their way up the Hudson and came upon Lake George and they loved it," she says. "In Ti, there was a community of Italian immigrants." There, he raised his 10 kids, helped rebuild Fort Ticonderoga, and worked on the area's most elaborate homes until moving in with Ray's family in Lake George.

"His friends would come over and I'd sit up with all these old men as they smoked their pipes and played cards all night. My grandfather knew everything about every-

Celebrity chef Rachael Ray grew up in Lake George. *Courtesy of the Food Network*

thing: cooking, landscaping, gardening. He taught my mother everything he knew. Anyway, I was really bored when I went to school because I had been hanging out with 80-year-old Italian men, and I thought they were my contemporaries."

That experience has much to do with Ray's cooking, influenced by flavors she's familiar with—"lots of olive oil and garlic." She says, "My style of cooking definitely reflects where I live. It's very earthy. I lean toward the woodsy spices: rosemary and thyme and sage. And I chop everything big. Most of the year I live off one-pot menus like soups and stews and things that go hand in hand with living on a mountain."

Adirondack cuisine, says Ray, is more about atmosphere than ingredients. She says she couldn't live without Hicks Orchard, in Granville, particularly "their cider doughnuts, really hot." She's been going to Sutton's Marketplace, in Queensbury, since it was a roadside apple press. Of Jacobs and Toney's Meat Store of the North, in Warrensburg, Ray says, "A sandwich there is twice the size of your skull!" Also in Warrensburg, Oscar's Smoke House—"their smoked turkey breast, their Canadian bacon; everything they make is fantabulous. That horseradish cheddar, give me a break with that!" And she says everyone should put a calendar from Martha's Dandee Cream ice cream, in Queensbury, on the fridge and plan "what flavors are what days so you don't miss the peanut butter days or the black raspberry days."

The inn's wine list is extensive; meals are truly an experience. The menu changes each season, but starters may include duck leg confit or the Baha cracked crab in the shell martini with ponzu-scented cocktail dressing. Entrées have been applewood-smoked bacon bearded prawns or double venison loin chops. There is, of course, a dress code.

Pizza Jerks (518-668-4411; www.pizzajerks.com; 59 Iroquois Street) serves fresh, delicious pies; management swears its pies are better than anyone else's, or your money back. You can get grub to go, have it delivered, or eat in. Try the specialty pizzas, such as the Tree Hugger (fresh spinach, pesto, garlic, and onions), the Carcass (every meat in the shop), or hot subs, chicken wings, or for dessert, silly sweet stix (baked dough strips with cinnamon sugar and icing).

Ridge Terrace Restaurant (518-656-9274; www.theridgeterrace.com; 2172 Ridge Terrace Road) sits firmly in the history of the east side of Lake George. Regulars as well as summer friends celebrating a day at the Saratoga races choose this venerable eatery for dinner. Even with reservations, you are likely to spend time in the lounge. Request seating on the enclosed porch and you'll enjoy the gleam of the highly varnished log structure and serenity of the gardens. The food is well prepared and generous. Ridge Terrace's menu is like time traveling—beef with béarnaise or bordelaise sauce, veal with cream sauces, entrées that were in the front line of fine restaurant cuisine 30 years ago. All desserts are made here.

Lake Luzerne

UpRiver Cafe (518-696-3667; 29 Main Street) is in Papa's Ice Cream Parlor's old digs. Now the place is brighter, with good lunches and delicious dinners that might include almond-encrusted salmon in a Thai peanut sauce, or duck in a maple glaze. The deck out back over-looks a pretty stretch of the Hudson River with Rockwell Falls, and diners agree this is a sweet spot for fine fare. Luzerne Music Center concert-goers can bring their Monday night series tickets and get a discounted meal.

Pottersville

Café Adirondack (518-494-5800; www .cafeadirondack.com; 8015 US 9) spe-cializes in "Coastal Southern seafood." Recommended in summer are the café's Seafood Diablo and its seared tuna, not to mention reservations.

Schroon Lake

Drake's (518-532-9040; www.drakes motel.com; 1299 US 9), a no-nonsense restaurant on the north side of Schroon Lake village, has been a popular spot for almost half a century. The cuisine is Ital-ian/American, with an extensive array of seafood dishes. Appetizers of note are steamed mussels and Italian-style roasted red peppers in fresh garlic and olive oil with garlic bread. For entrées, try classic Italian chicken dishes such as cacciatore, parmigiana, and Marsala, plus a handful of vegetarian selections, such as eggplant parmigiana and baked ziti. Or try the Alaskan king crab legs, seafood Newburgh, sautéed scallops, or have a big ol' New England lobster (check out your dinner victim in the tank on the way in). Good desserts— Ticonderoga bread pudding, "Chocolate Confusion," and New York cheesecake, among others—are made on premises.

The Morningstar Bistro (518-532-0707; www.morningstarbistro.net; 1079 Main Street) is just a block from Schroon Lake's park and public beach, though it could very well be in some bucolic corner of French countryside. This quaint little eatery is owned and operated by Myriam Friedman, who's from Algeria by way of Paris and a kib-butz in Israel, and now Adirondack crepe lovers are rejoicing that she picked Schroon Lake to share her culi-nary expertise. Sandwiches, named after old Schroon Lake hotels, are fantastic (the Scaroon is made with roasted red pepper and avocado; the Ondawa is a turkey melt; the Edgewater is topped with grilled salmon and cucumber and wasabi dressing); salads are fresh and fun; and the crepes . . . enough of a rea-son to head to Schroon. Order a savory crepe—Swiss or Cheddar or Brie and avocado—or a sweet one (or two) filled with marmalade, Nutella and banana, lemon butter, fruit and Grand Marnier.

Pitkin's (518-532-7918; 1085 US 9) is the place where the homemade soups are thick with real stuff (not cornstarch), pies are heavenly, coleslaw and potato salad and barbecue are the best around. This place might look like your average North Country diner with giant lake trout and panoramic photos on the walls, but you get authentic Texas-style barbecue, beef brisket, pork ribs, and chicken. On Thursday nights in the summer, the lines of ribs fans snake down Main Street, in anticipation of the Thursday rib special, and the wait for a table can be long.

Stony Creek

Stony Creek Inn & Restaurant (518-696-2394; www.stonycreekinn.net; 6 Roaring Branch Road), a 150-year-old southern Adirondack institution, is one of the neatest spots between Saratoga and Montreal. On Sunday night, the joint really jumps, when there's great Mexican food and local bands. Long a mecca for square dancers and the home stage for the regionally renowned Stony Creek Band, the inn presents everything from straight country to rhythm and blues, old-time fiddle to salsa. All this music—a rarity in the area—attracts crowds from far and wide. Along with hot tunes, the Stony Creek Inn has some unbeatable specials: check out Wednesday's "Five & Dime" menu, which offers $5 burgers (in all sorts of styles) and $10 dinners (roast tip sirloin, chicken, etc). Closed Mondays and Tuesdays.

In Warrensburg, Brunetto's Restaurant (518-623-1041; 3579 US 9) has traditional, meat-and-potatoes-type fare in huge portions. Lizzie Keays (518-504-4043; www.lizziekeays.com; 89 River Street) serves tasty meals in the refurbished Empire Shirt Factory. Also in Bolton Landing's Frederick's is open year-round, and a casual lakeside spot for cocktails (518-644-3484; www.fredericksrestaurant.com; 4870 Lakeshore Drive). Also in Bolton is family restaurant Son of a Sailor (518-240-6017; 4933 Lakeshore Drive), where locals like to eat. In Chestertown, Anywhere's a Better Place to Be (518-494-5888; www.anywheresabetterplacetobe.com; 6332 US 9) has good wings. In Warrensburg, Bill's Restaurant (518-623-2669; 3915 Main Street) makes a fine roast-turkey sandwich and serves breakfast all day. And family-run Oscar's Adirondack Smoke House (1-800-627-3431; www.oscars adksmokehouse.com; 22 Raymond Lane) is a regional institution. When Rachael Ray's in town, she stops here for smoked bacon and aged Cheddar cheese.

To Do

Attractions and activities in Lake George & the Southeastern Adirondacks

Consider *The Last of the Mohicans*. The harrowing trip from what's now called Cooper's Cave, in Glens Falls, to the fort at Ticonderoga went along the Hudson River, crossed over the Tongue Mountain range, skirted the west side of Lake George, and reached Lake Champlain at its narrowest spot. The adventure is now firmly etched in American letters, but few of us connect the journey with actual sites in the Adirondacks. James Fenimore Cooper visited Warrensburg and Lake George in 1824 to research his story and observe the landscape. Many of his landmarks are inaccessible today, but you may catch a few glimpses if you follow in his tracks, on modern-day US 9. Painter Georgia O'Keeffe experienced Lake George with her photographer husband, Alfred Stieglitz, creating elemental scenes of water, rock, sky, and undulating hills. Although her Adirondack tenure was a short period in a long and productive life, this region launched O'Keeffe's signature style. In 2013 The Hyde Collection

Adirondack Shooter

The home base of Carl Heilman II, one of the Adirondacks' most intrepid, talented landscape photographers, is Brant Lake, in the southern Adirondacks. Heilman's a regular contributor to regional publications, such as *Adirondack Life* magazine, and has published numerous coffee-table photography books on this region, plus instructional guides on how to capture these scenes. Order a book—his *Lake George* and *The Adirondacks* are gorgeous—check Heilman's tour schedule, or sign up for one of his popular photo workshops at www.carlheilman.com.

Adirondack photographer Carl Heilman II offers workshops across the park.

Courtesy of Carl Heilman II, www.carlheilman.com

(www.hydecollection.org), in Glens Falls, is featuring O'Keeffe's Lake George work in a much-anticipated exhibition.

Today the Lake George region still has a lively arts scene, with galleries, museums, a folk school, an opera colony, even jazz in the park. The Lake George Arts Project (518-668-2616; www.lakegeorgearts.org; Old County Courthouse, 1 Amherst Street, Lake George) has had a lot to do with that, organizing sculpture shows, exhibiting artists with national renown in its courthouse gallery, offering free outdoor concerts in Shepard Park—including the Lake George Jazz Festival—and throwing fun, well-attended benefits such as the rock-and-roll and chili cook-off called Bands 'n Beans (March), and the Black Velvet Art Party (November), a celebration of terminal tackiness.

ARCHITECTURE

For many travelers, Warrensburg is the gateway to the Adirondacks. Along Main Street (US 9), there are stately 19th-century homes, from Greek Revival and Gothic cottages to Italianate villas and Queen Anne mansions. The oldest building in Warrensburg, diagonally across from the car dealership on US 9, is a former blacksmith shop, dating back to 1814. Along the Schroon River (NY 418 West), you can see remnants of the village's industrial center in several old mill buildings; the Grist Mill (518-623-8005; www.gristmillontheschroon.com; 100 River Street), now an excellent restaurant, still has grindstones, conveyors, chutes, and grain-grinding apparatus, plus a great river setting. Also on US 9, Chestertown has a historic district with colorful Greek Revival houses and restored storefronts.

CINEMA

Carol Theater (518-494-0005; Riverside Drive), in Chestertown, shows first-run films and kids' matinees from Memorial Day through fall. In Schroon Lake, the Strand Theater (518-532-9300; Main Street), a restored art deco building with state-of-the-art sound system is open May through October, plus some off-season weekends.

An-Tiki

The **Tiki Resort**, in an A-frame motel with artificial palm trees and faux-Polynesian wood carvings, has been around since 1963. Today hundreds of Tiki nostalgia buffs come here for the annual June **"Ohana—Luau at the Lake,"** a weekend-long celebration of 1950s-, '60s- and '70s-era tikiana. (*Ohana* is a Hawaiian word meaning "extended family.") Hosted by the Fraternal Order of the Moai, a nationwide organization of people interested in the pop-Polynesian aesthetic, the event includes performances by surf-rock bands, outdoor vintage-movie screenings and, of course, a luau—with proceeds benefiting the Rapa Nui people of Easter Island.

Visit the Tiki Resort at 2 Canada Street, in Lake George. The Waikiki Supper Club's Polynesian dinner show runs nightly in July and August, except Thursdays. See www.tikiresort.com or call 518-668-5744 for reservations. Information on the annual Ohana–Luau at the Lake event can be found at www.luauatthelake.com.

The Adirondack Folk School, in Lake Luzerne, teaches adults the traditional arts of the Adirondacks. Courtesy of the Adirondack Folk School

CRAFTS AND FINE ARTS INSTRUCTION

Adirondack Folk School (518-696-2400; www.adirondackfolkschool.org; 51 Main Street, Lake Luzerne) is a relatively new, nonaccredited, not-for-profit continuing education campus along Lake Luzerne's Main Street, where adults can learn the traditional arts of the Adirondacks. Classes in quilting, building rustic furniture, weaving, blacksmithing, quilting, wood carving, playing banjo, caning chairs, braiding rugs, making soap, and basketry are offered year-round.

LECTURE SERIES

An Adirondack education is possible through numerous public lectures at libraries, museums, town halls, and other sites. The Adirondack Mountain Club Lake George Member Services Center (518-668-4447; www.adk.org) often hosts talks on wildlife, recreation, and more. Also popular in this region are the programs presented by the organizations that protect lovely Lake George. If you're interested in learning more about how to preserve this fragile basin and its surrounding lands, check out the following organizations: The Lake George Association (518-668-3558; www.lakegeorgeassociation.org); Lake George Land Conservancy (518-644-9673; www.lglc.org); Lake George Watershed Coalition (518-461-2200; www.lakegeorge2000.org); and the Fund for Lake George & Lake George Waterkeeper (518-668-9700; www.fundforlakegeorge.org).

LIBRARIES

Caldwell Lake George Library (518-668-2528; 340 Canada Street, Lake George) offers films, lectures, and workshops in addition to books.

Horicon Free Public Library (518-494-4189; 6604 NY 8, Brant Lake) is a tiny, picturesque cobblestone building perched on the edge of the lake.

MUSEUMS

The Sembrich (518-644-2431; www.operamuseum.org; 4800 Lake Shore Drive, Bolton Landing) celebrates the great Polish soprano Marcella Sembrich, but also Bolton Landing's early 1900s role as a mecca for opera stars and composers, such as Louise Homer, Samuel Barber, and Gian Carlo Menotti. From 1921 to 1935, Sembrich, made her home here. Born Marcella Kocha ska, she was a European sensation, and in 1898, she joined New York's Metropolitan Opera. Sembrich founded the vocal departments of the Juilliard School in Manhattan and the Curtis Institute in Philadelphia; during the summers, a select group of students came to her cottage studio. The studio, now a charming little museum, houses a collection of music, furniture, costumes, and opera ephemera related to Sembrich's brilliant career, including tributes from the leading composers of the day. Don't miss a stroll around the lakeside trail for a peaceful moment. Music lectures and a concert series are held in summer. Open mid-June through Labor Day.

In Warren County you'll find numerous small museums to visit. The Bolton Historical Museum, in Bolton Landing (518-644-9960; boltonhistorical.org; NY 9N), is housed in a former Catholic church. Nineteenth-century photos of Lake George hotels by Seneca Ray Stoddard give a taste of the Gilded Age; more contemporary photos show sculptor David Smith at work in his Bolton Landing studio. There's an assortment of furniture, clothing, agricultural implements, and items relating to the town's days as a summer retreat for musical superstars.

In Brant Lake, the Horicon Museum (518-494-7286; NY 8) is a well-kept nine-room farmhouse full of antiques, agricultural implements, prints, photos, toys, and dolls, open from Memorial Day through Labor Day. The Frances Kinnear Museum (518-696-4520; 2144 Main Street), open year-round in an 1880s Victorian Lake Luzerne home, is similarly chockfull of local memorabilia; the town is also home to two summer museums: the Pagenstacher Pulp Mill Museum (518-696-2645; Mill Street), set in a park near the lake, and the School House Museum (518-696-3051; Main Street). In Chestertown, local history comes alive from July to August at the Town of Chester Museum of Local History (518-494-2711; Town Hall, Main Street/US 9), with neat displays on village life. Ask about photographer Itsuzo Sumy, a Japanese bachelor who took endearing pictures of people and events in the area from the late 1930s to the 1960s.

In Lake George, in the old courthouse, the Lake George Historical Association Museum (518-668-5044; www.lakegeorgehistorical.org; 290 Canada Street) contains three floors of exhibits, including 1845-vintage jail cells in the basement. Also in Lake George is Fort William Henry Museum (518-668-5471; www.fwhmuseum.com; Canada Street), a restored log fortress dedicated to French and Indian War history, with life-size dioramas, assorted armaments, and lots of action: military drills, musket and cannon firing, and fife-and-drum bands. The fort is open daily, spring through fall.

In Schroon Lake, the Schroon–North Hudson Historical Society (518-532-7615; 1144 US 9) is open Wednesday–Sunday from June through Labor Day. Stony Creek's Stony Creek Historical Museum (518-696-5211; Lanfear Road & Creek Center) celebrates this place's past in a historic home.

In Warrensburg, the Warrensburg Museum of Local History (518-623-2928; 3797 Main Street) highlights the town's early industries, from garment factories to saw mills.

MUSIC

In September, the Lake George Arts Project sponsors the popular Lake George Jazz Festival in Shepard Park.

Courtesy of the Lake George Arts Project

On the second weekend in September, the Lake George Arts Project–sponsored (www.lakegeorgearts.org) Lake George Jazz Festival, in Shepard Park, is the place to be. The bands—often Latin or Afro-Caribbean stars—are topnotch, the vibe is cool, and the price is free. The arts project also sponsors music in the village park on summer nights, from reggae to blues to Celtic rock.

Lake George Music Festival (518-791-5089; www.lakegeorgemusicfestival .com) is a brand-new nonprofit organization whose mission is to bring classical music to the residents of Lake George Village and surrounding communities. For a week in August, concerts, featuring chamber groups and an orchestra, are held throughout the southern Adirondacks—in churches, hotels, galleries, schools, and private homes. Performers include professionals from symphonies around the world, plus current music students, who learn from these master musicians.

Luzerne Music Center (518-696-2771; www.luzernemusic.org; 203 Lake Trout Road, Lake Luzerne) is a classical music summer camp and chamber music festival on a 20-acre campus on Lake George. Throughout the summer members of the Philadelphia Orchestra, on faculty at the camp, perform in a chamber music series and give lessons and master classes to campers, ages 11–18. Luzerne's CEO and president is Elizabeth Pitcairn (www.elizabethpitcairn.com), a Luzerne Music Center alumna, an international performer, and owner of the famous Red Mendelssohn, made by Antonio Stradivari in 1720. (It's myth that the violin, purchased for $1.7 million for Pitcairn by her grandfather at a 1990 Christie's auction, is painted with the blood of the violin maker's wife, who died in childbirth. The instrument, which inspired the film *The Red Violin*, received its name for its burgundy varnish.) The

A Lake George Pilgrimage

The Pilgrimage for Restoration brings hundreds of the faithful to the Adirondack Park each September for four days of walking, prayer, and fellowship. The route—from the village of Lake George to the Shrine of Our Lady of Martyrs, at Auriesville, 40 miles west of Albany on the Mohawk River—commemorates the life and martyrdom of the saint Isaac Jogues, a 17th-century French Jesuit missionary who was captured, tortured, and eventually murdered by the Mohawks, one of the five original nations of the Iroquois Confederacy. Jogues is believed to have been the first European to see the heart of the Adirondacks.

Luzerne Music Center's recitals and concerts are superb. In 2011, violinist Sarah Chang performed; in 2012, John Corigliano, who wrote the score for *The Red Violin*, conducted a concert at the camp.

Schroon Lake Arts Council (518-532-9259; www.schroonlakearts.com; Dock Street, Boathouse Theatre, Schroon Lake) presents evening summer concerts, open jams, and dance performances in the historic Boathouse Theater; in August is its festival of folk music, storytelling, and rustic crafts.

Seagle Music Colony (518-532-7875; www.seaglecolony.com; 999 Charley Hill Road, Schroon Lake) was established in 1915 by Oscar Seagle, famed baritone and voice teacher. Vocal music is still the primary program, with coaching and master classes in opera and musical theater for conservatory students and aspiring performers. Every Sunday evening in the summer, the nondenominational Vespers concerts showcase exceptional choral singing; public concerts featuring scenes from opera and musical theater are held June through August.

NATURE CENTERS

Up Yonda Farm (518-644-9767; www.upyondafarm.com; NY 9N, Bolton Landing) is a lovely lake-view property that functions as an environmental education center. The site, operated by Warren County, is busiest during warm weather, with guided trail walks, after-dark tours, and programs on birds, butterflies, and other beasts.

SEASONAL EVENTS

Lake George Winter Carnival (518-240-0809; www.lakegeorgewintercarnival.com) spans from January through February, with kid-oriented activities, fireworks, music, races, and a polar bear plunge.

Bands 'n Beans (518-668-2616; www.lakegeorgearts.org) is a Lake George Arts Project benefit that includes numerous local bands and a massive chili cook-off at Roaring Brook Ranch, in Lake George, in March.

Americade (518-798-7888; www.tourexpo.com) is reportedly the world's largest multibrand motorcycle-touring rally. Held in and around Lake George in early June, there are guided rides on Adirondack back roads, seminars, swap meets, contests, music, parades, and banquets. Bikes range from tasteful special-edition Harleys worth tens of thousands of dollars to rusty "rat bikes" that look like found-object sculptures.

Summerfest (518-668-5755; www.lakegeorgechamber.com) features music, arts and crafts, and games for kids in Shepard Park, in Lake George, on the last weekend in June.

Stony Creek Mountain Days (518-696-3575; www.stonycreekny.org) highlight Adirondack skills and pastimes with lumberjack contests, craft demonstrations, square dancing, and storytelling, followed by fireworks, held in Stony Creek the first weekend in August.

Adirondack Folk Music Festival (518-532-9259; www.schroonlakearts

Americade, in Lake George each June, is reportedly the world's largest multibrand motorcycle-touring rally. Courtesy of Americade

Courtesy of Nancie Battaglia

Elvis in Lake George

Elvis look-alike contests, tribute competitions, vendors peddling black wigs, large sunglasses, and sparkly jumpsuits? King revelers come to Lake George each spring for the **Lakegeorge.com Elvis Festival** (518-681-7452; www.lakegeorgeelvisfest .com). Through the years, the event has had various organizers and names, but fans can agree that Lake George and Elvis are a natural fit.

.com) is an all-day affair in Schroon Lake that also includes rustic furniture and crafts, in mid-August.

Warren County Country Fair (518-623-3291; www.warrensburgchamber .com) is a family-oriented fair, with the usual 4-H and agricultural exhibits, a horse show, historical displays, traditional music, a pony pull, carnival rides, and fish-and-wildlife exhibits, held in August at the fairground on Horicon Avenue outside Warrensburg.

Fiddlers' Jamboree (518-623-9961; www.thurman-ny.com) is a high-spirited September weekend of bluegrass and fiddle bands, dancing, workshops, and kids' activities.

THEATER

Lake George Dinner Theatre (518-668-5762 ext 411; www.lakegeorge dinnertheatre.com; Holiday Inn, 2223 Canada Street, Lake George), an Actors Equity Company, has, for more than 40 seasons, presented one show a season in a semiproscenium setting. Productions are thoroughly competent, as is the food at the Holiday Inn's banquet room.

WRITERS' PROGRAMS

Fiction Among Friends (518-623-9305; www.persisgranger.com) hosts an Adirondack Mountain Writers' Retreat, in Thurman, that offers workshops and an in-residence component. Wiawaka Holiday House Women's Retreat (518-668-9690; www.wiawaka.org), in Lake George, has poetry and other writing workshops, and hosts readings by regional authors. The Writer's Voice (518-543-8833; www.silver bay.org), a nationwide program of the YMCA, has a center at Silver Bay Association, on the northern end of Lake George. Workshops by highly regarded poets, travel writers, novelists, and essayists are slated for spring and summer.

Recreation

Adventures in Lake George & the Southeastern Adirondacks

Boating galore on a big lake, a historical underwater diving trail, hiking treks up and around one of the most picturesque landscapes in the East, an extreme zip-line, even waterparks and Frankenstein—this region of the park has something for everyone.

ADIRONDACK GUIDES

If you'd like an expert to lead you on a biking, hiking, paddling, or fishing trip in the Lake George and southeastern Adirondack region, see www.nysoga.com.

The Wild Side of Lake George

The 70,000-plus-acre **Lake George Wild Forest** is an adventurer's playground. Great hikes surround the lake, especially if you like to climb for rewarding vistas. On the west shore the Tongue Mountain Range in the town of Bolton, with First and Fifth Peaks, to name a couple, has numerous vantage points. The summit of the range's French Point Mountain shows most of Lake George. To the water's east is Black Mountain, the highest rise in the wild forest. Although the fire tower atop it is off-limits, from the rocks to the tower's north is a spectacular 180-degree view of Lake George. Farther south,

Pilot Knob Ridge Preserve in the Lake George Wild Forest.

Courtesy of Carl Heilman II, www.carlheilman.com

Sleeping Beauty, where peregrine falcons nest on the cliffs, gives a great perspective of the southern basin.

Motorboats rule the southern reach of the lake, but there's quiet water, too. Islands in the Narrows are inviting, especially during the off-season, before the Fourth of July and after Labor Day. This stretch is good for kayaking, though beware of waves that can swell to 4-foot whitecaps in stormy weather. A tamer paddle, from Northwest Bay Brook through the wetlands and into Northwest Bay, which opens into Lake George, is a pretty trip. In Hague, Jabe Pond is an easy body of water to sample in a canoe and it's accessible by car.

See chapter 8 for guidebooks to this region for more trip ideas.

BICYCLING

There are endless thrilling, gorgeous rides—on skinny tires or fat ones—in these parts. Pack Forest in Warrensburg is good for mountain biking. The Warren County Bikeway (518-623-2877), an old trolley line linking Lake George village with Glens Falls, is a cyclist's and in-line skater's dream. It's smooth, peaceful, and well engineered; there are picnic groves, historical markers, and, as you enter the Falls, an ice-cream stand. To the 9-mile bikeway you can add another nine of vehicle-free riding on the Feeder Canal towpath. For experienced road riders, climbing Tongue on two wheels is a thrill. One popular group trip goes from Bolton, on Route 9N, over the long ridge of Tongue, past Silver Bay to a dock below Ticonderoga. There *The Mohican* picks up weary riders and transports them to the village with a fascinating narrated voyage. The Bicycle Discovery Cruise—usually in August—is 40 miles; the boat ride is five hours. For details contact Lake George Steamboat Company (518-668-5777; www.lakegeorgesteamboat.com). See chapter 8 for guidebooks and other resources for bike trip ideas.

BOATING

This is Lake George, where you've just got to cruise in your Chris-Craft, zip around in your motorboat, or launch your paddleboat. Many state campgrounds have boat ramps. If you have a reserved campsite, there's no extra charge to launch a boat.

Note also that motorboats (over 10 hp) and sailboats (longer than 18 feet) used on Lake George must have a permit, available from local marinas or the Lake George Park Commission (518-668-9347; www.lgpc.state.ny.us).

The *New York State Boater's Guide* contains the rules and regulations for inland waters, and is available from offices of the New York Department of Transportation. Some statewide laws for pleasure craft follow:

- You must carry one personal flotation device for every passenger in your boat. Children under 12 are required to wear life jackets while on board.
- Any boat powered by a motor (even canoes with small motors) and operated mainly in New York State must be registered with the Department of Motor Vehicles.
- When traveling within 100 feet of shore, dock, pier, raft, float, or an anchored boat, the speed limit is 5 mph. (Maximum daytime speed limits are 45 mph, and nighttime, 25 mph, although on many lakes with rocky shoals, or on water bodies that are also popular with nonmotorized craft, lower speeds are prudent.)
- Powerboats give way to canoes, sailboats, rowboats, kayaks, and anchored boats.
- The boat on your right has the right-of-way when being passed.
- Running lights must be used after dark.
- Boaters under 16 must be accompanied by an adult, or, if between 10 and 16 and unaccompanied, they must have a safety certificate from a New York State course.
- Boating under the influence of alcohol carries heavy fines and/or jail sentences.
- Littering and discharging marine-toilet wastes into waterways is prohibited.

BOAT TOURS

The season generally runs from early May through October, and many cruises require that you call ahead for a reservation. Lake George Shoreline Cruises (518-668-4644; www.lakegeorgeshore line.com; 2 Kurosaka Lane, Lake George) has several boats to choose from, including the adorable *Horicon* and the new *Adirondac*; narrated day-

Lake George Steamboat Company's paddle wheeler *Minne-ha-ha*. Courtesy of Nancie Battaglia

time and dinner cruises; wedding cruises available; and the *Horicon* departs at dusk on Thursdays in the summer for fireworks cruises. Lake George Steamboat Company (518-668-5777; www.lakegeorgesteamboat.com; Steel Pier, Lake George) has three enclosed boats, including the huge *Lac du Saint Sacrement* and the paddle wheeler *Minne-ha-ha*. The *Mohican* makes a four-and-a-half-hour-long tour of the lake daily in the summer and navigates through the Narrows, among the islands each afternoon. In addition to providing shorter narrated trips, boats have cocktail lounges and offer dinner, pizza, and moonlight cruises with live music; wedding packages are also available.

Invasion of the Lake-Choking, Tree-Mangling Imposters

AQUATIC INVASIVE SPECIES:

Aquatic invasive species are a major threat to Adirondack lakes, ponds, and rivers. Not native to this region and having no natural predators, invasive species spread uncontrollably, displace native plants and animals, and degrade habitat and deteriorate water quality and recreational opportunities. At least eight aquatic invasive plants are in Adirondacks waters. **Eurasian watermilfoil** (*Myriophyllum spicatum*), **curlyleaf pondweed** (*Potamogeton crispus*), **water chestnut** (*Trapa natans*), and **European frogbit** (*Hydrocharis morsus-ranae*) form thick, impenetrable mats. Although native to Europe and Asia, these plants arrived in the United States as popular aquarium plants or ornamentals used in water gardens. Once released into the environment, they quickly spread. Plant fragments or seeds easily attach to recreational watercraft or cling to gear and are transported to new waterways.

Adirondack waters also harbor aquatic invasive animals. **Zebra mussel** (*Dreissena polymorpha*), **spiny waterflea** (*Bythotrephes cederstroemi*), and **Asian clam** (*Corbicula fluminea*) are invasive invertebrates from Europe and Asia. The primary pathways to the United States for these and other aquatic animal invaders are the ballast water of ocean-going vessels, the aquarium trade, or live seafood market; once released, they, too, can attach to watercraft and gear or be transported in water in bait buckets or live wells.

Fortunately, two out of three Adirondack waters surveyed are still free of aquatic invasive species. A real opportunity exists to prevent widespread degradation. Individual actions make a difference. Check, clean, drain and dry all watercraft and gear before moving between waters, and dispose of unwanted bait in the trash. Report sightings of aquatic invaders to the **Adirondack Park Invasive Plant Program** at 518-576-2082.

TERRESTRIAL INVASIVE SPECIES:

Terrestrial invasive species—from plants and pathogens to mammals—put ecosystems and the services they provide to human communities at risk. Not native to this region, invasive plants such as **Japanese knotweed** (*Fallopia japonica*), **purple loosestrife** (*Lythrum salicaria*), and **garlic mustard** (*Alliaria petiolata*) are prolific spreaders that form dense single species stands along stream corridors, wetlands, and woodlands. More recent plant invaders such as **yellow iris** (*Iris pseudacorus*), **giant hogweed** (*Heracleum mantegazzianum*), and **swallow-wort vine** (*Cynanchum* spp.) are now taking hold. Ornamental plantings are the primary source of terrestrial invasive plants. Roots, fragments, or seeds are also spread via roads or construction projects that create disturbed areas or use infected soils.

Tree-killing forest pests and pathogens are also of great concern because the rapid rate of introductions and spread may be faster than forests can adapt. Discovered in New York in 2009, **emerald ash borer** (*Agrilus planipennis*) attacks all species of ash, which comprise 7 percent of New York forests. **Asian longhorned beetle** (*Anoplophora glabripennis*) attacks a broader range of species, including maples and other hardwoods. Its distribution is limited in the United States, but if it spreads, it could devastate forests and the wood products industry.

Feral swine or **Russian boar** (*Sus scrofa*), a new arrival in the region, escaped from licensed private hunting preserves and are established in more than 40 states. Their parasites, diseases, and feeding behavior pose risks to natural areas, agriculture, and human health.

Protect Adirondack woods and wildlands from terrestrial invasive species. Individual actions make a difference. Use local firewood. Never pick roadside wildflowers. Landscape with noninvasive plants. Clean shoes and gear upon leaving a natural area. Report sightings of terrestrial invaders to the **Adirondack Park Invasive Plant Program** (518-576-2082).

—Hilary Smith directs the Adirondack Nature Conservancy's Adirondack Park Invasive Plant Program. Learn more at www.adkinvasives.com.

The Department of Environmental Conservation (518-402-9428; www.dec.ny.gov) operates public campgrounds in the park, all of which are open from Memorial Day through Labor Day. Many campgrounds open earlier, and some operate late into the fall.

Facilities at state campgrounds include a picnic table and grill at each site, water spigots for every 10 sites or so, and lavatories. Camping is allowed year-round on state land, but you need a permit to stay more than three days in one backcountry spot or if you are camping with a group of more than six people. You may camp in the backcountry provided you pitch your tent at least 150 feet from any trail, stream, lake, or other water body. (See "low-impact camping," page 146.)

Reservations can be made for a site in the state campgrounds by contacting Reserve America (1-800-456-CAMP; www.reserveamerica), though DEC campgrounds will cheerfully take you on a first-come, first-served basis if space is available; before July 4 and after September 1, it's usually easy to find a nice site without a reservation.

DEC public campgrounds do not supply water, electric, or sewer hookups for recreational vehicles. If you require these amenities, there are privately owned campgrounds in many communities. The following camping fees are for 2012:

Eagle Point (518-494-2220; US 9, Pottersville). On Schroon Lake. Boat launch, showers, swimming. $22 camping fee.

Hearthstone Point (518-668-5193; 3298 Lakeshore Drive, Lake George). On Lake George. Showers, swimming. $22 camping fee.

Lake George Battleground (518-668-3348; 2224 US 9, Lake George). Historic site. Showers; an easy walk to downtown and tour boat docks. $22 camping fee.

Lake George Islands (numerous sites on Narrow Island, 518-499-1288; Glen Island, 518-644-9696; and Long Island, 518-656-9426; 18 Boathouse Lane, Bolton Landing). Access by boat; tents only; swimming. No dogs allowed. $28 camping fee.

Luzerne (518-696-2031; 892 Lake Avenue, Lake Luzerne). On Fourth Lake. A Hudson River impoundment. Showers, swimming, canoe and rowboat launch; no powerboats allowed. $22 camping fee.

Rogers Rock (518-585-6746; 9894 Lake Shore Drive, Hague). Historic site on Lake George. Boat launch, access to rock climbing cliff. $22 camping fee.

CAMPS

There are all manner of kids' summer camps in the Adirondacks, of course. Adirondack Camp (518-547-8261; www.adirondackcamp.com), at Putnam Station, uses Lake George as its playground. On Pilot Knob, YMCA Camp Chingachgook (518-656-9462; 1872 Pilot Knob Road) has been a fixture since 1914. If you're in the Adirondacks during July or August, and would like to visit a particular camp with your prospective happy camper, you should call ahead. See www.acacamps.org for a list of camps accredited by the American Camp Association.

CANOEING AND KAYAKING

Where to begin with Lake George? It's vast, it's gorgeous, and the possibilities are endless. There are more than 200 islands in this lake, ranging from windswept rocks sprinkled with blueberry bushes to 30-acre havens with lean-tos. Many are state owned, available for camping and picnicking for a fee and by reservation. The campsites are in great demand but you can book an island for a day for $10 when you get a permit from the Department of Environmental Conservation office on River

Road in Warrensburg or at Long, Narrow, or Glen Island ranger stations. Day permits (good from 9 AM to 9 PM) can be purchased at Norowal Marina, in Bolton Landing.

It's dangerous to paddle from the congested village waterfront, where Jet-Skis buzz and powerboats throw huge wakes. Head a few miles outside of town to Lake George Kayak Company (518-644-9366; www.lake georgekayak.com; 4973 Lake Shore

Paddling at the base of Deer Leap.
Courtesy of Carl Heilman II, www.carlheilman.com

Drive), the go-to spot in Bolton Landing for canoeing, kayaking, and stand-up paddling. The shop provides lessons, guided trips, rentals, and more. The Adirondack Mountain Club Member Services Center (518-668-4447; www.adk.org; 814 Goggins Road, Lake George) also offers spring, summer, and fall canoe workshops in different locations for all ages; guided canoe tours are available for women, youth, and Elderhostel groups.

When you're planning any trip, allow an extra day in case the weather doesn't cooperate. Remember that you're required to carry a life jacket for each person in the boat; lash an extra paddle in your canoe, too. Bring plenty of food and fuel, a backpacker stove, and rain gear. See chapter 8 for paddling guidebooks and other resources to this region.

DIVING

No amount of wishful thinking could turn the chilly Adirondack depths into crystal-clear Caribbean seas, but there is plenty to discover beneath the waves in Lake George. In fact, it's the site of New York's first underwater heritage preserve and home to numerous 18th- and 19th-century shipwrecks. The Underwater Blueway Trail promotes and preserves New York's maritime heritage. Shipwrecks and rock formations are marked with buoys, guiding lines, and signage. Volunteers for this project include members of Batteaux Below, historians and divers who created dive sites in Lake George beginning in the 1990s. Among the preserve sites at the bottom of Lake George are the 52-foot British artillery ship the *Land Tortoise,* which sank in 1758; the Sunken Fleet of 1758, smaller bateaux used to transport troops; and the 45-foot tour boat *Forward* that sank in the 1930s, today used as an underwater classroom for beginner divers.

The following dive operators can help with equipment, instruction, and maps to the Underwater Blueway Trail: Adirondack Scuba Champlain (518-884-4056; www .adirondackscuba.com; 98 Rowland Street, Ballston Spa); Diamond Divers (518-505-3483; www.divelakegeorge.com; Bolton Landing); Dive Center (518-562-3483; www.divechamplain.com; 4013 US 9, Plattsburgh); and Jones' Aqua Sports (518-963-1150; 482 Willsboro Point Road, Willsboro). The New York State Divers Association (www.scubany.org) also provides scuba diving resources.

FAMILY FUN

Adirondack Extreme Adventure Course (518-494-7200; www.adirondackextreme .com; 35 Westwood Forest Lane, Bolton Landing) is a high-wire treetop adventure park, with ropes courses and zip-lines for adults and kids. Open in temperatures above 20 degrees.

House of Frankenstein Wax Museum, on Canada Street, is a Lake George institution.

Courtesy of Nancie Battaglia

Lake George Floating Classroom (518-668-3558; www.lake georgeassociation.org), aboard the *Rosalia Anna Ashby*, allows kids and their families to learn about Lake George and how to keep its water clean. Open May through October.

House of Frankenstein Wax Museum (518-668-3377; www .frankensteinwaxmuseum.com; 213 Canada Street, Lake George) is just one of those Lake George places you've got to visit. Open daily Memorial Day through Columbus Day.

Magic Forest (518-668-2448; www.magicforestpark.com; US 9, Lake George), for little ones, has rides and games, plus Santa's Hideaway, and is home to the Adirondack Park's only diving horse, Lightning. Open Memorial Day through Labor Day.

Natural Stone Bridge & Caves (518-494-2283; www.stonebridgeandcaves.com; 535 Stone Bridge Road, Pottersville) is caves, with a mineral shop, a playground and picnic area, and mining activities. Open daily Memorial Day through Columbus Day.

Water Slide World (518-668-4407; www.waterslideworld.net; US 9 and 9L, Lake George) has a wave pool, water slides, and bumper boats. Daily mid-June through Labor Day.

FISHING

Begin your fishing education with the *New York State Freshwater Fishing Regulations Guide*, published by the Department of Environmental Conservation (www .dec.ny.gov; DEC, 625 Broadway, Albany, New York 12233). The booklet details all the seasons and limits for various species. Everyone 16 and older who fishes in the Adirondacks must have a New York fishing license, which can be purchased on the DEC's website, at sporting goods stores, and town offices. Nonresidents can get special five-day licenses; state residents 70 and older may get free licenses.

The DEC site also has helpful hotlines for anglers, describing the top fishing spots and what's hitting where on which kind of bait.

See chapter 8 for fishing guidebooks. Or see I Love New York's comprehensive *Adirondack Fishing* guide at www.fishadk.com.

To get in the proper frame of mind for fishing, nothing beats a trip to a local fish hatchery. In the southeastern Adirondacks, the Warren County Fish Hatchery (518-623-2877; 145 Fish Hatchery Road, Warrensburg) is open daily, with a nice picnic grove.

There are numerous fishing guides and charters in this region. Check out Lake George and outlying towns' chambers of commerce for listings.

GOLF

In this region the courses include:

1000 Acres Golf Club (518-696-2444; www.1000acres.com; 465 Warrensburg Road, Stony Creek). Nine holes; par-35; 3,900 yards.

Bend of the River Golf Course (518-696-3415; 5 Park Avenue, Hadley). Nine holes; par-35; 2,700 yards. One of the first courses to open in the spring.

Country Meadows Golf (518-792-5927; www.countrymeadowsgolf.net; NY 149, Fort Ann). Twelve holes; driving range.

Cronin's Golf Resort (518-623-9336; www.croninsgolfresort.com; Golf Course Road, Warrensburg). Eighteen holes; par-70; 6,100 yards. Cottages on site.

Green Mansions Golf Club (518-494-7222; www.greenmansionsgolf.com; 207 Darrowsville Road, Chestertown). 9 holes; par-36; 2,700 yards.

In Bolton Landing, the Sagamore's 18-hole Donald Ross–designed course is challenging and picturesque.   Courtesy of the Sagamore Resort

Queensbury Country Club (518-793-3711; www.queensburygolf.com; 907 NY 149, Lake George). Eighteen holes; par-70.

The Sagamore (518-644-9400; www.thesagamore.com; Federal Hill Road, Bolton Landing). Eighteen holes; par-70; 6,900 yards. Designed by Donald Ross; challenging and lovely.

Schroon Lake Municipal Golf Course (518-532-9359; Hoffman Road, Schroon Lake). Nine holes; par-36; 3,000 yards.

Top of the World (518-668-3000; www.topoftheworldgolfresort.com; 441 Lockhart Mountain Road, Lake George). Nine holes; par-36; 2,900 yards.

Miniature Golf

Historians take note: Miniature golf was reputedly launched in downtown Lake George at the intersection of Beach Road and US 9 in the early years of the 20th century. Lake George remains the Pebble Beach of Adirondack minis, and half a dozen courses are nearby. You can try Around the World in 18 Holes (518-668-2531; www.aroundtheworldgolf.com; Beach Road); Lumberjack Pass Mini Golf (518-793-7141; www.lumberjackminigolf.com; US 9); Gooney Golf (518-668-2589; www.goonygolf.com; US 9); Pirate's Cove (518-668-0493; www.piratescove.net; 2115 US 9); Putts N Prizes (518-668-9500; 8 Beach Road); and Magic Castle Indoor Golf (518-668-3777; 273 Canada Street).

HIKING AND BACKPACKING

There are dozens of guidebooks to help you decide where to go (see chapter 8). Take note: Rattlesnakes live in the Tongue Mountain Range near Lake George; keep your eyes open when crossing rock outcrops on warm, sunny days. These Eastern timber rattlers are quite shy and nonaggressive, but try not to surprise one.

When venturing into the woods and mountains, always be prepared. Your pack should contain a flashlight, matches, extra food and water, map, compass, and extra clothes (wool or fleece for warmth; leave the cotton at home). At most trailheads, there's a register for signing in. Always tell someone your hiking plans.

The Adirondack Mountain Club (518-668-4447; www.adk.org; 814 Goggins Road, Lake George) offers hikes with naturalists; fall foliage hikes; wilderness overnights; and weekends for women, youth, and senior citizens.

Tick, Tick, Tick

Cases of **Lyme disease** have been recorded in the Adirondacks, and hikers should take precautions against exposing themselves to deer ticks (*Ixodes dammini*). The ticks can be found in deep woods, although they prefer to stay on their host animals, white-tailed deer and deer mice. Dogs—especially exuberant ones that go crashing through the brush—are more at risk than humans; you can have your pet inoculated against Lyme disease.

Courtesy of Adirondack Life

You can minimize your exposure to ticks by wearing long pants (with cuffs tucked into your boots) and long-sleeve shirts, using a good insect repellent, and staying on the trail. If you wear light-color clothing, the ticks are easier to spot, and you can check yourself and your kids for the vermin while you're in the woods.

Deer ticks are very tiny, no bigger than a sesame seed. They don't fly. If you find an eight-legged crawling creature on your body, it could be a spider, a wood tick (not a carrier of Lyme), or an arachnid locally called a "ked," which, despite its scary-looking crablike pincers, is harmless.

Humans face the highest risk of tick contact in spring (though local veterinarians say they're seeing an increase of ticks on dogs in autumn). If you find a tick attached to your skin, pull it out steadily with a pair of tweezers or your fingers, grasping as close to the tick's mouth as you can.

Save the creature in a jar—your doctor will probably want to see it. Apply a topical antiseptic to the bite. A tick must feed for several hours before the disease is transmitted.

If you see on your skin a clear area encircled by a red rash and are feeling flulike symptoms, you may have contracted Lyme disease. Visit your doctor or a medical center for a Lyme test, but be aware that it takes several weeks after a bite for your body to show antibodies. Lyme symptoms mimic many other ailments, so it's difficult to get an accurate diagnosis; most medical practitioners will begin a course of antibiotics if they believe you've been exposed.

HORSEBACK RIDING AND WAGON TRIPS

If you have your own horse, the Department of Environmental Conservation has trail networks across the park, and even operates campgrounds that accommodate man and beast. For a description of these trails, contact the DEC (518-897-1200; www.dec.ny.gov). One rule applies for bringing in out-of-state horses: proof of a negative Coggins test is necessary.

A legacy of the dude-ranch days in the southeastern Adirondacks, Painted Pony Rodeo (518-696-2421; www.paintedponyrodeo.com; Howe Road, Lake Luzerne) presents professional rodeo competitions Wednesday, Friday, and Saturday nights in July and August, rain or shine. This is the home of the country's oldest weekly rodeo, complete with trick riding and roping, clowns and novelty acts. There's more equine action, particularly riding through acres and acres of trails, at 1000 Acres Ranch Resort (518-696-2444; www.1000acres.com; 465 Warrensburg Road, Stony Creek). Bailey's Horses (518-696-4541; NY 9N, Lake Luzerne) offers Western trail rides, lessons, hay wagon or carriage rides around Lake Vanare, winter trail rides, and trips to Lake George horse trails by reservation. Bennett Stables (518-696-4444; NY 9N, Lake Luzerne) gives trail rides. Circle B Ranch (518-494-4888; www.circlebranch

.com; 771 Potterbrook Road, Chestertown) does wagon, sleigh, and hayrides. Circle L Ranch (518-623-9967; 869 High Street, Athol) is a horse-pack outfitter; it provides half- and full-day trips. Rydin'-Hy (518-494-2742; Sherman Lake, Warrensburg) gives trail and sleigh rides. Saddle Up Stables (518-668-4801; www.ridingstables .com; 3515 Lake Shore Drive, Lake George) offers trail rides.

Public horse trails include the Lake George Trail System on the east side of Lake George, off Pilot Knob Road, with 41 miles of carriage roads on an old estate, plus lean-tos. Also, Lake Luzerne, off NY 9N near Lake Luzerne hamlet, on Fourth Lake, has a campsite with a corral, and 5 miles of trails on state land that connect with many miles of privately owned trails. Pharaoh Lake Horse Trails, in the Pharaoh Lake Wilderness Area, east of Schroon Lake, include 12 miles of sandy woods roads, plus lean-tos.

HUNTING

Native Americans, colonial scouts, and 19th-century travelers regarded the Adirondacks as happy hunting grounds. Early accounts describe shooting deer year-round for cooking at camp and for swank Manhattan restaurants. Old pictures show small groups of men displaying dozens of dead bucks.

Today there are seasons for deer, black bear, snowshoe hare, coyote, bobcat, and other small mammals, plus ruffed grouse, woodcock, wild turkey, and waterfowl. The booklets outlining game seasons are available from the Department of Environmental Conservation (www.dec.ny.gov); licenses can be purchased from sporting goods stores, town offices, or the DEC. Nonresidents may purchase five-day licenses. If you have never had a New York State hunting license, you must show proof that you have attended a hunter education course. Turkey hunting requires a special stamp from the DEC; waterfowl hunters must possess a Federal Migratory Bird Hunting Stamp.

Wilderness, primitive, and wild forest areas are all open to hunting. Hunters—even if they have a brand-new, state-of-the-art GPS unit—should be proficient with map and compass. Global-positioning units don't always work well in thick forest, and batteries wear out.

If you'd like to hire a hunting guide, check out www.nysoga.org.

RACES AND SEASONAL SPORTING EVENTS

Adirondack Sports & Fitness (518-877-8788; www.adksportsfitness.com) is an excellent source both for upcoming races and results of everything from snowshoe to cross-country-ski events to paddle fests to the Prospect Mountain Uphill Run. Always call or check websites to be sure these events are still on, as plans can change season to season.

New Year's Day Polar Plunge Swim (518-240-0809; www.lakegorgewinter carnival.com; Shepard Park, Lake George) means hundreds of brave swimmers plunging into icy Lake George.

Prospect Mountain Road Race (518-668-2195; Prospect Mountain Memorial Highway, Lake George) sends runners 5.5 miles uphill all the way, in early May.

Adirondack Distance Run (518-792-7396; www.adirondackrunners.com) is a 10-mile road race along Lake Shore Drive, in early July.

Lake George Triathlon (www.adktri.org) is a shorter version of the real thing, in early September.

Adirondack Marathon Distance Festival (1-888-724-7666; www.adirondack marathon.org), a 26-mile run around Schroon Lake, happens in September.

SAILING

Lake George offers great sailing in the midst of beautiful scenery and has marinas for an evening's dockage or equipment repairs. Sailing on island-studded waters can be tricky, since in the lee of an island you stand a good chance of being becalmed. Wind can whip shallow lakes into white-capped mini oceans, too. A portable weather radio should be included in your basic kit; Adirondack forecasts (out of Burlington, Vermont) can be found at 162.40 megahertz.

You can purchase Coast Guard charts for Lakes George and Champlain, but not for most of the small interior lakes. Some USGS topographical maps have troughs and shoals marked, but these maps are of limited use to sailors. Your best bet is to ask at boat liveries for lake maps, or at least find out how to avoid the worst rocks.

For hardware, lines, and other equipment, Yankee Boating Center (518-668-2862; www.yankeeboat.com; 3578 Lakeshore Drive, Lake George) is well stocked with everything from the essentials to brand-new boats. It also has a sailing school, and rents day sailers and cruisers. The Sagamore Resort (1-866-385-6221; www.the sagamore.com; 110 Sagamore Road), in Bolton Landing, has a sailing school. Y-Knot Sailing (518-656-9462; www.yknotsailing.org), at YMCA Camp Chingachgook, in Pilot Knob, offers sailing instruction, races, and workshops to sailors of all levels of experience and physical ability.

SCENIC HIGHWAY

Near Lake George village, Prospect Mountain Veterans Memorial Highway (518-668-5755; www.visitlakegeorge.com; off US 9) snakes up a small peak to a terrific 100-mile view stretching from the High Peaks to Vermont and the Catskills. It's a state-operated toll road open daily from late May through the fall.

SKIING: CROSS-COUNTRY AND SNOWSHOEING

For suggestions on backcountry ski trails see the guidebooks and other resources in chapter 8.

State campgrounds—closed to vehicles from November through May—offer snow-covered roads with gentle grades. Or a licensed guide (www .nysoga.org) will know where to go.

Before setting out on any of these wilderness excursions, prepare your pack with quick-energy food; a thermos

Whitehall Sliders

Whitehall High has the country's only high-school bobsled team. In winter, the dozen or so Whitehall student-athletes compete in Lake Placid every week in a league that includes about 20 other sliders in the Olympic Regional Development Authority's junior bobsled program.

filled with hot tea or cocoa; extra hat, socks, and gloves; topo map and compass; matches; flashlight; and space blanket. Dress in layers of wool, polypropylene, or synthetic pile. Don't travel alone. Sign in at the trailhead register. Let friends know your destination and when you plan to return.

Caroline Fish Memorial Trail (518-494-2722; Dynamite Hill, NY 8, Chestertown) is an 11-kilometer town trail, lighted for night skiing.

Friends Lake Cross-Country-Ski and Snowshoe Center (518-494-4751; www .friendslake.com; 963 Friends Lake Road, Chestertown) has 32 kilometers of groomed trails; with rentals and instruction.

Rogers Rock State Campsite (518-623-1200; NY 9N, Hague) means 10 kilometers of groomed trails; part of the trail is lit for night skiing.

Schroon Lake Ski Trails (518-532-7675) allow backcountry skiing in Pharaoh Lake and Hoffman Notch wilderness areas.

Warren County Trails (518-623-5576; Hudson Avenue, Warrensburg) is a 16-kilometer network along the Hudson River.

Courtesy of Ted Comstock, Saranac Lake

SNOWMOBILING

Many trail networks throughout the park cross private timberlands, as well as the state forest preserve. Public lands designated as wild forest areas are open to snowmobiling; wilderness areas are not. See the Department of Environmental Conservation's website, www.dec.ny.gov, for rules, regs, and links to Adirondack snowmobile trails.

Know your machine; carry an emergency repair kit and understand how to use it. Be sure you have plenty of gas. Travel with friends in case of a breakdown or other surprise situations. Never ride at night unless you're familiar with the trail or are following an experienced leader. Avoid crossing frozen lakes and streams unless you are absolutely certain the ice is safe. Some town or county roads are designated trails; while on such a highway, keep right, observe the posted snowmobile speed limit, and travel in single file.

Bring a topographic map and compass as well as a local trail map; survival kit with matches, flashlight, rope, space blanket, quick-energy food, and something warm to drink; extra hat, socks, and mittens.

Among the places that offer guided tours or snowmobile rentals are ½ Mile Ranch (518-696-3113; www.halfmileranch.com), in Lake Luzerne, and Bolton Landing Snowmobile Tours (518-644-9941).

WILDERNESS AREAS

These portions of the Forest Preserve are 10,000 acres or larger and are open to hiking, cross-country skiing, hunting, fishing, and other similar pursuits, but seaplanes may not land on wilderness ponds, nor are motorized vehicles welcome. In this region, there's

Pharaoh Lake. 46,000 acres; east of Schroon Lake hamlet. Extensive trail system, thirty-six lakes and ponds, lean-tos, views from Pharaoh and other nearby mountains.

WILD FOREST AREAS

More than a million acres of public land in the park are designated as wild forest, which are open to snowmobile travel, mountain biking, and other recreation:

Lake George. On both the east and

Lake George's Vicars Island, Deer Leap, and Sabbath Bay Point from Harbor Islands

Courtesy of Carl Heilman II, www.carlheilman.com

Don't Touch That Critter!

In recent years, rabies cases have been reported in the northern and southeastern corners of the Adirondacks. The disease seems to be spread by raccoons, foxes, and skunks in upstate New York.

However, humans are not at great risk for rabies exposure, as contact with sick wildlings can be avoided. If you come across a wild animal acting unafraid or lying passively, by all means stay away from it. Don't touch dead creatures you may find.

Dogs must be inoculated against rabies. Keep your pet under control when traveling through the woods.

west shores of the lake, north of Bolton Landing. Contains the Tongue Mountain Range on the west, and the old Knapp estate, with 40-plus miles of hiking and horse trails, on the east.

Wilcox Lake. West of Stony Creek. Miles of snowmobile trails and old roads; ponds and streams for fishing.

WILDLIFE

The usual suspects are in this part of the Adirondacks: varying hares, weasels, mink, raccoons, fisher, pine martens, otters, bobcats, porcupines, red and gray foxes, coyotes, white-tailed deer, plus terrestrial and aquatic birds. But unlike most other parts of the park, Eastern timber rattlesnakes live here, on Tongue Mountain. They are a protected species, as past practices and a misunderstanding of these creatures has threatened their southeastern Adirondacks habitat. Pay attention to your surroundings when hiking over rock outcrops on sunny days. These rattlers are quite shy and nonaggressive, but take care not to surprise one.

Eastern cougars, extirpated from New York State in the late 1800s, are constantly the chatter of Adirondackers. There are often reports of these mountain lions in this region, though the Department of Environmental Conservation had yet to collect physical evidence of these elusive predators—until December 2010, when a mountain lion was sighted in a Lake George backyard. His tracks led DEC personnel to a spot where hair samples were gathered for DNA analysis. In June of the following year, a 140-pound male cougar was killed by a car in Connecticut. It turned out to be the same animal, whose genetic markers indicated he had traveled from South Dakota.

Shopping

Adirondackana and more in Lake George & the Southeastern Adirondacks

Canada Street, Lake George village's main drag, is a Day-Glo kaleidoscope of T-shirt sellers, ice-cream stands, and souvenir joints; if you can't decide what to get the folks back home there's a psychic advisor who might be able to help. More traditional Adirondackana can be found outside the village. Antiques, also. And for shopaholics who need their outlet-shopping fix, there's that, too.

ADIRONDACKANA AND ANTIQUES

Among this sampling of regional shops, some are in private homes, so be sure to call ahead.

In Lake George, Ralph Kylloe Antiques and Rustics Gallery (518-696-4100; www.ralphkylloe.com; 1796 NY 9N) is Adirondackanapalooza, with its exceptional rustic furniture and décor for the home.

Antiques-shoppers should check out the excellent Black Bass Antiques (518-644-2389; www.blackbassantiques.com; 4920 Lakeshore Drive), in Bolton Landing, for books, antique fishing tackle, Lake George souvenirs and photographs, and other general Adirondack items.

Atateka Books & Collectibles (518-494-4652; 1329 Friends Lake Road, near NY 8) has paper ephemera, books, and smalls, in Chestertown.

In Schroon, the Emporium (518-532-9900; 1063 Main Street) is a large shop with antique furniture, clothes, glass, you name it.

Dusty Rhoads Antiques (518-532-9555; 1454 Charley Hill Road) buys, sells, and repairs antiques.

Warrensburg is home to Discoveries (518-623-4567; www.discoveriesusa.com; US 9 & NY 28, 1 mile north of town center), with its miscellany, from kitchen to bath, glassware, sporting goods, and furniture. Riverside Gallery (518-623-2026; www.riversidegallery.com; 2 Elm Street) sells old prints, paintings, reproduction furniture, picture framing, and Adirondack gifts. And Yesteryear Main Street Books (518-623-2149; 3922 Main Street) offers rare books, country furniture, and accessories.

ART GALLERIES AND ARTISTS' STUDIOS

Lake Shore Gallery (518-644-9480; www.lakeshoregalleryboltonlanding.com; 4985 Lakeshore Drive) features paintings by regional artists in Bolton Landing. Also in Bolton is watercolor portraitist Vivian Simonson (518-644-3106; www.vivian simonson.com; 4580 Lakeshore Drive).

Lake Luzerne's Lynn Benevento Gallery (518-696-5702; www.lynn benevento.com; 4 Bridge Street) shows local landscapes, wildflowers, and town scenes available as original paintings or limited-edition prints.

Thurman is where Diane Golden (www.dianegolden.com) creates her funky assemblages.

Assemblage by Thurman artist Diane Golden. Courtesy of Diane Golden

BOAT BUILDERS

In Brant Lake, Gar Woods are constructed and restored by the talented Turcotte brothers' GarWood Custom Boats (518-494-2966; www.garwoodcustomboats.com; 20 Duell Hill Road).

The Hacker Boat Company (518-543-6666; www.hackerboat.com; 8 Delaware Avenue) gives demonstrations and tours at its Silver Bay marina and factory.

Reuben Smith's Tumblehome Boatshop (www.tumblehomeboats.com; 684 NY 28), in Warrensburg, does high-end restoration and builds historic and classic wooden boats.

CLOTHING

The masses seem to go to "Million Dollar Half Mile," and it's just a quick toss of the gold card from Lake George Village. Separate plazas on both sides of US 9 (near its intersection with NY 149) add up to outlet heaven for the dedicated shopper. See a full list of the current stores—among them, Timberland, Eddie Bauer, Carter's, Coach, Bass, Harry & David, Lane Bryant, Yankee Candle—at several complexes of outlet malls at www.factoryoutletsoflakegeorge.com.

FAIRS AND FLEA MARKETS

Garage-salers take note: World's Largest Garage Sale (518-623-2161; www.warrens burgchamber.com; throughout Warrensburg) is the mother of all town-wide sales. The traffic backs up to Northway Exit 23 for this blowout, the first weekend in October. More than 1,000 vendors, plus many local families, offer a bewildering array of items for sale. Plan to walk once you get to town; there are shuttle buses from the parking lots. Christmas in Warrensburg (www.warrensburgchamber.com) includes crafts sales, and area shops open extended hours the first weekend in December.

FURNITURE MAKERS

Among the furniture makers in this region—which you should contact before visiting, as many studios are in private homes—are Jason Henderson (518-321-4445), of Bolton, who incorporates a modern twist to Adirondack rustic; Thomas W. Brady (518-644-9801), also of Bolton, who makes elegant contemporary furniture; Don Farleigh's the Pine Plank (518-644-9420), which offers chairs, in Diamond Point; and Barry Gregson's Adirondack Rustics Gallery (518-532-0020; www.adirondack rusticsgallery.com), in Schroon, where you can find rustic tables, chairs, settees, beds, corner cupboards, and sideboards, made of burls, cedar, white-birch bark, and assorted woods.

GENERAL STORES

Adirondack General Store (518-494-4408; www.adkgeneralstore.com; 899 East Shore Drive), a company store for a tannery dating back to the 1850s, is now an authentic country store that mixes the antique and the modern in a charming blend. You can hang out by the woodstove when it's cold; read the paper on the porch when it's warm; buy a nice gift; or get milk, eggs, bread, and such for camping in Pharaoh Lake Wilderness Area. The deli's very good.

Paradox General Store (518-532-7462; 759 NY 74) has a deli, gifts, and camp necessities.

POTTERY

Pottery dinnerware can be found in Chestertown at David and Sharon Coleman's Fawn Ridge Pottery (518-494-4373; www.fawn-ridge-pottery.com; 34 Fawn Ridge Road); Bill Knoble's Red Truck Clayworks (518-494-2074; www.redtruckpottery .com; 11 Dennehy Road) is where you can get truly fine stoneware.

In Hadley, Tom O'Brien (518-696-5997; www.obrien-fineart.com) creates portrait sculpture in bronze, terra cotta, carbon steel, and stainless steel.

7

If Time Is Short

A WHIRLWIND TOUR to see the Adirondacks can mean an awful lot of time spent in the car rather than getting to know a few nice places. Maybe it's best to carefully consider your tastes and concentrate your energy within a 40-mile area.

If you're a history buff and want to stroll through attractive, well-preserved towns and old forts, then head for the Champlain Valley, especially Ticonderoga, Crown Point, Westport, and Essex. Great restaurants and lovely bed & breakfast accommodations in Essex and Westport offer an excellent counterpoint to more rustic experiences. If you crave sweeping mountain vistas, aim your sights at the High Peaks, highlighting Keene Valley, Keene, and Lake Placid. The view from downtown Lake Placid, with chains of craggy peaks marching around the village, is unlike any other town in the park. If you like clean, island-dotted lakes, use Upper Saranac, Cranberry, Long, Blue Mountain, Indian, Raquette, Piseco, or Lake Pleasant as a base. For a terrific overview—literally—charter a floatplane from Long Lake or Inlet or take flight above the High Peaks from Lake Placid.

Recommended drives include NY 22 along Lake Champlain, NY 73 between Keene and Lake Placid, NY 30 between Long Lake and Lake Pleasant, and the Blue Ridge Road between Interstate 87 (the Northway) and Newcomb. Take a trip up the toll roads on Prospect or Whiteface Mountains; the views before you get to the summit are amazing, and accessible. Incidentally, the Northway provides quite possibly the most scenic high-speed road experience in the Northeast.

A few suggestions for places to see or stay:

LODGING

Dartbrook Lodge (518-576-9080; www.dartbrooklodge.com; 2835 NY 73, Keene), in the High Peaks, embodies the Adirondack aesthetic in high-end rustic cabins. Its on-site Dartbrook Rustic Goods showroom and The ADK Cafe are also hits.

The Hedges (518-352-7325; 11 Hedges Road, Blue Mountain Lake), with its beautifully restored rustic architecture, good cooking, and wine list. It's a very private spot on the lake where families have vacationed since the 1920s.

The Lake Placid Lodge (518-523-2700; www.lakeplacidlodge.com; Whiteface Inn Road, Lake Placid), a stylish Great Camp–style lakeside destination with the same high standards for food and wine, rooms, and cabins.

The Hit List: 10 Must-Do Adirondack Classics

Following are classic ways to experience this place:

1. Row a guideboat. Tupper Lake guideboat builder Rob Frenette says you can see, test and covet antique or shiny-new models of these traditional craft at the Willard Hanmer Guideboat Race and parade on Lake Flower, in Saranac Lake.

2. See a Great Camp. Adirondack Architectural Heritage executive director Steven Engelhart recommends Camp Santanoni, in Newcomb, because it has everything you'd expect of these quintessential landmarks: rustic buildings; secluded, lakeside setting; and a compelling history.

3. Visit a waterfall. *Adirondack Waterfall Guide* author Russell Dunn suggests picturesque Beaver Meadow Falls and colossal Rainbow Falls, both in Essex County and on tributaries that flow into the East Branch of the Ausable River. Just a mile apart, they can be appreciated from their bases—where you'll get the best view, says Dunn—during one hike.

4. Sleep in a lean-to. For the ultimate snooze in one of these iconic structures, central Adirondacks–based New York State Forest Ranger Greg George offers what he calls nice, remote sites at John Pond in the Siamese Ponds Wilderness Area, near Indian Lake, and Cascade Pond, off the Northville-Placid Trail, near Blue Mountain Lake.

5. Climb a fire tower. Marty Podskoch, who wrote *Adirondack Fire Towers: Their History and Lore*, gives a quartet of must-see structures: the restored one atop Bald Mountain, in Old Forge, which is accessible via a fairly easy trek; Hadley Mountain's tower, near Lake Luzerne, where you can consult an interpretive guide; in Newcomb, Goodnow Mountain's allows a spectacular scene of area peaks; and the sky cab on Snowy Mountain, near Indian Lake, is where, a hundred years ago, one of the Adirondacks' first fire-tower observers was stationed to spot backwoods blazes.

6. Tote a pack basket. Old-school guides used these carryalls because they're comfortable, durable and roomy. Marcia Waligory, of West Martinsburg, in Lewis County, weaves and sells the potbellied baskets at www.adirondackpackbaskets.com. Transport a picnic, an infant, a pet in one of these packs.

7. Paddle a motorless lake. Peter Hornbeck, of Hornbeck Boats, in Olmstedville, lists Lake Lila and Henderson Lake as his top picks. The former for its sheer beauty, with sandy beaches, islands and gorgeous views; the latter because of its "awesome" High Peaks vistas.

8. Explore a new state land acquisition. Although unofficially open to the public for years under Domtar Industries' ownership, Lyon Mountain, in Clinton County—with 14,400 acres for hiking, hunting, and skiing and a new trail to its summit—is now a public resource, according to the Adirondack chapter of the Nature Conservancy's Connie Prickett.

9. Hike one of the 46 highest peaks. Phil Corell, treasurer of the Adirondack 46ers—he's hiked 21 rounds of the 46, plus five circuits in winter—suggests Gothics and Colden. He says their open rock summits and central locale in the High Peaks Wilderness Area offer unobstructed views of surrounding mountains.

10. Watch the sunset from an Adirondack chair while sipping an Adirondack cocktail.

Recipe for an Adirondack, from A. S. Crockett's 1935 The Old Waldorf-Astoria Bar Book:

> **2 oz. gin**
> **2 oz. orange juice**
> Pour the gin into an old-fashioned glass filled with ice. Top with orange juice.

Mirror Lake Inn Resort and Spa (518-523-2544; www.mirrorlakeinn.com; 77
Mirror Lake Drive, Lake Placid) is right in town and a quick walk to the shops on
Main Street. It's elegant, and it does everything well: lovely rooms, great pub food,
a spa, a sweet little beach on Mirror Lake, and the Adirondack Food & Wine
Weekend.

CULTURAL ATTRACTIONS

The Adirondack Museum (518-352-7311; wwww.adkmuseum.org; NY 28/30, Blue
Mountain Lake), open from late May through Columbus Day, is a must see: no visit
to the Adirondack Park is complete without spending a whole day here. The scope of
the exhibits ranges from classic watercraft to fine arts to indigenous crafts.

Fort Ticonderoga (518-585-2821; www.fort-ticonderoga.org; 30 Fort Ti Road,
Ticonderoga), a handsomely restored fortress, played important roles in the French
and Indian Wars and the American Revolution; it's in a beautiful promontory on
Lake Champlain. Plan your visit on a nice day so you can enjoy the view. Open early
May through late October.

The Wild Center (518-359-7800; www.wildcenter.org; 45 Museum Drive, Tupper Lake), a beautiful new state-of-the-art museum, is devoted to the natural history
of the region. The live otters steal the show. Workshops, lectures, and events are
scheduled throughout the year.

Sagamore Great Camp (315-354-5311; www.sagamore.org; Sagamore Road, 4
miles off NY 28, Raquette Lake) is the real deal: A grand rustic estate in the heart
of the wilderness. Guided tours are given twice daily in summer; inquire about May
through October schedule. Concerts, workshops, and other activities are offered on
many weekends.

RESTAURANTS

Interlaken Inn (518-523-3180; www.theinterlakeninn.com; 39 Interlaken Avenue,
Lake Placid), Lake Placid's hideaway hotel, has a lovely dining room, cozy bar, and
fantastic food.

The Owl at Twilight (518-251-4437; 1322 CTY 29, Olmstedville) has super,
imaginative food—some might say the best in the Adirondacks. The restaurant sometimes closes for an entire season, so always call ahead.

The William West Durant (315-354-5532; Pier One, Raquette Lake), a wonderful tour boat that presents a movable feast, cruises Raquette Lake, the fourth largest
lake in the Adirondacks. Open May through October.

8

Information
NUTS, BOLTS, AND FREE ADVICE

CONSULT THIS CHAPTER to find the answers to questions about important community services and organizations, and for an array of miscellaneous facts and figures.

USEFUL NUMBERS

AMBULANCE, FIRE, STATE AND LOCAL POLICE

Throughout the Adirondack Park, 911 service should get you help. But keep in mind that cell service in the woods and on mountain and along some stretches of I-87 is spotty at best.

The New York State Police has offices throughout the Adirondacks. If no local officer is available, calls are forwarded to a 24-hour central dispatcher. Numbers are:

Chestertown 518-494-3201
Elizabethtown 518-873-2111
Indian Lake 518-648-5757
Keeseville 518-834-9040

Moriah 518-546-7611

Old Forge 315-369-3322

Ray Brook 518-897-2000

Schroon Lake 518-532-7691

Ticonderoga 518-585-6200

Tupper Lake 518-359-7677

Westport 518-962-8235

Willsboro 518-963-7400

The national hotline for Poison Control is 1-800-222-1222.

AREA CODES

The area code for the eastern two thirds of the Adirondacks, including Lake George, Warrensburg, Schroon Lake, Elizabethtown, Westport, Keene, Lake Placid, Saranac Lake, Tupper Lake, Long Lake, Blue Mountain Lake, Indian Lake, North Creek, Speculator, Wells, and Northville is 518. For communities in the northwestern and west-central Adirondacks, such as Cranberry Lake, Star Lake, Raquette Lake, Inlet, Eagle Bay, Big Moose, and Old Forge, the area code is 315.

HANDICAPPED SERVICES

For disabled New Yorkers, free passes to state-operated camping, swimming, golf facilities, and historic sites are available by applying to the Office of Parks, Recreation and Historic Preservation (518-474-0456).

The John Dillon Park (www.johndillonpark.org) is open to anyone with a disability, his or her family, friends, and caregivers. You need a permit, which you can get for free, and the lean-tos and trails are designed for people with disabilities. The park, with Grampus Lake and Handsome Pond, has more than 2 miles of nice trails with good surfaces for wheelchairs. Also, the Department of Environmental Conservation's campground at Scaroon Manor, in Schroon Lake, has trails and campsites for those with mobility concerns (518-457-2500; www.dec.ny.gov). Contact the DEC about the universally accessible trails for people with mobility impairments at Ausable Marsh, Lampson Falls, Francis Lake, Moss Lake, and Silver Lake Bog.

HEALTH CENTERS AND HOSPITALS

Most local health centers are open weekdays; Hudson Headwaters centers (www.hhhn.org) are open Saturdays as well. Many town health centers have answering services that can help with emergencies any time, day or night.

Central and Southwestern Adirondacks

Central Adirondack Family Practice, 315-369-6619; South Shore Road, Old Forge

Indian Lake Health Center, 518-648-5707; www.hhhn.org; Main Street and Pelon Road, Indian Lake

Long Lake Medical Center, 518-624-2301; NY 28N, Long Lake

Nathan Littauer Hospital, 518-725-8621; www.nlh.org; 90 East State Street, Gloversville

North Creek Health Center, 518-251-2541; www.hhhn.org; Ski Bowl Road, North Creek

Adirondack Health Center, 518-359-3355; 115 Wawbeek Avenue, Tupper Lake

Clifton-Fine Hospital, 315-848-3351; 1014 Oswegatchie Trail, Star Lake

Tupper Lake Health Center, 518-359-7000; www.amccares.org; 55 Church Street, Tupper Lake

High Peaks and Northern Adirondacks
Adirondack Medical Center, 518-523-3311; www.amccares.org; 29 Church Street, Lake Placid

Adirondack Medical Center, 518-891-4141; www.amccares.org; 2233 NY 86, Saranac Lake

Mountain Health Center, 518-576-9771; www.amccares.org; NY 73, Keene

Newcomb Health Center, 518-582-2991; Winebrook Hills, Newcomb

Wilmington Health Center, 518-946-7080; Springfield Road, Wilmington

Champlain Valley
Champlain Valley Physicians Hospital Medical Center, 518-561-2000; www.cvph .org; 75 Beekman Street, Plattsburgh

Elizabethtown Community Hospital, 518-873-6377; www.ech.org; 75 Park Street, Elizabethtown

Moriah Health Center, 518-942-7123; www.hhhn.org; 27 Hospital Road, Mineville

Smith House Health Care Center, 518-963-4275; 39 Farrell Road, Willsboro

Ticonderoga Health Center, 518-585-6708; www.hhhn.org; 102 Racetrack Road, Ticonderoga

Classic watercraft in Lake George.   Courtesy of Nancie Battaglia

Lake George and Southeastern Adirondacks

Bolton Health Center, 518-644-9471; www.hhhn.org; 11 Cross Street, Bolton Landing

Chester Health Center, 518-494-2761; www.hhhn.org; 6223 US 9, Chestertown

Glens Falls Hospital, 518-926-6670; www.glensfallshospital.org; 102 Park Street, Glens Falls

Schroon Lake Health Center, 518-532-7120; www.hhhn.org; 24 Fairfield Avenue, Schroon Lake

Warrensburg Health Center, 518-623-2844; www.hhhn.org; Health Center Plaza, 3767 Main Street, Warrensburg

MAGAZINES AND NEWSPAPERS

Adirondac (518-668-4447; www.adk.org; Lake George) is a bimonthly magazine published by the Adirondack Mountain Club, with articles on local history, outdoor recreation, and environmental issues.

Adirondack Explorer (518-891-9352; www.adirondackexplorer.org; Saranac Lake) is a tabloid-size magazine on newsprint that covers paddle trips, hiking and skiing treks, and the environmental issues.

Adirondack Life (518-946-2191; www.adirondacklife.com; Jay) is an award-winning bimonthly magazine, plus two special issues: *Annual Guide to the Great Outdoors* and the *Home Issue.* Known for excellent color photography; publishes essays, short stories, columns, and features on history, outdoor recreation, architecture, culture, local life, regional products, politics, and environmental issues by nationally known writers.

Central and Southwestern Adirondacks
Adirondack Express (315-369-2237; www.adirondackexpress.com; Old Forge); *Adirondack Weekly* (315-369-9982; Old Forge); *Hamilton County News* (518-548-6898; Speculator); *North Creek News* (518-251-3012; www.denspubs.com; North Creek); *Times Union of Albany* (518-454-5694; www.timesunion.com; Albany); and the *Daily Gazette* (518-374-4141; www.dailygazette.com; Schenectady).

Northwest Lakes
Tupper Lake Free Press (518-359-2166; www.tlfreepress.com; Tupper Lake); *Watertown Daily Times* (315-782-1000; www.watertowndailytimes.com; Watertown).

High Peaks and Northern Adirondacks
Adirondack Daily Enterprise (518-891-2600; www.adirondackdailyenterprise.com; Saranac Lake); *Lake Placid News* (518-523-4401; wwwlakeplacidnews.com; Lake Placid).

Champlain Valley
Lake Champlain Weekly (518-563-1414; 4701 US 9, Plattsburgh); *Plattsburgh Press-Republican* (518-561-2300; www.pressrepublican.com; Plattsburgh); *Valley News* (518-873-6368; www.denpubs.com; Denton Publishing Co., Elizabethtown).

Lake George and Southeastern Adirondacks
Glens Falls Post Star (518-792-3131; www.poststar.com; Glens Falls); *Lake George Mirror* (518-644-2619; www.lakegeorgemirror.com; Lake George).

RADIO STATIONS

National Public Radio

Three NPR affiliates reach different parts of the Adirondacks:

WAMC-FM, 90.3; 518-465-5233; Albany NY; also translator WANC, 103.9 (Ticonderoga) and WCEL, 91.9 (Plattsburgh).

WSLU-FM, 89.5 (Canton), 91.3 (Blue Mountain Lake and Thousand Islands), 88.9 (Paul Smiths), 88.3 (Peru), 90.1 (Keene), 96.3 (Keene Valley), 93.5 (Lake George), 91.7 (Long Lake, Lake Placid, Tupper Lake), 88.1 (Lowville), 90.9 (Malone), 97.3 (Newcomb), 104.3 (North Creek), 88.7 (Old Forge), 90.5 (Saranac Lake), 95.3 (Schroon Lake), 97.5 (Speculator), 101.7 (St. Huberts); 315-229-5356; www.ncpr.org; Canton, NY. The best news and feature coverage for the entire Adirondack Park by any media outlet; maintains an excellent Adirondack News Bureau at Paul Smith's College.

WVPR, 107.9; 802-655-9451; Colchester, VT. News coverage for the eastern Adirondacks and relatively reliable weather forecasts.

Commercial Radio Stations

WLPW-FM, 105.5; 518-891-5186; www.theclassicrock105.com. Lake Placid. General. (Signal broadcasts through WRGR-FM, 102.3, Tupper Lake as well.) The radio show *The Pat McAvoy Experiment,* on Saturdays from 10 AM to 7 PM, is a local favorite.

WNBZ-AM, 1240, 518-891-1544. Saranac Lake. General.

WSLK-FM, 106.3, 518-891-1544. Saranac Lake. Country.

TELEVISION STATIONS

There are no television stations broadcasting from within the Adirondack Park, and TV reception in areas not covered by cable or satellite service can be awful. The Plattsburgh NBC affiliate, WPTZ, reports on news from Lake Placid, Saranac Lake, and elsewhere in the eastern Adirondacks during the *Today Show* and in evening slots. WCAX, the Burlington, VT, CBS affiliate, has a reporter filing stories from the Adirondacks on a relatively regular basis.

ROAD SERVICE

For AAA members, there are local offices in Glens Falls, 518-792-0088; Johnstown, 518-762-4619; and Plattsburgh, 518-563-3830. Local police and emergency services can help you find a tow truck.

TOURIST INFORMATION

Taking care of visitors is the number-one industry in the Adirondacks, and communities have become quite skilled at educating the public about their unique offerings. Warren County (which encompasses Lake George and the southeastern Adiron-

---

Adirondack Blogs

There are many, but just a handful are truly helpful. **Adirondack Almanack** (www.adirondackalmanack.com) has a vast well of contributors who post on every Adirondack subject imaginable. Phil Brown, of **Adirondack Explorer** (www.adirondackexplorer .org), writes great posts about his Adirondack recreational adventures. And *Adirondack Life*'s weekly blogs (www.adirondacklife.com) cover history, nature, recreation, and whatever's on its editors' minds.

dacks) publishes a colorful guide with a calendar of events, lists of hiking trails, boat-launch sites, museums, libraries, attractions, campgrounds, and much more; call 518-761-6366 for a copy. Likewise, the Lake Placid/Essex County Visitors Bureau (518-523-2445; www.lakeplacid.com) has an extensive promotional packet.

> ### Visitor Information
>
> For more information about Glens Falls and around, contact the **Adirondack Regional Chamber of Commerce** (518-798-1761; www .adirondackchamber.org); for Saratoga Springs, call the city's **Visitor Center** (518-587-3241; www.saratogasprings visitorcenter.com).

Franklin County publishes a four-color booklet with general background information plus publications detailing services and outdoor recreation; these are available from the tourism office at 518-483-6788. Clinton County has a magazine-size guide, available by calling 518-563-1000. Hamilton County has a series of pamphlets about hunting and fishing, snowmobiling, craft shops, dining, and lodging, plus a magazine-format booklet, available by calling 518-648-5239.

Following is a selection of chambers of commerce and visitor information centers check out www.adirondacks.com for links to these towns and areas.

Central and Southwestern Adirondacks
Blue Mountain Lake Association: 518-352-7659

Central Adirondack Association: 315-369-6983; www.caany.com

Gore Mountain Region: 518-251-2612 or 1-800-880-GORE; www.goremtnregion .org

Indian Lake: 518-648-5112; www.indian-lake.com

Inlet: 315-357-5501; www.inletny.com

Long Lake/Raquette Lake: 518-624-3077; www.longlake-ny.com or www.central adirondacks.com

Speculator–Lake Pleasant–Piseco: 518-548-4521; www.adrkmts.com

Town of Webb: 315-369-6983; www.oldforgeny.com

Northwest Lakes
Tupper Lake: 518-359-3328; www.tupperlakeinfo.com

High Peaks and Northern Adirondacks
Lake Placid/Essex County Visitors Bureau: 518-523-2445; www.lakeplacid.com

Saranac Lake: 518-891-1990 or 1-800-347-1992; www.saranaclake.com

Whiteface Mountain Regional Visitors Bureau: 518-946-2255 or 1-888-WHITE FACE; www.whitefaceregion.com

Champlain Valley
Essex County Visitors Information Center: 518-597-4646; www.lakeplacid.com

Ticonderoga-Crown Point: 518-585-6619

Westport: 518-962-8383; www.westportny.com

Bolton Landing: 518-644-3831; www.boltonchamber.com

Chestertown–Brant Lake–Pottersville (Adirondack Regional Chambers of Commerce): 518-494-2722 or 1-888-404-2722; www.adirondackchamber.org

Hague Ticonderoga: 518-543-6239 (in summer only); www.hagueticonderoga.com

Lake George: 518-668-5755 or 1-800-705-0059; www.lakegeorgechamber.com

Lake Luzerne: 518-696-3500; www.lakeluzerne-chamber.org

Schroon Lake: 518-532-7675 or 1-888-724-7666; www.schroonlake.org

Stony Creek: 518-696-4563; www.stonycreekchamber.com

Warrensburg: 518-623-2161; www.warrensburgchamber.com

BIBLIOGRAPHY

Diverse authors have been inspired by the Adirondacks, from Robert Louis Stevenson, who completed *The Master of Ballantrae* when he was a tuberculosis patient in Saranac Lake, to Nathanael West, who penned part of *Miss Lonelyhearts* during a sojourn in Warrensburg. Sylvia Plath chronicled her ski accident at Mount Pisgah in *The Bell Jar*. Keene resident Russell Banks is the leading light of Adirondack literature with *The Sweet Hereafter*; *Rule of the Bone*; *Cloudsplitter*, based on John Brown's life; *The Darling*; and *The Reserve*. Ian Fleming's *The Spy Who Loved Me* is set in a dreary motor court near Lake George; L. Sprague DeCamp's horror-fantasy *The Purple Pterodactyls* has a definite Adirondack flavor. Mystery writer John D. MacDonald, of Travis McGee fame, even wrote a book about his cats' spending their summers in Piseco.

Literary Works

Banks, Russell. *The Darling*. New York: Harper Perennial, 2005. 400 pp.
———. *The Reserve*. New York: Harper Collins, 2008. 287 pp.
Barrett, Andrea. *The Air We Breathe*. New York: W. W. Norton, 2007. 320 pp.
Cooper, James Fenimore. *The Last of the Mohicans*. Numerous paperback editions. New York: Bantam Classics, 1982. 384 pp.
Doctorow, E. L. *Loon Lake*. New York: Random House, 1980. 258 pp.
Dreiser, Theodore. *An American Tragedy*. Paperback editions available. New York: Signet Classics, 1964. 832 pp.
LaBastille, Anne. *Woodswoman*. New York: E.P. Dutton, 1976. 277 pp.

History

Bellico, Russell. *Chronicles of Lake Champlain*. Fleischmanns, NY: Purple Mountain Press, 1999. 415 pp., historic vignettes, photos, maps, drawings.
Bond, Hallie. *Boats of the Adirondacks*. Blue Mountain Lake, NY: Adirondack Museum, 1995. 334 pp.
Brown, Phil. *Bob Marshall in the Adirondacks: Writings of a Pioneering Peak Bagger, Pond Hopper and Wilderness Preservationist*. Saranac Lake, NY: Lost Pond Press, 2006. 308 pp., photographs and maps.
Brumley, Charles. *Guides of the Adirondacks*. Utica, NY: North Country Books, 1994. 320 pp., photos, list of guides.
Donaldson, Alfred L. *A History of the Adirondacks*. Two-volume set originally published in 1921; reprinted, Fleischmanns, New York: Purple Mountain Press, 1993. 766 pp.

Jerome, Christine. *An Adirondack Passage: The Cruise of the Canoe* Sairy Gamp. Lake George, New York: Adirondack Mountain Club, 1999. 246 pp., photos, maps.

MacKenzie, Mary. *The Plains of Abraham: A History of North Elba and Lake Placid, Collected Writings of Mary MacKenzie*. Utica, NY: Nicholas K. Burns Publishing, 2007. 397 pp.

McMartin, Barbara. *The Great Forest of the Adirondacks*. Utica, NY: North Country Books, 1994. 266 pp., photos, charts.

———. *The Privately Owned Adirondacks: Sporting and Family Clubs, Private Parks and Preserves, Timberlands and Easements*. Lake View Press, 2004. 304 pp.

Nelson, James L. *Benedict Arnold's Navy*. New York: McGraw Hill, 2006. 386 pp.

Prochnik, George. *Putnam Camp: Sigmund Freud, James Jackson Putnam, and the Purpose of American Psychology*. Other Press, 2006. 480 pp.

Schneider, Paul. *The Adirondacks*. New York: Henry Holt, 1997. 340 pp.

Starbuck, David. *Massacre at Fort William Henry*. Hanover, NH: University Press of New England, 2002. 152 pp., photos, sketches, diagrams.

Terrie, Philip G. *Contested Terrain*. Syracuse, NY: Syracuse University Press, 2008. 223 pp.

Natural History

North Country Books (www.north countrybooks.com), in Utica, publishes a series of field guides on native birds, mammals, trees and shrubs, wildflowers, and mushrooms. All of the books are paperbacks with numerous color photos.

Peregrine falcon   Jeff Nadler

Bell, Allison W., and Slack, Nancy G. *Adirondack Alpine Summits: An Ecological Field Guide*. Adirondack Mountain Club, 2007. 80 pp., color photographs.

DiNunzio, Michael. *Adirondack Wildguide*. Elizabethtown, NY: Adirondack Conservancy/Adirondack Council, 1984. 160 pp., illus.

Jenkins, Jerry. *Adirondack Atlas: A Geographic Portrait of the Adirondacks*. Syracuse, NY: Syracuse University Press, 2004. 296 pp. 450 color figures, maps, and tables.

McKibben, Bill. *Wandering Home: A Long Walk Across America's Most Hopeful Landscape: Vermont's Champlain Valley and New York's Adirondacks*. Crown Journeys, 2005. 160 pages.

McMartin, Barbara. *The Adirondack Park: A Wildlands Quilt*. Syracuse, NY: Syracuse University Press, 1999. 94 pp., color photos, maps.

View from the top of Whiteface Mountain, which can be reached by foot or car, on the White-face Veterans Memorial Highway. Courtesy of Johnathan Esper, www.wildernessphotographs.com

Stager, Curt. *Field Notes from the Northern Forest.* Syracuse, NY: Syracuse University Press, 1998. 272 pp., illus.

Terrie, Philip G. *Wildlife and Wilderness: A History of Adirondack Mammals.* Fleischmanns, NY: Purple Mountain Press, 1993. 176 pp., photos.

Recreation

The main sources for Adirondack guidebooks for hiking, snowshoeing, and cross-country skiing are the Adirondack Mountain Club (ADK), based in Lake George, and North Country Books, out of Utica. The Forest Preserve series by various ADK authors covers seven different regions of the park, from the High Peaks to the Northville–Lake Placid Trail; these pocket-size paperbacks have plenty of detail and each comes with a separate topo map showing trails. You can order this at www.adk.org or at most regional bookstores or outfitters. Wild River Press (www.wildriverpress.com) publishes the Discover the Adirondacks series, written by the late historian/hiker Barbara McMartin and updated by Bill Ingersoll. These are livelier to read, with notes on the human and natural history of a particular destination.

Aprill, Dennis. *Good Fishing in the Adirondacks.* The Countryman Press, 1999. 224 pp., photos, maps.

———. *Short Treks in the Adirondacks and Beyond.* Utica, NY: Nicholas K. Burns Publishing, 2005. 160 pp.

Densmore, Lisa. *Hiking the Adirondacks: A Guide to 42 of the Best Hiking Adventures in New York's Adirondacks.* FalconGuides, 2010. 232 pp.

Dunn, Russell. *Adirondack Waterfall Guide: New York's Cool Cascades.* Black Dome Press, 2003. 248 pp. photos.

Goodwin, Tony. *Classic Adirondack Ski Tours.* Lake George, NY: Adirondack Mountain Club, 1996. 127 pp., maps.

Lake George steamer *Sagamore.* Courtesy of Ted Comstock, Saranac Lake

Haas, Jeremy, and Jim Lawyer. *Adirondack Rock.* Self-published, 2008 (www .adirondackrock.com).

Jamieson, Paul, and Donald Morris. *Adirondack Canoe Waters: North Flow.* Lake George, NY: Adirondack Mountain Club, 1999. Includes new state acquisitions. 368 pp., maps.

Kick, Peter. *25 Mountain Bike Tours in the Adirondacks.* Woodstock, VT: The Countryman Press, 1999. 190 pp., photos, maps.

McKibben, Bill, Sue Halpern, Barbara Lemmel, and Mitchell Hay. *25 Bike Rides in the Adirondacks: Bicycle Adventures in the East's Largest Wilderness.* Woodstock, VT: The Countryman Press, 1995. 174 pp.

Mellor, Don. *Climbing in the Adirondacks: A Guide to Rock & Ice Routes.* Lake George, NY: Adirondack Mountain Club, 1996. 318 pp., photos, maps.

Morrissey, Spencer. *The Other 54: a Hiker's Guide to the Lower 54 Peaks of the Adirondack 100 Highest.* Dacksdescents Publishing, 2007. 256 pp., black-and-white photos, color maps.

Starmer, Timothy. *Five-Star Trails in the Adirondacks: A Guide to the Most Beautiful Hikes.* Menasha Ridge Press, 2010. 304 pp.

Stoltie, Annie, and Ward, Elisabeth. *Dog Hikes in the Adirondacks: 20 Trails to Enjoy with Your Best Friend.* Shaggy Dog Press, 2010. 64 pp.

Index